GREEN BANS
RED UNION

Hon Dr Meredith Burgmann was President of the Legislative Council of NSW (Labor). She was previously a Senior Lecturer in Politics at Macquarie University and first woman President of the Academics' Union in NSW (now NTEU). She was actively involved in the green ban movement and was arrested defending the Victoria Street ban. She has written extensively on industrial relations and women's issues and published books on misogyny and ASIO.

Dr Verity Burgmann is Adjunct Professor of Political Science in the School of Social Sciences at Monash University and Director of the Roger Coates Labour History Project at www.reasoninrevolt.net.au. She is the author of numerous studies of labour and social movements, including 'In Our Time' (1985), *Power and Protest* (1993), *Revolutionary Industrial Unionism* (1995), *Power, Profit and Protest* (2003), *Climate Politics and the Climate Movement* (2012) and *Globalization and Labour in the Twenty-First Century* (2016).

GREEN BANS
RED UNION

THE SAVING OF A CITY

MEREDITH BURGMANN & VERITY BURGMANN

NEWSOUTH

A NewSouth book

Published by
NewSouth Publishing
University of New South Wales Press Ltd
University of New South Wales
Sydney NSW 2052
AUSTRALIA
newsouthpublishing.com

National Library of Australia
Cataloguing-in-Publication entry
Creator: Burgmann, Meredith, 1947– author.
Title: Green bans, red union: The saving of a city / Meredith Burgmann and
    Verity Burgmann.
Edition: 2nd edition.
ISBN: 9781742235400 (paperback)
      9781742242644 (ebook)
      9781742248103 (epdf)
Subjects: Green Bans – History. Builders Labourers' Federation – NSW Branch
    – History. Building workers – Trade unions – New South Wales – History.
    Environmental activism – New South Wales – Resident action.
Other Creators/Contributors: Burgmann, Verity, author.

Design Josephine Pajor-Markus
Cover images BLF Green Ban demonstration, Sydney 1973; Sydney skyline at dusk. Photo by DAVID ILIFF. License: CC-BY-SA 3.0.

CONTENTS

LIST OF ILLUSTRATIONS

ABBREVIATIONS

ABCE&BLF	Australian Building and Construction Employees' and Builders
ABCWF	Australian Building Construction Workers' Federation
ABLF	Australian Builders Labourers' Federation
ABS	Australian Bureau of Statistics
ACF	Australian Conservation Foundation
ACTU	Australian Council of Trade Unions
ALP	Australian Labor Party
AMWU	Amalgamated Metal Workers' Union
AWU	Australian Workers Union
BLs	builders labourers
BLF	Builders Labourers' Federation
BTG	Building Trades Group
BWIU	Building Workers' Industrial Union
CBD	Central Business District
CBCS	Commonwealth Bureau of Census and Statistics
CCAC	Commonwealth Conciliation and Arbitration Commission
CPA	Communist Party of Australia
CPA (M-L)	Communist Party of Australia (Marxist-Leninist)
CRAG	Coalition of Resident Action Groups
DMR	Department of Main Roads
FEDFA	Federated Engine Drivers and Firemen's Association of Australasia
GM	General Meeting
HVCRAG	Hunter Valley Coalition of Resident Action Groups
MBA	Master Builders' Association
MLA	Member of the Legislative Assembly
NERG	Newcastle East Residents' Group
NIMBY	Not In My Backyard
NSWBLF	New South Wales Builders Labourers' Federation
PDC	Parkes Development Corporation
SCG	Sydney Cricket Ground
SCRA	Sydney Cove Redevelopment Authority
SMH	*Sydney Morning Herald*
SPA	Socialist Party of Australia
UCATI	Union of Construction, Allied Trades and Technicians
VSAG	Victoria Street Action Group

PREFACE AND ACKNOWLEDGMENTS TO THE 1998 EDITION

When federal BLF Intervention against its New South Wales branch abruptly ended the 'green bans period' of the NSWBLF in 1975, Meredith ended up with much of the union's archival material in her sitting room, for the NSWBLF officials had had to vacate their Trades Hall office within 24 hours. She had been embroiled politically and socially with the union for five years and had cried along with the 2000 others at the final Town Hall meeting, which she tape-recorded. As an academic in the Politics Department at Macquarie University, Professor Don Aitkin persuaded her she was in a unique position to write a doctoral thesis on an exciting and important subject. Not only did she have in her possession most of the union's archives, she had lived through the experience as one of their many frenetically active supporters. Thus much of this book is drawn from Meredith's PhD thesis (completed in 1981), 'A new concept of unionism: the New South Wales Builders Labourers' Federation 1970–1974'. This thesis should be consulted by any person interested in a more detailed organisational and industrial history of the union, for this book greatly condenses the thesis in order to provide a considerable amount of new material on the wider political activities of the union, especially the green bans.

Meredith began looking for the rest of the NSWBLF archives, some of which she found in extraordinary places. The Executive Minutes from 1963 to 1971, for example, were in the cellar of the Sussex Hotel with beer dribbling over them. Working with BLF documents was not easy, for the NSWBLF was distinguished by its imprecise attitude towards its organisational and administrative paper work. The union's clear priority was active engagement in concrete struggles and campaigns, not the meticulous keeping of minutes and records – it could not even get its own name right. In 1967 the Industrial Registrar acknowledged receipt 'of a document purporting to be the Annual Return of the Australian Builders Labourers' Union', but pointed out that: 'as the name of the union registered under the *Trade Union Act, 1881*, as amended, is the Australian Builders' Laborers' Federation, NSW Branch, the said document is returned herewith'. Because the union itself most often used the form 'Builders Labourers' Federation', this is the convention adopted here, except where quotations and names of documents demand otherwise. Even the journal, usually *Builders' Laborer*, changed its spelling and exact title in cavalier fashion from issue to issue. The only point on which the union officials showed any strong preference was the elimination of the apostrophe following 'builders'. They argued that 'the Federation belongs to the labourers but the labourers don't belong to the builders'.

The other primary sources used, such as posters, pamphlets, letters and other pieces of documentary evidence, were gathered by Meredith from a large number of places. Apart from her own gleanings, many were lent by helpful unionists and duly photocopied. She also collected the ephemeral material about the builders labourers produced by other unions and left groups, including those opposed to the union such as the federal BLF and the BWIU, and the hostile literature produced by the Master Builders' Association. Thus Meredith had collected a valuable archival record of the union's recent history, much of which has now been donated to the Noel Burlin Archives of Business and Labour at the Australian National University. In addition, she consulted all the Sydney daily newspapers for the period and, when appropriate, provincial or interstate papers. She perused the publications of the Communist Party of Australia, the Communist Party of Australia (Marxist-Leninist), the Socialist Party of Australia, the Master Builders' Association and the federal body of the Australian Builders Labourers' Federation. She examined court records where necessary and utilised relevant information from the Commonwealth Bureau of Census and Statistics.

These myriad sources were greatly augmented by the interviews, some more than four hours long, which Meredith conducted between 1975 and 1981 with 46 NSWBLF members, five NSWBLF office staff, nine officials from other unions, one federal BLF official, one employer representative (who wishes to remain anonymous), and 11 resident activists and other supporters. Of the 46 builders labourers, 26 had never worked as officials for the union. Of the 20 officials interviewed, many had only been officials for short periods because of the union's policy favouring temporary organisers. As a result, Meredith discussed in depth with a considerable number of rank-and-file militants their own feelings and attitudes about what occurred. She also asked them how other labourers on their job-sites viewed certain acts – such as the green bans and women in the industry – to get some indication, even if second-hand, of the response of not so active members. Without leading, she tried hard to discover what the labourers felt were for them the most significant actions of the union. Several stressed that the interview had started them thinking, and often they would return some days later with more interesting stories or a forgotten leaflet. The experience of the rank-and-file unionists in struggle, as revealed in these interviews, is especially valuable, since ordinary union members do not write election pamphlets or set out policy in union documents, and only rarely do they write their memoirs.

While Verity has also carried out research on the green bans in particular, via newspapers and other sources, the richness of the material on which this book is based reveals primarily the unusual combination of advantages enjoyed by Meredith, as political scientist, participant and principal archivist. Meredith would like to thank her two PhD supervisors: Don Aitken, who persuaded her to write about the NSWBLF, despite her initial reservations that she was far too close to the subject matter; and Bob Connell, without whose encouragement and advice she would never have finished. She is grateful, too, for the helpful comments received at that time from her colleagues, notably Stewart Firth, Murray Goot, Winton Higgins, Tom Parsonage, Sabine Erika and Ted Wolfers. She wishes also to thank friends and family for their advice, assistance, support and endurance, particularly Glen Batchelor, Lorna and Victor Burgmann, Verity Burgmann, Beverley Firth, Pat Fiske, Heather Goodall, Helen Randerson, Ward Oliver, Pete Thomas, Paul Torzillo and Nadia Wheatley. She thanks all the men and women of the NSWBLF, especially those who allowed her to interview them and lent her papers, journals, pamphlets and other material.

Meredith's election to the New South Wales Parliament prevented her from turning her thesis into a book. In 1995 Jack Mundey persuaded her to hand the job over to her little sister – a political scientist and labour historian. Verity's role has been, firstly, to reduce Meredith's wildly over-length thesis and change its original chronological structure to develop a thematically based narrative; secondly, to research and write considerably more about the green bans and the union's other political and social activities, for the emphasis in Meredith's thesis was on the union's organisational development and industrial strategies; and, thirdly, to revise the conceptual framework within which we present this story, in the light of recent political trends and intellectual concerns. In this task, conducted over the past three years, Verity wishes to acknowledge gratefully the special assistance and advice of Stuart Macintyre, Andrew Milner, Jack Mundey and Joe Owens, and to thank John Dryzek, Ruth Fincher, Don Garden, George Hurchalla, Jane Jacobs, Bruce Scates and Graham Willett.

The team at UNSW Press and James Drown, the editor, have been great to work with. We are grateful for the institutional support given by the Political Science Department at Melbourne University and the assistance there of Rita De Amicis, David Lutz, Natalie Madaffari and Wendy Ruffles. We also appreciate the generosity of the University of Melbourne in assisting this project with a publications grant of $2000.

Finally, we offer this book in memory of Bob Pringle and the many other NSWBLF and green ban activists who are no longer with us.

Meredith Burgmann and Verity Burgmann

INTRODUCTION TO
THE NEW EDITION

Twenty years ago when the first edition of *Green Bans Red Union* was published, we were uncertain whether its relevance would continue and its message grow. We need not have wondered. The green bans and the heroic workers who initiated and defended them have become iconic in the present-day struggle of communities to control the environment in which they live. Not just in Australia but internationally, the story of the NSW Builders Labourers' Federation (NSWBLF) and their world's first environmental action struck a chord.

In recent times the problem of global warming has directed urgent attention to issues of environmental protection and emissions reduction. People around the world have waited impatiently for political leaders to tackle climate change but have been largely disappointed in their demands for meaningful action against the corporations who gain profit by polluting the planet.

Four decades ago the power of workers to prevent environmental damage – when politicians ducked the task – was forcibly demonstrated in the green bans movement of the NSWBLF, which refused to work on environmentally irresponsible projects and based this pioneering action on the concept of 'the social responsibility of labour'. Workers' organisations overseas are starting to contemplate green bans in the fight against global warming and are discovering the inspiring story of the NSWBLF.

The power of labour to protect the environment is commonly discounted in discussions of ecological problems, including climate change. For example, German sociologist Ulrich Beck's classic 1992 book *The Risk Society* ignores the role that organised workers could play in confronting ecological irresponsibility. He writes about the importance of 'public debate', 'dissenting voices' and 'alternative experts' to prevent environmental hazards. Yet public outrage in the instance he discusses in his book – a lead crystal factory dropping flecks of lead and arsenic on the German town of Altenstadt – got nowhere. If you lived in Altenstadt, would you rather rely on the workers in the factory refusing to continue working until the emissions ceased or on 'public debate', 'dissenting voices' and 'alternative experts'?

The residents of Sydney in the green bans period had already despaired of public debate and had found that dissenting voices and alternative experts were simply ignored, – until the builders labourers entered the scene and withdrew their labour. The power of these builders labourers at the point of production prevented the destruction and inappropriate development of large areas of environmental and cultural significance in the city.

As Sydney once again grapples with important community issues including the destruction of working class communities at Millers Point; the massive dislocation of inner city areas by the major freeway WestConnex; and the move towards privatisation of Sydney's favourite Art Deco masterpiece The Bondi Pavilion, we realise that the issues are the same as those confronted by the builders labourers in the 1970s.

In fact, the Sirius building at the Rocks, which was purpose-built as public housing as a result of NSWBLF bans, has just been emptied of public tenants and slated for possible demolition by the conservative state government. The WestConnex sounds very similar to the Western Distributor and North Western Distributor that were planned to trifurcate inner-city Glebe in the 1970s but which were stopped by a combination of BLF action and new Whitlam minister Tom Uren. The voice (and muscle) of organised labour is needed once more.

Looking at the green bans in an international context makes it is easy to forget their very practical local significance. Our beautiful Sydney is much more beautiful because of the BLF and their green bans. The bans saved our historic Rocks, Woolloomooloo, Victoria Street and the suburb of Glebe. They preserved parks and green space like Kelly's Bush and Centennial Park. They saved heritage buildings such as Lyndhurst, the Pitt Street Church and most of Martin Place.

The legacy of their bold action endures. To avoid ongoing green bans, governments responded with better laws and regulations around environmental and heritage issues, in particular the 1978 New South Wales Heritage Act and the 1979 Environment Planning and Assessment Act.

The green bans movement was immensely significant, but has tended to overshadow the union's other extraordinary achievements. The NSWBLF confounded the caricature of unions as organisations uninterested in issues beyond the workplace and unconcerned with forms of oppression other than class. It combined industrial militancy and a tendency to encroach seriously on managerial prerogatives with ultra-democratic organisational processes such as limited tenure of office and decision-making by general meetings. And it also retained its serious commitment to environmental protection and the rights of women, migrants, Aborigines and gay people.

The NSWBLF was a pioneer in the history of international trade unionism, a precursor of the 'social-movement unionism' that arose at the very end of the twentieth century. It meets the five characteristics of social-movement unionism outlined in Kim Moody's study of this international phenomenon of the 1990s: militancy; internal democracy; an agenda for radical social and economic change; a determination to embrace the diversity of the working class in order to overcome its fragmentation; and a capacity to appeal beyond its membership by using union power to lead community struggles. As we rightly celebrate the NSWBLF's momentous green bans, it is worth acknowledging that it was much more than this: the NSWBLF was, in all aspects, a union ahead of its time.

Finally, we would like to thank all those wonderful environmentalists and union activists in Australia and around the world who continually harassed us about republishing our book which had become impossible to buy, except online and for an exorbitant amount.

We also wish we could thank our self-appointed proofreader Gough Whitlam who, having agreed to launch our book in 1998, sent us a list of typos, which readers will be pleased to know we have corrected.

Meredith Burgmann and Verity Burgmann
November 2016

PART 1

PEOPLE BEFORE PROFITS

THE WORLD'S FIRST GREEN BANS

Green bans', 'builders labourers' and 'Jack Mundey' were household terms for millions of Australians during the 1970s. Sydneysiders in particular were polarised on the questions surrounding green bans and those who imposed them. To many, the New South Wales Builders Labourers' Federation (NSWBLF) represented the hideous spectre of working-class power maliciously halting progress, and restraining the liberty of property owners to undertake development, from which the public would benefit. To many others the builders labourers (or BLs) articulated the general interest of all except the greediest developers in preserving the built and natural environment from wanton destruction.

The union's guiding principle, which aroused such strong emotions and which underpinned its environmental activism, was the concept of the social responsibility of labour: that workers had a right to insist that their labour not be used in harmful ways. Strongly associated with this principle was a conviction that the organised labour movement should concern itself with all manner of social and political issues, to contest exploitation and oppression in the wider society and not just in the workplace. The union did not merely impose green bans – refusing to work on environmentally injurious constructions – it also insisted upon the right of women to work in the industry on an equal basis with men, and frequently used its power to aid groups such as prisoners, homosexuals, Aborigines, students, the women's movement, and poorer home-buyers, even imposing a range of non-environmental bans in defence of these oppressed, marginalised or vulnerable people.

The NSWBLF was one of Australia's oldest unions. It was formed in the

1870s and registered under the New South Wales *Trade Union Act* of 1881 as the United Labourers. In 1912 it became the Builders Labourers' Union; and in 1926 it joined with labourers' unions in other states to form the Australian Builders' Labourers' Federation (ABLF). By the early 1970s the ABLF had a national membership of around 30,000 and covered all unskilled labourers and certain categories of skilled labourers employed on building sites: dogmen, riggers, scaffolders, powder monkeys, hoist drivers and steel fixers. Between 1970 and 1974 the New South Wales branch, with about 11,000 members, operated outside the traditional confines of the trade union movement, guided by many capable and committed officials but in particular by three outstanding union leaders: Jack Mundey, Joe Owens and Bob Pringle. Strongly influenced by New Left ideology (which emphasised equality, personal liberation, participatory democracy, environmentalism and direct action) the unskilled manual labourers of the NSWBLF used their industrial muscle to put their union's advanced policies into action.

Above all, the union is remembered for its most spectacular application of the concept of the social responsibility of labour: the green bans. By October 1973, these bans had halted projects worth 'easily $3000 million' (at mid-1970s prices) according to the Master Builders Association (MBA). By 1975 bans had halted $5000 million of development, saving New South Wales from much of the cultural and environmental destruction it would otherwise have suffered.[1] The bans were a deliberate confrontation with the power of capital. In the absence of sufficiently sensitive planning and conservation regulations, the builders labourers took it upon themselves to dispute employers' rights to build what they liked where they liked, and they were prepared to defend their bans on picket lines and at demonstrations.

Their action was the first of its type in the world. The international *Dictionary of the Environment* entry on 'green bans' comments they were 'very effective in Australia, where they were first attempted' and the *Australian National Dictionary* notes that the use of the term, now international, was recorded earliest in Australia.[2] The green bans were an entirely home-grown contribution to international environmental politics and radical practice, constituting 'one of the most exciting chapters in trade unionism world wide'.[3] Indeed the NSWBLF in this period can be seen as a prototype for the 'social-movement unionism' of the 1990s, which is characterised internationally by militancy, internal democracy, an agenda for radical social and economic change, a determination to embrace the diversity of the working class in order to overcome its fragmentation, and a capacity to appeal beyond their memberships by using union power to 'lead the fight for everything that affects working people in their communities and the country'. Social-movement unionism constitutes, in short, a rehearsal for self-emancipation from below.[4]

The union was extraordinarily outward-looking, even enduring negative consequences for themselves in the form of foregone employment over the imposition of bans: 'Green bans were altruistic' as Mackie noted.[5] The Australian black movement was gratified by the degree of the union's commitment to Aboriginal rights. Homosexual liberationists found the stereotype of the homophobic building worker confounded by the union's practical support for their cause. Women who entered the building industry appreciated the genuine egalitarianism of many of their new work mates. However, the union did not engage in such actions for purely altruistic reasons: because its class consciousness and radical awareness were especially strong, it saw itself as expressing the real collective self-interest of most people in confronting all manner of oppressions and preventing environmental degradation. In doing so it impressed and inspired constituencies far beyond its membership and even beyond the working class. Many New Left academics decided, on the basis of their interaction with the union, that the proletariat might be the midwife of history after all. The 'middle-class matrons' of Hunters Hill discovered this union of manual labourers was more sensitive to the natural beauty of Kelly's Bush and more aware of the need for its preservation than conservative politicians and newspaper editors, and they were radicalised permanently by their experience. Justice Rodney Madgwick remarked at the time on their 'moral force'. While the union's many activities on the part of oppressed groups undoubtedly contributed to this force, the central moral question the union posed for the wider public was whether the pursuit of profit, invariably presented as 'progress', should override all other claims.

Jurgen Habermas's account of the development of the 'bourgeois public sphere' considers the way in which the rhetoric of economic 'privacy' protects some interests from public challenge. Thus issues seen as private ownership prerogatives are shielded from broader debate.[6] It was precisely such private ownership prerogatives that the green ban movement most notably contested, and herein lay the glorious temerity of the NSWBLF. In challenging employers' prerogatives, and successfully showing these traditional rights to be harmful to others and detrimental to the environment, the union confronted the very basis of the power and class relations that the public sphere habitually protects.

NSWBLF and residents blockade Playfair Street, The Rocks, 24 October 1973.
Jack Mundey and the author Meredith Burgmann in the foreground. In the background are
Nellie Leonard, John Clare, John Cox and Peter Wright. (Courtesy Fairfax)

In denying and thereby contesting employers' longstanding perceived right to employ others to build whatever and wherever the profit motive dictated, the NSWBLF and its thousands of active members and supporters formed an alternative public sphere, or what Nancy Fraser has described as a 'subaltern counterpublic': an arena 'where members of subordinated social groups invent and circulate counterdiscourses to formulate oppositional interpretations of their identities, interests, and needs'. Subaltern counter-publics have a dual function in stratified societies: as spaces of withdrawal and regroupment; and as bases and training grounds for agitational activities directed towards the wider public. It is precisely in the dialectic between these two functions, she writes, that their emancipatory potential resides, for this dialectic enables subaltern counterpublics to offset the advantages enjoyed by members of dominant social groups in stratified societies.[7]

The union and its supporters clearly constituted such an alternative public sphere, attracting the support of disparate elements such as union activists, inner-city pensioners, Marxist academics, hippies, housewives, and acclaimed writers and intellectuals. Kay Anderson and Jane Jacobs note in their criticism of narratives about the green bans (which privilege a tale of class-based resistance led by male unionists) that the green ban movement had a scope extending well beyond a narrowly defined class struggle. They also stress the degree to which the movement not only transcended class boundaries, but gendered constructions of urban space that provide spatial expressions of the way women are consigned to the private sphere of the home and men to the public sphere of paid work. With women so prominent amongst the resident action groups, whose requests for assistance were the rationale for most green bans, Anderson and Jacobs argue that the green bans constituted a repositioning of 'the flexible terrain upon which geographies of "publicity" and "privacy" are negotiated', because such urban activism took these 'community mothers' beyond domestic concerns into 'a framework of broader citizenry in which the orbits of publicity and privacy are under constant negotiation'.[8]

The green ban movement, by transcending class and gender divisions in a most dramatic way, yet being based on the power wielded by those engaged in productive labour, can be seen to function as a space of withdrawal and regroupment, and as a base for agitation directed towards the general public. However, while Anderson and Jacobs understandably take issue with the depiction of the builders labourers' involvement with the resident activists as 'a kind of heroic, rescue operation' (whereby the women are 'escorted into the public sphere of politics' by the builders labourers)[9] there would have been no green bans without the NSWBLF.

This is the crucial difference between an alternative public sphere and social-movement unionism. Social-movement unionism often includes the formation of a subaltern counterpublic (because its constituencies are wider than its membership) but it directs this agitated and agitating public towards specific goals through actions undertaken primarily by a union. It was because the green ban movement constituted a subaltern counterpublic mobilised by social-movement unionism that it was not merely challenging and popular but also – through the power of that union to withdraw its labour – extremely effective.

Builders labourers marched from First Fleet Park to Premier Askin's Office, in October 1973 (left to right: Seamus Gill, unknown, Joe Owens, Bob Pringle, Duncan Williams).

A new phrase was needed for such a significant new action. Precisely because these bans were not imposed in any direct sense in the interests of the workers concerned, who were even denying themselves work in the process, the usual terminology of 'black ban' seemed inappropriate. Indeed, the altruistic and ecologically aware nature of the action demanded a completely new nomenclature. In February 1973, more than eighteen months after the movement had started, Mundey coined the term 'green ban' to distinguish it from the traditional union black ban imposed by workers 'to push their own issues'. He argued that the term was 'more applicable as they are in defence of the environment'. A greater sensitivity about racist language had also made use of 'black' less attractive. One of the Battlers for Kelly's Bush refers to Mundey's 'brilliance' in coining the term, reckoning it 'a turning point in public support', removing as it did the 'ugly connotation' of black ban. Mundey realised the imposition of a green ban had 'much more positive social and political implications' than those associated in the public mind with black bans. Affirmative rather than negative, the neologism helped the message behind the action to be heard. Green bans, unlike black bans, contained both an environmental element and a social element: they expressed the union's determination to save open space or valued buildings and to ensure that people in any community had some say in what affected their lives.[10]

By mid-1973 'green ban' was being used regularly to describe the union's actions. The *Canberra News* was possibly the first to use the term when it reported on 23 May 1973: 'Mr Mundey said today that the "green" ban on Black Mountain had the backing of most Canberra people'. The *Adelaide News* commented on the new term on 20 August 1973. By this stage the eastern states' media were playing with a range of colours to describe the activities of the NSWBLF: on 28 October 1973 the *Sunday Mirror* claimed 'Jack (Green Ban) Mundey' was threatening to place an 'amber ban' on a city hotel; and the NSWBLF's unsuccessful attempt to persuade Tasmanian unionists to ban the damming of Lake Pedder was touted as a 'blue ban'. At this time, press use of the term 'greenies' designated supporters of the NSWBLF green bans,[11] from which point it later broadened to embrace environmentally concerned people in general.

The power of the term was acknowledged by those against whom the bans were directed. During the 1973 New South Wales state election campaign, when the green bans were a hotly contested issue, both employer and state government authorities attempted, with little effect, to rename them 'red bans' to stress the dangerously radical orientation of the union and the revolutionary implications of the bans.[12] The union's other main opponent, the federal organisation of its own union – whose employer-sponsored Intervention against its New South Wales branch late in 1974 was to bring this remarkable period to a close – declined to use the term 'green bans' precisely because it was associated with the New South Wales branch and emblematic of its wide cross-class support. The federal BLF insisted on the long-winded 'environmental bans' or persisted with the negative designation of 'black bans'.

The modern European green movement has its origins, at least etymologically, in the activities of the NSWBLF. Speaking in the Senate on 21 March 1997, Senator Bob Brown of the Australian Greens recalled:

> Petra Kelly the feisty, intelligent, indefatigable German Green came to
> Australia in the mid-1970s. She saw the green bans which the unions, not

least Jack Mundey, were then imposing on untoward developments in Sydney at the behest of a whole range of citizens who were being ignored by parliaments. Thank glory that, because of their action in the mid-1970s, such places as the Rocks, one of the most attractive parts of Sydney, still exist. She took back with her to Germany this idea of Greens' bans, or the terminology. As best we can track it down, that is where the word 'green' as applied to the emerging Greens in Europe came from.

Bob Brown and Peter Singer claim the significance of the green bans movement was more than etymological, that Kelly did not merely import vocabulary into Germany: but was so inspired by the green ban movement that it was mainly responsible for her launching the German Green Party; that she would often speak about the impact that the green bans had upon her and her philosophy; and that she was especially impressed with the linkage achieved between environmentalists and a progressive trade union movement.

Similarly, when Paul Ehrlich visited Australia during the green bans period, he considered the phenomenon of workers uniting with resident action groups and conservationists in direct action to protect the environment 'the most exciting ecological happening, not only in Australia, but overseas as well'.[13] In the light of the failure of green politics in the past two decades to achieve similar spectacular alliances between trade unionists and, in Mundey's words, 'enlightened middle-class people',[14] the success of the green bans has continuing implications for green political practice today and in the future.

Because the union's activism was concerned not merely with the environment, but a wide range of social issues, the subject matter of this book raises many currently fashionable concerns about the rights of women, indigenous Australians and homosexuals, while confounding many of the paradigms within which these concerns are expressed. New social movement theory has tended to view these matters as lying beyond the parameters of trade union action and has effectively discounted the role of the labour movement in achieving broader social changes. The NSWBLF's achievements in precisely the areas dear to new social movement activists contradict the assertions of many theorists who dispute the efficacy or even possibility of organised working-class action in pursuit of such aims. Only a certain sort of union could initiate, develop and maintain green bans. The NSWBLF sponsored the green bans, not simply because the environmental consciousness of its leading ideologues was especially high, but because it was a dramatically different kind of union. The NSWBLF's philosophy and practice challenged not just developers but employers, governments and traditional trade union structures. To comprehend the green bans, the union that produced them must be understood: a union that developed what Mundey described as a 'new concept of unionism'.[15] The publicity accorded the green bans has obscured the other ways in which this union was remarkably different from other unions, even those generally regarded as being left-wing. If the circumstances that prompted the bans had not arisen, the innovative organisational forms and the peculiarly militant strategies pursued by the union would still deserve their place in history for the very real challenge they represented to customary labour movement and industrial relations practices.

For instance, rank-and-file control of union affairs and limited tenure of office for union officials were as threatening to the established trade union bureaucracy as the green bans were to the developers. The unionists' contempt for arbitration procedures and enthusiasm for direct action, industrial sabotage and workers' control of jobsites, not only created considerable unease among the union bureaucracy but provoked immediate retribution from enraged employers and their allies in government. Such opposition was quite apart from the angry reactions in these same circles to the green bans. The hostility the union aroused in public and the antagonism it encountered from within the ranks of the labour movement were due at least as much to these more generally challenging aspects of the union as to the green bans. The ultimate demise of the NSWBLF was not a victory merely for those who opposed its green bans, but for all who feared its new concept of unionism. Similarly the support and enthusiasm for the NSWBLF was engendered not simply by its green bans, but also by these features that were as essential to it as the principle of the social responsibility of labour.

Only a union that was growing in strength as a union, with a union leadership that enjoyed the support and welcomed the active participation of the membership, could countenance such a contentious form of union action as the green bans. Its successes in improving membership levels and participation rates, and its remarkable achievements in improving wages and conditions through militancy, clearly aided its wider radical political and social agenda. Such activity came more naturally and easily to a union that was also very committed to and successful in pursuing normal trade union aims, albeit by abnormally democratic and combative means. These two aspects of the NSWBLF – the politically radical and the militantly economistic – were interconnected outcomes of its remarkably new concept of unionism.

THE PRECONDITIONS
FOR RADICAL UNIONISM

I must be asked why the green bans movement emerged at this time, in this place, in this union. Andrew Jakubowicz has examined the eruption of the movement in the context of urban struggle and class politics.[1] The emphasis of this study is on the union, and it investigates why the NSWBLF took the leap which dramatically extended the concept of unionism, while other left unions remained bound by traditional parameters, and why it was the NSWBLF and not other unions that physically confronted capital on the question of socially useful labour.

The media opinion of the time was that the militancy and political activity of the NSWBLF was simply a product of the building industry boom. However, this does not explain why other building industry unions, notably the Building Workers' Industrial Union (BWIU), failed to respond to the same stimulus. If the cause was the strategic position builders labourers held within the industry, it does not account for the fact that the BLF in the other states remained unaffected and were even hostile to such radical gestures. If the influence of a de-Stalinised Communist Party within a generally radicalised political climate was the answer, why did most other Communist unions remain unchanged?

A peculiar conjuncture of factors explain the phenomenon: the general economic and industrial relations conditions; the building boom and technological and structural changes within the industry; the radical ideological influences on the membership and leadership of the union; the recent history of the union, that made it especially responsive to these conditions; and the way in which the occupation of being a builders labourer inclined them to unconventional activity.

THE ECONOMY

Just as unionists in many other industrialised countries experienced militancy in this period, Australian workers were making significant progress in improving their real wages and conditions through industrial action. Working days lost annually per employee in industrial disputes in Australia had averaged around 0.2 during the 1950s and early 1960s, but rose dramatically to 0.46 in 1969 and to a high of 1.29 in 1974. This successful strike activity demonstrated to many for the first time the efficacy of collective action and induced many unions to seek over-award payments by negotiating outside the system. This tendency was encouraged by low unemployment, and the fact that people entering the workforce during the late 1960s had no memory of the depression or war years, and therefore had higher expectations than previous generations of workers. The high inflation rates of the period also encouraged militant wage demands in both the blue- and white-collar sectors: a pattern replicated internationally. Significant wage rises were being demanded, and more often, usually with success precisely because the inflationary times allowed employers to pass the cost increases on to customers.[2]

The militancy, consequent upon a high degree of job security in a booming and inflationary economy, was encouraged further by the effective removal after 1969 of any threat that industrial courts would use their penal powers against militant unions. This was the significance of the unions' triumph in the 1969 general strike which contested the gaoling of Melbourne tramways union leader Clarrie O'Shea for his union's refusal to pay fines levied by an industrial court. Jack Mundey announced in August 1970:

> I think tactics in strikes, particularly since 1949, have been so tailored as to give a high priority to the penal powers threat, and thus the need to 'get them back to work' to avoid fines.... With the removal of some of the teeth from the penal powers in May 1969, longer strikes including general strikes are likely to become the order of the day.

Moreover, the penal powers had increasingly chained union activity to the grind of the arbitration system. Mundey believed unionists, including the left, had fallen victim to 'arbitration-mindedness under the influence of the penal powers', and that the 1969 general strike was 'decisive in cracking the sense of frustration which was becoming universal among workers'. The Clarrie O'Shea case and the subsequent defeat of the penal sanctions cleared the way for militant action and the chance for unions to be 'on the offensive'.[3]

CHANGES IN THE BUILDING INDUSTRY

The conditions for offensive action by workers were particularly propitious in the building industry. The industry was relatively unaffected by the slight recession of 1971–72, and had experienced unprecedented boom conditions and full employment from the late 1960s until 1974. The builders labourers rediscovered the truth of the old maxim that militancy thrives in a favourable economic climate. 'Militancy worked differently to what I'd always thought,' Dean Barber discovered. 'When there's plenty of money around, the fridges are full and there's no worries about getting a job, that's when blokes become militant.'

The building boom facilitated militant activity and easier union organisation. More specifically, the developers' need for speedy completion of speculative projects, financed by venture capital loans at high interest rates, gave a tactical advantage to the building industry unions, which they were loath not to exploit. Kevin Cook observed: 'the boss wasn't really the boss, we knew it and he knew it'.

The flow of millions of dollars of foreign investment into Australia was encouraged by the Coalition Government's reluctance, despite a booming economy, to revalue the dollar, due to pressure from the Country Party, whose rural supporters would have been adversely affected. Development projects in the Sydney CBD soaked up much of this speculative investment, a process facilitated by taxation laws that encouraged commercial rather than domestic building and the especially lax town planning regulations in New South Wales. This had a dramatic effect on the state's construction industry, as described in MT Daly's *Sydney Boom, Sydney Bust*. Throughout Australia, the total value of new buildings approved jumped from $1734 million in 1965–66 to $2943 million in 1970–71, of which New South Wales' share was $1095 million (compared with Victoria's $677 million). While the number of approvals for houses, flats, shops and factories doubled in this period, the approval rate for offices almost tripled.[4]

Though the boom was most concentrated in office block construction in the Sydney CBD, it also spread to Newcastle during 1972. With large projects such as Lombard House and the Civic Centre underway, the union was able to make significant progress in the area. According to the northern organiser, Tony O'Beirne 'the membership jumped … We really organised Newcastle, we didn't let up till we got every site organised.' By the end of 1972 the major builder of the Lombard project was complaining: 'The whole future of the project may be in doubt because of this Sydney based militancy being waged in Newcastle through the local BLF officials'.[5] According to O'Beirne, the builders labourers were strongly imbued with the belief that their time had come, that 'it's happened in Sydney – it's now happening here'.

Construction in the rural areas of New South Wales, particularly in the northern region, began to accelerate by 1974 as developers turned some of their attentions to country towns. Small centres such as Wyong, Gunnedah, Casino and Coffs Harbour experienced their own mini-booms, a trend that was to continue throughout the 1970s. As the union responded quickly to the favourable conditions, union membership, organisation and militancy in these remote areas proceeded apace.[6]

The relationship between workers' militancy and boom conditions is revealed in statistics. For example, 1971 saw many new large building projects commenced in the city. Industrial action was very high throughout 1971 in general, but especially so in New South Wales and even more so in its building industry. In the first five months of that year, three out of every four working days lost were recorded in New South Wales; and about 45 per cent of the total days lost in all industries were lost in the building industry.[7]

With the rise in capital investment, the number of workers engaged in the industry also rose (though not in direct proportion to the value of new construction, due to new less labour-intensive technology). The number of builders labourers in New South Wales increased from 7101 in 1961 to 9302 in 1972.[8] The clustering of so many of the new projects around Circular Quay meant that, for the first time, large numbers of builder labourers were concentrated in one area. As Marx predicted long ago: 'with the development of industry the proletariat not only increases in number; it becomes concentrated in greater masses, its strength grows, and it feels that strength more'.[9] This feeling of strength was an important factor in militancy. Certainly, the largest jobs tended to be the most militant: when giving reasons why the big jobs were so, builders labourers reported 'a feeling of safety in numbers'. This local concentration of the workforce had ramifications for militancy over and above the safety in numbers experienced on each site. Large numbers of builders labourers drinking together in Quayside hotels fostered a culture of solidarity, enabling acts of militancy to be remembered, repeated and even organised. Often, radical NSWBLF philosophies were reputed to have originated in pubs such as the Ship Inn, the Paragon, and the First and Last.

Many builders labourers of all ages reported being radicalised by 'the big, militant, well organised city sites', which educated less experienced labourers.

Glenys Page, one of the newcomers, explained how 'there was always some-one on the site who could explain what was happening and what the company was trying to do to us'. She also described how, as militancy on the site progressed, 'the nature of the job changed. The workers, even men who'd worked for Watts for nine years, became more militant as time went on and were prepared to strike. We became stronger and more unified.' In any case, as Noel Olive observed, because the larger nature of the constructions lengthened the employment periods of all building workers, it encouraged a feeling that it was worthwhile to fight for decent wages, safety conditions and amenities.

Many of the newly recruited labourers found the better wages and conditions which the union was able to extract from the large developers tempted them to remain in the industry. Previously the occupation of build-ers labourer had been seen by most as a stepping stone. Migrants in particular would work as labourers until they learnt enough English to gain a better job. However those who came into the industry in the late 1960s and early 1970s often decided to stay, despite their original intentions. This had posi-tive ramifications for the union in the quality and experience of its members, as Dean Barber explained: 'At last we were no longer training militants for other unions. They stayed around and got involved.'

The building boom in no way alleviated the labourers' dislike for the 'enemy'. Journalist Paul Gardiner noted 'the remarkable hostility that exists between employer and employee' in the building industry at this time. Pro-fessor RN Johnson, Dean of Architecture at Sydney University, observed early in 1972 that the building industry's management was too 'autocratic and finance-oriented' and that many strikes in the building industry were caused by 'a growing alienation between management and workers'. The building boom and the technological changes in the building industry exacerbated the poor relationship between employers and employees because the old-style construc-tion companies (that hired all labour and played the traditional 'boss' role) were becoming displaced by large development companies. The sheer size of the projects, and consequently the companies that employed builders labour-ers, rendered the division between employer and employee increasingly stark and antagonistic. Dean Barber remarked: 'I didn't realise how big the enemy was until I became involved in big building. It's just more obvious in the build-ing game.' Many labourers, when giving reasons why they believed the new-style big jobs became militant, explained: 'you weren't in face to face contact with the boss like you were in bungalow building'. Clearly the loyalty to the boss, which labourers may have felt when small- to medium-scale construction companies dominated the building industry, was greatly weakened by the increasing role of gigantic and often multinational corporations.[10]

The proliferation of subcontractors, combined with the increased size of the main contractor, further exacerbated the poor relations between them and the workers. Subcontractors had always had a reputation for under-capitalisation, bankruptcies and bad debts, and they became even more notorious during the 1960s. John Hutton explains that the boom attracted into the industry 'ill-prepared and uncoordinated' teams of subcontractors. Not only were they ill prepared, many were downright dishonest, and confrontations between the NSWBLF and subcontractors over unpaid wages and other financial irregularities were common.[11]

Labourers were still employed on the 'one hour hire and fire rule', and the large contractors were just as likely as the old-style master builders to use this power of dismissal. Labourers therefore had few loyalties to their employer. They were far more likely to be devoted to their union precisely because of job insecurity: while their employers changed continually, they always belonged to the same union. As Dean Barber expressed it: 'We quickly absorbed the fact that we would always get more from the union than from the boss'. Employers, on the other hand, were more divided than before.

The changes in the industry that prompted greater attachment to the union on the part of the workers had encouraged a much greater differentiation among building industry employers. The MBA was undoubtedly the most significant employer organisation in the building industry in New South Wales, yet less than 40 per cent of eligible building employers at this time were members, and it was increasingly unrepresentative of those for whom builders labourers then worked. The *Financial Review* described the MBA at this time as adopting 'the tone and approach of the majority of its membership who are old, well established middle and small-scale builders, many of them family or private companies'.[12] Significant very large companies such as Civil & Civic, Parkes Development and Holland Constructions were not members of the MBA during crucial periods in the 1970s.

This situation was to cause major rifts among building employers, especially during the 1973 lockouts and the 1974 deregistration proceedings. It was not unusual during the early 1970s for the establishment media to make reference to the 'fragmented employer groups'.[13] Thus the NSWBLF, stronger, more unified and more resolute than in the past, was arrayed against employers with substantial disagreements about how best to exploit their workforces. While the degree of class antagonism in the building industry was encouraged rather than ameliorated by the technological changes accompanying the boom, the employers' capacity to restrain and discourage union militancy was eroded, both by the boom conditions and the structural changes among employers.

This situation clearly improved the building unions' position, but boom conditions alone cannot possibly explain the obvious difference in industrial philosophy and behaviour between the NSWBLF and the other major union in the building industry, the BWIU. With approximately 50,000 members nationally and 22,000 in New South Wales in 1974, the BWIU was the principal tradesmen's union. It also effectively controlled the industrial and political outlook of most of the small and obscure craft unions, many of which were still state based organisations. In the early 1970s the number of unions in the Building Trades Group (BTG) of Labor Council fluctuated between nine and eleven, but the BWIU dominated the BTG with the assistance of six small craft unions that were associated with it, some with memberships of less than 400. The NSWBLF's major ally among building industry unions, the Federated Engine Drivers and Firemen's Association of Australasia (FEDFA), which had about 1200 of its 5500 members employed in the building industry, was in the Metal Trades Group rather than the BTG of Labor Council.[14]

The dominance of the BWIU among building industry unions did not reflect the deteriorating position within the industry of the tradesmen it represented. Builders labourers were more favoured by the technological changes accompanying the boom than were the tradesmen, and this is of greater significance than the boom as such in explaining NSWBLF militancy. The nature of the new developments was such that, while all building industry workers improved their bargaining power, builders labourers further improved their industrial muscle in relation to the tradesmen. The new construction methods of the boom period transformed the relations between tradesmen and labourers, to the advantage of the labourers, because these changes required: larger scale preparatory demolition and excavation, carried out by builders labourers; a greater degree of labourers' autonomy in the workplace; increased use of concrete, which was handled by the builders labourers; and greater reliance on certain ticketed builders labourers in skyscraper construction.

The increased importance of large-scale demolition and excavation preceding construction meant that very large numbers of workers, who were builders labourers in practice, were needed to get projects underway. Although the new methods reduced the overall amount of labour, they did require large numbers of workers on site in the very early stages. Thus the NSWBLF was not only strengthened by the greater numbers of demolition and excavation workers, but it was in a strong position to influence the mood of each workplace from the start. The demolition and excavation work attracted a huge influx of labourers, often migrants, who had never before worked on building sites. With no predetermined attitudes as to how a building site should operate, they were, according to Duncan Williams, quick to appreciate the effectiveness of advanced action. Militant organisers and job delegates were able to set the pace among a large and relatively inexperienced pool of labourers. For many labourers 'growing with the job' was an important factor in their increasing commitment to the union. Glenys Page explained: 'I got more involved on the job because I was there at the early stages when a lot of things were being thrashed out among the workers and with the Company … eventually I was elected a delegate'. By the time large numbers of tradesmen arrived to work on such sites, patterns of militancy had already been established by the NSWBLF, which tended to continue for the duration of the project.

The most important aspect of the new building methods was not that labouring jobs proliferated at the expense of tradesmen's positions, but that builders labourers no longer assisted tradesmen: instead they worked autonomously in other skilled or semi-skilled occupations. The tradesmen were experiencing a relative loss of skill and status rather than a loss of jobs, for the new methods encroached upon their old skills while relying on the newly acquired skills of the labourers. The use of glass, aluminium and concrete, as well as pre-formed concrete and other prefabricated sections which arrived onsite pre-cut and already painted or coloured, was increasing in both commercial and domestic construction. Aluminium replaced timber joinery and plastic pipes, stud-nailing machines and other innovations substituted for the craftsmanship of tradesmen. The special problems of transporting the prefabricated units to the central city sites resulted in greater industrial strength accruing to the dogmen and crane drivers, as they had to be on-site waiting for them because of lack of storage space. One disgruntled architect complained: 'The crane driver and the dogmen … can tie up the whole site'.[15] A simple refusal to work overtime or a strategic sick day became an industrial weapon of great potential.

Even more nerve-wracking for employers was the ease with which the physical properties of concrete could be used to such good industrial effect by those in charge of pouring it: the builders labourers. If a concrete pour is commenced but not completed, the wrongly set concrete has disastrous consequences on a building site. The ability of builders labourers to walk off, or threaten to, before completing a pour was an important bargaining point. Previously used only in foundations, concrete was now used in many ways. O'Beirne described how quickly the tactic, and with it the realisation of the power this gave the labourers, spread from Sydney to Newcastle: 'breaking concrete pours … we said "that's just the most fantastic thing that's ever happened, why didn't we think of that?"'. With union coverage of almost all concrete work, the NSWBLF was aware of the special strength this gave it in negotiations or confrontations with employers: a power that contributed to the general mood of militancy at this time.

Finally, the most obvious way in which the building industry was transformed was in the construction of skyscrapers, which commenced in Sydney in the 1960s with the AMP building (207 metres) and the MLC Centre (262 metres), projects that were quickly dwarfed by even taller buildings in the 1970s. The height of the new structures assured riggers, scaffolders and dogmen of long-term work on each site, producing a large body of these skilled or ticketed builders labourers, who began to see the building industry as their lifetime occupation. It was this core of ticketed labourers who provided the impetus for many of the struggles. The height of the skyscrapers and the new technology also demanded increased skill on the part of these BLF members, once again at the expense of BWIU tradesmen. Builders labourers used their ticketed position in a tight labour market to bargain mercilessly with the developers, for they had the ability to bring most high-rise sites to a virtual standstill within a few hours of stopping work. Joe Owens, a dogman, referred to this combination of circumstances as the union's 'peculiar industrial muscle' and spoke proudly of its use to promote 'a deliberate challenge to the existing authority'.[16]

The tradesmen were less than thrilled about such developments. They complained that:

> The production on most major construction projects could be stopped
> almost at an instant by the action of a very few key members of the BLF. It
> was relatively easy for this particular union leadership to ban demolition of
> buildings, to suspend crane work or hold up concrete pours by involvement
> of [a] small group of workers.

The tradesmen conceded that the other building unions 'did not have the same industrial power.'[17] Although new areas of skill opened up for some tradesmen, such as air-conditioning and sprinkler fitting for the plumbers, and lift installation for the metal workers, the BWIU craftsmen became increasingly superfluous. Rarely were the old skills of these carpenters and bricklayers required on the large building projects. As Rod Madgwick observed, 'carpenters on city building sites are a bit of a joke, all they have to do is hang doors and sometimes not even that. Even bosses knew it.' Thus the craftsmen experienced a diminution of their ability to control the industry, and of their own autonomy. Stripped of 'craft knowledge and autonomous control', the tradesmen lost opportunities to exercise 'discretion' in the work place, which is considered essential for groups of workers likely to 'push the frontier of the workmen's control further into the employers' territory'.[18] Their new vulnerability increasingly led them to adopt conservative industrial attitudes.

In a reverse process, the NSWBLF reacted to the builders labourers' rise in status. Just as rank-and-file tradesmen felt threatened by deskilling, labourers felt the power that their new industrial position brought them. The labourers were not losing the power to exercise 'discretion': in many ways they were gaining it. As Ralph Kelly proudly explained to Pat Fiske in 1980:

> It required so much labour to actually place the materials on site that the strength of the BLs was growing rapidly. We were developing skills that were becoming necessary with the new technology. We became scaffolders, riggers, hoist drivers, dogmen, steel fixers and concrete finishers. We were builders labourers but it was not an artisan's job. It was a labourer's job, a new kind of labourer, a skilled construction worker, a builders labourer!

The changing relationship brought about a new feeling of confidence, which was clearly enunciated in the builders labourers' attitude towards possible amalgamation with the BWIU: it would have to be based on 'respect for the builders laborers as equals, and not as second-class building workers'.[19] The feeling of equality with the tradesmen not only bolstered the morale of builders labourers as individuals, it greatly encouraged them to feel pride in their union: when interviewed many labourers mentioned their newfound selfrespect before they even mentioned green bans. Tony O'Beirne: 'My brief period in the BLs gave me a different idea of how I should be treated'. Darcy Duggan: 'We got our identity back and we weren't being cudgelled by other unions'. Mick McEvoy: 'The spirit was different. We were saying "we're the BLF" and ain't nobody kiss my arse.' Bob Baker: 'It certainly convinced lower-paid workers that we weren't garbage, and that we had some rights'. Dean Barber explained how his consciousness was affected:

What I seen I admired. I seen a group of blokes prepared to get up and look authority in the eye and tell them to get stuffed. That was the first time I'd seen that even though I'd been in some stupid riots inside institutions but they were only one-off situations. Here was a group of blokes prepared to stay, look authority in the eye and keep fighting. Now for a lot of blokes, that's what they marched down the street about – not green bans.

This feeling was particularly strong among migrants. At one mass meeting in 1974 Viri Pires made an emotional speech in which he described how he was no longer just 'a wog', he was a builders labourer: 'I can hold up my head with pride and say I am a builders labourer'. This pride, which was some-times mistaken for arrogance, manifested itself in small but significant ways, as Seamus Gill observed:

> Years before, blokes didn't say they were builders labourers. If someone asked them in the pub they'd say 'I'm in the building game' or 'I'm just a labourer' but now they'd say, 'I'm a builders labourer' because there was a certain amount of dignity attached to it.

Overall, the technological changes that prompted greater antagonism towards employers on the part of building workers had also transformed the relation-ships among workers in the building industry, especially between the labour-ers in the NSWBLF and the tradesmen in the BWIU. The picture which emerges of the building boom in New South Wales is of a dynamic, well organised BLF, increasing numerically in relation to the tradesmen, but also in status and industrial bargaining power.[20] However, strategic importance is of no industrial benefit whatever without a radical ideological stance,[21] and without it little of lasting significance would have occurred.

IDEOLOGICAL INFLUENCES

Possibly the most interesting radicalising force operating on the NSWBLF was the ideological climate within which it was acting. Especially significant was the effect of the Communist Party of Australia (CPA). Because the CPA had long been influential within the building industry unions, the various splits and ideological schisms of the party had their reflections within the building unions. Owens recalls that the 1968 Soviet invasion of Czecho-slovakia 'caused total consternation in the building industry … there were even punch-ups on jobs'.[22] When the CPA transformed in 1971, with the departure of those most loyal to the Soviet Union, this was to have significant repercussions within the BLF.

An earlier CPA split had had profound consequences upon the BLF. The federal office of the BLF was in Melbourne, where Norm Gallagher (federal secretary since 1961) had dominated both the union's Federal Management Committee and the Victorian state branch under its like-minded secretary, Paddy Malone. Gallagher and Malone were among those who had left the CPA in 1963 to form the Communist Party of Australia (Marxist-Leninist), known generally as the CPA (M-L), or simply the M-Ls or Maoists. This split among Australian communists expressed the Sino-Soviet split of the time, with the CPA (M-L) upholding the People's Republic of China as the true defender of the hard-line communist principles associated with Stalinism, against the alleged moderation, tendency to detente with the capitalist west, and capitulation to liberalising pressures evinced by the Soviet Union under Khrushchev. The difference of ideologies between the Victorians and the NSWBLF at this time was always a significant factor in explaining not only the actions of these two sections of the union but also the relations between them.

For many others within the Australian communist movement, the weak and inconsistent reforms of the Khrushchev era that had antagonised those who formed the breakaway CPA (M-L) did not go far enough in the direction of true democratisation and de-Stalinisation of the Soviet Union. After the departure of the Maoists, the more radically democratic elements within the CPA, which also believed each country's communist movement should develop its own policies without reference to any communist government elsewhere, gradually gained the ascendancy within the party, under Laurie and Etic Aarons. The subsequent Soviet invasion of Czechoslovakia revealed the tensions that had already developed within the CPA: it did not cause them. The Aarons faction had already become increasingly dissatisfied with the 'narrowness, conservatism and timidity' of certain Communist union officials.[23]

The CPA thus germinated the split that was to occur in 1971, when those enamoured of the Soviet Union, who felt that no more change was needed and that Moscow's guidance should be sought on domestic matters, departed to establish the Socialist Party of Australia (SPA). It is these developments that account for the political orientation of the BWIU under Pat Clancy, for Clancy resigned from the CPA in August 1970 and most of the other BWIU officials followed him into the SPA when it was formed.[24] As the SPA's most prominent union leader, Clancy was subsequently dubbed 'Klansky' by those more sceptical of the Soviet Union's achievements. The influence of the SPA was felt beyond the BWIU, because the small craft unions tended to follow the BWIU. Thus the ideological split dramatically compounded the difficult relationship between the BLF and BWIU.

Given that neither China nor the Soviet Union had any interest whatsoever in the Australian building industry, and that most Australian building workers had no strong opinions on which nation in the communist world best preserved the principles of the Bolshevik Revolution, it seems bizarre that the purported 'lines' of Beijing and Moscow should loom so large in the calculations and motivations of Australian building union leaders. But Gallagher and Clancy and their supporters in unions across the country cannot be comprehended without reference to their sectarian political affiliations.

The complex and increasingly acrimonious relationship between the federal BLF and its New South Wales branch, due to the ideological differences between them, was exacerbated by Gallagher's determination to strengthen the power of the federal body. However, intervention was much more than a natural transfer of functions from a state branch to a federal organisation: it constituted a brutal standover. Moreover, although Gallagher was aided in his vendetta against the New South Wales branch by the tendency towards centralisation in the union movement, his principal allies were the building industry employers. Far from fearing future confrontation with a more centralised BLF, the employers were pleased to aid the Maoist federal body's desire to eliminate the unusually militant, independently minded and ultra-democratic New South Wales state branch, whose increasingly autonomous nature mirrored the mood of the most militant elements within the generally progressive forces of the CPA at the time.

It is significant that the relationship which really blossomed under the new conditions was that between the NSWBLF and FEDFA. Members of both unions gained considerable status and strategic power from the new conditions and as Jack Cambourn, secretary of FEDFA pointed out, rank-and-filers of both unions worked together, especially FEDFA crane drivers and NSWBLF dogmen. This physical interaction was greatly fortified by political proximity via the mutual influence of the CPA, producing a combination of immense strategic importance. Both Cambourn, who had recruited Mundey into the CPA in 1955, and Vic Fitzgerald, the FEDFA organiser in the building industry, remained in the CPA and were actively involved in all the green ban struggles.[25]

The 1971 split in the CPA and the ensuing BLF–BWIU split left both the party and the NSWBLF open to the influence of the New Left ideologies that were a powerful force in the late 1960s and early 1970s, for the tensions that had developed within the party had essentially resolved themselves by the exit from the party of those hostile to the New Left influences upon the party. It is hard to encapsulate properly the euphoria which enveloped the left in those heady times, though Frank Moorehouse's *Days of Wine and Rage* evokes the temper of the period.[26] Nor was this temper a merely local phenomenon. Donald Horne made the point that:

> Even Wendy Bacon's *Tharunka* and Jack Mundey's green bans, though founded in local idiom and reflecting local traditions, and able to be explained in local terms, arose at the time they did from moods (of permissiveness and environmentalism respectively) that were similar to moods overseas.[27]

Mundey considered that events overseas, such as the American black power movement, had 'impressed' builders labourers and that the activities of students in many countries (including Australia) 'have also made an impact and been appreciated by advanced workers'. For his own part, he stressed the impression made upon him by the struggles of workers and students in France in 1968, which encouraged 'the style of *offensive* strike developed in our struggle'.[28]

In a muted way the new Federal Labor Government of Gough Whitlam, elected in December 1972 (18 months after the first green ban) expressed, and all too briefly reinforced, the radicalisation of Australian society and the impact of New Left ideology at this time. Within weeks this government recognised China, ended conscription, abolished race as a criterion of immigration policy, began reform of the health service, supported equal pay for women, banned racially selected sporting teams, abolished federal British honours, increased arts subsidies, put contraceptives on the medical benefits list, moved to stop the slaughter of kangaroos and crocodiles, and searched for a new national anthem.[29] The widespread feeling that change was not only desirable but possible, expressed in Labor's 'It's Time' election slogan, undoubtedly encouraged other ways – such as the green bans – in which people at this time, guided to differing degrees by New Left ideology, sought to improve both the world around them and their immediate circumstances.

Most of the central precepts which distinguished New Left ideology – personal liberation, participatory democracy, the struggle against racism and sexism, direct action forms of political activity, community decision-making, and environmentalism – were encompassed by the NSWBLF. All involved, according to Owens, the question of 'who makes the decisions'.[30] In this New Left climate the NSWBLF style flourished: Warwick Neilly remarked that the NSWBLF 'reflected the times'. The leadership all agreed that New Left ideology had influenced them but, when questioned about specific acts such as the introduction of limited tenure of office for branch officials, claimed 'it arose out of the struggles we'd had within the BLs'.[31] The NSWBLF leadership forged a distinctive and innovative industrial variant out of New Left ideology.

With the departure of the 'Old Left' comrades in 1971, the CPA was temporarily able to reposition itself as the leading expression of New Left ideas within the trade union movement. The peculiarly radical and militant temper of the NSWBLF owed much to the de-Stalinised nature of the CPA after 1971. Meanwhile the success on the ground of the new style NSWBLF fortified the New Left disposition of the CPA. Both party and union were responding to the same radical political environment in a mutually reinforcing process. This was facilitated by the fact that about one hundred New South Wales builders labourers were also members of the CPA, many of them joining the party after being radicalised by the union. Although the party's formal vehicle of influence within the union was the Building Branch of the CPA, the way in which CPA philosophy was most easily transmitted to NSWBLF activists was not through this branch, or through party schools or reading matter, but through pub conversations, and discussions over tactics at NSWBLF meetings.[32]

The new political freedom and independence discovered by the CPA after 1971 clearly had its industrial reflection in the NSWBLF, whatever the precise nature of the interaction between the two. In this situation the NSWBLF, unlike the BWIU or the federal BLF, was especially willing and able to struggle for all manner of reforms – industrial, political and social. Determined to shape events and not simply react to them, the union moved away from the traditional defensive or protective role of the trade union and towards an offensive stance that committed it to militant actions in the pursuit of both economistic and new social movement aims. Employers were to discover that the independent and radically minded NSWBLF was an unusually determined opponent.

THE RECENT HISTORY OF THE UNION

There were further factors specific to the union itself that contributed towards its radical disposition. Much of the NSWBLF's distinctive style and philosophy is prefigured in the rank-and-file militants' long struggle over the previous two decades, first to rescue the union from a corrupt and conservative leadership clique, and then to consolidate their own positions as the union's new leaders. The protracted and difficult campaign against the gangster regimes of the early post-war period greatly affected those who were to become the leadership after 1969, and brought about the existence of a union that was effectively a new organisation.

During the late 1940s and 1950s the union had been firmly under the control of a right-wing gangster element. In 1951 a Rank and File Committee was formed, encouraged by the CPA, to oppose this leadership that engaged in physical intimidation, corruption, excessive secrecy and ballot-rigging. The Rank and File Committee gained hundreds of supporters in this period: often it would have a majority at branch meetings, only to have their decisions ignored by the executive. Violence erupted in January 1961 when a general meeting was called to endorse three delegates to the union's Federal Conference. It was attended by 200 members and it was obvious that the Rank and File Committee's supporters had a clear majority over those of secretary Bill Bodkin. Mundey recalled the fracas:

> Bodkin kept descending the stairs and I kept picking him up, carrying him back and sitting him in his seat … It was the first democratic meeting ever held in the Builders Labourers... we kept them [the Bodkin group] sitting in their seats 'til 10 o'clock with the [police] down below … it was the first time we hit the headlines.

The Rank and File Committee organised enthusiastically during 1961 for the triennial branch election, coming to an agreement with some independent centre groups so that the Rank and File/Centre ticket represented a broad range of opposition forces. Mick McNamara, a left-wing member of the Australian Labor Party (ALP), was this coalition's nomination for secretary. The entire Bodkin team was defeated and the new team took office in November 1961, only to discover no office staff, few administrative records, burnt minute books, a bank account of £9 and debts totalling £15,000. (Much of the union's history of the 1960s is the story of the executive's uphill fight to repair the NSWBLF's financial position. By the late 1960s the branch was on a much sounder financial footing.) Mick McNamara, only 21 and Australia's youngest union secretary, relied heavily on Jack Mundey for advice and support. Mundey was elected temporary city organiser in 1962 and became a major force in the union. For the 1964 election, the Rank and File team, as the new leadership still called itself, included both CPA and ALP members, and the membership voted overwhelmingly for this ticket. Among the newcomers on the executive was Mundey, and later in 1967 Bob Pringle, Tom Hogan and Bud Cook were elected to the executive for the first time. In 1968 Mick McNamara resigned the secretaryship on health grounds, and Mundey was elected secretary. Bob Pringle became president in 1969 and, with Joe Owens elected as temporary organiser, the group that constituted the leadership in the 1970s began to emerge.[33]

NSWBLF secretary (1961–68) Mick McNamara with Arthur Calwell,
probably during the 1966 federal parliamentary election campaign.

Important changes in the way the union conducted its internal affairs
began to materialise during the later 1960s. These were an open democratic
structure of decision-making, and an emphasis on rank-and-file participation
– both significant legacies of the long fight against undemocratic decision-
making and the old right-wing leadership's blatant abuse of its power. Moreover, an increasingly militant industrial stance was becoming evident. The
rolling of the old regime had been so thorough that the union was, to all
intents and purposes, rebuilt as an organisation. Judy Mundey, who had
worked in the union office from 1961 until she married Jack in 1965, talked
of the male organisers and female clerical staff starting afresh in 1961 as 'raw
young things' learning the ropes together. Jack Mundey claims that the great
advantage of this situation was that 'there was no old entrenched hierarchy
in the union'.

In terms of theoretical analysis, the union could be regarded as a 'new'
union; the process of 'taming' was greatly inhibited.[34] While co-option and
incorporation can and do occur at all stages in a union's growth, these tendencies are less marked in the early stages. Certainly, the NSWBLF leadership bore the marks of their newness to union officialdom, moving in and
out of full-time union positions with apparent ease and no discomfiture.

Even before the union introduced its rule of limited tenure for officials, most of the senior officials (such as Bud Cook, Brian Hogan, Tom Hogan, Peter Barton, Roy Bishop and Duncan Williams) were in the habit of returning voluntarily to 'the tools' for lengthy periods. When Owens returned to the job from his position as an organiser in 1970, the union journal remarked that 'he could not be talked into remaining an official'.[35]

Thus the union leadership of the early 1970s was not a long-standing and entrenched oligarchy remote from the rank and file. Except for Mundey, not one official had held a position for more than a few years. It was a leadership able and willing to respond both to the radicalising influences from wider economic, industrial and social forces, and to the militant aspirations of the rank-and-file. HB Davis has argued that many campaigns have failed because conditions were not favourable, and that many discontented workers have remained unorganised because union leaders neglected to step in at the right time.[36] The NSWBLF leaders were not reluctant to seize the historical moment offered them.

The size of the union facilitated its radicalisation and rendered it relatively immune from the tendencies in union development towards bureaucratisation and conservatism. Despite the impression fostered by the media, the NSWBLF was not a large union. Membership rose from about 2500 members in 1961 to about 9000 in 1971, rising to a peak of 11,000 in 1973–74. Mundey regarded the union's size as significant: 'There was a lot we could do as a small union we couldn't have done if we were bigger'.[37] The NSWBLF did not experience the problem of the 'iron law of oligarchy' identified by Robert Michels as a necessary feature of large organisations, and described by Richard Lester:

> As the organisation grows in size and its activities and responsibilities enlarge …
> a hierarchy and bureaucracy tend to develop, and the relationship of top officials
> to the rank-and-file grows more impersonal … as the top positions come to
> require more administrative and manipulative talents, the oratorical agitators are
> superseded by skilful managers.[38]

On the contrary, because the union's size remained manageable, the union leadership was able to have daily contact with members in disputes and to maintain a close link generally with the rank and file. The union office, as the organising focus for a small and generally proximate membership (rather than the remote hub of a gigantic bureaucratic apparatus) was able to be organised so as to encourage members to 'drop in with their problems' or just to socialise. Tom Hogan recalled how, when the union office moved to Room 28 of Trades

Hall in 1971, they redesigned the interior so 'there was no counter between the organisers and the members like there is in other union offices'. Members took advantage of this welcoming atmosphere and would gather around the coffee machine during strikes or after work to discuss the union's activities.

Thus compactness enabled the democratic principles of the union leadership, forged in the battle against the previous regimes, to be realised and maintained. These democratic practices then kept the leadership in touch with the rank and file, in tune with their needs and aspirations. In particular, the loyalty of members who could remember the 'bad old days' was immense and long-lasting. The high regard in which the leadership was held by the rank and file, and the degree of trust and confidence between them, made the majority of union members receptive not simply to the militant industrial relations strategies preferred by the union leadership, but also to its radical social and political agenda.

THE OCCUPATION OF BUILDERS LABOURER

The occupational grouping of builders labourers had certain characteristics that in the favourable circumstances engendered militancy: youthfulness, larrikinism and itinerancy.

A general characteristic of builders labourers is their youth. Evidence suggests that being a builders labourer, always a physically demanding occupation, became even more so during the building boom. The union journal recorded in 1966 that 'because of the strain of multi-storey work, most of our delegates and active unionists are young … the pressure of building construction today makes it difficult for most men over 45'. During the 1970 margins strike, old-timer Theo Austin commented that the extraordinarily militant behaviour of the members 'showed that younger workers had what it takes'. Not just the vigilante squads that demolished scab-built labour, but also the union's full-time paid officials were young. In the 1970s all the organisers except Prendergast were in their twenties or thirties – very young compared with most other unions.[39]

Certainly the culture of the union was young. Mundey observed: 'When the BLs started to buzz it was a pretty young-thinking outfit'. According to Duncan Williams, the type of industry veterans who 'were old and staid and invariably pro-company and pro-boss' were few and far between. Most older workers, outnumbered by the new and youthful workforce, were caught up in the spirit of the times and became involved in radical industrial activity. Mundey claimed: 'even the older people like Dick Prendergast and others were generally in a mood of being young'.[40] Youthfulness not only encouraged industrial militancy, it meant the builders labourers were more receptive to the values of the youth culture of the time, which was inclined towards rebellion and unorthodox behaviour. Occasionally the experience of militant industrial action led directly to countercultural behaviour. Dick Whitehead tells the story of a conservative builders labourer who found himself involved in a crane occupation and was so affected by the experience he tried smoking marijuana, and had been smoking it ever since.

The 'Leagues Club incident' was also indicative of the union's susceptibility to the values of the youth culture. In April 1973 Bob Pringle was refused admission to the Eastern Suburbs Leagues Club, despite being a long-time member, because his hair 'fell below the collar line'. Pringle maintained the club's attitude was discriminatory, impinged on individuals' human rights and he began a sustained campaign to have the rule changed, arguing that 'under the present rules … Einstein, Captain Cook and even Jesus Christ, would have been barred'. He was successful in having the club call a referendum, which was narrowly lost. Pringle then argued the referendum had been unfair because female associate members of the club had been refused the right to vote. Tony Hadfield, a NSWBLF organiser and former Eastern Suburbs player, was also refused entrance for having long hair. (Although it was commonly assumed that the union banned work on extensions to the club as a reprisal, this was only ever used by the union as a warning and was never implemented as an actual ban.[41])

Pringle and the union had publicly committed themselves in support of 'the longhairs', which in those days carried clear connotations of youthful defiance. In terms of dress codes the incident indicated the union's lack of propriety on such matters, compared with other leftist workers' unions. Mick McEvoy believed that the BWIU, 'the so-called craftsmen, were tied up with notions of respectability, they actually disapproved of us, even the way we dressed'. To such unions, the dispute was undoubtedly read as yet another larrikin gesture on the part of a disreputable union.

The epithet of 'larrikin' was one which the labourers attracted: 'People try to make us out to be heavy-handed larrikins', Tony O'Beirne complained.[42] It was also a term they also used about themselves. Seamus Gill commented:

> The larrikin style was definitely there and I think we worried some of the respectable trade union officials. We didn't wear suits and ties or anything like that. I think a lot of that comes from working in a ratshit job to begin with – not the best of conditions.

NSWBLF organisers and officials did not dress or behave like other union officials. Outside Central Court in Liverpool Street after a court appearance in 1974 are (left to right) Johnny McCarron, Bobby Chandler, Joe Owens, Ian Makin, Tony O'Beirne, Bob Pringle, Dean Barber.

Other phrases redolent of larrikin characteristics, such as 'rough', 'lair', 'knockabout' were frequently used when the labourers were describing themselves, their actions and their attitude towards life: Tony O'Beirne observed that the Newcastle disputes had a flavour of 'energy and roughness'; Rhonda Ellis mentioned the 'lair factor' common to many of her male builders labourer counterparts; Seamus Gill commented that the conditions of employment in the industry 'tend to make you a bit more of a knockabout'. The irregular and outdoor nature of the work (at a time when there was ample stable indoor work for manual workers) attracted unconventional personality types, and this was especially true of some more skilled categories of work – dogman, rigger and scaffolder. These were also the most dangerous forms of employment. The larrikin culture was as strong, therefore, among the better-paid builders labourers as it was among the pick-and-shovel labourers. Evidence from the interviews suggests the ticketed labourers had the same attitudes and modes of self-identification as the unticketed labourers. According to Mick McEvoy this is because 'lairs are attracted to those sorts of jobs in the first place'.

McEvoy believed that the larrikin style came from a 'nothing to lose' mentality: 'If you're the lowest of the low then who gives a fuck', and as Mundey conceded when asked whether he regretted not being better educated: 'Every builders' laborer wants to be something else … It's a bastard of a job.'[43] The builders labourers can therefore be seen to constitute a class with nothing to lose but its chains, the living expression of alienated humanity that Marx saw as the one truly reliable force for social change. Yet Communist Party organiser Mick Tubbs remembers that many in the party were aghast at what they saw as the union's unwarranted larrikinism in their enthusiasm for industrial sabotage: 'Hands were thrown up in horror'. About his personal change of heart on the issue he said:

> I realised that it wasn't alienating them from their membership. It was part of the BLs to be that way. The average BL was a knockabout, a bit of a larrikin and providing it was kept within bounds, providing serious questions were considered seriously and sensibly, and realisable objectives were projected, then they accepted that [sabotage] as part of the industry … better to be that way than stuffy union officials.

In any case, as he remarked, 'in any other society some of the major developers would have been in gaol'.

The more itinerant nature of the work also created a workplace culture noticeably different from that of other unskilled workers such as process workers or even the skilled tradesmen in the building industry.[44] Labourers stressed in interviews that although long-term projects offered the opportunity for more stable employment, this did not really affect the basic insecurity of their position as builders labourers. Therefore, although the pace and size of construction in the early 1970s engendered longer-term patterns of employment that encouraged militancy, this relatively novel degree of job stability occurred in an industry traditionally reliant upon a mobile labour force ready to move from job to job and employer to employer. This had produced an itinerant culture among builders labourers, which remained strong even when, during the boom, job stability was at its best. It was accepted that labourers would suffer periods of unemployment between jobs, and that even in the course of a particular job employment was not secure. Dismissal rates in the industry had traditionally been high, and much higher among labourers than tradesmen. Mick Curtin referred to the 'semi-nomadic life of the Builders' Labourers, continually kicked from job to job'.[45]

While conclusive figures on itinerancy in the industry are not available, the 1975 Inquiry into Employment in the Building Industry suggests that employers regarded the builders labourers they employed as itinerant, and itinerant of their own accord: 'The employers' view was that the main reason for termination of employment was the voluntary act of the worker; the high turnover level was due to the independent nature of the building worker'. The union did not concur on the matter of volition, pointing out builders labourers needed to leave jobs close to completion to go to another project just beginning. Whatever the cause, the inquiry concluded that figures on labour turnover suggested that:

> the building industry has a higher percentage of persons whose jobs have lasted less than one year than industry as a whole. There is also a higher percentage of jobs of less than 13 weeks duration … The differences are greater between tradesmen and labourers in the building industry than between … comparable groups in other industries.[46]

Thus, the inquiry's findings reinforce the view that job duration for builders labourers was short compared with both the tradesmen in the same industry and with unskilled workers in other industries, and that this was especially true of the unticketed builders labourers.[47]

Itinerancy builds a culture with specific characteristics. A cursory analysis of the home lives of the 46 builders labourers interviewed certainly seems to confirm this view: only seven were married and living in a family situation and only four owned or were buying a house. Itinerant work not only induces a state of mind in those involved, it also attracts to it a certain type of personality. Many of the labourers mentioned the itinerancy of the industry as their reason for becoming builders labourers, and its attractiveness to such personality types undoubtedly increased with its capacity to employ easily and quickly. *Rydge's* maintained that the building boom attracted 'a lot of men from the sea with a tradition of radical unionism', and a building industry employer claimed that the full employment situation forced the industry to use workers who 'are neither interested in nor suitable for permanent employment'.[48]

Those deemed by employers to be unsuitable for permanent employment were presumably those who agreed with Roy Bishop's assessment of the situation: 'get what you can as quick as you can'.

The traditionally insecure nature of builders labourers' employment encouraged an impatient attitude to industrial action. At the same time, longer-term job prospects made effective industrial action more feasible, and even more worthwhile in terms of lasting gains than in the past. Thus the culture of itinerancy, based on traditional insecurity, mobility and periodic unemployment, was as important in modeling industrial attitudes as were the boom conditions of the time that ameliorated the situation. It was a powerful combination that produced a worker with a peculiarly militant temper and, in the political climate of the time, one also responsive to radical ideas: a larrikin with a social conscience.

THE GREENING OF THE UNION

Why did the 'new concept of unionism' developed by the NSWBLF manifest itself most spectacularly in the form of environmental bans? Clearly, a radicalised union of builders labourers who accepted the principle of the social responsibility of labour would necessarily question the products they themselves made. 'Workers,' Mundey persistently stressed, 'must be concerned about the end result of their work'.[1] In New South Wales in the early 1970s there were very good reasons for builders labourers to recoil from that which they were paid to do. The degree of general alienation experienced by builders labourers has already been discussed, but further consideration of the alienation effect helps to understand the militant environmental action undertaken by this group of workers.

THE CONCRETE JUNGLE

One important aspect of how the construction boom served to radicalise the builders labourers was the nature of the development taking place. What was being built and the way it was being built was having a profound effect not just on the leaders of the union but also on the rank-and-file labourers. It was increasingly obvious to them that the CBD was becoming massively overdeveloped. They could take Mundey's point that 'it's not much use getting great wages and conditions if the world we build chokes us to death'.[2] In addition the boom in commercial property was causing a major reshaping of central Sydney at the behest of an elite with control of finance capital and influence on governments.[3] Mundey described the process that builders labourers observed at first hand:

During the 1960s and early 1970s, our major cities underwent a transformation. Enormous amounts of 'hot' money, both from Australia and
overseas, were poured into property development. The construction of giant
glass and concrete buildings changed the face of our cities. This was most
evident in Sydney, much of whose charm and beauty were destroyed in the
name of progress.[4]

Workers on the city sites predicted a glut in office space well before the
financial pages of the daily newspapers were aware of it. As early as 1967
Bud Cook was complaining about the overproduction of office blocks, but
it was not until late 1971 that the oversupply began to attract serious public
comment.[5] Indeed, the union's concern with the problem helped advertise
its existence. The expression 'concrete jungle', used regularly by Mundey at
this time, was cited in the *Sydney Morning Herald*'s 'Sayings of the week' on
25 September 1971, when Mundey declared: 'The building industry can
only be described as a concrete jungle'. It was highly appropriate, then, that
Taming the Concrete Jungle was the favoured title for Pete Thomas' 1973
book, by which the union hoped to justify its green bans to a wider public.

When a 16-storey office-block in Woolloomooloo failed to attract a bid
at auction, then remained vacant for years afterwards, it became the topic of
many discussions among building workers. They were well aware that it was
they who were being required to construct the office-blocks, many of which
were superfluous. As long ago as 1968 the union had expressed its concern
that, despite increased building volume overall, 'the housing needs of the
Australian people remain unsatisfied'.[6] Thomas described the situation as the
union saw it in the early 1970s:

> ... people are desperate for homes, caught by a housing shortage that has
> been chronic, and the NSW Housing Commission chairman has confessed
> himself to be 'sick with worry' about the housing plight of low-income
> people. Yet, while this crying human need persists 'developers' have underway
> or in planning over $600 million worth of Sydney city office, retail, and
> other commercial construction projects, to add to an existing glut of empty
> office space.[7]

The oversupply of office-blocks was displacing inner-city working-class communities, as the popular green ban song 'Under concrete and glass' emphasised:

> *Under concrete and glass, Sydney's disappearing fast,*
> *It's all gone for profit and for plunder.*

Though we really want to stay they keep driving us away
Now across the Western Suburbs we must wander.[8]

Builders labourers could see that the destruction of the inner city was driving their class out of its traditional residential areas. Their class consciousness and environmental awareness were thus mutually reinforcing. The union's response to the environment, Mundey explained to the Workers' Control Conference in Armidale in 1973, was 'provoked by the frustrations of people living in cities and being confronted with the destruction of the so-called building boom'.[9]

Reflecting on that period, Mundey stressed the connection between the profit motive and wasteful inefficiency: 'Construction was for profit, not for use.' There were millions of square feet of vacant office space in Sydney's centre, 'while people looking for their first homes or flats could find nothing'. There were 40,000 on the New South Wales Housing Commission waiting list, but because of the shortage of finance and the high price of land it was able to construct only 5218 dwellings in 1971–72. The problem was caused by 'speculators or so-called developers'. In March 1974 it was revealed that, although the Commission had $20 million for urgently needed houses, it could not spend the money because there was 'a shortage of bricks and mortar – and men to put them together'. The same process of financial and manpower resources being diverted to the large-scale developments, and the consequent increase in prices of materials, had caused small-scale builders who constructed homes for individual buyers to go out of business, with serious repercussions for home buyers. The casualties were low-income earners living in matchbox flats in order to raise a deposit on a house, the price of which was rising faster than they could save. In the midst of this domestic housing crisis, there were 370,000 square metres of unlet office space in Sydney, and 24 per cent of CBD office space was unutilised.[10]

While alienation is generally considered to arise either from the relationship to the means of production or from the nature of the work, there is evidence that workers who question overproduction or waste in their industry experience an especially radical form of alienation. For instance, John Foster has argued that the Oldham cotton workers' criticism of overproduction and competition in their industry was significant in forming their anti-capitalist attitudes.[11] The nature of builders labourers' work heightened their awareness of waste in the industry, for it was primarily they who demolished the existing and often still useful buildings to make way for the office-blocks.

'Ordinary builders labourers', as Owens stressed, 'are the ones who break the ground, when this kind of Public vandalism takes place.'[12] It was therefore easier for builders labourers to see the contradictions inherent in the building boom, and the often dire consequences in human terms, than for the other building workers who were not so involved in demolition. At the same time, it was the builders labourers' involvement in demolition that gave them the power to prevent the environmental irresponsibility they came to abhor.

The Green Ban Float in the May Day Parade in 1975.
On the truck are Darcy Waters and Elvis Kippman.

The first environmental ban placed by the NSWBLF was as early as 1962, when a group known as the North Sydney Citizens' Rights Committee approached the union for support in its fight against the Department of Main Roads, which had summarily provided the affected people with only one month's notice to quit their homes to make way for the Warringah Expressway. Secretary Mick McNamara made an announcement that was later to achieve a familiar ring: 'Members of my union will not demolish any house or flat which is occupied and we control this section of the building industry'. However, a subsequent statement from McNamara indicated the distance between the union's position in the early 1960s and the green ban days: in explaining the ban on an invalid pensioner's home in the path of the expressway, 'Mr McNamara said his union did not oppose building the expressway, but it objected to people like Mrs Davies being evicted without suitable accommodation'.[13]

The union's environmentalism, which eventually encompassed an anti-expressway philosophy, was unformed at this stage. But throughout the 1960s there is evidence that issues of town planning were increasingly concerning the union. In a 1966 issue of the *Builders Labourer*, Mundey vehemently criticised the boom in office-block development and pleaded instead for the construction of socially useful projects. In the April/May 1967 issue, Bud Cook again criticised the number of office-blocks being built and called explicitly for the construction of schools, homes and hospitals. At a delegates conference in 1967, it was recorded that: 'Cde. Mundey … thought that we should demand that the Federal Government make more funds available for essential and useful work'. By 1969 Cook was attacking the State Planning Authority for 'scandalous' activities, arguing the urgent need for pensioner housing and complaining that working-class people were being forced to move further out of the city. By March 1970 Pringle was advocating 'War on pollution, not on people'.[14] With the green bans under way from mid-1971, the union continued to stress the need for proper planning. Much of the BLF literature of this period made reference to a speech to the MBA by the Federal Labor Government's Minister for Housing, Les Johnson, who had criticised the building of office-blocks at a time when there was a housing shortage.[15]

In May 1974 the union attempted to have a claim inserted into the National Award log stipulating that 60 per cent of the building industry's resources be diverted into construction of public amenities such as hospitals, kindergartens, creches and houses. 'This claim,' explained Owens, 'is designed to channel resources away from building useless office buildings which presently stand idle in all major cities and use our limited resources in the public interests'. In support of this demand Cook undertook a study in collaboration with the Teachers' Federation of what 'socially beneficial construction' was necessary for education purposes, and organisers attended teachers' meetings to pledge support to their struggle for better facilities.[16] The nature of builders labourers' work also acquainted them intimately with the direct consequences to building standards caused by the remorseless pursuit of profit. They also witnessed the lack of co-ordination and planning, and the way developers pursued their own interests with no properly independent, overall assessments being made of the compatibility and total impact of the individual investment decisions. The incessant competition between individual capitalists and the financial greed underpinning the boom repelled those who laboured long and hard to maintain this competition and sustain the avarice of their employers with such scanty remuneration for themselves. Builders labourers' longstanding antipathy towards developers undoubtedly served to maintain the momentum of the green bans.

As a union of building industry workers, increasingly alienated from their employers and appalled by the products they were required to produce, the NSWBLF came to believe it had a special responsibility to alert the wider community to problems within the building industry. It also concluded from its experience with a relatively unregulated industry that development should be controlled not by the builders alone but by the general public and by those who worked in it. At the 1971 ABLF conference, the New South Wales branch proposed 'A National Building Industry Enquiry', maintaining there was a crisis in the industry:

> … because of the complete lack of planning, the terrible problem of sub-contracting [and] the huge degree of bankruptcies occurring in all States … A call for an open enquiry will show our union's preparedness to debate the problems, the scandalous activities of 'developers' and 'builders' and win us public support in our drive to achieve greater control of the industry.[17]

Mundey, Owens and Pringle stated in 1975 that private ownership of land, both residential and commercial, and the attendant difficulties in restraining how individual landowners chose to utilise their private domains, was one of the major reasons for the need for green bans in Australian society.[18]

Public safety, the union argued, was also at stake. Quality of home building was compromised, Owens explained, because 'the good materials are going to commercial developments and the home building sector gets the oddments'. Yet commercial developments posed a greater threat to public safety because of the manner of their construction. Pringle caused a controversy in May 1974 when he reported in the Federal Department of Housing magazine *Shelter* that unsafe building methods were being used to cut costs and save time – a concern he had first expressed publicly in September 1973 in a Brisbane newspaper. He claimed he had found 'serious bulging and wall cracks in dozens of high-rise office and residential blocks in Sydney', which could cause wall facings to fall into the street from great heights. The union called for a 'full enquiry into building methods used for high rise buildings'.[19]

Three of the bans were directly concerned with safety for the wider community. In December 1973 the union banned reconstruction work on the Woolworths' supermarket in Warringah Mall, following a fire in which two female employees were burnt to death. Owens announced that 'the Federation would pull the burnt-out building down but it would do no other work until it had assurances that everything possible to prevent fire was incorporated in the new building'. The union, with support from the local labour councils, placed bans on construction work in Austinmer near Wollongong in January 1974, and in Newcastle in May 1974. Inadequate drainage of the sites rendered 'slippage' probable and water leakage inevitable, which would lead to dangerous foundations, cracks in houses, and possible land slides. The only work allowed on these sites was work aimed at solving the problem before any other construction proceeded.[20]

In the wake of these safety bans the union launched a campaign 'to protect people from shoddy or dishonest builders'. Owens revealed the union had at times received up to 24 complaints a day from people dissatisfied with home-building work done for them. The union promised to use its 'industrial muscle' to 'discipline house and home-unit builders' and announced it would co-operate with resident activists in 'protecting low-income home buyers who were financially stretched to the limit' and 'to stop rackets in the home building industry'. If necessary, the union would place a 'ban on any builder who offends frequently against the interests of home buyers'.[21]

FROM ALIENATION TO ENVIRONMENTALISM

From the long-running anxieties about the nature of the building industry, a broader environmental consciousness developed among the union's leaders. Facilitating this was Mundey's upbringing: from his early life on a small farm on Queensland's Atherton Tableland Mundey had learned to love the natural landscape and to respect its integrity, having witnessed the destruction of natural forests in the course of 'development' and the resulting soil erosion:

> I liked living in the country, riding horses, swimming in the streams and
> moving through the rainforest ... [but] There was another side to that
> beautiful environment. The cattle industry had been established by burning
> down the heavy stands of natural timber – maple, cedar, silky oak. This was
> still happening when I was young. It was nothing to look across at night and
> see hundreds of hectares being burnt off. The fires were highly visible and
> a spectacular sight because the burning-off was being done on top of the
> mountains ... That timber should have been retained. The subsequent erosion
> was the price paid for failing to appreciate the need to be harmonious with
> nature.

Moreover, his reluctant removal from this rural environment to that of Sydney
alerted him to environmental issues. Mundey had not come to 'the big smoke'
of his own accord: talent scouts from the Parramatta Rugby League Club had
enticed him to Sydney in 1951 to play for the club, and he appears to have
suffered environmental shock in the course of his relocation at the age of 19.
'City life wasn't easy to adjust to for the boy from Malanda. There were occasions when I would willingly have gone back to North Queensland.'[22] By his
own account, he became an environmentalist soon after his arrival, a position
later reinforced by his experience as a builders labourer:

> Though I had grown up in an area where there were still some rain forests, I had
> really taken them for granted until I got to Sydney. Then I became impressed
> by how beautiful they had been. The building boom of 1960 to '71 in Sydney,
> through which I had worked, convinced me that something was wrong. It made
> me aware that the environment of the city was changing, as I saw the sun was
> shining on fewer streets as the high-rise office blocks went up.

Encouraging Mundey's concerns was the fact that his young son suffered
from respiratory trouble which medical staff blamed on industrial pollution
in Granville, where Mundey had lived in the early 1960s. Mundey's feelings
and concerns were shared by his fellow labourers, even by those who had not
come from the country, as early as the mid-1960s when the Rank and File
team obtained the leadership:

> When we got control of the union, we made a decision at one of our executive
> meetings that we had to do something about the environment, but we didn't
> get much further than that. Then the Kelly's Bush thing came along and the
> answer was clear.[23]

Bob Pringle had also grown up in Queensland. He was born at Toowoomba in 1942, was educated at Enoggera, and after leaving school at 15, worked at many jobs in Queensland, including cane-cutting. He came to Sydney when he was 17. He was active within the ALP and NSWBLF on the issue of land auctions and land nationalisation, and always remained attached to outdoor activities, especially fishing and boating (an enthusiasm that was to claim his life in a boating accident in 1996).[24]

Joe Owens chose to leave the congestion and pollution of England's industrial north ('we were always crook as kids') departing the Durham coalfields in 1958 and coming to Australia as a seaman. Though Mundey claims Owens was influenced during the 1960s by a little-known environmental ban by seamen, who banned a wharf in protest against oil pollution in the harbour, Owens insists his environmental awareness was aroused by Mundey and others after he joined the CPA in the mid-1960s.[25]

The builders labourers' concerns were clearly informed by a growing environmental awareness that was beginning to affect many people's outlook. Mundey recalls:

> It was … in the 1960s that environmentalists started to arouse public consciousness about the finite nature of the earth's resources and their rapid depletion, the alarming increase in the world's population … and the myriad environmental problems caused by the outdated and predatory qualities of existing social systems.[26]

Among the books that alerted the public, and which greatly influenced Mundey during the 1960s, were *Silent Spring* by Rachel Carson, *Population Bomb* by Paul and Ann Ehrlich, and *The Closing Circle* by Barry Commoner.

It is possible that the occupation of builders labourer attracted people more likely to be sensitive to environmental concerns. Builders labourers had chosen outdoor employment in preference to the many other options available for manual workers in this period, and this may indicate a degree of empathy with the outdoors in general, although the majority worked on city building sites. Paul Hogan's ocker character, popular during the green bans period, worked as a rigger on the Harbour Bridge, and Hogan implies that these urban larrikins of the late twentieth century were heirs of the nomad tribe of bush workers of the nineteenth who had represented the stereotypical Australian in their enthusiasm for the bush and their scepticism about city life and its inhabitants. There is considerable anecdotal evidence that, although many builders labourers lived in inner-city working-class communities, their self-image was connected with the archetypal Australian character that valorised bush over city, space over congestion, and the outdoors over the confined.[27] Thus builders labourers were susceptible to environmental arguments, to embracing what Bob Goodin has described as a 'green theory of value' (whereby the last tree or last historic building is more valuable than the second last, and so on) which Goodin contrasts with the brown theories of value to be found in the neo-classical notions of utility.[28]

Builders labourers had personally experienced the operations of brown theories of value, and found them decidedly wanting. The rapaciousness of developers, their use of public assets for private gain, and their disregard for the environment and safety of others were well known to them. From this vantage point it was not difficult to embrace in inchoate fashion a green theory of value. In a hostile article on Mundey, Denis Minogue conceded that Mundey's period in office 'has been marked by an apparent awareness among laborers of the quality of life, possibly even by an abandonment of old principles that the dollar in your pocket and the beer in your hand was what really counted'.[29]

Mundey estimated about half of the union's members were actively 'interested in conservation and preservation'. When an MBA spokesman suggested in a letter to the *Sydney Morning Herald* early in 1972 that builders labourers did not support the leadership's environmental policies, 23 job delegates wrote an angry reply affirming membership support for the union's policies that aimed to ensure that workers' living conditions, not just their wages and working conditions, were adequate.[30]

A green theory of value confirmed the prejudices builders labourers already held about their employers. If the actions of developers could be understood and presented as irresponsible environmental vandalism, then a green theory of value served builders labourers' interests and articulated their hostilities as effectively as Marx's labour theory of value, to which they also intuitively subscribed. Further, given the heightened class consciousness of this particular group of workers, these green values were adapted to emphasise urban conservation: the last pieces of inner-city working-class housing, no less than graceful public buildings, had value. 'Workers had to look further ahead than wages and conditions and ensure that the environment was protected', Mundey insisted, because 'developers would do irreparable damage if they were allowed to go unchecked'.[31]

> Now before the city's wrecked these developers must be checked
> For it's plain to see they do not give a bugger,
> And we soon will see the day if these bandits have their way
> We will all be driven out past Wagga Wagga.

THE PROBLEM OF THE STATE:
NEW SOUTH WALES AND BEYOND

Corrupt and conservative governments could also be indicted by the union in its environmentalist gestures. Apart from the fact that 11 developers received knighthoods from New South Wales Premier Askin, it was not difficult at the time to point to collusion and corruption: Troy has itemised the Askin Government's resistance to the Federal Whitlam Government's initiatives to reduce land prices and increase public housing stock; and David Hickie has detailed the extent of Askin's criminal connections. Builders labourers commented that the New South Wales Government under Askin 'slavishly followed the whims and wishes of the property developers' and Askin 'would do nothing to control his friends the developers'.[32] While sponsoring and encouraging major redevelopment projects, the Askin Government also aided and abetted local councils in their tendency to favour the land development interests, which for a range of historical reasons had always been over-represented at local government level. Third parties in New South Wales had no legal right to appeal the decision of a local council or planning authority to grant a development application; but a developer whose application was denied (or approved only under conditions the developer found objectionable) could appeal to the specially established Local Government Appeals Tribunals. The union's opinion of the Askin Government was placed in a formal statement that Mundey insisted be written into the transcript of an Industrial Commission hearing on 18 September 1971:

> The industrial turbulence which has existed in this industry in the recent years stems from the failure of the NSW Government in particular, as well as employers to face up to the nature of the industry in the early seventies.
>
> The unplanned, environmentally destroying, unstable, chaotic conditions abounding in this industry must be changed in the interest of all parties associated with the industry as well as the general public, many of whom have suffered great hardship because of some unscrupulous 'developers' and 'builders' who have fleeced home and home-unit owners in various ways.[33]

The union's stance on the defence of Kelly's Bush was presented (retrospectively) by Mundey as the outcome of a long-standing concern with the effects on all Sydneysiders, including builders labourers, of this high-level corruption:

> we were ... concerned about Sydney's vanishing green spaces. In the late 1940s and early 1950s, the Cumberland County Council, which then oversaw most of the metropolitan area, planned a series of wide, green belts to surround the

New South Wales Premier Askin was a frequent target of green ban supporters, such as in this demonstration outside Gallagher's office in Melbourne on 1 November 1973 (from left to right: Jack Mundey, unknown, Seamus Gill, Mick Milokhuvic, Julia Moran).

inner metropolitan area. This plan was virtually destroyed through ineptitude, greed and corruption at various levels of government. Our members were living all over Sydney. We had every right to have a say in the future of our habitat.[34]

That Premier Askin and Local Government Minister Morton 'went mad' with anger over the Kelly's Bush green ban actually strengthened the ban because it 'galvanised the men', according to Mundey, due to their contempt for the Askin Government.[35]

Richard Roddewig's study of the green bans movement from a lawyer's perspective concludes that: 'Political, planning and legal factors gave rise to the green ban movement. They explain why Australian unions were the first in the world to use the strike weapon for environmental purposes.'[36] Sydney was the centre of this significant movement. The reason conservationists allied themselves with builders labourers in such a remarkable fashion was that, as Mundey explained at the time, people saw 'the hopelessness' of relying upon the State Government and local councils.

If the Government of the day adopted a responsible attitude on ecological issues, it wouldn't be necessary for resident action groups, progressive architects and town planners, unions with a social conscience and ordinary citizens to come forward and fill the vacuum.[37]

The union's existing concern about a chaotic and unplanned building industry which was aided and abetted by the State Government was expressed succinctly in the slogan of 'People Before Profits'. The union explained its position in the lead-up to the 1973 state election:

> Whilst there is a shortage of labor, materials and finance for houses, flats and units, developers, with Askin's support, ravage park land (Kelly's Bush and Eastlakes – banned), destroy historical buildings (ANZ bank in Martin Place – banned, CML – now retained because of ban), rob the city of cultural expression (Theatre Royal – replaced in new building because of ban, and Regent Theatre – banned) and decimate residential communities (Woolloomooloo, the Rocks, and Darlinghurst – banned).
>
> All this in the interests of a fast buck with no thought to the future of the city.
>
> People need protection – builders labourers support their needs by placing green bans.[38]

Dr Runcie of the Centennial Park Residents Association saw the green bans as a necessary response to deficiencies in the state's democratic processes:

> Not one of those who tout 'democratic channels' and the 'vote-once-every-three-years' strategies offer any answer to what democratic emergency powers are officially available to the citizen at the instant required ... The answer at present is green bans, which citizens will continue to seek from a union that acts instantly and with strength on their behalf ... Until our 'democratic channels' do a like job of instant citizen protection in the emergency riddled area, citizens from all walks of life and all political thinking, will cheerfully continue to benefit from the ... BLF'.[39]

New South Wales Labor leader Neville Wran conceded that: 'Until there is sensible and selective planning, coupled with a positive scheme to stabilise land prices, green bans will be more in the public interest than against it'. He pointed out that South Australian Labor legislation had stabilised the price of land, whereas the Askin Government 'has repeatedly refused to stop this scandal. It has joined with speculators and, by auctioning Crown lands, it has helped force up the price of land.' Hugh Stretton explained the dearth of bans in Adelaide by comparing South Australia's with the 'spectacularly bad government' of the eastern states, of which he said 'It's crooked and far to the right.'[40]

Among these spectacularly bad governments, New South Wales was the one most inclined to favour private developers' ideas about town planning, even promoting them as public ventures. The behaviour of the Askin Government does not in itself explain the peculiar strength of the green bans movement in Sydney, but its performance certainly encouraged the union's growing conviction that it was necessary to pause and take stock of the development process, and that only labour, not the state, would evince sufficient social responsibility to restrain the power of capital.

Few of the environmental bans imposed by the Victorian branch of the union were directed against public development proposals, whereas at least half the Sydney green bans were. Victorian Premier Hamer, unlike his New South Wales counterpart, was not corrupt. Roddewig argues that the Victorian Government became environmentally aware much earlier than the New South Wales Government. For example, plans for a massive Melbourne expressway network through inner-city areas were dropped in the late 1960s after initial planning proposals met with strong neighbourhood opposition. With the government in Victoria exhibiting greater ecological sensitivity and restraint, and with less investment money therefore pouring in to the southern capital, Melbourne bans tended to be smaller targets: individual buildings, parks or sites, rather than entire neighbourhoods. In consequence the combined value of banned projects was considerably less in Melbourne. The Melbourne movement was much less controversial and did not generally involve physical defence of bans by builders labourers as in Sydney.[41]

That said, the Melbourne movement was important and, in its initial action, predates even the Kelly's Bush campaign.[42] The Carlton Association was formed in the late 1960s to protect its residential character of terrace houses against commercial and industrial development, and it can be seen as a prototype for the resident action groups formed in Sydney in the early 1970s.[43] Even Norm Gallagher was intimately involved in the first of these Melbourne bans, from October 1970, in a way only he knew how. George Hurchalla tells the story:

> A block of land in Carlton, an inner Melbourne suburb, which was owned by the railways was to be leased out for a pittance to a developer for commercial purposes ... Upset, the local community called for help from the BLF. As the project was only of benefit to the developer, the BLF placed a ban on the site. In a row with the son of the employer, 'Big Norm' was forced to relive some of his boxing days from his youth until the police intervened and broke two of his ribs while carting him away. Refusing to pay the fine, Gallagher was

locked away for 13 days on charges of assault. Seeing the determination of the people of Carlton and the BLF, the railways were swayed into giving the land to the people as a park under the control of a people's committee.[44]

The New South Wales branch supported Gallagher over this arrest, although it was critical of the fact that the workers were not consulted before the Carlton bans were placed. As Pringle observed, there was also a degree of scepticism among builders labourers about anyone who went to gaol when they could avoid it by paying a fine: 'they thought he was grandstanding ... they said he was a mug for letting himself be gaoled'.

In one way, then, Gallagher could claim a first, as Mundey acknowledges. On the other hand the Melbourne movement was more a series of isolated events whereas in Sydney, 'we could see them all tied together'.[45] Moreover, Gallagher's personal involvement here makes his subsequent action in breaking the green bans of the NSWBLF all the more significant and sinister.

The other Victorian bans, many of which were placed on sites not actually threatened, included : Flinders Street Station; Tasma Terrace in Parliament Place (now the headquarters of the National Trust); the Treasury Building; the Princess Theatre and Windsor Hotel in Spring Street; a restaurant and carpark in the Royal Botanical Gardens; St Patrick's Tower in Cathedral Place; Gordon House for the homeless (until a replacement facility was built); quarrying at Arthur's Seat on the Mornington Peninsula;[46] a National Trust classified building at 61 Spring Street;[47] the Newport Power Station (lifted when the State Electricity Commission agreed to stricter pollution controls imposed by the Environmental Protection Authority);[48] the Regent Theatre;[49] Queen Victoria Market;[50] a row of Parkville terrace houses;[51] the City Baths;[52] the Beaurepaire Pool;[53] two century-old Cypress trees on the corner of Mount Eliza Way and Boundary Road;[54] Mac's Hotel in Franklin Street;[55] South Melbourne's historic 2.1-hectare Emerald Hill estate of nineteenth-century townscape housing;[56] 1.8 hectares of bush frequented by bellbirds in Blackburn Road (where Lend Lease aimed to build 29 home units);[57] the Commercial Bank of Australia building in Collins Street, with its historic dome;[58] terrace housing in Carlton;[59] the construction of a new morgue in a residential area of South Melbourne, on the corner of Napier Street and Church Street;[60] a vacant site in Cardigan Street, Carlton (which local residents wanted for a park instead of the intended flats);[61] the demolition of a house in Abbotsford in the path of the Eastern Freeway (until the Board of Works offered the partially deaf single mother a better price for her house);[62] Blanche Terrace in Fitzroy where Henry

Handel Richardson was born; a projected factory in Albert St, East Brunswick;[63] 8 hectares of bushland in South Warrandyte (which the government made a sanctuary);[64] the construction of a 563-kilometre natural gas pipeline from the Barrier Highway to Gunning;[65] the construction of a restaurant on Point Ormond;[66] all 'construction, repair and extension' of supermarkets that raised their prices from 19 August 1974 (a move strongly backed by the Citizen Action Federation);[67] houses in Mordialloc condemned to make way for a Coles supermarket;[68] demolition of the Yallourn township to mine more brown coal;[69] and old-style city hotels, 'to preserve some watering holes for workers', because the hotel where 'a man can go in his working clothes for a drink at a normal price is disappearing'.[70] In August 1974 Gallagher 'proudly' opened a 'Green Ban Gallery' in Trades Hall, featuring sketches by Joan Coxsedge who had been retained by the union to travel the country sketching historic buildings which, Gallagher said, 'must never be demolished'.[71]

Adelaide had three bans: in 1970 the Norwood velodrome was rescued from becoming high-rise flats (in opposition to residents' protests); the Unley Road shops site in Parkside was saved from becoming an eight-storey block of flats; and Highbury Park, which was to become a shopping centre, became a reserve instead.[72] An *Adelaide Advertiser* editorial conceded there was 'some public sympathy' for the builders labourers' green ban on the Parkside flats, but insisted nonetheless that the union was 'not the proper body to be determining whether it goes ahead or not'. The chairman of the Federation of Adelaide Metropolitan Residents' Association, TJ Strehlow, pointed out that there were no alternatives to such bans: the zoning that allowed high rise building was decided without adequate public discussion in most parts of Adelaide, so many people did not know they lived in a high-rise zone until such development commenced:

> The unions don't just move in. In such cases the local residents are fairly
> desperate and have usually exhausted all other means open to them. For
> a residents' association to change the zoning takes a lot of effort, skill and
> dedication and a successful residents' association is the exception rather than
> the rule.[73]

The Australian Capital Territory branch participated with other Canberra unions in three significant bans: stopping the destruction of Reid House, the old government hostel in Civic, to make way for a carpark; halting for a few days the construction of the Googong Dam on the Queanbeyan River, until adequate assurances were given about its effect on aquatic life in Lake

Burley Griffin;[74] and, for a few months under Mundey's influence, on the erection of the Black Mountain telecommunications tower (until 'big cash concessions' to work on the project enticed Canberra builders labourers to reject Mundey's entreaties as 'outside interference' and to agree to work on the controversial tower).[75]

Perth had two bans: the Palace Hotel, which the Commonwealth Bank wished to demolish and redevelop for its prime commercial site (it was bought four years later by Alan Bond to operate as an old-style hotel with staff in period costumes);[76] and the old buildings in the port area of Fremantle.[77] Hobart had one ban, to save Battery Point buildings dating from 1830 from being demolished piecemeal by developers in late 1973.[78]

In Queensland, the union placed its first ban in mid-1973 on three National Trust classified buildings in George Street, adjacent to the Royal Botanic Gardens, which were destined to make way for office-blocks: The Mansions (1890), Belle Vue Hotel (1886) and the Queensland Club (1884).[79] Visiting the scene of the impending development with a National Trust representative, Mundey urged Queenslanders to be alert to the perils of bad government:

> Unless Brisbane people are vigilant and aware of what developers are doing 'in the name of progress' they will find their city has been destroyed – the same as Sydney … The unions should be responsible and think beyond wages and conditions and support the National Trust in their aim to preserve what is historical … The question now is will Brisbane become a haven for the developer. In the absence of a responsible government the people should take responsibility.[80]

FROM DEMOCRATIC UNIONISM TO ECOLOGICAL ACTION

The New South Wales Government embodied the worst practices of town planning, accountability to the public, and environmental sensitivity of any government. In contrast, the NSWBLF expressed the determination of an unusually radicalised group of workers to hold employers and government answerable to workers, to the public at large and to the needs of the planet. The internal democracy practised by the union found a natural and larger expression in the green ban movement.

Owens observed that government 'elections did not ensure the community participated in decision-making', and in any case 'international corporations had more power than elected governments'. The imperatives of democracy required that organisations such as unions, which had the ability to restrain corporations and prompt governments to reconsider foolish decisions, had to concern themselves with 'important social issues' and 'become more active in opposing pollution and despoliation of natural resources'.[81]

Mundey explained how the union's ultra-democratic principles led inexorably to green bans:

> It is not good enough in a modern society to say that the only right an individual has is to vote once every three years in an election. I believe in everyday democracy. If a decision is incorrect, any individual or any organisation has the right to do all that's necessary to change that decision. Otherwise, how can decisions be altered? All such matters should be subjected to public scrutiny.
>
> All laws are changed, not by the 'great' thinking of legislators, but by the extra-parliamentary activity of ordinary men and women who want to see wrong righted.[82]

The union believed that no greater wrong existed than that the powerful few should spoil and despoil the environment of the powerless many. It presented environmental problems as stemming from corporate power, and thus having their origin in class inequality, while transcending class in their unfortunate effects.

It is in this context that the seemingly bizarre initiative of the union in placing the green ban on Kelly's Bush needs to be placed. This action could be portrayed as an example of a lumpenproletarian union using its industrial muscle to save not only the environment but also the land values of an upper-middle-class suburb. Mundey saw the decision to save Kelly's Bush as a statement that environmental and ecological values went beyond class differences. He recalled his arguments of the time: 'What is the good of fighting for wages and conditions on the job, if we live in cities devoid of parks and open space and denuded of trees', 'Our cities had to be for people, not for corporations to plunder and destroy. Kelly's Bush wasn't just for its neighbours, it should be public land and used by everybody who wanted to use it.'[83]

It was also considered that workers suffered disproportionately from environmental problems. Mundey stressed that, more than other sections of the community, workers had to 'put up with all the problems besetting urban cities such as pollution' because they lived in the least desirable localities, and so it made good sense that they should 'link up with other sections of the community, such as those involved in ecology'.[84] To academic observers the link did not make sense: Mark Haskell described it as an 'unlikely collaboration'; Leonie

Sandercock referred to the relationship between resident activists and the BLF as 'surprising' and, on the assumption there was nothing in it for the workers, anticipated 'that the alliance between middle class and working class is likely to be short lived'.[85] This common assumption, that the 'unholy alliance' (as it was increasingly depicted) benefited only the residents, formed the basis of the charge frequently made against the union: that it was neglecting the interests of its working-class members to suit the interests of the 'trendies'. Thus the legacy of the Kelly's Bush campaign in particular was to provide opponents of the green bans within the labour movement with ammunition to attack the working-class credentials of the NSWBLF.

Such ammunition was fired from both the right and the left. From the left the attacks were carried out as part of the sectarian disputes within the communist movement. The emphasis of the SPA's attack on the CPA and its show-piece union, the NSWBLF, was not only that they were ultra-left but also that they had become preoccupied with middle-class issues such as conservation at the expense of properly working-class concerns. The SPA regarded Mundey's appointment as Aarons' campaign manager (for the seat of Sydney in the 1972 federal election) as 'an attempt by the CPA to convert into votes some of the middle-class support which the BLF has gained from its very active conservation role in the electorate'.[86] From the CPA (M-L) perspective, bans such as those on Kelly's Bush and on Sydney and Macquarie universities over women's and homosexual rights, were grist to the Maoist mill: Gallagher dismissed the extensive public support enjoyed by the NSWBLF as coming from 'residents, sheilas and poofters'.[87]

The union's 'prolier than thou' critics maintained their chorus of disapproval, but the facts of the green ban campaign increasingly belied their accusations that the defence of the environment somehow benefited the affluent more than the poor and that all resident groups were as middle-class a phenomenon as the women of Hunters Hill. While the campaigns to defend the open spaces may have favoured middle-class rather than working-class interests, the campaigns to protect inner-city buildings overwhelmingly expressed the determination of working-class residents to stay put in their traditional communities. The movement also stressed the need to preserve these suburbs for poorer people as low-rental areas, and not as renovated neighbourhoods that would become magnets for the middle class fleeing the suburbs or seeking locations for offices. Most of the green bans were placed to protect traditionally working-class inner-city areas. Pringle clearly stated the union's priorities in imposing bans: 'The position of the union is firstly to support the residents of the area to provide a better environment and to save homes for the working people particularly'.[88] Moreover, the union argued persuasively that working-class people would benefit in the longer term from increased environmental awareness and improved town planning procedures generally.

In any case, the fact of union involvement with resident activism mitigated against the tendency of such activity to favour the middle class. Urban sociologists and geographers have rightly pointed out the class bias of 'not in my back yard' (NIMBY) politics, whereby local communities with middle-class resources are better able to contest the location of 'urban nasties' and compete for desirable amenities, thus exacerbating rather than challenging existing patterns of exploitation and inequality through this 'politics of turf'.[89] Studies of Sydney resident activism in the 1970s by Sandercock and Jakubowicz confirmed the fact of superior mobilisation on the part of middle-class professionals and their 'hegemony' in the debate over the distribution of resources. Lauren Costello and Kevin Dunn note in a 1994 study the salience of earlier observations that the 'cycle of exclusion of the poor and homeless from legitimate or adequate space within the city' continues and that land use disputes position the rich against the impoverished and the powerful against the alienated.[90]

However, the participation of the NSWBLF clearly disrupted the customary balance in favour of the middle class by equalising the bargaining power of resident activists across metropolitan Sydney. With the green ban as the ultimate weapon in stemming unwanted developments, middle-class resident activists had no greater clout than working-class activists, for projects were now contested objectively on the basis of their demerits rather than as unwelcome intrusions in middle-class localities. David Jencken argues that the Kelly's Bush ban immediately strengthened the position of working-class people elsewhere: 'From that time onwards, the people of inner Sydney who had previously been powerless against big developers and government found that they had an effective means of making their wishes known'.[91]

Moreover, the bans clearly favoured working-class interests in many instances because of the value the union placed on the rights of working-class communities. Given the high proportion of bans placed in the defence of workers' homes or habitat, it is most likely that the green ban movement did not merely neutralise the class effects of NIMBY politics but altered the balance so entirely that NIMBY politics was transformed in the process, revealing in Mundey's words, 'the potentially revolutionary character of ecological action, people in action'.[92] Sandercock conceded that the green bans were unusual because they aimed not merely to win a specific struggle but to achieve longer-term 'consciousness-raising'; they were constructive as well as conservative.[93] Due to NSWBLF involvement, therefore, Manuel Castells' optimistic depiction of urban social movements as forces leading to a change in the underlying economic or social structures, and as manifestations of class conflict with emancipatory potential, has relevance to the struggles of resident activists in Sydney in this period.[94]

Resident action groups were formed in many areas throughout Sydney during 1971 and 1972, leading to the establishment in 1972 of the Coalition of Resident Action Groups (CRAG) that co-ordinated protests and pooled resources. The formation of CRAG brought the professional expertise of the groups' members from more middle-class areas directly to the service of those in more working-class areas. Thus the cross-class alliance operated not merely between residents and the union but also among resident groups. In January 1973 a report in the *Daily Telegraph* estimated that resident action groups had been springing up in New South Wales at the rate of two a week for the previous six months. By 1974 there were more than a hundred operating throughout the greater metropolitan area and the 'unprecedented success' of the phenomenon of action groups in Sydney was seen to be due to two facts: the driving force of residents was comprised of 'middle-class, well educated extroverts'; and the 'unholy alliance' consummated with those the establishment would have thought least likely to have shared any common interests with the residents – builders labourers. Professor Neil Runcie, the founding president of CRAG, admitted that many middle-class members found it 'difficult' to be grouped together with the BLF. Similarly, some of the 42,000 members of the National Trust were disturbed by the nature of the newfound power enjoyed by the Trust in association with the BLF.[95] Generally middle-class prejudice was overcome, for as Murray Geddes, another of the founders of CRAG, explained: 'The BLF were exactly what we (the residents) needed. They weren't like other unions. They were really interested in the environment and what we had to say. They listened. The other unions' officials used to come along and give us "the line".' CRAG itself acknowledged its power was 'greatly strengthened' by the help of the builders labourers.[96]

The union regarded the creation of the resident action groups as an exciting development with great potential. Mundey wrote:

> New South Wales has in the past two years seen the emergence of resident action groups linking up with builders' labourers and other unions to become a powerful countervailing force against institutionalised bureaucracy and the power of the developers' dollar.[97]

The combination surprised employers and the government, who were accustomed merely to dealing with claims by unions for wages and conditions. Mundey believed that 'the phenomenon of having unionists come together with residents, in concerted action, formed a new alliance which was so powerful and is potentially still more powerful, that governments haven't found the way to handle it'. He stressed the diverse nature of the action groups, ranging from the upper-middle-class women of Hunters Hill to those 'the other end of the social ladder' at Eastlakes.[98] Troy describes the union's decision to respond to the women of Hunters Hill as 'a stroke of genius', for it brought together women of unimpeachable character with the rebels of the union movement. The 'strange chemistry of those two compounds' concentrated attention on the important principles involved in a way that neither element alone could effect, and gave the resulting green ban movement an extraordinary saliency and legitimacy, which was reflected in the emphasis on urban and residential issues in the Whitlam Government's reform programme.[99]

While most of the green bans were placed to protect traditionally working-class inner-city areas, the union itself did not consider as problematic the middle-class nature of some of the resident action groups, most notably the Battlers for Kelly's Bush. The Battlers were depicted in the media as a 'twin sets and pearls' group, and by Mundey himself as 'Upper Middle Class Morning Tea Matrons' from Hunters Hill. Mundey wrote with approval of the green bans' 'wide and growing support from people of diverse social and class backgrounds'.[100] The NSWBLF saw the movement as a people's movement on the offensive against the prevailing ideology of development at all costs.

Mundey and most of the union's activists were also confident that action against the developers and the conservative State Government would radicalise residents from middle-class areas, and in most cases they were correct. Betty James and Kath Lehaney, two of the middle-class matrons in question, often remarked on how their experience with the Kelly's Bush campaign changed their political outlook. Juanita Nielsen, initially wary of the effect on Victoria Street property values of the squatting campaign, was, as Wendy Bacon notes, won over to the radical agenda of the NSWBLF 'like many middle-class Sydney residents of the day'. Many of the resident action groups became involved in other social issues, such as low cost housing, public transport, tenants' rights and even prison issues.[101] Jakubowicz argues that the critical issue in attempting to analyse urban social movements lies in the dynamics of social change and class struggle; conflicts may become more subjectively class struggles.[102] The green ban movement, even in the instances

Jakubowicz deems the 'bourgeois bans', achieved this subjectivity through unceasing struggles.

There was in any case an over-arching and objective class dimension to the green bans, regardless of the nature of the area being defended, the class composition of the residents concerned or their consciousness. The union argued in 1971 that the 'lust for private profit' was threatening the planet: 'The struggle against pollution and for the preservation of the environment must bring about a confrontation with those who have a vested private interest in pollution, irrespective of the genuine public interest'.[103]

The green bans resisted the power of capital. They seriously thwarted the remorseless quest for profit at the expense of all other forms of value, which was a characteristic feature of a class-based system of exploitation of both people and the environment. The degree of resistance from developers to these bans is clear testimony to the extent to which the bans represented the ultimate form of encroachment upon employer prerogative on the part of a union which, as Part Two reveals, was becoming accustomed to such usurpation.

PART 2

A NEW CONCEPT
OF UNIONISM

ORGANISATIONAL PRINCIPLES AND PRACTICES

According to government statistics, the nunber of potential members of the NSWBLF at the end of the 1960s was 9102; the number of actual members was 4200. By 1973 the union could claim a membership of 11,000. Between 1969 and 1971, BLF membership nationally rose by 136 per cent, compared with an overall union increase of 7 per cent for the same period. There is no doubt that this huge leap in membership was mostly attributable to the building boom but, over the same period, the BWIU experienced only a 2 per cent rise and FEDFA nil.[1] Although these figures may not be entirely accurate, such a huge discrepancy cannot be dismissed as a statistical error. Furthermore, it is obvious from BLF records that the New South Wales branch grew out of proportion to the other state branches. The NSWBLF must bear a large part of the credit for this organisational growth.

It was obvious from the first day of Mundey's secretaryship in June 1968 that there would be greater concentration on organisational details: 'We have such a fine record of militant activity in the interest of the members at job level, we can and must improve the financial unionism, for if we fail, we cannot possibly do a real job and expand, improve our services to the Builders Labourers in NSW'.[2] Mundey's organisational standards were high (organisers were admonished for any deficiencies such as failing to ring in to the office, neglecting to fill out job reports, or not contributing enough articles to the journal) but he also gave credit whenever it was due. There was a need to be even better organised, he stressed, so that all jobs were visited regularly, including those in the outer suburbs. The dedication of the members of the executive and organisers was obvious.

Special all-day executive meetings, extra branch meetings and weekend meetings were arranged frequently. The pace of activity was frenetic, and the officials' working days often very long.[3] Their results, in terms of membership growth, were spectacular.

'NO TICKET, NO START

It was in the wake of the peculiarly militant and successful margins strike in the middle of 1970 that the union was able to initiate its serious crackdown on non-unionists and unfinancial unionists, testimony to the interconnection between hard-fought gains and union growth.[4] As Tom Hogan recalls, after the margins strike: 'We were insisting on "no ticket no start" while the BWIU were saying "fill this form in to pay later and you 'I'll be right"'. The 'no ticket no start' campaign was pursued with the builders labourers' usual vigour: a special branch meeting was arranged to discuss unfinancial membership and organisers were requested to attend; delegates' conferences were organised on the issue; and show-card days were held throughout September and October 1970. To these efforts of the leadership and the organisers, rank-and-file unionists added their own initiatives to the campaign: Keith Jessop reported to a branch meeting that there was 'extensive abuse of workers if after joining the Union they did not pay their dues'.[5] By the end of October the Public Works Department was a closed shop and successful confrontations with other employers had forced them to adhere to the union's policy of 'no ticket no start'. The New South Wales branch meeting on 3 November resolved that: 'From this date we will not work with other than fully paid financial Builders Laborers on any site'. Within a week of this resolution, the city and North Sydney areas were fully unionised. Mundey reported that pay-ins were excellent and announced proudly that 'a new situation now exists in the BLF'.[6]

The geographic concentration of the majority of actual and potential members within the CBD greatly facilitated organisation. Moreover, as these large projects provided longer-term jobs, members became less itinerant, creating a much more stable network of experienced job delegates: often the same people were elected delegate and co-delegate on a site for four or five years. As their competence grew, the basic work of organising the site was left in their capable hands, allowing the union's paid organisers, 14 at the union's membership peak, to concentrate their efforts on those areas which the union recognised had been largely neglected: the suburbs and the country areas.

Increasing the union's density on suburban building sites was made difficult by the nature of building in Sydney's sprawling suburban areas. Here it was predominantly single house construction, with occasional small blocks of home units, which involved a large amount of sub-contracting. The union's executive frequently discussed the problems of organising the suburbs, especially the western areas where Sydney was growing most rapidly, yet it was obvious that, although the suburbs remained problematic, a vast improvement had nonetheless taken place. Don Crotty mentioned that, at stop-work meetings, he met 'members from the Western suburbs who previous to the seventies had been billed by the union for years and had never seen an organiser ... and now they were coming along and getting involved'.

By comparison with the situation in the suburbs, organisation in country areas proceeded apace, despite the tyranny of distance and financial constraints on the provision of organisers. The executive agreed that the scale of building work in Wollongong and Newcastle warranted permanent full-time organisers in both, but that these organisers also had to be responsible for a vast hinterland. In May 1972 the executive appointed Tony O'Beirne, a young Newcastle labourer, as the northern organiser based in Newcastle. His area stretched from the Hawkesbury River just north of Sydney up to the Queensland border. Nonetheless, by 1974, areas as far-flung as Lismore, Coffs Harbour, Gunnedah and Wyong were properly unionised, in many cases for the first time.[7]

INTERNAL DEMOCRACY

Following Robert Michels and other elite theorists, who insist that large organisations will inevitably be controlled by a tiny minority, most academic commentators have emphasised the many constraints which thwart democratic aspirations within trade union structures. However, it is important not to lose sight also of those features which enable democratic aspirations to be realised: the way in which, as Alvin Gouldner has observed, an 'iron law of democracy' operates as effectively as Michels' 'iron law of oligarchy'.[8] Trade unions are among the most democratic organisations in our society, certainly more democratic in general than corporations, parliamentary parties and governments.

However, the democratically elected leadership of the NSWBLF was nonetheless unusual in its determination to expand and enhance internal union democracy, and to reduce the distinction between leaders and led, effectively transferring power away from itself and back to the rank and file who had elected it. When in power the NSWBLF leadership practised the democratic principles normally only preached in opposition. In its organisational principles and practices it anticipated the social-movement unionism of the 1990s, which also emphasises internal democracy and rank-and-file participation in reaction to the increasingly hierarchical forms of traditional unions. An anarcho-syndicalist bricklayer and member of the Union of Construction, Allied Trades and Technicians in Britain, was so intrigued by the innovative style of the NSWBLF he wrote about it in order to publicise its organisational achievements among British trade unionists, because the contrast with British unions was so striking: compared with his union, 'it sounds like a dream'.[9]

The major structural changes initiated by the NSWBLF were: the introduction of limited tenure of office for union officials; the use of temporary organisers; the emphasis on job-site autonomy; the opening of executive meetings to all members; the frequent use of mass stop-work meetings; the tying of officials' wages to the BLF award; and the non-payment of officials during industry strikes. In the country, area committees were established to improve links between members in these more remote areas and the organisers.

In recognition that it was often not formal constraints which most inhibited participation and democracy, the union leadership encouraged members to 'drop in' to the union's office at Room 28 at Sydney's Trades Hall and to participate in informal discussion on union matters with officials. This increased the leadership's accessibility, and rank-and-file perceptions of its accessibility: the ordinary member felt able to criticise and advise the leadership in a way unusual in Australian trade unionism.[10] The leadership also facilitated rank-and-file participation by reducing the formality of the large meetings (while nonetheless retaining enough to avoid the problems identified around this time as 'the tyranny of structurelessness'). For instance, non-English speaking immigrants were encouraged to participate by alteration of the traditional format for meetings.[11] Accordingly, these immigrants, much less intimidated than before, often spoke at union meetings, sometimes with interpreters and sometimes without. The difficulty most members, not just those with language problems, had previously experienced speaking in a large meeting was reduced by a simple change in mass meeting procedure, whereby members queued at microphones and spoke in turn rather than having to depend on catching the chairman's eye.

The spoken rather than the written word was the medium of NSWBLF democracy. Its members were unskilled workers, mostly uneducated, occasionally illiterate and often unable to read or speak English. The written word was simply an inappropriate tool in the circumstances. Not only were the members unaccustomed to the written word but the leaders themselves felt uncomfortable expressing themselves in print. The union operated nonetheless on the principle that all organising work, including the production of pamphlets and the editing of the sporadic union journal, be carried out by builders labourers and not appointed research officers as in most unions. (This brought about a situation where written work was largely neglected.)[12] However, in a membership of 11,000, concentrated predominantly in the CBD, the lack of written material was not a serious failing. Rather it contributed to the internal democracy of the union in that it created less differentiation between leaders and the led: it was easier for a rank-and-file member to refute an official's argument at a job-site meeting than to write a criticism of it.

The NSWBLF was moving against the trend of increasing bureaucratic and oligarchic practices in trade unions throughout the industrialised world. Moreover, this was a tendency being exacerbated in the Australian situation by the arbitration system, which as many commentators have suggested promoted centralism in unions and a tendency to rely on specialist advocates or outside experts to negotiate wage agreements.[13] Thus, in sharp contrast to most union bureaucracies in Australia in the 1970s, the NSWBLF leadership encouraged rank-and-file initiative and expressed faith in the membership's ability to make 'correct' decisions. This trust was reciprocated: the leadership was highly regarded by the rank and file for its hard work on wages and working conditions, its honesty, its accessibility, and its solidarity. The unusual consensus-style decision making was widely known about and commented upon among the members. Viri Pires noted: 'The media always talked about Jack Mundey deciding this or saying that but we knew that it had been a collective decision'.

The high degree of internal democracy and the militant industrial relations strategies were interconnected. According to Pete Thomas the basis of the union's militant strength was 'democratic control by the rank-and-file': the way in which the tenure of officials was limited, and the 11,000 members were regularly exercising their strength and initiative through job-site committees and stop-work meetings.[14]

While enthusiasm for the leadership was quite strong in the provincial centres and even in more remote areas, the support base for the new democratic and militant practices was clearly concentrated in the Sydney CBD, especially on the gigantic concrete and glass erections emblematic of the building boom. The boom conditions facilitated these democratic practices of the union: the generally low level of unemployment in the industry not only encouraged members' militancy, rendering them much more inclined than usual to risk employer displeasure, but it increased the periods of employment for individual rank-and-file members and job delegates, the crucial middle layer in any union. Thus the large-scale long-term developments greatly stabilised job delegates' positions, so that sites such as QANTAS, Royal North Shore Hospital or Dillingham (Clarence Street) rarely required the services of a union organiser. In these situations the autonomy of job-sites (which the union leadership favoured in principle) could easily and safely be translated into day-to-day practice. Other unions which enjoyed similar circumstances induced by the building boom were not so inclined towards the same internal democracy: the NSWBLF's radical organisational forms can not be attributed solely to the bouyancy of the industry.

The democratic procedures were not only observed during moments of industrial quiet. On the contrary, strike activity seemed to further stimulate the union's predilection for participatory and egalitarian forms of organisation. The distinctive internal practices of the union – its commitment to both rank-and-file involvement and the development of routines to ensure that officials' interests remained those of the rank and file – first became apparent during the 1970 margins strike. In the course of this strike the membership involved itself to a remarkable degree in decision making and militant activity. Mundey observed that many experienced leaders of other unions were surprised that, in a casual industry, the NSWBLF could maintain the involvement of so many in a five-week strike. In fact attendances at the mass meetings increased as the strike proceeded, with these meetings unanimously or overwhelmingly endorsing continued action.[15] The executive also organised activists' meetings, which soon took on a life of their own and engaged 250 or more members in constant activity. These meetings were held almost every morning and became the informal policy-making bodies in between the mass meetings during the strike. Bud Cook maintained 'Those people actively involved in the strike were making the decisions between general meetings … they were binding on the executive and the only way they could be cancelled was by a general meeting decision'. He stressed that 'no decisions came from the top level', that everything was 'kicked around and argued and finally a general consensus decision was made by everybody', which 'worked out very good' and 'the blokes were very happy about the whole scene'. Mick Curtin recalled that these activists' meetings would decide what recommendations the executive would make to each mass meeting. Mundey saw these developments as important: 'The openness and involvement was something very different'.[16]

The actions and practices of the officials were most important in promoting solidarity between all levels of the union. Unlike the officials of most other unions, they received the same wage as the members on the job. During the margins strike they resolved 'that officials' wages be stopped whilst the strike is on'. Not one official dissented from this decision, despite the fact that they were all working harder than ever. Mundey believed this decision 'helped a lot' and he reported to the executive that 'a new high had been reached in cooperation of officials and Rank and File'.[17] Ralph Kelly confirmed that the leadership's refusal to be paid during the strike gained them considerable respect, that their stocks soared enormously among the rank and file, even among those who had not previously been sup porters. Thus, as the *Builders' Labourer* pointed out in July 1970, 'builders labourers demonstrated their confidence in their elected leaders, while newspapers, employers and the police were telling us what to do'. The capitalist press could not achieve division and disenchantment in the face of the union's internally democratic practices. Pete Thomas observed in *Tribune* that 'the thing that stood out was that, after five weeks on the grass, their militant morale was as high as ever'.[18]

Over the next five years the leadership of the union stressed the extent to which the margins strike and the methods of collective decision making that evolved had changed the union dramatically. Mundey used the strike and the union journal to pound home a few points of democratic policy:

> It is an undeniable fact that the union leadership and the members are as one. Quite unlike many bureaucratic union leaderships it is our main aim to develop this position further … The leadership aims for 'total involvement' in decision making by the membership. We are opposed to 'top' decision making without reference to the membership.

How many other unions, Mundey enquired in that journal, really tried to involve their members in industrial action and real decision making? Given that the NSWBLF was a relatively small union, Mundey asked readers to 'imagine for a moment what struggles could be waged by the bigger unions with their greater resources, if they really involved their membership as we did in direct confrontation with the wealthy employers'.[19] Owens believed that the reason the MBA tried so hard to break the strike was their desperate desire to normalise the NSWBLF: 'they saw we'd be driven back to the BWIU and to the accepted norms … the employers knew the differences that existed'.[20]

A well-known NSWBLF adage reminded the officials: 'Never eat the boss's lunch unless you occupy the site and find it on his desk'. (Specifically, this advice springs from Mick Curtin's involvement in an occupation, an incident that many subsequently believed to be apocryphal: 'I finished up having the boss's lunch. I really enjoyed his sandwiches. I rang up the police and told them not to worry, that everything was under control and that I was having the boss's lunch at the moment and enjoying it.') The significance of the adage is the extent to which NSWBLF officials used it in debates among themselves about the difficulties of remaining outside the 'club' to which the NSWBLF considered employers and most other unions' officials belonged.

By tying officials' pay to BLF award rates, the leadership avoided the isolating effect of higher salaries, for as union leaders secure higher financial rewards for their jobs their sense of identification with the workers and the urgency of their problems inevitably suffers.[21] Nor did they seek the higher social status that is an integral part of the incorporation of union leaders.[22] The officials of the NSWBLF believed that any deviation from their previous lifestyle would be frowned upon by the rank and file and, as union president Bob Pringle put it, they would be quickly 'pulled into line'. The leadership continued to conform to working-class norms. Their response to their own position was unstated but nevertheless definite: their lifestyle changed not at all. They remained drinking in the same places, with the same people. They did not change addresses, nor their eating and dressing habits. Unlike other trade union officials who rarely started work before 8.30 am, they kept normal working-class hours by starting work at 7.00 or 7.30 am, which encouraged continuing interaction with rank-and-file members. The caretaker of Trades Hall complained to Pringle: 'Not only do I have to open the joint an hour earlier now that you're here but nine out of ten blokes that come through the door are headed for Room 28'.[23]

Most of the officials had worked in the industry for long periods, and relatively recently, by comparison with union officials generally. Not only were the habits and practices of the industry still second-nature to them, they were also well known among the members. The union's policy on such matters was firm: all officials, even industrial officers and publications editors, had to come from the shop floor. Only one NSWBLF official, Bill Holley, had more than an elementary education – a situation which again distinguished the leadership from those of other unions in the building industry, and from the federal and Victorian bodies of their own union.[24]

The distance between membership and leadership was decreased even further by the way in which the central core of full-time elected officials was supplemented by temporary organisers brought on to service specific areas such as Newcastle and Wollongong for particular events. The practice of appointing temporary organisers, whose appointment had to be endorsed at branch meetings, was formally adopted as branch policy at the August 1970 branch meeting. During 1970, Bob Pringle, Joe Owens, Brian Hogan, Tom Hogan, Don Forskitt and Bud Cook were all appointed as temporary organisers; and Owens and Tom Hogan in particular went back into labouring work for long periods between terms as organisers. Between 1973 and 1974, 39 organisers 'have come on and gone back to the job'.[25]

However, the most startling innovation was the move towards a limited tenure of office: the insistence that officials, after six years at the most, return to the job. By the time of the 1973 branch elections, the New South Wales branch had embraced limited tenure as a matter of principle. It was a structural negation of the 'iron law of oligarchy', and it received a cool reception within the wider union movement of the time. The idea for this departure from traditional union practice developed out of the fertile mind of Jack Mundey. 'The driving force that made me suggest limited tenure', Mundey explains, 'was my own experience of seeing modern, contemporary unionism

The ABLF Federal Executive in 1970 (standing: Vince Dobinson, Qld, Jack Mundey and Bud Cook, NSW; seated: Pat George, admin., Ron Davies, WA, Marco Masterson, Vic., Norm Gallagher, federal secretary, 'Speed' Morgan, Tas., Les Robinson, SA).
(Courtesy John Squire)

Organisational principles and practices | 69

and seeing the need for some inbuilt guarantee for limiting power and having inbuilt renewal'.[26] During a television interview in September 1971, he suggested such a practice would be a beneficial one for the entire union movement: 'To avoid development of union bureaucrats (and unfortunately not all are right-wing either) ... there needed to be greater movement of people between leadership and rank and file'.[27] The barb at 'left bureaucrats', the intimation that this phenomenon ought to be a political contradiction in terms, positioned the NSWBLF apart from other left unions. Union officials watching the programme were probably as appalled by this section of the interview as the executive members of the MBA (who had hired a television set to watch it during a meeting) were by Mundey's comments about the need for workers to undertake militant industrial action.[28]

Nor did Mundey fail to apply the principle to himself. Indeed he chose to apply the limited tenure rule retrospectively by announcing that his six years were already up. Described by many as 'the most foolish move Mundey ever made', he did not seek re-election in 1973 and, at the beginning of 1974, he returned to the building industry to work as a pick-and-shovel labourer. (Bert McGill and Dick Prendergast also stepped down after six years as organisers and returned to work as labourers.) Maintaining he was 'just another builders' labourer', Mundey commenced work on the new annex to St Vincent's Hospital, which he was fortunately able to describe as 'socially beneficial'. The daily papers featured photos of Mundey busy shovelling, wheeling and jackhammering.[29] Though he was frequently absent from this job to fulfil the many speaking engagements attendant upon his notoriety, his standing as a CPA candidate in the 1974 Senate election, his appointment to the Whitlam Government's Cities Commission and his election to the executive of the ACF, he was still employed on this site when Gallagher, in the course of Intervention, urged the manager to sack him.[30] The loss of his union ticket after Intervention made further employment as a labourer impossible to find. Besides, by then he was in his forties and without a classified skill, an unusual predicament for a union official, for most labourers who had been in the industry long enough to become officials had classified skills of some sort. With a formidable reputation as well, Mundey was virtually unemployable. He worked in manual jobs after Intervention, but never again as a builders labourer. Mundey always replied to critics that the limited tenure rule was designed to benefit the institution, not the individual.

Within the union itself both the SPA group and the Maoists opposed limited tenure. The SPA ideal of union leadership was embodied in the desk-bound and grey-suited figure of Pat Clancy, and this group criticised Mundey for not remaining in office: 'Anarchistic opposition of union leadership in general led to imposition of a rigid rule automatically removing union leaders from office just as they were becoming experienced and capable representatives of the union and the working class'.[31]

Writing with the benefit of hindsight, after Intervention had eliminated the New South Wales branch, Owens conceded that both he and Jack agreed with the criticism of limited tenure of office in that particular instance, yet insisted nonetheless: 'But that isn't a criticism of the idea. I also agree with Jack when he says "I should have knocked back some of the almost daily speaking invitations and spent more time on the job, but the important thing was the release of power".'[32]

Voluntary release of power was also an alien principle to the Maoists. Not only did this group distinguish itself by a reluctance to return to the job, many of the Maoist officials who replaced the likes of Mundey after Intervention had never been in the job, because they were university educated.

Although limited tenure had been discussed within the left,[33] it was only the NSWBLF which actually initiated the practice in Australia. The CPA had admittedly distanced itself from the especially authoritarian forms of organisation typical of the Stalinist period when its 22nd Congress in 1970 rejected the idea of 'monolithic' organisation, which 'stifles new ideas, democratic discussion and decision'.[34] Nowhere was the new CPA philosophy more obvious than in the NSWBLF, but this is not to suggest that the CPA initiated or even suggested to the NSWBLF the reforms that promoted democratic discussion and decision.

The relationship between the union and the party was a complex two-way affair. For instance the NSWBLF had been as quick as the Aarons group within the CPA to condemn the Soviet invasion of Czechoslovakia.[35] Both the NSWBLF and the CPA had for several years been responding to the New Left influence, with its emphasis upon participatory and egalitarian political structures. After the 1971 split within the CPA, both were grappling with a totally new situation. The CPA had lost many of its senior cadres just as the NSWBLF had lost the paternal (some say smothering) influence of the BWIU. The influence of such dominant NSWBLF personalities as Jack Mundey, Joe Owens, Tom Hogan and Bud Cook was bound to have had more effect on the party than the presence of CPA functionaries Mick Tubbs and Joe Palmada at CPA Building Branch meetings would have had on the union, for following the defection of the BWIU trades-men, the Building Branch was dominated by the NSWBLF.[36]

According to Owens the most significant aspect of the post-Czecho-slovakian situation for the CPA, but even more so for the NSWBLF, was its fluidity: 'We'd broken from the tradition. There were no rigid rules, no guidelines. Everything was decided as it came along.'[37] The NSWBLF expe-rience with democratic decision-making processes prompts the inquiry (in the words of Gouldner) whether this situation was one of those 'random occurrences, mere historic butterflies which flit through events with only ephemeral beauty'.[38] Considering subsequent developments within the union movement, notably the increasing distance in terms of social back ground and life experience between officials and those they purportedly rep-resent, and the extent to which the resulting rank-and-file dissatisfaction and alienation has been identified as one of the principal causes of union decline in the past two decades, the NSWBLF's ideas about the need for officials to come from the job and return to it do appear salient yet fragile.

The extent of rank-and-file support for the members of the leadership is manifested in the outcomes of the internal branch elections during this period. Nobody opposed Mundey at the well-attended Rank and File preselection on 16 August 1970 for the triennial elections, although Don McHugh from Can-berra stood against him at the election in October 1970. McHugh's rationale for resigning from the CPA the following year was: 'I don't agree with Mundey or his "direct action" brand of Communism … That lot are … too Trotsky-ist.'[39] Mundey easily defeated McHugh for the position of secretary 684 votes to 148. Elected unopposed were: Bob Pringle as president; Ron Donoghue as vice-president; Bud Cook and Dick Prendergast as trustees; Alan Luthy as guardian; and Brian Hogan, Tom Hogan, Joe Owens and Don Crotty to the executive. Prendergast, Brian Hogan and McGill left the moderate Lynch far behind for the three organisers' positions; for the three delegates to Federal Council, Lynch, Mundey and Pringle were elected, and McHugh defeated.[40] Once the 1970 election was over, the Maoist opposition scarcely made its pres-ence felt, disruption on the executive was non-existent for the next few years and the officials worked in harmony throughout this time.

The next triennial elections, in 1973, provided the opportunity for the organised pro-Gallagher team to oppose the branch leadership and all it rep-resented. The leadership team, otherwise known as the Rank and File Com-mittee, ran Pringle for the presidency and Owens for the secretaryship, and included seven CPA members, four ALP members, an anarchist and two militants of no fixed political abode.[41] It ran a campaign that emphasised the importance of the green bans, the move to achieve permanency for builders labourers, and the right of women to work in the industry.[42] This team was returned by a majority of about two to one: Pringle received 1270 votes to Donaghue's 622, and Owens defeated John McNamara 1258 to 634. Of those eligible to vote, 20.15 per cent did so, a high return for a union of itinerant unskilled members.[43]

SOLIDARITY

Another important pressure towards conservatism which the NSWBLF avoided was that of sectionalism. The union's notion of solidarity was not restricted to its own small portion of the labour movement. In the interests of this wider trade union movement and of working-class people generally the NSWBLF habitually supported other unions' struggles and vigorously opposed demarcation disputes as a matter of principle. Just as it believed in union helping union so also was it determined to avoid union fighting union. With such principles consciously in mind, the NSWBLF endeavoured to 'do the right thing' by other unions and labour movement bodies, even those with whom it had significant ideological differences.

Consequently, though the name of the federal union changed officially on 1 January 1971 to the much more comprehensive title of the Australian Building and Construction Workers' Federation (ABCWF), the New South Wales branch, which had resisted the name change, rarely used it. Although the Federal Management Committee resolved that the new name should be used in all union propaganda, the New South Wales branch executive continued to use the old name because it believed the new name would imply the intention to 'body-snatch': the NSWBLF in particular persistently 'eased BWIU fears that the name change could be the prelude to body snatching'.[44]

The NSWBLF's goodwill towards other unions was demonstrated in its display of traditional union solidarity during the lengthy plumbers' strike in July and August 1972. Labourers consistently refused to allow scabs onto building sites. (As a result of this action, dogman Danny Rose was dismissed for preventing a foreman carrying out plumbing work.) The union also held support meetings and arranged collections for the striking plumbers.[45] Moreover, the union refused to pour concrete when cores or downpipes were in place, since directions on where to place such cores would have been given either by a scab plumber or a foreman doing plumbers' work; NSWBLF members would not pour concrete until the offending cores were removed.[46]

In August 1974 workers on the two large Dillingham sites in Sydney walked out in solidarity with Dillingham employees in Newcastle, who were in dispute over a BWIU member who had been refused employment because he was on a black list. This dispute was won because Dillingham workers acted in a united fashion, not just between job-sites but also between unions: labours in Sydney had taken action in support of a tradesman in Newcastle.[47] The NSWBLF also supported other unions not in its immediate vicinity that were engaged in struggles, such as the Victorian Tramways Union, the Waterside Workers, the Canberra nurses, the Painters and Dockers, and the Miscellaneous Workers Union. The range of support included financial assistance, letters of encouragement, meetings on job sites, inviting representatives to speak at executive meetings, and even strike action.[48]

The union's commitment to solidarity and co-operation between unions naturally inclined it to be critical of the functioning of the New South Wales Labor Council, whose procedures stifled debate and whose attitudes clearly discouraged militant industrial action.[49] Despite the fact that NSWBLF officials regarded the New South Wales Labor Council as the bastion of working-class conservatism and right-wing Labor intrigue, they nonetheless considered it important that the union remain part of it and avoid, if possible, the isolation that their radicalism was likely to induce. The leadership emphasised the importance of the union's continuing involvement, with Mundey urging executive members to attend as delegates. Pringle even stood in 1970 as left-wing candidate for trustee in the annual Labor Council elections.[50]

Thus the union's expulsion from Labor Council in June 1971 was felt as the cruellest cut of all, especially since the union was unfairly blamed for the violent and rowdy behaviour in the Council's public gallery of a small number of builders labourers, most of whom were actually Maoist opponents of the union leadership and all of whom were promptly suspended by the union for their conduct.[51] This casting out of the NSWBLF by Labor Council indicated the extent of the much-dreaded isolation that the union was already experiencing at this relatively early stage, and the strength of the forces from within the labour movement working against it and its radical agenda. Formally, the union's response to the expulsion was principled: having received a legal opinion that its suspension was illegal, the executive decided not to proceed to obtain an injunction 'because it is not good to put an injunction on another working class body. That would be a worker v. worker situation. We work outside of the courts.'[52]

The NSWBLF also distinguished itself by an aversion to demarcation disputes. This was so marked that on the rare occasions when it found itself in the throes of such a dispute it usually conceded that area of work to the rival union with unusual haste.[53] Given the extensive technological changes occurring, it is remarkable how few disputes occurred between the BLF and the tradesmen's unions in the New South Wales building industry at this time. Because of its ideological objection to demarcation disputes the NSWBLF avoided the problems that occurred in other states over issues such as plasterers' work and plumbing installation. For example, late in 1971 it backed away from a dispute with the BWIU over the delicate issue of the ratio of labourers to tradesmen in the formwork field, and it frantically attempted to prevent 'the collision course that N. Gallagher and P. Clancy were headed for over demarcation'.[54]

Another example of the branch's determination not to 'poach' or 'body snatch' was its reluctant demarcation dispute with the AWU over tar-sealing work on building sites, a 'grey' area of coverage where the workers concerned had indicated their preference for joining the BLF. Accordingly, in October 1971, the AWU, through its control of the concrete batching yards, placed an indefinite ban on all concrete going to jobs with BLF labour. AWU secretary Lew McKay admitted that the rates of pay for tar sealing and asphalt work under the AWU award were lower, and Mundey proposed that these workers join both unions, with the employer paying the additional dues. However, the AWU would not accept this compromise and reiterated its determination to maintain the ban until the AWU terms were met.[55] The NSWBLF executive discussed the problem, and Mundey recommended that bitumen paving be the sole right of the AWU. It formulated a resolution that conceded bituminous work but which also urged the AWU leadership 'to ensure there is no drop in the wage rates, conditions and accident pay to the workers concerned' and expressed the desire that 'our two unions can work together for the mutual benefit of our respective memberships and all workers generally'. After considerable debate, the branch meeting endorsed the executive resolution and Mundey informed the AWU that the NSWBLF had made a concession so as to avoid the close down of the whole building industry. The concrete ban that had lasted five days was subsequently lifted and relative peace returned to the building industry.[56]

Had the NSWBLF believed that demarcation disputes were worthwhile, the AWU could not have beaten them in any all-out tussle. The NSWBLF had a more militant workforce and was stronger in the construction industry.

Moreover, the fact that the disputed workers would receive more pay under BLF coverage than under the AWU award would easily have secured their support, and that of other militants. The significance of this demarcation dispute, one of the very few in which the NSWBLF became involved, is that it was brought to a rapid conclusion by a generous NSWBLF concession because it disapproved of demarcation disputes. The AWU found itself the unworthy opponent of a union determined to use its industrial muscle to confound and dismay employers, not other unions, and to pursue far-reaching industrial and political objectives, not its own organisational aggrandisement.

While anxious to encourage other unions to adopt its radical stance on industrial and political matters, the NSWBLF, precisely because of this heightened class consciousness, shied away from growth at the expense of other unions. An AWU official, Digby Young, acknowledged in interview that the NSWBLF did not body snatch, that 'the Mundey group always did the right thing by us'. In marked contrast, the Gallagher-installed leadership that replaced the NSWBLF officials in 1975 cited the reluctance to engage in demarcation disputes as one of the faults of the Mundey, Owens, Pringle leadership. Steve Black promised in 1980 'We will continue to stop other Unions from poaching our work, particularly the BWIU, AWU and the Ironworkers' Union. We should press on with recovering BL's work lost by previous leaderships.'[57]

The principled basis upon which the Mundey-Owens-Pringle leadership detested demarcation disputes was its class-conscious approach to union matters. It was an approach that also fostered class-conscious sentiment among NSWBLF members, and encouraged the attitudes that underpinned the union's commitment to class-based action in defence of the environment.

The extent to which the NSWBLF continued to function effectively by traditional union criteria was facilitated by its pursuit of the radical organisational agenda associated with the 'new concept of unionism', for this agenda entailed a commitment to the interests of the collectivity – the union and the wider labour movement – and disdain for bureaucratic and hierarchical practices that increased the distance between leaders and rank and file. Accordingly, the union improved its density and the rank and file responded to the emphasis on internal democracy with considerably higher levels of involvement, commitment and support for the union and its activities. The internal organisation of the union therefore remained remarkably stable, even in the midst of feverish industrial turmoil created by the union's militant and presumptuous industrial strategies.

INDUSTRIAL RELATIONS STRATEGIES

The organisational strength of the union was greatly increased under the Mundey leadership, and this was to stand the union in good stead as it embarked upon unconventional forms of union activity such as green bans. But the militant industrial relations strategies also augmented the power of the union and encouraged a degree of loyalty to its elected leadership, which also sustained the union in its imposition of bans for the union's militancy was undoubtedly effective in improving the material circumstances of its members. These industrial relations principles and practices, like its organisational ones, were as radical and innovative as the political and social agenda associated with the NSWBLF.

WITHOUT MILITANCY WE WILL NOT
IMPROVE THE LIFE OF THE WORKER

The promised new concept of unionism was displayed clearly in the union's hostility to the arbitration system and its concomitant emphasis on direct action strategies. Jenny Healey, who had worked in the BWIU office before moving to that of the BLF, commented that 'the BLF was always prepared to take action on the spot whereas other unions like the BWIU liked to sit down and talk it over for a while'. Not only were NSWBLF members more frequently in dispute with their employers, the type of activity undertaken and the style of the struggle was changing. Mundey summarised the situation: 'We were pushing things up to the employers. We as a union had changed, not the objective conditions.[1]

The leadership was highly critical of the arbitration system, which prevented workers at this boom time from reaping the full benefits of their strengthened bargaining position: Bud Cook advocated 'casting aside the outdated Arbitration Court system'; Mundey spoke of the need to 'bypass arbitration and resort to collective bargaining'; Owens wrote that 'arbitration has no future' and that it was 'being slowly and surely carted off to the funeral pyre'. A general meeting in March 1970 resolved to keep up pressure on Labor Council 'and the Right Wing' about the need to circumvent arbitration.[2]

The experience of the margins strike in the middle of 1970 was to strengthen the union's aversion to arbitration and its commitment to direct action methods. During this strike Mundey consciously broke with his past associates such as Clancy when he spoke of the way traditional industrial activity had frequently operated against the workers' interests:

> ... when a group of workers was involved in a struggle (and I could give many examples), after a few days or a week an array of union officials ranging from extreme right to extreme left would turn up and urge them ... to ... return to work to avoid the penal powers being slapped on the whole union or body of unions involved. The 'left' officials usually justified this as being 'in the interests of the class as a whole' as against those of the few score or few hundred workers actually involved. This may have been true in some periods and instances, but it became a habit and an excuse. There was too much readiness to settle rather than set out to win disputes.

He also attacked 'left' union officials when speaking of the problems created among militant workers by the 'arbitration mindedness that developed'. He claimed that:

> Most militant workers have been critical for years of the general passivity displayed in strikes, and the failure of communists and others on the left to really force the issues ... These workers found it difficult to differentiate who was who, who was left, right or centre when all urged return to work when it came to the prospect of a longer strike.[3]

Not only did the union eschew arbitration, on occasions it even refused to discuss matters. For instance, the workers at Frankipile, whose militancy had recently secured them significant over-award payments, became involved in industrial action in August 1970 when the company sacked a delegate. The company initiated proceedings in the industrial court to open the way to possible penal action, probably in the belief that this action would dampen moves for a further prolonged strike. However, as Pete Thomas described the scene:

The case was listed for hearing. The Commonwealth Arbitration Commission solemnly assembled; the employers' legal men, headed by a QC were there but the union wasn't. The union's deliberate absence caused a flurry. Phones ran hot. But it was the employer who backed off. The delegate was reinstated and a bans-clause application was abandoned.[4]

The union adopted a similar tactic during a strike at Dillingham's QANTAS site a few weeks later. After one session at the Commission, Mundey explained that 'the Court hearing was attended only as a tactic' and that the union 'would accept only favourable decisions'. An executive meeting in November 1970 decided upon non-appearance in the industrial court in relation to the Dillingham dispute, even though Dillingham was moving for penal action over the strikes on the QANTAS project. The union's telegram to Justice Moore advocated that the company agree to genuine negotiations 'and not engage in antiquated penal action proceedings'.[5] The dispute was won by the union without penal action being incurred.

Just as the union officials showed little deference towards traditional arbitration procedures, the rank and file became imbued with a similar disrespectful attitude towards the boss at each workplace. This was enhanced by the union leadership's policy that rank-and-file initiative in industrial disputes was to be encouraged.[6] The strikes of 1970 and 1971 had developed an independence among the members. Tom Hogan, city organiser, recalled: 'At that stage [1971] stop-pages would occur and you'd only find out two hours later that they'd stopped. Once I went to seven stop-work meetings in a day. There was a tremendous amount of initiative taken by the men on the job.'

Even without active leadership encouragement it is likely that the status and power of rank-and-file members in relation to officials would have been heightened. It has been noted that, in times of depression and unemployment, the focus of power and influence within unions shifts upwards towards full-time officials.[7] The corollary of this is obvious: in boom conditions the employer's vulnerability to militant demands and inability to suppress job-site activity through victimisation or the threat of dismissal greatly enhances the position that rank-and-file activity can occupy in union strategy. Yet the NSWBLF leadership was unusual in welcoming and encouraging, rather than attempting to discourage, such rank-and-file militancy.

In adopting this approach the NSWBLF was acting in concert with changes in CPA industrial policy, wherein emphasis was shifted downwards towards rank-and-file organisation (as opposed to the previous CPA policy of capturing leadership in trade unions). This may be seen as making a virtue out of necessity (the 1971 split had denuded the Sydney branch of virtually its entire traditional industrial base) but these new industrial policies had been signalled before the split occurred. The CPA's policy statement, *Modern Unionism and the Workers' Movement*, had warned early in 1970 against 'undue emphasis on official trade union positions and relative neglect of rank and file organisation and the development of their initiative'.[8]

The union's commitment to practical organisation at a job level, and the militant message it espoused, prompted a high-level response from government long before the issue of the green bans ever arose. Employer interests other than those of the building industry were concerned to confront the threat to established industrial relations practices that the NSWBLF posed, and to strengthen MBA resistance to this rogue union. It appears that the 1970 margins strike had made a deep impression on employers, who incurred a loss of over $60 million during the dispute. According to Premier Askin the new *Summary Offences Act* was inspired by the BLF margins strike. Police were also issued with new equipment following the strike, 'especially to get the BLs', as Mick McNamara put it.[9]

Police harassment of builders labourers during industrial disputes was a pattern that had begun to develop during 1970. In November several members were arrested by the police during industrial action at a Leighton Industries job in Baulkham Hills. When Bud Cook was fined $1000 the union issued a press statement pointing out that Cook was fined the same amount as BHP had recently been fined for polluting the Hunter River, but that BHP did not receive a bond and could pollute the river again, whereas Cook had 'a savage restrictive five year bond imposed on him'. The union expressed its serious concern with the increasing use of the *Crimes Act* and the *Summary Offences Act* in industrial disputes, but insisted: 'We will not be intimidated and state emphatically we will continue our militant policies in support of improved living standards and a higher quality of life'. It blackbanned all other Leighton's projects and argued that the only condition it would accept was the withdrawal of all charges against the workers involved. Eventually, after an extensive campaign, the company backed down and the bans were lifted.[10]

More unwelcome attention from the police occurred when they visited the union's office following Jack Mundey's interview on the ABC 'Monday Conference' programme in September 1971, where he had argued the need for workers to undertake militant industrial action and develop new tactics: 'Without militancy we will not improve the life of the worker ... I for example would like to see offensive strike action taking place in the service industries, the trains and buses. I would like to see them keep running during strikes and not collect fares.' He suggested that, during strikes, factories that manufactured goods and foodstuffs should continue to make them but instead give them to pensioners 'and the needy in our society'.[11] As the principal spokesperson of a disconcertingly militant union, Mundey's utterances were of intense interest to the state and the employing class. The police had a list of 17 questions with them. They refused Mundey a copy and he refused to give them oral answers. However, he stated in interview: 'The main points of the intended police questions were on my ideas on militant forms of strike action, occupations, combating scabs, retaliation on scab-built buildings, and agitation for workers' control and abolition of the penal powers'.[12]

The election in December 1972 of a Federal Labor Government, under Prime Minister Gough Whitlam, was greeted by the union with some ambivalence. This was due to its fears that such a welcome change after 23 years of Coalition governments might encourage trade unionists to place too great a reliance on reforms from above, rather than on direct action from below. While builders labourers had been encouraged to work for a Labor victory and the union had donated to ALP funds (and equally to CPA funds), Mundey was hesitant about declaring unequivocal support for the incoming government, due to its possible impact on the industrial wing of the labour movement. On the Channel 9 programme, 'Federal File', Mundey stressed there was a danger that the ACTU under Hawke would be 'too co-operative' with the new Federal Labor Government, that there was a continuing need for workers to take direct action, and that the industrial movement would and should be demanding 'a bigger share of the cake and more social progress for the workers'.[13]

STRIKING FOR HIGHER WAGES

Continual, successful wage campaigns were conducted by the union from 1970 to 1974. As Owens recalled, the branch at this time was 'setting out with a conscious policy to clear up wages and conditions'. Mundey reported in December 1969: 'Strike action is "in", and in all states we should break with agreements that tie us hand and foot and by word or deed obstructing our right to strike'. According to *Tribune*, the declarations from the floor of a 24-hour stop-work meeting in March 1970 'reflected the militant mood'. As one member said: 'if we don't get what we demand, then we'll all go out together, and the sooner the better'.[14] Clearly, a new-found confidence and confrontationist mood permeated the industry.

It was not simply that militancy brought successful wage demands, but these triumphs reinforced militancy, and in the case of the NSWBLF the militancy was such that it overleapt the conventional bounds of unionism. The overtly profitable nature of the new building developments also encouraged huge wage demands. The union made its position clear in March 1970: 'We will no longer accept low wages while employers, investors and developers in the industry are making record profits'.[15] As John Niland noted, unions covering higher productivity industries are hardly reluctant to seek wage increases in line with that higher productivity: 'A sense of injustice emerges when they are held to a wage level reflecting the national average'.[16] The union kept its members alert to the gross discrepancies in the fortunes of their employers and themselves. It surveyed the financial affairs of 259 companies during 1970–71 and produced the results for its members in a leaflet, revealing that in the last half of 1971 Jennings Industries boosted its net profit by 80 per cent, Lend Lease by 94 per cent, Hanover Holdings by 152 per cent, and Mainline Corporation by more than 300 per cent.[17]

Moreover, the new developments were financed in such a way that stoppages were a serious threat to profitability. Because developers relied on credit at high interest rates, the difference between bankruptcy and profit was often the simple matter of a few weeks either side of a completion date. The builders labourers knew they could inflict serious injury upon developers through the withdrawal of their labour and in this situation they were naturally inclined to press home their advantage. It is also possible that the circumstances prompted them to take the view that, precisely because they had this power to disrupt, they therefore deserved to be paid considerably more than they were. Frank Parkin suggests that the 'disruptive potential' of an occupational grouping can form the basis for an 'alternative standard of distributive justice', that is the development of radically different ideas about appropriate wage levels from those normally held about the relationship between status and income. The wages militancy of the builders labourers attests to the cogency of Parkin's hypothesis that among industrially powerful groups there exists 'a subterranean theory of distributive justice which provides tacit moral justification for organized labour's attempts at usurpation'.[18]

The union's militant stance on wages was characterised by a determination to pursue higher levels than those stipulated in the base rate award, by extracting additional payments at each job site, and also to close the gap between the wages paid to tradesmen and labourers. In both these aims, and in the manner in which they were successfully achieved, the union indicated

Builders labourers march to the Master Builders Association headquarters during the 1970 margins strike (left to right: Mick Curtin, Peter Barton, Vince Ashton, Jack Mundey, unknown, unknown, Joe Owens).

its transformation from a conventional union that obeyed the rules of the industrial relations system to one that defied these regulations and sought to establish radically different codes and practices.

While the pursuit of site-based and sectional over-award payments was a continuing feature of the union in this period, the battle to reduce the discrepancy between tradesmen's and labourers' wages was fought initially in one almighty confrontation in the late autumn and early winter of 1970. Concerted and concentrated as it was, the psychological impact of this strike upon all concerned – employers, tradesmen and labourers – was immense.

The five-week builders labourers' margins strike of May–June 1970 was regarded by most builders labourers as the event that heralded the emergence of a new style of union. Yet although all those interviewed believed that the 1970 margins strike was the event which altered their collective consciousness, they could never adequately explain why. As Richard Hyman has warned, no general theory is available to relate the struggle for material reforms to the development of consciousness. He has argued nonetheless that involvement in a specific victory or defeat, in itself of little obvious world historical significance, may have critical consequences in terms of workers' subjective confidence and aspirations.[19]

The dispute was the earthquake that expressed and released the pressures that had been building up due to the transformations in the way builders labourers were relating to the tradesmen, which in turn reflected the fact that through new processes and the accompanying new skills the labourers had gained a strategic advantage within the building industry at the expense of those tradesmen. The NSWBLF argued late in 1969 that wages must be increased 'because of the versatility of the work performed by our members, and because of the key part we play in construction', and that the gap between tradesmen's and labourers' pay must be reduced.[20]

Mundey's criticisms of 'craftism' (or craft-consciousness) extended beyond the building industry. He saw the issue in general terms: 'what relativity of wages should exist between tradesmen and non-tradesmen? It is in the latter category that we find the most exploited of the industrial workers in the steel works, metal factories, motor car plants etc., where the profits are enormous.'[21]

The NSWBLF assault on traditional relativities clearly placed the BWIU in a difficult situation. The tradesmen were not just being threatened on the job by loss of control and skill, they were being threatened in their home and social lives by a relative drop in living standards. Although the BWIU's discomfiture is understandable, it does cast doubt on the claim made by it that enmity between the two unions was caused when the NSWBLF embarked on a course of 'adventurism' and 'one-outism'.[22] It is obvious from the 1970 strike onwards that the BWIU felt antipathy towards the labourers. The claim that precipitated the margins strike was for $6.00, which would have reduced the old relativity, whereby builders labourers earned about 75 per cent of tradesmen's pay, to an astonishingly narrow 90 per cent. The true significance of the attempt to change the relativities was not simply the amount of money, but the change in status implied. Mundey summed up the situation when he spoke of the need for real industrial unionism, 'free from craft hangovers and with the laborers being accepted as a real force in the industry, not just as assistants'.[23]

The fact that the BWIU tradesmen were not fully supporting the labourers' struggle became obvious by the third week of the strike.[24] During this week, in the middle of the hardest-fought strike in building industry history, the NSWBLF officials had a meeting with Communist Party BWIU officials at which Clancy advised the builders labourers to return to work. 'He told

The occupation of Ray Rocher's project during the margins strike, 28 May 1970, became known as 'The Siege of Shirley Street' (in window, left to right: unknown, chief spruiker 'Tony', Bob Pringle, Joe Owens, unknown, Dick Keenan, Danny Simpson; next window: Johnny McNamara, John Belcher). Radio 2BLF was also established during this incident.

us to pack it in,' Owens recalled, 'it was the beginning of the real break with the BWIU. We no longer looked on them as our ideological mentors.' In recommending that the builders labourers go back to work at a key moment in the struggle, Mundey believed Clancy was clearly 'embarrassed by our militancy'. For Pringle, who had previously felt that Mundey was unduly critical of the BWIU, this consultation with Clancy changed his mind: 'There he was, sitting behind his desk, twiddling with his paper-weight … criticising our actions and quoting from Sharkey's book about generalling a strike. That was the end of it for me.'[25]

The high level of organisation the labourers required for their innovative forms of industrial activity had never been necessary for the BWIU's less itinerant membership. The progress of the margins strike highlighted the extent of the NSWBLF's militancy and the advantages this brought to the membership. When the union met with the MBA in the early stages of the strike, on 11 May, there had been little preparedness on the MBA's part to concede anything substantial. But 'when the labourers disappointed their expectations for return … they got a big shock' and 'they got an even bigger one from the vigilante groups and so they had to change their tune'.[26] The employers were outrun: on 8 June, in the fifth week of the strike, the labourers returned to work after private discussion with employers produced an agreement that provided immediate interim increases, constituting approximately half of the final margin increase, ranging from $1.75 to $2.50, and an immediate brief work value case to be conducted for riggers, scaffolders and concrete finishers. The expected national increases from the agreed formula were $6.30 for riggers and $5.80 for most of the others. An increase in the 'follow the job' allowance was promised and the new award was to date from 1 July. The MBA had conceded more or less everything the union had demanded.[27]

The work value case began immediately and its ultimate decision almost eliminated the differential in pay between the most highly paid labourer (the rigger) and the tradesman: a rise in status for the labourer that was to have profound psychological and industrial effects. Builders labourers interviewed mentioned feelings and responses such as 'no longer being a second class citizen', 'no longer being lowest of the low' and 'no more just "shit" labourers'. Their enhanced status was not just a reflection of labourers' improved industrial position, but an expression of their changed position within the much more complex economic hierarchy of margins, relativities and loadings on which so many inter-union relationships are based. Subsequent wage demands made by the union no longer accepted the inferior wage relationship expected of 'unskilled' labourers. In October 1971, following a 16-day strike, agreement was reached with the MBA on wage increases ranging from $6.60 for the top rate to $6.20 for the third rate: this represented 99 per cent of the tradesmen's rate for most ticketed builders labourers and 88.5 per cent for labourers. (In Britain at this time labourers earned about 77.2 per cent of the pay of tradesmen .) These margins, won after a long and difficult struggle by the NSWBLF, flowed through to builders labourers in all states.[28]

By contrast with the cataclysmic encounter of the margins strike, the battle for over-award and other additional payments constituted, in Brian Rix's words, a 'daily series of little victories'. Site-based campaigns became commonplace, instigated generally by rank-and-file workers at each workplace and then supported by the union leadership. Inspired by the new mood of militancy, workers were taking the initiative on their own job sites, and this was welcomed by Mundey in spite of resulting pressures upon officials: 'This intense activity demonstrates the militancy of our Union'.[29]

Among individual work sites, the high-rise QANTAS building commenced during 1970 in Clarence Street by Dillingham Constructions became an important focus for industrial activity, and an important pacesetter on wages and conditions. The gigantic structure, with a semi-governmental institution as the client and a huge multinational developer as the main contractor, was to offer workers plenty of scope to push their demands. As Mick McEvoy, one of the early labourers on the site, explained, 'they could feel safe behind the structure of the building'. Moreover, 'QANTAS was completely committed to that building, they'd sunk so much money into it. They could not pull out. Everybody realised that – the client and the men.' The workers at the QANTAS site won important struggles, guided by experienced unionists such as Brian Rix, Mick Curtin, Reg Mason, Duncan Williams and Noel Olive. A site-allowance strike began in August 1970 and lasted for almost four months. Sharing the MBA's fears that such an over-award payment would become generalised if conceded, Dillingham resisted with grim determination. Organisation around the strike was accordingly intense: subscription lists were distributed and job meetings were held almost daily. In October, the site was blackballed. Unfortunately, the Jinks previously forged with the tradesmen became undone at this point, and the BWIU backed out despite the clear wishes of a large majority of workers at a combined meeting of both unions that the strike continue. Symbolic of the extent to which the NSWBLF leadership now differed from that of the BWIU was its unanimous decision not to appear in court proceedings over this dispute. Instead Mundey sent a telegram and despite the minor furore this unorthodox action caused the dispute was eventually won, with Dillingham paying a site allowance of 11.25 cents per hour.[30]

Although significant gains were being made on strongly unionised, militant jobs, other areas were lagging: a testimony to the still highly unsettled state of the industry at that time. Indeed Tom Hogan believed that a number of employers were actually paying under-award rates, and even more were paying what was known as the 'fourth rate'. The union had been attempting for some time to eliminate this rate under the award, which permitted employers to pay less to the pick-and-shovel or jack-hammer labourers-men they deemed completely unskilled. Many of these labourers were in excavation and demolition work, and a large percentage were recent immigrants, so the union expended additional efforts to ensure these workers were well organised. The success of the margins strike, which had greatly improved pay for the more skilled labourers, added impetus to this particular campaign.[31] The general meeting held on 3 November 1970 passed a policy motion: 'We resolutely reject the suggestion that any builders laborer has no skills whatever and declare the fourth rate inapplicable at all times'. In the CBD, where the bulk of members worked, the fourth rate was eliminated by the end of 1970. However in outlying districts and in poorly unionised sections of the industry employers continued to pay the fourth rate and its eventual disappearance was gradual rather than dramatic.[32]

At the other end of the builders labourers' pay scale from the pick-and-shovel labourers were those whose market position and disruptive potential were heightened by the new developments in the building industry. An especially militant sectional campaign carried on throughout 1970 was that of riggers, scaffolders and dogmen claiming higher rates. Dogmen initiated a 24-hour stoppage early in 1970 and announced that, if the matter went to arbitration, they would not consider themselves bound by any unfavourable decision. The striking dogmen marched from the Trades Hall to Martin Place, handing out leaflets describing the dangers of their work, and their claims. Dogmen also used tactics such as banning Sunday work, early starts and late finishes; refusing to work through smoko or lunch; and breaking concrete pours when they ran over time. Given their strategic position, these manoeuvres were frustrating and financially damaging for the individual employers, who were inclined to seek peace at almost any price, against the urgings of the MBA. Owens recorded that 'most employers have indicated their willingness to pay, but claim that the Master Builders will not allow them to do so'. The dogmen were back in dispute in December 1970 with yet more demands. To some extent their gains flowed through to benefit other building workers, even those deemed 'unskilled' by employers, so most of the officials agreed that no apologies should be made for such sectional campaigns, because 'more unionism and better pay has resulted'.[33]

In the boom conditions of the building industry over the next few years, the gains won by the NSWBLF in 1970 and 1971 were easily maintained. Overall, in the 1970–75 period, militant direct action undoubtedly earned 'a bigger share of the cake' for builders labourers. Between 1970 and 1973 Mundey's leadership secured substantial wage rises for all members, and up to $27 a week for some. In Owens' first year as secretary the trend continued with a $29 wage rise to an average of $124 a week. The new award negotiated shortly before federal Intervention raised builders labourers' pay to an average of $150 a week.[34] As Pete Thomas concluded:

> Gains have been won by direct bargaining, backed by the union's militant strength. Results have proved – in hard cash and other gains – the correctness of the union aversion to arbitration, with its protracted, legalistic and costly procedures and its frustrating decisions.[35]

In August 1974 Mundey called for a 'Spring Offensive' on wages, culminating in a national strike. Although this call received some support from job delegates, many trade union officials joined the more usual opponents to hurl abuse at him. John Ducker, Bob Hawke, Laurie Short, Pat Clancy and Norm Gallagher all publicly criticised Mundey and his proposal. Gallagher, for his part, announced: 'As a union leader, Mundey is dead, and you can't rule from the grave'.[36] (Gallagher 's bom bast frequently contained a strong element of wish-fulfilment.)

The opposition of Bob Hawke, as president of the ACTU, was more properly representative of the union bureaucracy's inability to embrace the likes of Mundey, to accept the challenge to normal union behaviour posed by the NSWBLF. This was not the first time that Hawke and Mundey had expressed their differences: Hawke had used the platform as guest speaker at the BWIU State Conference in September 1971 to attack a recent NSWBLF strike. Mundey's reply to Hawke reflected the fundamental differences between them:

> ... at the very time of your remarks, the employers in NSW were attempting to foist a 'no strike' clause upon this branch and we were in the midst of repulsing an attempt to deregister the union ... you certainly didn't avail

yourself of any discussions with the N.S.W. leadership – yet saw your way clear in the full blaze of the mass media to have your dig at the N.S.W. Branch … Maybe the chiding was for the benefit of the electorate at large; however, as the industrial leader your first obligation surely must be to the Trade Union Movement.[37]

The nature of this obligation was interpreted somewhat differently by Mundey and Hawke, as their subsequent personal histories reveal; likewise their respective understandings of the functions of the trade union movement were diametrically opposed.

INDUSTRIAL SABOTAGE

The extent to which the union developed new industrial relations strategies can be seen in the union's preparedness, in certain situations, to carry out industrial sabotage. This was used to good effect during the margins strike. The activities of the vigilantes, who systematically and methodically demolished scab-built constructions were, in the manner of their organisation, indicative of a radical solidarity and high degree of membership participation. The use of scab labour had not previously been such a clear threat to industrial action in the building industry, because strikes (through the sheer economics of the penal clauses) had hitherto been short-lived affairs. In the new long drawn-out stoppages, strike breaking was not only more likely to occur, but also constituted a much more serious threat to success. In the margins strike the MBA used scabbing as a deliberate policy to attempt to smash the strike,[38] and it became apparent by the end of the second week that this strike-breaking activity was not being effectively curtailed. It also became obvious that unless it was stopped, the strike would be broken. Bud Cook remembers rank-and-filers complaining: 'What's the good of going on strike if blokes do our job'. Mundey argued the union was clearly obliged 'to stop the small number of tradesmen and non-unionists from performing our work'.[39]

The question was how. In the suburbs the large number of small jobs made picketing an impractical tactic. Though the flying gang picket (a small mobile picket line moving from job to job) had been reasonably successful in, as Bud Cook explained, 'getting blokes off jobs', it was unable to keep them off. When the need to stop sites working was raised at a stop-work meeting, the leadership replied that a handful of officials could not stop it, only rank-and-file participation could. Accordingly, sixty or so rank and filers stayed back after the meeting to go round to these jobs. 'We were pretty naive,' Tom Hogan recalled, 'we went out in twos … the hard-line scabs around just ran over the top of us'. The rank-and-file activists could see that these small groups were easily threatened and therefore ineffective. Then, one morning, according to Hogan, 'a meeting of about 50 of us took place ... we said "bugger it we are not going to get intimidated any more, we're going out together" and I suppose that morning was the real birth of the vigilantes'.[40]

Most strike-breakers were inclined to stop working when a larger force of strikers descended on a site: 'when they saw about twenty cars pull up, twenty car doors slam'. But again the problem was how to ensure that work did not resume once the force had left. The only tactic left for the strikers in these circumstances was to make continued employment of scab labour an uneconomic proposition for employers. As Mundey argued: 'We did not set out on a wanton destruction rampage, but attacked only buildings where employers were attempting to use scab labour to break the strike'.[41] The builders labourers saw the action they took as a simple necessity, and the numerous stories told about the birth of the vigilantes echo this sentiment. In Mick Ross's words: 'There was nothing else to do but take direct action and stop their jobs'.

Every participant in this strike had their own first memory of vigilante activity, often their own distinctive version of how the vigilantes came into being, and their own involvement in this process. These stories were the product neither of self-aggrandisement nor faulty memories; rather they are a good indication of the ad hoc nature of the vigilante movement.[42] The membership generally believed that sabotage was necessary and justifiable. When asked whether their tactics alienated other members their answers were all similar: Tom Hogan: 'The other rank and filers didn't disagree ... in fact mass meetings started to grow'; Mick Curtin: 'There was no argument at all they fully agreed with it'; Mick Ross: 'There wasn't opposition to destruction of property ... the unity was very good'; Darcy Duggan: 'There was very little feeling against "vigilante violence" ... only from those not involved in the strike'; Tom Hogan agreed that 'rank and filers did not worry about men pushing over walls' but added that the two old-time officials, Lynch and Austin, 'felt that this had gone too far ... they stood for protection of private property'. Though initially wary of the tactic because of the expected bad publicity, Mundey became persuaded that vigilante action helped unify the striking workers.[43] Certainly, meeting attendances rose as the vigilante movement developed and many rank and filers eagerly joined in.

Vigilante activity confounded the distinction between union leadership and union rank and file and, in so doing, was symptomatic of the democratic mood of the time. 'They didn't have great leaders to instruct them,' wrote Owens, 'every day they met and formed their methods of action for the day'. As Tom Hogan recalled of the vigilante movement: 'one wouldn't know who was union official and who was rank and file', only if the union official 'walked fast enough' would he 'get in front and do the talking'.[44]

Moreover the daily meetings of vigilantes made decisions that were regarded as policy, until the next general meeting. Accordingly the decision to go out to jobs en masse was made subject to endorsement at the next mass meeting, which readily assented on the condition there be no physical attacks on people. As Owens put it: 'Destruction of property was better than getting into physical confrontation with fools who allowed themselves to be used as scabs'. While admitting 'most blokes would have had no compunction about giving a scab a bat over the head with a lump of four by two', they also knew too well that such action would alienate public opinion. Accordingly the vigilantes made no assaults upon people: the only person 'biffed' was a builders labourer on a picket line, and the company apologised to the union for the incident.[45]

Indeed no activist could recall any incident, either in this strike or subsequently, where a labourer had attacked an employer or strike breaker. Most labourers used phrases such as 'the policy was pretty principled 'and gave the impression that refraining from hitting scabs was an act of great forbearance.

Vigilantes take over a building site during the 1970 margins dispute
(bottom left: Alan Luthy; furthest column: Paul Langeman; centre column: Dick Keenan).

Such restraint notwithstanding, the employers, the State Government and the media frequently accused the vigilantes of violence against individuals. Repeatedly Mundey challenged both Premier Askin and Police Commissioner Allan to produce one individual who had been assaulted by striking labourers. 'It was almost a nightly occurrence I was on the box saying … "just bring me one", and they couldn't bring one'.[46] Continual denials, however, had little effect on a media anxious to sensationalise events and, in many cases, to demonise the builders labourers.[47]

The union was only concerned to deny violence against people; they were otherwise unrepentant about damage to property erected by scabs. On 19 May the union paid $596 for a half-page advertisement in the Mirror: 'if employers are provocative enough to use non-union labour during the strike, those employers must face the consequences. In such cases the correct word is RETRIBUTION NOT VIOLENCE'. The advertisement was on page 48, but the next day the builders labourers were on page 1. The *Sydney Morning Herald*, for its part, railed against 'ugly and decidedly un-Australian' tactics.[48] Headlines from the three major Sydney newspapers declared: 'Building Strike, Violence Goes On'; 'Strike Emergency, Riot in City'; and 'Riot Squad Out: $10,000 Damage in Rampage'.[49] The statements of employers and politicians were similarly exaggerated: Les Ball from the MBA claimed that the union's actions were reminiscent of the gangster activities of US trade unions in the past; the president of the Employers' Federation maintained the vigilantes' behaviour was 'completely foreign to the concept of law and order which is a characteristic of democratic Australia'; Premier Askin said his Government would not tolerate lawlessness, rioting and bloodshed in the streets.[50]

The membership remained unperturbed. Indeed the number of vigilante raids increased as the margins strike wore on, involving up to 400 men by Mundey's reckoning. Indicative of the vigilante movement's popularity is Tom Hogan's observations that three months after the strike there had apparently been 5000 vigilantes, and by 1977 when he was interviewed he presumed there were 25,000, because so many builders labourers wanted to claim involvement. The extent to which the movement proved itself was apparent in the immediate post-strike edition of the union journal, where vigilante actions were recorded as 'highlights' and sabotage incidents openly boasted about.[51]

The strike, and those which subsequently embraced industrial sabotage, widened the gulf that had begun to develop between the NSWBLF and traditional unions, especially the BWIU which deplored the way in which the

NSWBLF had 'secretly planned and implemented their policy of violence against property'. Mundey commented: 'conservative tradesmen's leaders threw up their hands in horror at the "terrible crime" of a few scab-built walls being pushed over'.

Laurie Aarons admits there were many in the CPA hostile to the vigilantes' activity, notably those who were to depart with the SPA the following year and who used the issue of industrial sabotage in factional argument: 'It was seized on as an illustration, not as how the BLs and Mundey were committing anarchist errors but how the leadership of the CPA was encouraging and even misleading these people into anarchist errors'. The SPA expressed its vehement opposition to the destruction of scab-built erections during strikes: 'a reversion to old, futile practices that have been previously discarded in the labour movement'.[52]

On the contrary, the practice was embraced with enthusiasm by builders labourers as a welcome addition to the union's armoury of industrial tactics, and the resulting break with the BWIU was hailed as a positive effect of the strike. For Peter Barton, who remained with the CPA: 'The break with the BWIU did our union the world of good. The Clancys and the McDonalds were bogging us down.' Many labourers reported feelings of 'elation' or of having 'the cobwebs blown away'.[53] Tom Hogan believed that 'never again as a union can we go back to the old style'. For Owens it represented a break with 'the old idea that a union was a series of officers with strict authoritarian control over the membership', a transformation encouraged by the autonomy of the vigilante groups that 'had to make decisions on their own'. Mundey maintains the strike 'brought about a qualitative change … the membership started to become self acting … It was a very aggressive strike. It was not a go-home stay-home strike.' Ralph Kelly stressed the significance of the vigilantes learning to use switchboards, typewriters and maps in the process of co-ordinating their activities.[54]

Another result was that the union grew, and its organisation was greatly improved by an influx of enthusiastic and able militants, including many of the experienced vigilantes who subsequently became job delegates or temporary organisers. Many new names appeared in branch meeting minutes in the following months and by March 1971 Mundey could report to a general meeting that the percentage of financial members was the highest ever.[55] Although it was a stunningly successful strike in the demands won, Mundey insisted that the most significant aspect of the strike was that 'completely new methods of struggle were adopted during and after'. The vigilante action 'set a standard of aggressive strike activity' that could lead to workers' control and as such threatened to 'really rattle the employing class'. No longer could the employers do 'behind the door' deals with the union. 'They have a far too healthy respect for our fighting capacity even to try it.'[56]

The achievements of the vigilantes prompted the union to undertake similar action in other campaigns, with similarly successful results. By its nature the use of vigilantes to demolish scab-built construction was an activity that barely needed repeating. During a strike over a disputes procedure in August–September 1971, vigilante activity was deliberately low key, but in any case scarcely necessary. As *Tribune* commented: 'A feature of the strike was the virtual absence of scabbery. This testified to the effectiveness of the vigilante actions in previous strikes.'[57]

Other forms of industrial sabotage were also countenanced from time to time. For instance, in December 1972 a bundy clock, used to record arrival and departure times of employees, on the Aliens Castlereagh Street job was smashed, and in September 1973 the MBA notified the Commission of a dispute that had prompted the 'removal of a time clock'. Actions such as these, and widespread simple non-compliance with the bundy system, eventually eliminated their use in the building industry. The breaking of concrete pours remained a popular strategy, and the very possibility of this perturbed nervous developers.[58] The judicious use of industrial sabotage in the course of the campaign for better on-site amenities (discussed in detail in Chapter Six) was crucial to the success of this campaign and is a startling testimony to the power bestowed on workers who commit the occasional 'anarchist error'.

ENCROACHMENT STRATEGIES

In its policy statement at the 23rd Congress in April 1972 the CPA observed that 'more challenging methods of struggle' had been developed in the 1970 and 1971 building strikes. Though it avoided direct reference to vigilante activity, it noted the experience of strikers denying employers the use of scab labour and argued the need for democratic workers' control over capitalist decision making, such as the right to hire and fire: 'The new trend to challenging hitherto accepted "rights" of employers to authoritarian control is shown by the big proportion of strikes against managerial policies'.[59] In embracing the notion that significant gains for workers could be achieved by on-site activity, the CPA distinguished its position from that of the SPA, which insisted that since workers did not control the means of production under capitalism, real workers' control was not attainable, and therefore the struggle was a fruitless exercise; and it was 'necessary to resist the tendency to follow this discredited path of anarcho-syndicalism and Trotskyism'.[60] As Angus McIntyre pertinently suggested, the SPA regarded 'workers' control' as a threat to the established trade union structure. Accordingly, the BWIU opposed workers' control on job sites.[61]

The NSWBLF aimed to translate rhetoric into action more than other CPA-influenced unions at this time, and it began developing serious strategies for encroachment upon managerial rights.[62] From 1971 such strategies were being pursued regularly at individual job sites. Some of these tactics, such as resistance to dismissal and de-facto union hire were initiated by the leadership. Others, such as work-ins, developed on specific job sites and were often aimed at limiting management prerogative.[63] On an ABC 'Lateline' discussion with Upper Clyde Shipyards work-in leader Jimmy Reid, Mundey emphasised that most work-ins were defensive acts which occurred over retrenchments, but that NSWBLF work-ins were also often offensive, with labourers' demanding more than the mere right to work, insisting upon greater control of their workplace.[64] The branch motion on 'Workers Control' proposed to the union's Federal Conference in 1973 supported 'workers' rights to control the industries in which they work'; endorsed the worker control centres established by militant workers and radical academics in various states and urged members to participate in their activities and discussions; and resolved to 'push further in all states the issues of election of foreman, leading hands, safety officers and first-aid officers on jobs'.[65]

It was this encouragement of workers' encroachment upon managerial prerogative that received the most vehement response from those in the best position to judge the effectiveness of such policies. The New South Wales Employers' Federation journal replied to the CPA's definition of worker control in an editorial: 'Worker control may appeal to hoodlums and standover men and supporters of participatory democracy … But in the final analysis it is fundamentally necessary that management be permitted to do the job it has been trained to do.'[66]

The NSWBLF was not particularly disposed towards permitting management 'to do the job it has been trained to do', but its experience of true worker control was limited to a few short-term incidents. Therefore the policies it did pursue, and with considerable success, are best understood as strategies for encroaching upon employer control.[67] The NSWBLF contested the employers' right to hire and fire at will and to appoint their own choices to key positions in the workforce: it 'reserved the right' to campaign for permanency of employment in the trade, and the election of foremen and safety officers.[68]

The union had already earned itself a reputation with employers for contesting employers' rights to dismiss troublemakers. But when fighting individual dismissal cases the union had simply been behaving like a normal, albeit militant, trade union. Far more innovative was the way in which the NSWBLF in this period questioned the employer's rights to hire and fire on the grounds of work available, and to dismiss workers not just for union activity, arriving late or having too many days off, arguing with the foreman or not working as directed, but for reasons completely beyond the workers' control, such as supplies being held up, finance running out, accidental overemployment, strikes by other workers, or a reluctance to pay for public holidays. Traditionally, redundancy cases were fought on the grounds of seniority: the union tried to force employers to accept the 'last hired, first fired' practice. However, increasingly within the NSWBLF redundancies were opposed outright. Tom Hogan explained the union's position as it developed in that period: 'no longer were we prepared to say the boss has got the right to sack us as long as he gives us an hour's notice'.[69] This traditional issue thus took on a more significant meaning: a challenge to the employer's right to hire and fire, and constituting a serious encroachment on the established decision-making structure within the industry.

One struggle over dismissals, which occurred on the Costains Macquarie project in July 1972, produced the complaint from the MBA that the union was 'not prepared to concede that the company has the right to employ or dismiss employees as they see fit'.[70] A similar incident took place on Dillingham's Martin Place site later in 1972 when retrenchment notices were handed out to four labourers. Organiser Dave Thomason 'put to the men that they refuse to accept that [the] company could not keep [the] men'. This position was adopted by the members and the company eventually backed down.[71]

The right of management to hire and fire was also contested successfully in November 1972 at Lombard's in Newcastle. Here the main points at issue were the employment of a female nipper, June Philpott, and the re-employment of ten carpenters who had been declared redundant. The labourers struck in support of the dismissed carpenters, though they were BWIU not BLF members, and would not resume work until they were re-employed and all workers paid for lost time. The carpenters and labourers announced that they would report for work daily, but only work if the carpenters were employed. This action lasted for a week and was described as a 'sit-in' by the two Newcastle daily papers. Once again, direct action was successful and the ten carpenters were re-employed. Furthermore, the workers' staunch support for June Philpott's right to be employed as nipper (one stop-work meeting voted 21 to 4 to continue this dispute) also triumphed eventually over obstacles such as injunctions and civil court actions from the builder.[72]

Refusal to accept dismissals continued to cause altercations of varying intensity with employers during 1973. For instance the dismissal of seven riggers caused 300 labourers on 14 Concrete Constructions sites to engage in protracted stoppages in January. In September 1974 police were called to the Longspan site at Bankstown: the men were 'working in' four labourers who had been sacked because of job slow-down 'due to miscalculations by Longspan'. Four builders labourers were arrested and the site went on strike. The dispute was successfully resolved, but only after bitter struggle.[73]

Occasionally, resistance to management prerogative took the more aggressive form of 'work-ins'. In February 1972, 50 labourers on the Concrete Constructions Centrepoint job, known as Lanray, were dismissed for striking over a special rates claim:

> They were notified that all money owing would be posted to save them the trouble of ever coming near the site again. But the blokes had other ideas. They all met on the site the following morning and decided on a reverse whammy. The decision was they were going back to work, but the foremen weren't.[74]

Tom Hogan, the organiser on the site at the time, explained:

> We sacked every foreman on the site. We left the manager [Lindsay Pearson] there in isolation because someone had to pay us. We said, 'You're all fired and we'll be doing no production until such time as safety gets up to scratch'. The foremen remained there by the gate with a forlorn look on their faces. They didn't believe it at first. They'd try to give orders and we'd say 'Run along son, we're busy'.[75]

In less than an hour the labourers had elected five foremen from among themselves, an extra nipper and a first-aid attendant. Within 20 minutes, Concrete Constructions director, Ted Cooper, arrived on site, saw what was happening and promptly rang the union office. According to Owens, 'Cooper rang me up and said, "We've got a very unusual situation here ... they've gone back to work and elected their own foremen". I said "What's wrong with that?" and he replied "But they're not doing what the company tells them".'[76]

The result of the phone conversation was an offer by the company to reinstate all the workers immediately and negotiate the original pay claim. However, a condition of re-employment was that the men reinstate the company's foremen. Even after securing what was a major victory, the men were undecided about that condition:

> It wasn't a unanimous decision that we'd accept the foremen back even then.
> It must have been about a 60/40 decision. We went much better without
> them. A new confidence was there. Some form of workers' control was
> necessary to implement it ... I'm not suggesting it was perfect ... but more
> and more we were beginning to feel our strength, that we didn't have to bow
> down every time we heard the boss speak.[77]

A few months later, a comment in the Disputes Book suggests that the foremen never regained their authority: 'Men decided that job would stop if
foreman was not transferred or replaced'.[78]

A major work-in occurred at the Opera House in April 1972. Here the
labourers, supported this time by the metal workers, elected their own foremen
and safety officers. When the work-in petered out through lack of materials,
the conditions under which normal employment was resumed were dictated by
the workers. The company foremen, who had been sympathetic to the workers' occupation, were taken back as charge hands with no disciplinary powers.[79]

By 1973 employers' concerns about workers' control parallelled their
growing distress over the imposition of green bans. Work-ins, demonstrations and workers' control conferences were taking place in many industries.
The CPA sponsored a Workers' Control Conference in Newcastle at Easter,
which was a resounding success, attended by 446 delegates from four states,
including NSWBLF officials.[80] Mundey spoke at this conference and at
another Workers' Control Conference in Armidale in July, where he claimed
the notion 'struck fear into the hearts of the employing class'.[81]

The Liberal Party, much agitated over the matter, produced a policy
paper on workers' control which claimed that in the case of the NSWBLF
it already existed.[82] The Bulletin reported 'growing agitation ... for worker
control' and cited 'the disruptive activities of the BLF in NSW serving as a
model of how employers can be crunched'.[83] The Employers' Federation and
the MBA saw the two big building industry lock-outs in May and October
1973 as a serious contest between the employers and the workers for control of the industry: their resistance was accordingly more stubborn and the
resulting conflicts more severe.[84]

On 5 May 1973 the MBA announced it was cancelling all week end
work for BLF members and accused the NSWBLF of encroaching on
employer prerogative by using nuisance tactics. 'The issue at stake,' Rydge's
observed, 'is the union's efforts to impose worker control of the building
industry'.[85] In response to these overtime bans, the union defended its

commitment to establishing workers' control: 'builders labourers who spend their entire life in the industry should have control of the industry'.[86] The MBA now claimed: 'We realise that if we lose this fight everything is lost ... This is a fight for the industry itself.'[87] The MBA was determined to outwit the union's campaign, commenced early in 1970, to extend the practice of 'union hire' to the point where it provided a degree of permanency for labourers in the building industry.[88] It made little attempt to hide its fear of the sinister-sounding 'union hall hire' as it preferred to call it. Ray Rocher explained in 1979: 'We didn't then, nor do we now ... take acceptance of the philosophy of union hall hire ... Worker control was just an extension of union hall fire in fact ... so we saw it as unacceptable in the industry.' The MBA complained to the BTG of Labor Council that it was having to endure a campaign by the NSWBLF 'in respect of union hall hiring' and it threatened large-scale dismissals since its members were 'quite adamant' they must protect their rights to determine employment matters.[89]

In announcing the overtime bans, the MBA alleged the NSWBLF was enforcing workers' control by insisting on the right to nominate men for particular jobs. The MBA inserted large advertisements in the morning papers appealing to 'responsible union members on the job ... to restore stability to the industry'. MBA officials declared they were 'almost in a state of war' with the NSWBLF and the 'preposterous' demand for union hire was 'a direct confrontation on the employer's democratic and undeniable right to select his own employees'. Then, on 24 May, employers locked out 6000 labourers on 800 projects in Sydney.[90] The MBA advertised yet again in all the major newspapers, featuring a quotation from the 'Communist promoted' Workers' Control Conference at which Mundey had recently spoken, arguing that 'worker control, not permanency is the issue' and accusing the union of 'sabotage', 'intimidation of workers', and 'property damage'.[91]

With the New South Wales building industry virtually shut down, the Federal Government proposed the establishment of an independent inquiry into permanency to be chaired by Mr Justice Aird. The union and the MBA consented to conditions for resumption of work that effectively re-established the status quo. The union genuinely believed the permanency inquiry was a substantial achievement, and had the federal BLF continued to support the New South Wales branch's campaign for permanency, it might have attained the significance the state branch anticipated. However, the ultimate result of the inquiry was disappointing in both the length of time taken and its lack of resolution. Permanency as an issue in the building industry died with the New South Wales branch in March 1975.[92]

The MBA's attack on workers' control had no success in quietening builders labourers on the jobs, as the next two years of encroachment struggles were to show. Builders labourers resorted to work-ins in response to the other big lock-out starting in October 1973, imposed by the MBA in response to the green bans. The work-ins began on 7 November 1973, with 19 labourers arrested on the Lamay and City South Telephone Exchange projects. Elsewhere, such as at the QANTAS building, labourers on work-ins were not arrested, although the Sun reported that more than 400 police were patrolling the building sites. Sites that remained at work levied themselves to provide strike pay for builders labourers who were locked out. Those arrested were represented in court by Jim Staples, who felt compelled to inform the magistrate: 'I know that the song goes "When they gaol a man for striking it's a rich man's country yet", but when they gaol a man for working it's a mad man's country yet'. The work-ins continued, with labourers taking over sites, sometimes peacefully and sometimes after an initial confrontation.[93]

The industrial dispute that created the most excitement and attention in 1974 occurred in Wyong. Like many spectacular industrial incidents, it began quietly enough. A labourer was dismissed when he returned to work on the Shopping Plaza project after being absent on compensation. A meeting of workers decided to 'work in' the sacked labourer. The company, Miruzzi South Seas, called the police and dismissed all 67 workers on the site. Sixty police arrived and made several arrests. At this stage a number of the workers managed to position themselves in the jib of the crane and announced they would remain there until the job was re-opened for all workers, without loss of time, and the charges dropped against those who were arrested.[94] Amid enormous publicity, four labourers occupied the crane for the next 63 hours. About thirty labourers and supporters from Sydney were arrested while attempting to get food and medical supplies to the men. Police eventually withdrew from the site at 4 am on Sunday morning, to loud cheers from the large crowd gathered around the site in pouring rain.[95] The workers on the site organised work the next day along self-management lines and held a meeting of residents to decide whether they wanted a shopping plaza or a hospital. Although the workers believed a hospital would be more useful, they accepted the residents' vote and agreed to go ahead with the plaza.[96]

Workers' control at the Plaza site lasted for six weeks, and the men only ended their occupation after certain agreements were reached with the company. They were to receive generous site and wet weather allowances; they had the right to elect their own foremen, leading hands and safety officers; they were to have one hour a fortnight for site meetings; the unions were to be consulted on 'hire and fire'; and the building contractor was only to be allowed on to the site for discussion with the supervisor of works, and was excluded from any dealing with the workers.[97]

It was not until the serious opposition to the union, from within and without the labour movement, forcibly manifested itself during 1974 and early 1975 that the union's capacity to provide its members with improved wages and conditions was threatened. Chapter Twelve traces the way in which the breaking of the union and its green bans was achieved by the combined effects of action and inaction on the part of sections of the labour movement that were as threatened by the organisational and industrial relations practices of the NSWBLF as the developers were by the green bans and employers generally by its militancy. Ultimately it was only the federal BLF's Intervention that solved the employers' problems, by obliterating the branch that had enraged them so much.

CIVILISING THE INDUSTRY

In the early 1970s the NSWBLF embarked upon an aggressive campaign to improve the general conditions under which builders labourers worked, by up-grading safety and amenities. Despite some progress that had been made during 1969 when it first announced its intentions to 'Civilise the Building Industry', conditions had remained poor. It was after the 1970 margins strike that the union realised the time was right for gains to be made on work conditions, and it initiated discussions on the matter with the MBA. However, since most employers showed no inclination, free of industrial pressure, to improve conditions, the union decided to resort to direct action.[1]

This campaign was not pleading to employers to provide a safe and decent working environment, but an insistence that such was the right of those who laboured in the building industry. Indeed the poor conditions of the industry were part of the reason why such a belligerent crusade could be launched, since these circumstances had helped produce the especially vociferous and assertive workforce determined, among many other aims, to end them. The *Builders' Labourer* of July 1970 pointed out that the union's militancy was encouraged greatly by the instability, insecurity and harsh environment of the industry, which were exacerbated further by a 'general paucity of amenities'. Mundey outlined the union's developing position:

> Further we should have a real say in the industry. Not only on the need
> to register builders, but to programme the entire building industry in the
> interest of building workers and the general public, not in the interest of
> greedy so-called 'developers', loan sharks and jerry builders, who really are

agents who sub-contract every conceivable part of work out. Their sole concern with the industry is to make the fastest available dollar.

A statement of objectives the union insisted on placing before an Industrial Commission hearing in September 1971 announced: 'We ... are genuinely concerned with civilizing this concrete jungle, and bringing human dignity to those who now work in this very insecure industry ... To these ends we will untiringly work.'[2] This civilising mission asserted workers' rights to 'have a say in the industry', a theme that was also to haunt the developers affected by green bans.

HEALTH AND SAFETY

Although the building boom afforded workers increased industrial muscle, it also encouraged employers to neglect health and safety issues. With the need to complete projects in the shortest possible time, developers and contractors alike were inclined to cut corners with regard to safety precautions in particular. As a job delegate from EA Watts wrote: 'speed is what employers look for mostly'. Ray Rocher of the MBA conceded that 'some jobs at times are allowed to be in an unsafe condition'.[3] While the building industry has always been a particularly dangerous area of work, the nature of the new buildings compounded old safety problems and produced new ones. It was not simply that there were so many buildings being built too quickly, they were much higher than previously, their foundations were dug deeper into Sydney's soft sandstone, and demolition work was being carried out at an unprecedented rate.

With the growth in city skyscrapers came an alarming increase in the number of on-site accidents, the height of the new structures taking its toll on the labourers. Death by falls accounted for an increasing percentage of building industry deaths each year. Dogmen were most at risk, but virtually any occupation on the multi-storey projects was hazardous unless safety standards were rigidly observed. An additional problem, previously not encountered, was that of wind turbulence caused both by the height at which work was now being carried out and by the skyscrapers themselves changing wind patterns and creating unpredictable wind-tunnels.

Increased depth was another feature of the building industry in this period. Excavation created health problems for builders labourers as foundations and below-ground construction bit deeper into the sandstone shelf on which Sydney is built, causing occupational diseases such as 'dusting' (silicosis) and respiratory problems that did not become widely recognised until years later. Among excavation workers, industrial deafness and throat problems also increased, caused by operating, and shouting above, noisy jackhammers.

The relatively new field of demolition work attracted unskilled contractors, who took advantage of the State Government's reluctance to introduce a licensing system for demolishers, despite the obviously dangerous nature of the work. Under-tendering from these 'wreckers' encouraged neglect of even the minimum safety standards prescribed by the Department of Labour and Industry. Reputable demolishers such as Whelan the Wrecker gave evidence to a parliamentary investigation in 1970 of the 'malpractice' that occurred in the industry: that other demolition companies were underbidding on tenders because they were able with impunity to neglect safety procedures, pay 'cash in hand' to avoid paying employees' income tax, and pay lower workers' compensation insurance than they should. The loser was 'the worker who does all the heavy dangerous work'.[4] Demolition companies, like excavators, came to the forefront as targets in the union's campaign.

That the new developments created particularly dangerous working conditions is borne out by the statistics. In the year ended April 1973, 44 building workers were killed in New South Wales. On just one site in Sydney, 178 accidents were reported in nine months. The Department of Labour and Industry was simply inadequate for the task: it had too few inspectors and the union was convinced it did not enforce safety regulations sufficiently.[5] Safety was also a serious issue in other states, but the problem was especially acute in Sydney because of the scale and nature of the new construction work.

These adverse conditions emphasised the important role of the union in the fight against the employers. With the department apparently incapable of protecting workers, the union, through its aggressive emphasis on safety, increasingly came to perform this role. In so doing it tapped a deep reservoir of support from its membership. While workers had differing ideas about the degree to which employers were entitled to exploit them, none conceded employers the right to put workers' lives at risk. Tony Hadfield remarked: 'It's bad enough having to go to work, let alone having to die there'. The ceaseless struggle over safety standards 'attracted workers who would not otherwise have been involved', explained Glenys Page, a rank-and-file labourer. 'They could see they were affected in a direct sense.'

Often the union was accused of fighting for conditions in excess of the Department of Labour and Industry's standards. But the extent of rank-and-file support for the union's hard line on the issue indicated just how important the safety issue was at this time.[6] The workers were instinctively inclined to fight over safety matters and when they discovered the union was prepared to struggle long and hard on the issue, many militants and loyal unionists were created. Moreover, the experience of battling for improved safety at a job level encouraged job solidarity. Glenys Page stressed 'nothing unites a job more than a safety issue'. Such struggles, which clearly raised union consciousness and aided union organisation, also encouraged a more generalised class consciousness as workers confronted an employer's seeming indifference to what was for them a life-and-death issue. Campaigning around safety thus strengthened the union directly and indirectly: it was not just that the union grew in influence, membership and the degree of its members' attachment to it, but the workers' themselves were often changed in the process, preparing them to support the union's further claims, in the form of green bans, for workers to 'have a say in the industry'.

The rank and file also displayed their concern about health issues short of life-and-death matters in an increasingly militant response to extreme weather conditions. For instance, spontaneous mass walk-offs from building sites in the metropolitan area occurred early in February 1973 when the temperature reached 40 degrees. Pringle endorsed these actions, warning employers that the workers would strike if they were not paid for the day. In practice, there was an inverse correlation between degrees of militancy and degrees Celsius at which workers would quit: the more militant the job site, the quicker the workers absented themselves, some walked off at 33 degrees but others only did so in the mid-to-high 30s. While no agreements were ever reached with employers over this matter, the militant sites in this period were able to impose their own rules about what constituted unbearably hot working conditions, and employers did not dare refuse to pay them for the time lost.[7]

While heat was easy to measure, the definition of 'rain' occupied a considerable amount of industrial court time during the early 1970s. (Indeed having failed to agree on a definition of rain, the court preferred instead to refer to 'inclement' weather.) Builders labourers had always disliked working in the rain on health and safety grounds, and now their greater militancy on this matter prompted a court ruling that, if the weather was 'inclement' for 4 hours, the workers should be 'paid off' and allowed to go home. Again, in practice, whether the weather was considered inclement depended on the level of militancy of each job-site. For example, labourers at Mainline decided to re-define 'wet weather' and succeeded in forcing the foreman to agree to ring the weather bureau and, if the bureau believed it would continue to be wet, to allow the men to go home. Most large sites during the early 1970s at least secured agreements in principle that builders labourers would be paid for any rain-induced inactivity.[8]

In most cases the campaign to improve health and safety involved direct confrontations with employers, at which the NSWBLF was adept. However, the union was also involved in the attempts by other building industry unions to insist upon greater supervision by the state of the construction industry. These unions gave evidence in 1970 to a New South Wales Parliamentary Select Committee, calling for the registration of both builders and subcontractors, and the NSWBLF continued to call for stricter government controls. Mundey and Pringle issued a press statement which argued: 'The MBA has failed to control its own members and has been found wanting in its ability to enforce even the barest conditions of safety and amenities ... we call for a Royal Commission into the whole industry'.[9] But little was forthcoming from the state. Both the ineffectuality of the government instrumentalities and the militancy of the union is illustrated in the case of free-fall hoists. Although these hoists had a shocking accident record, the Department of Labour and Industry would not ban them, so the union did. Accordingly, union members refused to drive these hoists. However, since employers were unrestrained in this matter by the department, some continued to use free-fall hoists, particularly in outlying areas where the union was not so strong.[10]

The successes of the union's 'Civilise the Industry' campaign were due principally to direct action aimed at employers. Mundey stressed the need to insist on proper safety precautions before projects commenced, with the threat of an absent workforce if the site was not acceptable in terms of safety.[11] But many important disputes also took place at existing sites, which indicated a growing militancy on the issue of safety. Apart from the partially successful attempt to ban free-fall hoists, safety campaigns included the banning of 'riding the hook'; the fitting of water attachments to jackhammers to eliminate dust and of silencers on jackhammers and other noisy equipment; the appointment of full-time safety and first aid officers on high-rise city jobs; and the demand for accident pay.

The situation of dogmen highlighted the peculiar juncture of circumstances in the Sydney building industry at this time that rendered safety such an important issue. Employers were notoriously reluctant to hire two dogmen for every crane, one at the top and one at the bottom, so the sight of dogmen 'riding the hook' from top to bottom of the new gigantic structures was all too common. Dogging had always been a hazardous occupation, but with the increased speed in production techniques, and the greater heights at which they were now required to work, it became even more so. In March 1970, former dogman Joe Owens reported on 'conditions that dogmen face as they work at heights, in high winds (regulations set no limit on velocity of wind in which work can go on) and with every contractor on the job putting on the pressure so as to keep up with his own tight schedule'. He explained: 'With loads such as panels there is the risk of wind starting the load spinning and getting the fall rope twisted with the dogman's bellrope, fouling up his means of communication'.[12]

Throughout 1970 there were repeated calls, particularly from Brian Hogan and Owens, for the banning of dogmen riding hooks, a demand firmly resisted by employers unwilling to hire the extra dogmen required. Accordingly, during 1972 the union embarked upon a concerted campaign to enforce the use of two dogmen on each crane. Though the number of dogmen killed 'riding the hook' had remained significant, this campaign did not enjoy the support of the Department of Labour and Industry. On the contrary, one departmental inspector, after visiting the Kell & Rigby Mount Street site during a dispute in the middle of the year, assured the company there was no need for two dogmen to be employed on the site, an opinion the MBA tendered in writing to the New South Wales Industrial Registrar. Disputes over the issue also occurred at TC Whittle's Hammerson site in July and on another Kell & Rigby job at the University of New South Wales in August. Since these disputes constituted attacks on staffing prerogatives, the builders resisted them fiercely.[13] At a meeting between the MBA and the union on the issue, Owens received a negative reaction to his lengthy submissions: 'The spokesmen for the Employers made it quite clear that while they did not deny that some Companies adopted the 2 Dogmen per crane system, the Association as such could not agree that it would be acceptable as a general rule'. The union journal deemed this 'callous resistance'.[14]

The arbitration system displayed an attitude similar to that of the employers and the Department of Labour and Industry. Mr Justice Sheehy, delivering his opinion of the Kell & Rigby dispute, found himself 'unable to recommend the use of two dogmen in all situations'. Not easily deterred by the united front of employers, public servants and the judiciary, the union continued its campaign by simply enforcing its own safety requirements. Direct action techniques such as banning sites that flouted these union-imposed rules and refusing to work cranes insufficiently manned led to eventual victory. By 1973 the dangerous practice of 'tiding the hook' was virtually eliminated and two dogmen per crane became the rule rather than the exception.[15]

While the higher buildings posed particular perils for dogmen, the deeper burrowings downward presented new hazards for labourers in excavation work. Much of this work, deemed unskilled by the employers and remunerated at the lowest rate for builders labourers, was carried out by recently arrived immigrants. In pursuit of much healthier conditions for those of its members who were involved in such work, the union embarked upon a campaign in 1973 to have silencers fitted to jackhammers and reduce dust levels. (In so doing, the union was also acting in pursuit of a more pleasant environment generally, since the menace of increasing levels of noise and dust pollution was being felt by people in the vicinity of the sites.)

In April 1973 the union threatened to ban work on all sites where equipment was not fitted with any necessary noise and dust control devices by 1 May. In its press statement the union pointed out that because excavation work was increasing and going deeper than previously, 'there has been an alarming increase in the number of excavation workers being ... affected by silicosis'. It also mentioned 'noise-induced deafness' as a further danger to workers' health. On 3 May the union inspected excavation sites to ensure compliance with its demands, the story's newsworthiness gaining the union publicity for these inspections. A hard-hatted and somewhat embarrassed Jack Mundey was photographed testing 'the quietest jackhammer in Sydney'.[16] To increase job-site vigilance, the union journal printed Greek and Italian translations of its new regulations about noise and dust. By July, 50 jobs throughout the city had experienced stoppages in relation to the issue. The campaign was hard-fought and took some time to produce results, but by August 1974 the employers' journal *Rydge's* had acknowledged its effectiveness.[17]

Another safety issue that had formed part of the initial 'Civilise the Building Industry' campaign of 1969–70 was the policy of getting full-time safety officers and full-time first aid officers appointed on all high-rise jobs in the inner city. Strong employer resistance had thwarted these aspirations, but early in 1972 workers on the Westfield site at William Street went on strike for a week after two serious accidents on successive days, and eventually Westfield was forced to employ a full-time safety officer. The precedent was set: other large jobs demanded safety officers and employers succumbed, sometimes after stoppages and sometimes without such prompting. But constant vigilance and militancy was required. As late as February 1974, there was a lengthy and ultimately successful strike, prompted by Dillingham's refusal to employ a female safety officer on the Clarence Street site.[18]

Occasionally, when employers were uncooperative, tactics other than strikes were used; 'newer forms of action were necessary', as Mundey remarked.

On the PDC Rawson Place job the workers decided a full-time first aid officer was essential, so they resolved that if the company refused to accept this, they would stop work for the day in protest, and the following morning 'would work in with him'. Like so many other direct action tactics, this working-in forced the employer's hand. The union's Disputes Book entry for the following day was short but to the point: 'First aid man entered first aid shed and has since been employed as first aid officer'.[19]

That particular struggle had taken place with the support of all the workers on the job, from the BWIU and FEDFA. However other disputes occurred where it was only the builders labourers pushing the demand for safety and first aid officers, despite the fact that it was in accordance with BTG policy. Mundey believes the reason the BWIU was not prepared to support these initiatives was that the NSWBLF was demanding that safety officers be elected by the workers, 'because it is to the workers that they are responsible'. This, Mundey happily admitted, was 'a clear challenge to the boss'. The bosses agreed with Mundey's assessment: the demand for elected safety officers was one of the reasons why the MBA was at this time moving to have the NSWBLF deregistered.[20]

In July 1972 a prolonged dispute took place at the Costains Macquarie site at the corner of Sussex and Liverpool streets, because the company objected in principle to the fact that the first aid officer was 'nominated by the union', as was the leading hand. When the company refused to employ the two men, the builders labourers stopped work. The company responded by calling in Wal Glover from the MBA, an indication that both the company and the MBA saw the issue as one that needed to be resisted strongly. The labourers eventually resumed work and worked-in the two men they wished the company to employ. (One of the labourers told the *Tribune* reporter that, when the dispute was over, 'we'll have to consider whether or not we take the company back'.) Two weeks later the dispute was still unsettled and the MBA notified the Industrial Commission again.[21]

Early in 1973, another incident involving the insistence upon 'union hire' of a safety officer caused a strike on a large Concrete Constructions project that lasted almost a month.[22] Indeed the union's full-scale campaign during 1973 for 'union hire' insisted that not only leading hands but also safety officers should be chosen by the union rather than the employer: 'We believe we are more competent to control safety on projects, to elect people whom we believe can best safeguard safety and to elect people who are best fitted to be leading hands on the job'.[23]

Since the pursuit of profit was primarily responsible for adverse safety conditions, the demand for accident pay was a peculiarly opposite response on the part of workers. Hitherto employers had relied upon the state, in the form of workers' compensation payments, to meet their obligations to injured workers, but the building industry unions now insisted that employers provide accident pay to meet the shortfall between award wages and 'compo'. The BTG had launched a campaign for accident pay in April 1970, but the NSWBLF stressed safety issues even more than the other building unions, probably because its membership was most at risk. Owens expressed their feelings when he announced: 'It is high time builders accepted their responsibility and made up the compo payments to award wages. Their balance sheets show they can well afford it.'[24] Owens was commenting on a successful dispute over accident pay at Chillmans in Sussex Street in February 1970. Another such struggle around this time was that of the builders labourers on a Mogul Construction job in North Sydney, who according to the delegate Don Crotty were 'the first workers in Australia to win full accident pay'. These actions of the rank and file early in 1970 paved the way for a broader but equally successful accident pay campaign in 1971.

On 4 February 1971 a mass meeting carried a resolution demanding that all employers in the industry agree to 'full accident pay', pointing out that three employers had already agreed to this. The issue then became incorporated in the joint building unions' campaign that began in March 1971, 'for $6 and Accident Pay'.[25] A mass stop-work meeting of all building industry unions on 13 May was a huge success, with only about two dozen of the 3500 present voting against the resolution: 'The employers' refusal to agree to our claim that a building worker be paid award wages when off work injured, leaves us no alternative but to continue the strike'.[26] The crowd of unionists, some in wheelchairs, then proceeded from Wentworth Park to the MBA offices in Newtown, where they held a noisy demonstration. Mick McEvoy believed that the march 'scared hell out of the builders ... although we lost a few BLs in the pubs along the way'. The *Sydney Morning Herald* printed a large photo graph of the demonstration under the caption, 'The multi-lingual March', because of the numerous placards printed in foreign languages. The ACTU backed the strike; federal building union leaders hinted at the possibility of a national stoppage if the New South Wales workers' demands were not met; and the New South Wales Labor Council unanimously supported the struggle.[27]

However, in the third week of the strike, BWIU secretary Pat Clancy held discussions with Judge Sheehy of the State Industrial Commission, who promised to hear the accident pay case in one day if the strikers returned to work. On 19 May the BTG drew up a recommendation to return to work on this basis. Mundey opposed the resolution at the group's meeting, but it was carried 9 votes to 1. Mundey was expressing the opinion of militants who felt nothing definite had been promised and that the members were in excellent fighting spirit, and who were convinced 'there was more in it for us if we held out longer'.[28] A NSWBLF leaflet described the 'angry reaction' of the Sydney mass meeting on 20 May, when Clancy put to them the group's recommendation to end the strike: 'Many unionists felt that they were not being told the full story, and that the mere fact of an arbitration judge agreeing to hear and decide the case the next day was not sufficient reason to drop their guard and go back to work'. This Sydney meeting carried a rank-and-file amendment to stay out on strike for another week, and the BTG recommendation was never put to a vote.[29]

The Sydney militants, believing they had voted to remain on strike, were therefore stunned to discover that the BTG was tallying the voting figures from all the stop-work meetings throughout the state, and in dubious ways. For instance, votes recorded at Gosford and Newcastle for motions favouring another stop-work meeting were counted as votes for a return to work;

Voting to remain on strike during the accident pay dispute, Wentworth Park, 20 May 1971. Migrant workers from the Public Works Department and Concrete Constructions are at the front of the picture. (Courtesy *Sydney Morning Herald*)

Wollongong was deemed to have voted 84 to 40 for a return to work, though no count had been taken there; and the 618 minority in Sydney who had not voted to remain on strike were assumed to favour a return to work, although a number of them were clearly in favour of the amendment (never put to the meeting) for another stop-work meeting. By this procedure, the BTG officials estimated that 'the overall NSW percentage for a return to work was 63 percent'. Anger at what many workers believed was a sell-out mounted throughout the day as the strikers gathered in hotels, criticising the terms of the return to work.[30] 'We felt bitter', recalled Ralph Kelly.

The union's conviction that the outcome would have been more favourable had the workers stayed out was substantiated the next day. Although Sheehy granted the unions' claim for accident pay loading, a large group of employer organisations took immediate action in the Supreme Court to prevent the decision being carried out. The position was not clarified until 22 October, when the final appeals were dismissed; and the relevant clauses were not written into the Builders' Labourers (Construction on site) Award until 6 December 1971.[31]

Moreover, Sheehy had decided full accident pay should be restricted to six months. The NSWBLF had been barred from participating in the negotiations with Sheehy, due to its temporary suspension from Labor Council. Had it been present, it would have opposed this time limit and demanded that a mass meeting be held so workers could discuss the matter. Owens explained the builders labourers' position: 'if any worker is off for six months or longer, then that worker is seriously hurt and he's the one that needs full pay when he's on compo, much more than anyone off work for a lesser time'. Bob Petty felt the six-month limit was due to the return to work, that 'we could have got more if we had stayed longer'. Ralph Kelly, with similar feelings, described the decision as 'the final nail in the coffin of co-operation with the BWIU'. Owens was convinced that, had they been given the option, the workers would have 'fought again' on the issue. 'They were ready to go, there was a lot of feeling. It was a highly emotional issue. There wasn't one who hadn't been on compo in previous years and they would have struggled and achieved a much better deal than they got.' But as Bud Cook pointed out: 'once Clancy had settled there was nothing we could do'. The MBA saw the six-month limit as an enormously important aspect of the accident pay decision, its circular to members on accident pay underlining the clause referring to this restriction.[32]

Employers realised the significance of the accident pay decision for all industries. Accordingly the MBA argued that the State Government should legislate to increase workers' compensation payments. The *Financial Review* summed up the situation: 'The revolutionary character of the NSW building workers' claim is what accounts for the strength of employer opposition, and, of course, for the enthusiastic support of other unions'. Mundey had stated early in the strike that employers in other industries saw the campaign on compensation as a spearhead that would affect them too. The *Sydney Morning Herald* agreed: 'A breakthrough by the unions in obtaining their demands of full pay for building workers off duty through injury could open the flood-gates to other industries'. Open the flood-gates they did: indeed the results of the accident pay strike flowed to every other worker in New South Wales, and then in Australia.[33]

AMENITIES

Amenities on building sites at the beginning of the 1970s were primitive or non-existent, and the drive to improve them was an important part of the wider campaign to civilise the industry, and one which gained the leadership considerable support.

One of the more enlightened developers, Civil & Civic, admitted in 1970:

> The standard of site accommodation provided by most builders for their workers on site is deplorable. Steps have been taken in our Company over the last several months to improve the level of site accommodation that we offer our workmen. Prior to this some of our conditions on site were below standard.[34]

Mick McEvoy describes the conditions for Sydney building workers: 'You had no washroom, changed in the tool shed, no such thing as a separate eating place ... these are small things to people outside but they're big things when you spend one third of your day on the work site'. It was in the provision of substandard amenities that the 'get rich quick' mentality of the development boom most clearly manifested itself, for the conditions under which the employees worked, which had always been poor, had not improved as the value of development, and the profits made by the employers, had increased.

As many historical experiences testify, the demand for 'civilised amenities' has often been the catalyst for outbursts of militant action. Certainly such concerns in the United States were important in the radicalisation of the Western Federation of Miners and the United Farm Workers early in the twentieth century, and of shearers, wharfies, miners and others in Australia.[35] Mundey himself ascribed the 'shocking conditions' in which he worked as one of the major causes of his own radicalisation. Owens saw the union's militancy stemming from the long period of struggle 'in a raw industry where every inch of conditions was a battleground'.[36] Mick Tubbs, who observed the union's struggles as a CPA organiser, recalled: 'The men really resented their bad amenities. The hatred [of the employer] was really there. It just needed to be given an opportunity to come out.' Tubbs added that 'it was an1azing how quickly things changed when the hatred did explode'.

The first opportunity for this explosion to occur was provided by city organiser Tom Hogan's campaign against substandard amenities sheds in 1970: one of the most spectacular series of incidents on the part of an increasingly spectacle-prone union. Hogan describes how the 'great compressor incident' of 1970 came about:

> An excavator in Clarence Street had eight obviously newly arrived Italian migrants as labourers. The job consisted of a hole, a compressor, eight jackhammers and a hose. Not a tap, not a toilet, not a shed in sight. I saw the boss and told him he would have to have the job up to scratch by the next day. But the next day nothing had changed … I couldn't speak to any of the workers because they had not one word of English. So I stopped the compressor, uncoupled the hoses and started to pull it forwards. The workers stepped forward to help … the boss started to laugh until suddenly we got a bit of pace up and veered right. He nearly collapsed. It was a beautiful shot. It went down about fifteen foot and landed on its end. It jerked the motor back two foot and stood there pointing skywards. That action alone would have cost builders in the city millions of dollars to get amenities up to scratch.

Hogan returned the next day and found four fully lined sheds, three toilets and a full row of wash basins. 'The workers were immensely pleased but we still couldn't talk to each other.' (For the next few weeks, he was followed around building sites 'by about twenty police'.) Hogan claimed this action had the effect of introducing decent sheds onto building sites:

> Builders started ringing us saying 'can you please give us two weeks, we can't get the sheds up in time'. So we rang up shed people and in fact new companies sprang up selling amenities on building sites. They came into our office saying 'Does this meet with your approval?'

The 'great compressor incident' served as a warning to employers of the dire consequences of making employees work in substandard conditions and as an example to the workers that this kind of retaliation was guaranteed to get results.

Such action was infectious. In October 1970 Danny Simpson announced at the branch meeting that 'tomorrow morning Summit workers intended tipping over unacceptable sheds'. The Summit site was being excavated by Brambles, a giant company that in Hogan's opinion: 'would get certain jobs up to scratch if a few militants happened to be working on it, but all the rest would be a shambles'. At the Summit site the labourers had a tin shed only 8 feet high and 6 feet square (2.40 and 1.80 metres) as a change-room for 14 men.[37] Because of the way excavation workers travelled from site to site, there were 'interconnections between jobs so the whole of the rank and file got to know what the situation was'. Accordingly, when the Summit workers called for all Brambles jobs in the city to stop work, the response was overwhelming. Again, Hogan describes the scene:

> Brambles had about fourteen jobs in the city at that time. They all stopped and came up to the Summit. About the last five jobs I visited to pull out had already done so before I got there and were on their way up to Kings Cross. At least two hundred, mainly migrants, marched right through the Botanical Gardens to Kings Cross and we had our usual marshalls of the N.S.W. police force alongside us. When the marchers got up to the site they saw the one tiny shed and the Summit workers explained the circumstances to them. So they said, 'well we've judged the shed and its guilty, it's got to go down'. They grabbed it, all 200 put a hand on it. I tried but I couldn't get in. So the shed was pushed down and beautiful new sheds were erected that afternoon.

Hogan acknowledges it was a gratifying experience 'to be there and see what the rank and file in action could actually get, and get in a hurry'.

The employers were not amused. Mundey was called to a compulsory State Commission conference over the compressor and shed incidents, where he explained to the Commissioner that 'new approaches had now to be made where amenities were non-existent'. Indignant though employers were at these incidents, they responded to them in ways that proved their efficacy. By November 1970 Mundey was able to report to a NSWBLF general meeting that the compressor and shed incidents had been 'most effective'.[38]

Notwithstanding their effectiveness, these acts caused consternation among other unionists within the left generally, and especially within the CPA. The CPA went through a certain amount of soul searching over these events, just as it had in formulating its reaction to the vigilantes. Mick Tubbs believes there was no real attempt with in the party to dampen the union's methods, although the issues were often raised in discussion. The Aarons group in control of the party was unlikely, even within party circles, to oppose openly acts by the BLF when that union was solidly in their anti-Soviet camp. There were others within the CPA who wholeheartedly espoused the rights of workers to take such action. Stella Nord claimed 'we felt that if this was the way the bosses treated workers then they had no right to the equipment anyway'.

These colourful incidents aside, the union's campaign to civilise the industry was nonetheless serious. The union maintained its formal pressure on the MBA and the sectional employers' organisations to keep their members in line over the matter. More and more disputes occurred over amenities and these were rather more productive of results. If disputes did not start as pure amenities disputes, they often included better amenities in the final list of demands.[39] The November 1970 branch meeting passed four important policy motions, of which two concerned amenities: that work should not begin on any site until amenities were brought up to the required standards; and that from 1 January 1971 the only acceptable sheds on any site were to be those fully lined and with adequate heating, lighting, ventilation and so on. In December 1970 Mundey reported on 'the present campaign waged in relation to amenities on jobs and the success achieved in this matter'. At the same meeting Bud Cook referred to the 'big break throughs' that had occurred over the provision of amenities, especially in the fields of demolition, excavation and concreting.[40] Although the struggle over amenities continued throughout the 1970s and constant vigilance remained the price of decent working conditions, the blitzkrieg of 1970 ensured that conditions were never again as bad as they had been before .

The union's mopping-up operations over amenities included a typical piece of builders labourer larrikinism in Newcastle in October 1972. The labourers on the Civic Centre project were demanding that the main contractor provide showers for the men, which was by that stage a standard condition in Sydney. Tony O'Beirne explained to the *Newcastle Sun* that 'major builders come here from outside thinking we are boys from the bush. They seem to leave award rates and conditions at the Hawkesbury.' The men were working with jackhammers in an excavation 4.5 metres deep: 'in fine weather they were covered with dust and in wet weather in mud a foot deep … Because they had no shower facilities they had to wear dirty clothes home.'[41]

The *Newcastle Morning Herald* described how these labourers drew attention to their plight, with an accompanying large photograph of hairy-chested, semi-naked builders labourers.

During the campaign for better conditions and amenities eight builders labourers from the Civic Centre project rigged up a shower on Newcastle Town Hall steps in October 1972 (left to right: Bernie, Brian and Phil Hogan).

Eight builders' laborers risked pneumonia when they staged a protest demonstration on the steps of Newcastle City Hall yesterday afternoon. Clad in underpants and shorts, they showered with cold water from a hose as light rain fell and the mercury dropped to about 19 degrees.

The newspaper report added that the men would continue to shower each afternoon on the City Hall steps until their employer provided a shower room. While the Labor Lord Mayor of Newcastle declared he 'would not tolerate any more foolish actions by these laborers', the company responded within two days by installing showers. Like most of the union's more extravagant direct action antics, the approach had succeeded.[42]

Another broad amenities campaign was launched in June 1974 because the leadership feared that standards in such matters were tending to decline again. It explained in a circular to all builders in the state that it was 'necessary to remind builders of the union's regulations on conditions and amenities'. True to form, in its circular to organisers it advocated that decisions on standards must be made by the workers concerned: 'DON'T LET THE BOSS DECIDE FOR YOU'.[43] Unfortunately for the health, safety and comfort of builders labourers throughout the state, federal Intervention shortly thereafter ensured that they were no longer in as good a position to challenge the bosses' decisions on such matters .

The very real gains of the New South Wales branch 's campaign to civilise the building industry had contributed greatly to the radicalisation of its members. The officials, who had all worked on the job themselves for considerable periods, knew how important safety and amenities were for the rank and file, so they understood the importance of what was called 'shithouse seat organising'. Improvements such as hot showers and properly lined sheds, quieter jackhammers and more first aid officers were always considered to be important victories. Part of the pride that builders labourers experienced in being 'BLs' and not just labourers was that, during the early 1970s, their working conditions became equal to, and often better than those of the tradesmen. Even more than the wage increases they had won, it was the improved working conditions that were most often cited as the major symbol of their improved status. The gaining of human dignity, through struggle, was an important ingredient in the development of their political consciousness.

The labourers correctly perceived from where their improved conditions and status stemmed: that it was their collective actions that had brought these benefits. 'We got stuck into the builders,' Ralph Kelly stressed, 'We demanded hot showers and we got them. We demanded lined sheds, fridges, stoves, and improved safety – and we got them.' Whenever builders labourers spoke of their improved conditions, they never once saw the employers as the benefactors. They saw clearly that the developers, despite record profits, would have given them exactly nothing if left without union pressure. Just as the Petrograd workers perceived after July 1917 that 'They dare not give us bad bread now',[44] the builders labourers knew it was only their exercise of collective power that had prompted their employers to accord them dignity and respect. As Laurie Aarons put it, the BLF was up against the most backward section of Australian industrial capital, the developers. The issues were not obfuscated by pleasant conditions and amiable employers. This reinforced both the membership's loyalty to the union and its hatred of the boss: 'exposure of abuses in some backward trade … serves as a starting point for the awakening of class consciousness'.[45] Such exposure also served as an important starting point for the awakening of environmental consciousness.

PIONEERING SOCIAL MOVEMENT UNIONISM

Since the mid-1970s new social movement theorists have argued that the labour movement is no longer a social movement, that class no longer has the mobilising power it once had, and that identities based on gender, race, ethnicity and sexuality have eclipsed class. Trends within academic thinking reflected transformations within political life: from the late 1960s the rise of the new social movements – such as the anti-war, women's, homosexual liberation and black rights movements – appeared to have seized the political initiative from the labour movement. Accordingly the labour movement's capacity to effect social change was contrasted unfavourably with these new social forces. It was deemed the 'old' social movement, and these theorists even suggested that the labour movement was not only 'institutionalised' into the political system (and therefore incapable of providing social opposition) but that labour now shared interests in common with capital: they were both involved in the production process and committed thereby to maintaining capital growth, which was necessarily destructive of the environment.[1]

Thus it is interesting to examine the way in which the NSWBLF successfully transcended the stark dichotomies erected in new social movement analysis, which would argue that traditional labour movement concerns, such as wages and conditions, job control and job security, are generally at odds with those of the new social movements, such as women's rights and saving the environment. Drawing on caricatures of trade unions as bastions of homophobia, machismo, racism, ethnocentrism and ecological irresponsibility, the distinction between old and new is frequently depicted as that between bigoted workers who never thjnk about anything but their material self-interest and the enlightened supporters of new social movements whose concerns embrace more than the merely economic and who care about other people.[2]

Of course the NSWBLF existed before (although only just before) new social movement theorists commenced their assault upon the old social movement of labour. Clearly it would be too much to claim that its record therefore constinited a refutation of all such new social movement theorising. New social movement activity undoubtedly inspired the NSWBLF, however the degree to which the NSWBLF accepted new social movement issues as legitimate and fundamental concerns for workers and their unions, and made these campaigns the union's own, cannot be accommodated within the framework of new social movement theorists.

Rather, the NSWBLF of the 1970s prefigures the development of 'social-movement unionism' in many parts of the world in the 1990s, which as Kim Moody observes, 'uses the strongest of society's oppressed and exploited, generally organized workers, to mobilize those who are less able to sustain self-mobilization'.[3] Robin Kelley's study of Justice for Janitors and coalitions of union and community against racism in the United States, Sam Gindin's research on the Canadian car workers, Gary Seidman's study of workers' movements in Brazil and South Africa, and Kim Moody's *Workers in a Lean World* all provide some examples of the extent to which organised labour is reasserting itself in militant and broad-ranging ways in social-movement unionism. These writings are also indicative of the rekindling of academic interest in the capacity of the old social movement of labour to effect social change, not only on behalf of workers but on behalf of much wider constituencies, whose interests are now seen to be clearly aligned with labour against the neo-liberal austerities imposed by globalising capitalism.[4] As Bob Pringle expressed the NSWBLF viewpoint: 'The strong should support the weak in issues that involve everybody'.[5] Although the issues of the early 1970s were sometimes different from those of the late 1990s, the NSWBLF's orientation fits precisely the characteristics of social-movement unionism. It was a union ahead of its time.

Apart from the far-reaching social movement actions undertaken by the NSWBLF, the union's capacity to think beyond its own immediate interests is demonstrated in its constant attempts to engage the wider labour movement in activities aimed at improving the conditions of people outside the union movement. In 1970 alone the union called the attention of Labor Council to a range of issues it felt were important and warranted combined union action: education, free hospital care for pensioners, the problem of pollution from a chemical factory at Greystanes, fund raising for a kidney machine project, and unsafe scaffolding at the Boy Scouts Jamboree. Mundey urged the federal BLF 'to involve ourselves in support of the Trade Unions of New Guinea and assist in their development'.[6]

The union was especially supportive of the many recently arrived immigrants who worked as labourers in the building industry, concerned not only to counter any vestiges of prejudice against them but also to assist them to overcome the disadvantages they experienced.[7] Apart from routine provision of interpreters at branch meetings and the publication of union material in the principal languages of these immigrants, the issue of discrimination and its effects was confronted directly in the branch's publicity: 'we must fight ... for equality on the job, in society, AND IN OUR OWN TRADE UNION!'[8]

NSWBLF propaganda persistently drew connections that encouraged workers to think systematically about patterns of oppression. For instance, during a series of job-site disputes with Dillingham during 1974, one leaflet placed Dillingham's treatment of building workers in Sydney and Newcastle in the broad perspective of international capitalist exploitation and alerted workers to the detrimental effects on other people and places. It detailed Dillingham's profits from US military aggression in South-East Asia, and the harmful effect of its mining operations on the Australian environment and on Aboriginal workers. Another leaflet emphasised the destructive nature of the company: 'These people tear down workers' homes to build giant office blocks for investment purposes'.[9]

This capacity to think beyond wages and conditions was persistently expressed in practice. The NSWBLF displayed a readiness, independently of other union support and with no conceivable benefit for its own members, to use the physical skills and capacities of its members or the strategic power of the union as an organisation to defend the interests of the powerless. For example, it would not tolerate high-handed eviction: in 1971 it became involved in the political and physical defence of the Glebe Old Men's Home; later the same year the rank and file involved themselves when two Chinese women were evicted from their flat and the Tenants Union approached the BLF for assistance. Bob Pringle discovered that the owner of this building was a director of Stocks and Holdings, so the union response was typical: stop-work meetings were immediately held on Stocks and Holdings sites throughout the city. These meetings 'had the effect of quickly finding a new flat for the Woo sisters, plus reimbursement of any loss they suffered through being evicted from their home'. As the left-wing newspaper *Scope* pointed out: 'Once again a trade union has stepped in to take up the cause of people who would be otherwise without muscle to oppose the system'.[10]

'Without muscle to oppose the system' is also an appropriate description of many new social movement activists. Whatever the failings or otherwise of the old social movement in terms of inclination to effect social change, there is no doubt that its power to do so is superior to that of the new social movements. Ralph Miliband argues that the new social movements can achieve little without the power that alone can contest ruling-class power. This is the power of the producing class, its ability to effect political change based on its strategic location in the economy, the necessity of its labour and the havoc that can be wreaked through its withdrawal.[11] Such power was forcefully displayed by the NSWBLF in its imposition of the green bans. Moreover the wide-ranging nature of the other campaigns it initiated and social issues it raised, and its preparedness to use the unique power available to workers at the point of production, indicate that the NSWBLF was a social movement in its own right. It was neither old nor properly new, because it exploded such distinctions, but a movement worthy of separate treatment, analysis and categorisation: a social-movement union a quarter of a century in advance of others of its type.

The union's unusual degree of altruism, its well-developed sense of responsibility towards the community at large, expressed itself most significantly in radical actions to secure social change and greater social equality, even while its industrial activity continued at a high level. Indeed the unionists' preparedness to engage in radical action in the interests of others was facilitated by the union's spectacular record of achievement on behalf of its members. While builders labourers were receiving regular wage rises and their working conditions were improving, their ability and eagerness to involve themselves in the political activities of the union were enhanced. Far from deflecting unionists' attention away from broader issues (as new social movement theorists suggest) the 'economistic' struggles of this union drew its members into active political struggle. Brian Rix maintained the leadership's success in 'demanding $6 and getting $6' commanded respect and support from the rank and file, inducing a readiness to respond to the union's radical social and political agenda.

The NSWBLF transcended traditional union roles and concerns, blurring the boundary that normally separated a union from the wider radical public. It became the principal and strategically central social movement of the period in Sydney: the strongest and most successful in its development of the green bans; and the one to which other radical causes turned for help and inspiration. As the anti-Vietnam War campaign wound down with the withdrawal of Australian troops, the NSWBLF became the centre of radical activity, and increasingly so as it widened its scope to include women's issues, prisoners, blacks and homosexuals. Mundey insisted that 'for a union to be meaningful it must speak up on all issues affecting the life of not only the members of a union but all Australian people'.[12] Precisely because it was a union, not a single-issue movement, it was able to encompass all manner of radical causes, and form an alternative public sphere that acted as the base for various agitational activities directed towards wider publics.[13] Many of the New Left who had been radicalised by the campaigns against the Vietnam War and the 1971 Springbok tour were beginning to feel the need for a new focal point. The NSWBLF's blend of idealism and morality, combined with working-class toughness, was an irresistible mixture for the basically middle-class New Left. Within this milieu the student movement and the Sydney libertarians were two groups significantly affected by, and supportive of, the activities of the NSWBLF.

For the student movement of the time, contact with the NSWBLF constituted its only real experience of the much-vaunted 'worker-student alliance'. The builders labourers, who were often with the students in their various political campaigns, were the only manual workers most of these radical students ever met. Empathy with the radicalised students and antipathy towards social hierarchies prompted the union at the request of Macquarie University students to place a ban in 1974 on the construction of a partition which would have segregated staff from students in the previously integrated University Bar. Student activists were also welcome in the union office. The union supported the radical students, so these students supported the union in its campaigns. Like many of the green ban episodes, the union's links with the student movement indicated its preparedness to breach class barriers and to form cross-class alliances in the cause of social change.

The other important section within the left that saw the union's direct action methods as something new and exciting in working-class struggle was the libertarian group based on the old Sydney Push,[14] now reinvigorated by recent struggles against censorship and centred around the University of New South Wales student newspaper, *Tharunka*. Roelof Smilde believed that the NSWBLF's 'direct action approach' was what appealed to most libertarians.[15] *Tharunka* editor Wendy Bacon heard about the shed and compressor incidents and sought an interview with Brian Hogan. As it turned out, the issue of *Tharunka* in which the interview with Hogan appeared happened to be the one chosen by police for prosecution as an allegedly obscene publication. Since the issue had been distributed widely on building sites, Mundey was asked to give evidence that builders labourers were unlikely to be offended by the material in that issue.[16] This was the beginning of the strong association between the Sydney libertarians and the NSWBLF. The union put into practice what was mainly idealistic theory for the New Left. Wendy Bacon described the process:

> New Left-type politics, taking control of your own life, community politics – what seemed to flow on from all that was the BLF. It was the lifeblood, the only thing that gave us a fighting chance … the BLF was taking on the whole thing of property and capital in a direct way. It was so much more direct and clear cut than anything I'd been involved with before.

The interaction between New Left ideology and NSWBLF practice was, in the context of Sydney in the early 1970s, a two-way process, since the Sydney New Left was affected by its experience with the union. Although New Left ideas had indeed informed the NSWBLF's outlook, it was precisely these New Left ideas that were reformulated by the experience of the many who became involved with the union, for the union demonstrated the power that a determined working class can wield. Among people conversant with Marcuse's doubts about the capacity of the proletariat to be the midwife of history, the NSWBLF persuaded many of them that the working class was, after all, the one with radical potential. At the very least, the union convinced many left-wing intellectuals that New Left ideals, such as humanitarianism and all manner of egalitarianisms, could co-exist within the same structure as the traditional union virtues of good tactics, powerful oratory, toughness under pressure and hatred of the boss, and that these New Left ideals were all the more powerful and influential when embraced by those with real resources at their disposal.

The interaction between New Left ideals and NSWBLF practice was mediated most obviously through the Communist Party, whose leadership was now greatly influenced by New Left philosophies of personal liberation and egalitarianism. Just as the CPA was rewriting its organisational and industrial policies, so too was it reconsidering its relationship with the new social movements. This revisionism also reflected and encouraged the union's developing position. In 1970 the CPA Congress emphasised the need for trade unions to involve themselves in 'action on social and political issues going beyond the traditional concern of unionism'. The 1972 Congress listed areas properly of concern to unions, which included 'taxation … health, education … foreign policy, war and armaments; racism in Australia and abroad; preservation of the ecological environment and the struggle against pollution in all its forms'[17].

The union, unlike the party, could start working on this wish list. As Viri Pires described the relationship: 'The CPA is very small. It can have ideas but it can't do much with them. It was the BLF which tested the ideas.' The union became the CPA's show-piece. That the CPA hoped to capitalise on the undoubted popularity of Mundey and the green bans movement was exemplified in its propaganda material for the 1974 Federal Senate election campaign, which featured a photograph of Mundey speaking in front of a banner pro claiming 'Support BLF Green Bans': the slogan for the campaign was 'Vote Red for a Green Australia'.[18] The party's New Left orientation was fortified by the success and popularity of the NSWBLF on the ground and by the builders labourers who joined the CPA: having been radicalised by the union, they ensured the continuation of NSWBLF influence within the party. Thus, although the union's ideology was shaped by the party, the union's activities influenced party thinking as much as the party's ideology affected the union.

While the union's major political activity from 1972 revolved around the environment, it remained active on other political fronts. Its Christmas cards sent out in 1971 ('Let us fight in 1972') listed the main issues for the New Year in addition to conservation as including: pensioner power, prison reform, the defeat of the McMahon Government, zero population growth, Papuan New Guinean independence, workers' control of industry, the 35-hour week and full employment. 'Mr Mundey has a lot on his plate for 1972', commented the *Sydney Morning Herald*.[19] Mundey continued to extol the line that unions should be political: 'The Builders' Labourers' Union feels strongly about unions and the whole workers' movement involving themselves more deeply in all political, moral and social questions affecting ordinary people'.[20] Although other unions in this period sometimes lent support to radical causes, the important difference between the NSWBLF's involvement in political issues and that of other left unions was that it was actively participating and at many levels.

THE ANTI-VIETNAM WAR MOVEMENT

From 1967 the NSWBLF had expressed both its opposition to 'US aggression' in Vietnam and Australian involvement in the war, and its support for the anti-war movement in Australia and the demand that Australian troops be returned home. It also urged members 'to consider joining actively in a peace organisation'. The union offered enthusiastic support to the moratorium movement from its commencement and attempted to interest Labor Council in the case of a student victimised for anti-war activity. The branch meeting of 9 June 1970 passed a unanimous resolution declaring disgust at the actions of construction workers in the United States for attacking anti-Vietnam War demonstrators. By the time of the September moratorium march, the New South Wales branch was urging the federal BLF to issue a national directive in support of the moratorium movement.[21]

That such purely political agitation was not counterposed in the union's mind to 'proper' industrial activity is apparent in the branch executive's response to the May 1970 moratorium march, which occurred less than a week before the margins strike began and in the midst of frenetic preparation for that encounter with employers. While acknowledging the difficulties involved, there was no hesitation on the part of any executive member in calling on the membership to participate in the march. They even organised to have officials address meetings of members on the subject. Again despite hectic industrial activity in 1971, the union became increasingly involved in agitation against the Vietnam War. One of the union's members, Michael Matteson, was a draft resister who was prominent in the anti-war movement. The union congratulated him for his refusal to comply with the *National Service Act* and pledged him and all other non-compliers the union's 'complete support'.[22] It was active in anti-Vietnam War organisations, it sponsored advertisements, held job meetings and its members were regularly arrested at moratorium marches. Mundey successfully moved a resolution through the Federal Management Committee calling upon the ACTU and the ALP 'to intensify activity against the National Service Act; and that we especially call upon the ACTU to lead with all forms of action, particularly direct action, to further raise public opinion against this Act'.[23]

Among its agenda items for the 1971 Federal Conference was a branch motion reaffirming 'our Union policy of opposition to the criminal war being waged against the people of Indo-China, and against the Liberal Party's policy of involving Australia'. Further, the motion demanded the unconditional withdrawal of all foreign troops from the area; immediate abolition of conscription; support for all young men refusing to comply with the National Service Act; and the release from custody of all men gaoled for refusing to comply. 'We call on all young men to defy this Act.'[24] In 1972 the builders labourers turned their occupational skills to good political effect: when student draft resisters set up a draft sanctuary on the top floor of the University of Sydney's union building, it was Pringle and other builders labourers who constructed the barricades on the stairs to prevent police arresting students.[25]

In July 1972 Mundey was arrested for 'intent to incite people to fail to

Tom Hogan holds a cheeky sign during the rally in July 1972 to support those who had signed the 'Incitement not to register for National Service'. The Chatswood Branch of the Police Association had voted to oppose conscription.

register for National Service'. Although 12 other poeple were arrested during the demonstration, including Pat Clancy, all the media showed photos of Mundey. One particular picture, of Mundey making a defiant V-sign, was widely disseminated. Interviewed in the course of the subsequent court proceedings, which fined the 13 protesters a total of $60, a remorseless Mundey mentioned he was asking union members to stop work at 3.30 pm on Friday to attend an anti-conscription rally in the city.[26] In January 1973, although Australian withdrawal had commenced, the union joined enthusiastically in a campaign against American business interests in protest against the US bombing of North Vietnam: job-site meetings were held on projects controlled by two of the biggest American firms, Dillingham and Mainlines. On behalf of the union, Pringle explained action was necessary 'to try and stop this homicidal bombing of North Vietnam'.[27]

THE ANTI-APARTHEID MOVEMENT

Soon after becoming secretary of the union, Mundey wrote to John Ducker, acting secretary of Labor Council, stating that the NSWBLF felt Labor Council should 'call upon Australian sporting organisations to refuse to play against South Africa whilst ever that country adopts a racist approach to sport'.[28] The Springbok rugby union tour of Australia in the winter of 1971 provoked an immediate reaction from both officials and members. Mundey moved, successfully, that the Federal Management Committee 'urge our Members and other workers to engage in protest action against the South African Touring Team whilst the South African Government continues its cruel, Racial discrimination'. The NSWBLF was one of the few unions openly to advocate the physical interruption of matches. Mundey announced publicly: 'We think it is not good enough to just demonstrate and protest. We feel at least some of the games must be physically stopped. We consider we will go down in the eyes of the world as a racist country unless some of the games are stopped.' He promised that teams of workers would try to disrupt the games, and that he was 'hopeful that he could get leaders from other unions to join the protest'.[29]

Pringle was particularly active in organising the anti-Apartheid protests: he attended the central organising meetings of the Anti-Apartheid Movement and helped produce a leaflet sponsored by the BLF, the wharfies and the printers encouraging unionists to join the anti-Apartheid protests and outlining the appalling wages and conditions endured by black South African workers. Pringle also gained instant notoriety among the rugby crowd, and earned the admiration of the anti-Apartheid protesters, for his action in attempting to cut down the SCG goal posts with a hacksaw the night before one of the games, effecting cuts of several inches on one post before being arrested and charged with 'maliciously injuring one aluminium goalpost'.[30]

When the rugby tour was over, anti-Apartheid activists concentrated their efforts to have the impending South African cricket tour cancelled. In August 1971 black Zimbabwean campaigner Sekai Holland (who later worked as a builders labourer) addressed a NSWBLF Sydney branch meeting on the matter, but a number of workers present walked out when she rose to speak; among these were those who had shown vociferous opposition to the branch leadership. Mundey told the meeting it was disturbing that, in a militant union, so many had walked out. 'It illustrated the depth of racism in the country and among workers, and showed the need to debate the issue on the jobs.' Owens, equally appalled, wrote to Tribune about the incident:

> There is, undoubtedly, a deep undercurrent of racialism in the Australian worker … However, unions such as the [BLF], in fronting up to the problems of racialism, are going a long way toward changing the thinking of workers, and whilst some degree of initial opposition can certainly be expected, it is a small price to pay in driving home this important issue to unionists.

In November 1971 the branch noted in a motion to the BLF Federal Conference that some trade union officials during past periods of unemployment had been 'conned into supporting right wing policies of assisting capitalism in its own crisis, by restricting women workers' right to work, especially married women; sharing the job at reduced wages; and fostering anti-migrant and racial attitudes towards other workers'.[31]

In 1972 Pringle stood trial for sawing through the SCG goalposts. He and his co-defendant, ironworker John Phillips, were kept in custody during the three-day trial, as if other goalposts were at risk. They were convicted of malicious injury and Judge Head held over his sentence until the following day. The union held a special executive meeting, which decided to ask labourers to walk off the job to attend the sentencing. Mundey also announced that if Pringle was sentenced to gaol the union would call for a national strike. More than 100 police, including detectives from the Subversive Activities Squad, were present at the court. Pringle and Phillips were fined $500 each and placed on $1000 good behaviour bonds. An estimated crowd of 400 builders labourers booed the verdict.[32] To the crowd and reporters, Mundey condemned the decision as 'a miscarriage of justice' that revealed 'the extent to which racism exists within our society'. He maintained it was 'the spontaneous action of workers walking off jobs that stopped the racist judge from sending these two men to jail'.[33]

The following day, Liberal Attorney-General McCaw announced that he was seeking advice on whether action could be taken against Mundey for contempt of court. McCaw made it clear that, whatever the crown law officers advised, his own opinion had already been formed: 'I believe this man Mundey, wants to destroy the institutions [the courts] to which I have referred. He has made an effort to do it on other occasions. This community

On 22 August 1972, Johnny Phillips and Bob Pringle leave Darlinghurst Court Quarter Sessions, after being fined $500 each for attempting to cut down the SCG goal posts during the Springbok tour. (Courtesy *Sydney Morning Herald*)

is in real danger from people like Mr. Mundey and those who share his views.' Consequently, Mundey was charged in September, the Crown submitting that Mundey's remarks 'constituted a very serious contempt of court' and that they 'far exceeded legitimate criticism of a judge'.[34]

While proceedings were adjourned, a massive 'Defend Jack Mundey Campaign' developed, launched by a group representative of the support the union had generated: black activists, environmentalists, clergymen, unionists, draft resisters, a writer (Frank Hardy), an anti-Apartheid campaigner, student activists and feminists. The campaign raised the issues of freedom of speech, and racism in Australia and South Africa, and asked people to sign a statement repeating the allegations that Mundey had made, in order to make themselves similarly liable to be charged with contempt of court. Notwithstanding the risks involved, this statement was signed by 553 people, including two members of parliament. Money and messages of support were received from all over Australia. Predictably, those most indebted to the BLF were heavily involved, such as activists from resident groups, Aborigines and students, but so too were academics, lawyers, migrants and Nobel Laureate Patrick White (who walked into the union office one day and donated $100 to the Defence Committee). The Defence Committee also invited people to sign a statement declaring that they believed 'that actions taken by the BLF and Jack Mundey as its Secretary to preserve the environment against activities of big property developers have aroused political hostility in influential circles'.[35]

When Mundey appeared in court in October 1972, riot squad detectives patrolled the Supreme Court and the public gallery was packed with builders labourers. Judge Hope set 15 November as the date for the trial. The union asked metropolitan job organisers to have delegations from their jobs attend the court. Mundey continued to maintain that 'the real issue was the question of racism and apartheid'. Hope reserved his decision, handing it down just before Christmas, possibly to avoid large-scale demonstrations. He found Mundey guilty on only one of the two charges, describing his statement that labourers in court had influenced the verdict as 'scandalising contempt', and ordered Mundey to pay two-thirds of the cost of proceedings. The verdict received massive statewide publicity, being reported in detail in all Sydney and many regional papers.[36]

In the meantime the union continued to support the efforts towards multi-racial sport in South Africa. For instance in October 1972 it sent a message to the llth National Championships of the Southern African Lawn Tennis Union: 'We completely support the aims of multi-racial sport and we see your present actions as positive in the fight against Racism and Apartheid. We hope that you will overcome all the barriers that you will obviously encounter.' At its Federal Conference in 1973, the New South Wales branch urged the BLF, in keeping with its declared policies 'against apartheid, racism and colonialism' to call for trade bans on South Africa and Rhodesia and for government action to close the Rhodesian Information Centre in Sydney 'and to prevent its re-emergence in any form as an agency of the evil Smith regime'; to express its support for the liberation struggles in Southern Africa; and for each branch to sponsor the Southern Africa Liberation Centre. The branch collected signatures for a petition sent by the Liberation Centre to the Minister for Foreign Affairs in September 1974, urging the government to extend financial aid to the south-ern African liberation movements, close Australian trade offices in South Africa and withdraw rights from South African Airways to operate in Australia.[37]

ABORIGINAL RIGHTS

As a union of unskilled manual labourers, the NSWBLF had a signifi-cant Aboriginal membership. Under Mick McNamara's secretaryship, the union started to take its responsibilities towards these members seriously. In 1962 the executive agreed to send an Aboriginal builders labourer, Monty Maloney, who had recently represented the union and the BTG on a delegation overseas, to the 5th National Conference on Aboriginal Affairs in Adelaide in April. Around this time the union also committed itself to support the principles and demands of the Federal Council for the Advancement of Aborigines and Torres Strait Islanders.[38] From the mid-1960s, Ray Peckham (another Aboriginal member), Alan Williams and Ralph Kelly were especially active in support of indigenous rights.

In 1965 the NSWBLF successfully moved at the union's Federal Conference the following motion:

> We call on the Federal and State Governments to grant full citizenship rights to the aboriginal people. All discrimination against aborigines should be a crime in law. Further, we call on Governments to give special assistance … to compensate them for past injustices and to rapidly help them to take full advantage of citizenship. Further, we call upon the Trade Union Movement and other progressive sections of the Australian people to give the utmost support to the programme of the Federal Council for Advancement of Aborigines and Torres Strait Islanders. The pertinent points that require special support from our Union are: The restoration of Aboriginal lands; granting of land titles; preservation of Aboriginal communities; development of Aboriginal industries such as co-operatives, improved living and working standards, including equal pay rates; provision of all community and social services on reserves, provision of special education facilities; legislative reforms to give Aboriginal people equal electoral rights; provision of proper housing; prevention of any further alienation of Aboriginal lands without the agreement of the people concerned and with full compensation.[39]

During the Gurindji strike at Wave Hill in 1966, fund-raising efforts were strong with two projects alone contributing over $600 and the Aboriginal leaders from the Northern Territory received rousing welcomes on the many New South Wales job sites they visited at the invitation of the BLF.[40]

With land rights now placed on the political agenda by the Gurindji strike, the New South Wales branch meeting resolved to move at the 1967 Federal Council that 'the communally held land by Aborigines be declared inalienable lands, and only the Aboriginal people be given the complete rights to control their own affairs', and that 'they should have the right to live on such land or live in the community as they choose with complete freedom of movement'. The resolution called also for 'equality before the law with protection from all discrimination for all Aborigines', and for extensive government-funded schemes, administered without discrimination, 'to train the Aboriginal people in trades, professional and all other types of work, with

One of the meetings called by the NSWBLF in support of the Gurindji land claim, probably during 1967. Captain Major (seated) and Dexter Daniels (standing) addressed building sites all over Sydney.

proper homes and child recreational facilities being made available'.[41]

From this point onwards, Aboriginal organisations frequently enlisted NSWBLF support, invariably generously given, for a wide range of projects and initiatives.[42] In June 1968 the NSWBLF was one of the sponsors of a large public meeting on Aborigines' Land Rights, chaired by Ray Peckham, who had been 'paid off' by the union to work on projects 'in furtherance of the Aborigines' cause'. Mundey thus took issue with Frank Hardy's speech at this meeting – for 'lashing all white unionists and sneeringly making remarks about our racist tendencies' – while readily admitting 'much more remains to be done'. With Ray Peckham recently elected convenor of the Federal Council for the Advancement of Aborigines and Torres Strait Islanders' trade union sub-committee, Mundey urged Labor Council to 'hear Bro. Peckham on the Aborigines' Land rights issue' and to support that cause generally. The following month the union cotributed financially to assist Aboriginal activist Dexter Daniels attend the 9th World Youth Festival. In August 1968, the branch executive decided 'to give all possible assistance to the appeal to assist the Northern Territory Aborigines to win back their land 'and circulated 100 appeal petitions to the membership.[43]

Known as a union that encouraged its Aboriginal members and supported them in anti-racist activity, and one that habitually assisted the wider black movement, as it was then called, the union became closely involved with the Sydney black movement from the late 1960s onwards. It formed close links with local black leaders such as Paul and Isabelle Coe, Billy Cragie, Gary Foley, Norma Ingram, Tony Koorie, Lyn Thompson and Gary Williams. One of the union's organisers, Kevin Cook, was also a prominent and well-respected leader in the local black movement. Cook's standing facilitated the union's ability to establish non-racial structures within the union, to encourage anti-racist attitudes at membership level, and to maintain meaningful links with the Sydney black community. Pringle was especially generous in providing bail for arrested Aborigines: 'It was evident every time', he informed the Sun, 'that these people had been the subject of excessive zeal'.[44]

When Aboriginal protesters wanted help in advertising the 'black moratorium' on 14 July 1972, the union arranged for banners to be hung on the jibs of cranes around the city. One dogman, Roy Bishop, was dismissed for refusing to take a sign down. (He was reinstated and dismissed several times before the situation was resolved.) Pringle was arrested during the black moratorium march in Sydney, receiving a black eye, bruising and abrasions, and a four-hour stint in a police cell. In a subsequent leaflet, 'The Black Awakening', Pringle objected to the way in which this march was not allowed the same freedom of movement as the Anzac Day march, the changing of the guard at Martin Place each Thursday or the Waratah Festival; that it was forced onto the footpath by the police and when anyone overflowed on to the road they were hassled or arrested by the police.[45]

Pringle was also involved in the Aboriginal Embassy demonstration in Canberra later in July, when black activists and white supporters endeavoured on successive occasions to prevent police forcibly removing the tent embassy erected on the lawns in front of Parliament House. Of this 23 July struggle, Pringle, lucky to escape with minor abrasions and bruising, recalled: '362 Robots of the law marched out in military fashion and turned about in unison and then mechanically smashed us. Many people were seriously injured.' At the confrontation on 30 July, one speaker argued the police had a job to do and should not be ridiculed. Pringle spoke next and suggested rather that the police, who were 'a bunch of racists, fascists and pigs', were in a position analogous to that of the NSWBLF: 'if it is good enough for us to refuse to work on jobs that were not in the interests of the public, it is good enough for them to refuse duty when it is not in the interests of the nation'. His comments received great applause from the crowd.[46]

During this period of intense agitation on the part of the black movement, the union showed its continuing support by donating frequently to Aboriginal causes. In January 1973 it systematically collected money from builders

A banner advertising the black moratorium in July 1972. Dogman Roy Bishop was dismissed for refusing to take down the sign, but was later reinstated. Bob Pringle was arrested during the march.

labourers on job sites for the Wee-Waa Appeal, in support of the 2000 striking cotton chippers, predominantly black, in outback New South Wales who were earning a flat rate of $46 per week for 10 hours per day, in appalling conditions. In acknowledging this kind of fund-raising initiative, Aboriginal activist Lyn Thompson wrote to the union on behalf of the Black Moratorium Committee: 'The aboriginal Cause has a long way to go yet, and with the moral and financial support given to us such as the Builders' Labourers give, we will soon start solving a lot of our problems'.[47]

In December 1972, the NSWBLF and the plumbers' union supported 18 Aborigines occupying two Chippendale terrace houses that had been bought by a development company. Bob Bellear, as spokesperson for the group, explained the occupation was in support of Aboriginal land rights and would constitute Sydney's 'Aboriginal embassy'.[48] In the same month, a black ban was placed on the demolition of empty houses occupied by Aborigines in Eveleigh and Louis streets, Redfern. A big developer, IBK, had bought most of the houses to renovate as expensive townhouses and had evicted the Aborigines. Bob Bellear and Dick Blair contacted Pringle and the NSWBLF informed IBK that all work on the project would be banned. This ban greatly aided the black movement's resistance to the developer, which led ultimately to the Federal Government buying the disputed houses from the developer and granting the area to the black community in March 1973 as an Aboriginal housing scheme under Aboriginal control. Gordon Bryant, the new Whitlam Government Minister for Aboriginal Affairs, had visited the area and discussed the issues with the NSWBLF and the local black community. This Redfern Aboriginal Community Housing Scheme, provided much-needed low-rental accommodation, comprising 65 houses in the block bounded by Louis, Caroline, Eveleigh and Vine streets. At least ten Aboriginal builders labourers were employed on the reconstruction and renovation work. Many of the back fences were pulled down to create a communal recreation area. One of the two factories in the area was converted into a hall-workshop-gym and cultural centre; the other became a pre-school run by Aboriginal mothers and a medical centre linked with the Aboriginal Medical Service. The corner store became a co-operative shop, selling food cheaply. The whole project was managed by an elected co-operative committee. It was proudly declared to be the first successful Aboriginal land rights claim in Australia. As Tom Hogan wrote of this thoroughly satisfactory solution: 'On the Redfern end of town, white supremacists tried by all means including petitions to stop blacks being properly housed. The racists were defeated.'[49]

It was the New South Wales branch that proposed to the Federal Conference in 1973 that the union declare its support 'for full Aboriginal advancement in all forms and calls on the Federal Government to enter into genuine negotiations for a treaty to ensure that Aboriginal rights are accorded and upheld'.[50] When the New South Wales Liberal Party chose as its 1973 state election symbol two hands clasped, Pringle pointed out to the Sun that the symbol was an adaptation of the symbol recognised worldwide as that of the International Labour Organisation and of the World Federation of Trade Unions, and that the significant change made by Premier Askin was to show both hands as white, whereas the labour movement symbol depicted one white and one black hand. Given Askin's record as Police Minister, when he 'did nothing to stop flagrant police excesses when arresting Aborigines in the Redfern area', Pringle argued the adaptation 'directs one to the conclusion that the Askin Government is racist'.[51]

Kevin Cook's many positions within the black movement included presidency of the Black Theatre Art and Culture Centre, which was established in Redfern in 1974. In the first issue of its magazine, Mereki, Tom Hogan wrote on behalf of the NSWBLF, congratulating the Black Theatre 'for their guts and determination in demanding that the Black voice of Australia be heard', and assuring the theatre 'of our continued support in your fight against racism and for the self-determination of your people'. Referring to the union movement's emblem of the black and white hands clasping, he noted how important it was to 'strengthen that grip', referring to the struggles of black Australians against developers in Redfern and on Palm Island and the union's struggles to prevent workers' homes being demolished. 'A common enemy has arisen for Black and White. These types of attacks bring our organisations and our memberships closer together … Separately we have fought tyranny … together we shall overcome.'[52] When the union was indeed in trouble, the response from black Australians was overwhelming: no less than 38 separate Aboriginal organisations pledged support for the New South Wales executive of the union in its struggle against deregistration.[53]

PRISONERS' RIGHTS

Late in October 1973 the New South Wales Penal Reform Council sent an urgent telegram to the NSWBLF asking it to impose a ban on the almost completed $1 million concrete and steel maximum security block 'Katingal' at Long Bay Gaol, until the issues raised by 'this monstrosity' could be discussed publicly. Pringle agreed the block was 'barbaric' and appeared to be 'concerned with revenge on the individual rather than with rehabilitation'; Mundey announced the union would impose the 'blackest of black bans' on this project that belonged to the 'medieval past'.[54] The Council for Civil Liberties and the committee that provided courses for prisoners also appealed against the construction of this block that would house 40 prisoners unable to see daylight, confined to windowless cells for 18 hours a day, and 'subjected to a dehumanising process'. Since the building was almost completed, the participation of other building unions was crucial in maintaining a successful ban, for builders labourers were not as powerful in this instance as in the commencing stages of a project. The BTG resolved in January 1974 that no concrete would be poured to form the block's roof, the last stage, until the design was made more 'humane', and Labor Council endorsed this position. NSWBLF and BWIU workers at the gaol stopped work pending talks with the Minister for Justice.[55]

With reassurances that only the 'most intractable' prisoners would be confined in the block, the Labor Council, and subsequently the BWIU and the BTG, succumbed to public opinion and backed away from the ban. Only the NSWBLF remained determined to 'fight the issue' and retain the ban. The Penal Reform Council alleged the other union bodies had been hoodwinked by the Minister for Justice, who should resign because he was diverting funds away from probation and parole services to build Katingal.[56] The NSWBLF reaffirmed its ban on the 'inhuman hell cells' where toilet bowls doubled for wash basins, accused the Labor Council of being gutless over the issue, and called for an inquiry into an alternative use for the block.[57] It attempted to maintain the ban – Dean Barber recalled that Tony Hadfield single handedly tried for some time to 'use the muscle we didn't really have' in the face of the other unions' backdown – but was unable to prevent the completion of the block. In May 1974 the NSWBLF included among its claims in the national award log that prisoners in Australian gaols be entitled to representation and award conditions when engaged on construction or building maintenance work. When prisoners at the maximum security section of Bathurst Gaol set fire to their cells, the union placed a ban on any rebuilding of the burnt-out gaol. Owens travelled to Bathurst with George Petersen MLA to lend support to students at Mitchell College concerned to impress upon the public the need for reform in the New South Wales penal system. Owens explained he was opposed to the existing method of maximum security in New South Wales gaols because of its repercussions on the individual.[58]

The union's position on maximum security blocks and on Katingal in particular was vindicated by the Nagle Royal Commission into New South Wales Prisons, which reported four years later: 'The cost of Katingal is too high in human terms. It was ill-conceived in the first place, was surrounded by secrecy and defensiveness at a time when public discussion should have been encouraged. Its inmates are now suffering the consequences.'[59] Upon Judge Nagle's recommendation, Katingal was closed in 1978.

HOMOSEXUAL LIBERATION

In June 1973 the union placed a ban, known as the 'pink ban', on all new construction work at Macquarie University over the expulsion of a homosexual student from the Anglican residential college on the campus. Jeremy Fisher, the treasurer of the campus Gay Liberation Group, had been a resident of Robert Menzies College until its Master, Dr Alan Cole, had discovered Fisher's role as a gay activist. Cole had insisted that Fisher could not remain at the College unless he undertook to lead a celibate life and seek to have his 'perversion' cured by seeking psychological and spiritual help. Fisher refused to meet these conditions and was accordingly expelled. The executive of the Macquarie University Students' Council asked Dr Cole to change his decision. They stated they were not asking that he change his personal opinion of homosexuality, but that he refrain from imposing this on the private lives of college applicants and residents: but he refused. The council then approached the NSWBLF executive, which recommended a ban. This recommendation was endorsed at a state branch meeting and also unanimously by the builders labourers working on the campus, who agreed the ban should remain until the university made an 'unequivocal statement' that there would be no discrimination against homosexuals and 'human dignity' was restored. 'Universities are places for people to learn – they should not discriminate against individuals,' explained Mundey to the press, 'The ban will remain until the authorities at the University allow homosexuals to study there the same as anyone else'. The ban threatened construction of a $500,000 lecture theatre, extensions worth $26,000 to the gymnasium, a $150,000 maintenance depot and a $170,000 science workshop. The University Council formed a committee to investigate the case, which favoured Fisher's reinstatement, so the ban was lifted – but Fisher had decided he did not wish to return to the college.[60]

Judging from the interviews conducted with rank-and-file builders labourers, it was this ban that found least acceptance among the membership: a frequent response from those interviewed was an expression of total support for the bans, 'except for that one about homosexuals'. But as Dean

Barber pointed out, there must also have been support for it for the men to walk off the job. Pringle suggests the debate at the meeting that endorsed the ban indicated the unionists were more concerned 'about the dictatorial attitude of the Master of the College rather than the actual issue of homosexuality'. The labourers, he informed *Gay Liberation Press*, 'like society generally, were not sufficiently radicalised on issues of sexual oppression'. As a lesbian working in the industry, Janne Reed recalled the experience of a young man on a job who was labelled homosexual because he was a very gentle person, and suggested there was a strong correlation between union consciousness and acceptance of homosexuality. 'There were a lot of militants who supported him but most workers were really bad to him.'[61]

The union's preparedness to jeopardise members' work prospects by placing a ban over the issue of homosexual rights was remarkable, and appreciated as such by the gay movement. Bob Pringle was interviewed about the union's policy on homosexuality by gay movement reporters, who were clearly exhilarated by the union's stance because builders labouring, 'probably more than any other industry, has masculinity as its foundation'. Yet these reporters were critical that the depth of anti-homosexual feelings among workers still made it difficult for homosexual labourers to be open about their sexuality and that the NSWBLF executive seemed hesitant to 'push a great barrel about homosexuality'. Pringle explained: 'We as an executive believe that it is a presumption of any sort for society to be the moral judge for an individuals sexual preference'. However he made it clear that, while the union would stand up for homosexual rights wherever appropriate, the broader battle had nonetheless to be fought by the homosexual liberation movement: 'The issue is yours, not ours. We will help, support and do all we can, but we will not fight the issue for you.'[62]

Nonetheless the branch sponsored a motion to its Federal Conference in 1973 contesting the heterosexist double standards of the time: 'Conference calls on all sections of government to alter existing laws to allow homosexuals the same privacy in their personal relations as heterosexuals and be subject to no more control under the law'. Also in 1973, it moved a motion at the New South Wales ALP State Conference calling for legalisation of homosexual relationships and an end to discrimination. During 1974 the union was active in support of Penny Short, whose Teachers' College scholarship had been withdrawn because she was a lesbian: many NSWBLF activists marched in the demonstration against the Education Department's decision to suspend her scholarship.[63]

When the homosexual rights organisation, Campaign Against Moral

Persecution, issued a 29-page report in April 1974 entitled *Homosexuals Report Back* in response to the Sydney Anglican Diocesan attacks on homosexual people, it sent a copy of this report to the NSWBLF. This was a natural response in light of the union's central position within the radical milieu of the time and, more specifically, the union's practical support for the cause of homosexual liberation. When the National Homosexual Conference held in Melbourne in August 1975 debated the issue of relations with other organisations, the 'direct material support to NSW Gay Lib. by the then progressive leadership and rank and file BLs' was cited by delegates to the conference as an example of why homosexual women and men should support unions seeking social change. Owens' final speech as secretary to the packed meeting of 2 November 1975 mentioned the Macquarie University ban as one that, because of the strength of homophobic attitudes in the building industry as in society at large, had created a stir and made 'a difference'.[64]

THE WOMEN'S MOVEMENT

The union demonstrated support for the burgeoning women's movement in numerous ways. From 1971, both the *Builders' Labourer* and the *Rank and File Rag* featured articles about women's issues and advertisements for women's day marches, the women's unemployment centre, abortion demonstrations and so on. Caroline Graham described how the Women's Electoral Lobby approached the union for help in raising funds for an abortion rights advertisement: 'The response was typically generous: not only did we receive a large cash donation, but the union president Bob Pringle, helped our representative to compose and lay out the advertisement'. The union officials often marched on International Women's Day, (sometimes to the accompaniment of ribald remarks from labourers high on city building sites).[65]

In an action that, in the context of the time, constituted a feminist gesture, the union was forthright in its support of the Kings Cross strippers' strike in November 1973, a form of solidarity not greatly appreciated at Trades Hall. The leadership and activists even participated in picket lines and demonstration, which was considered not very respectable behaviour by most of the other unions. When the Staccato Club was fire-bombed during the strike, the union banned any reconstruction work until the strippers' claims were met and in protest against the bashing of an Actors Equity official. The branch requested its 1973 Federal Conference to pass a motion 'That the persecution of prostitutes by the law and their exploitation by Court fines cease'.[66]

The union's active support of women's liberation was expressed most publicly in June 1973. For some time, authorities at the University of Sydney had been resisting attempts by two tutors, Jean Curthoys and Liz Jacka, to launch a women's studies course in the Philosophy Department, despite the fact that the staff concerned and the proposed course had been approved by the relevant undergraduate studies committee. When the Professorial Board vetoed the course, Mundey deemed the decision 'sexist' and, following an approach from concerned students, announced a ban on all further construction work at the university. This placed in immediate jeopardy extensions to the medical faculty building and a proposed $3 million theatre complex. Coming only one week after the Macquarie University ban in defence of homosexual rights, Mundey explained the union treated the bans as 'top priority' because it had a social conscience – and considered that universities should reveal theirs:

> In these days of social enlightenment and reform, the wiping out of
> these discriminations should start at the universities. Now we find that
> discrimination is being promoted at the universities. The ban will stay
> on all further construction until the decisions are reversed.[67]

Mundey affirmed this ban to a 2500-strong meeting of students striking in support of the proposed course on 29 June. Since the university urgently required the completion of certain buildings, the dispute was resolved internally and the ban lifted.[68] The course commenced in 1974 as one of the pioneering courses in this field of study that is now commonplace at universities throughout the world.

The union's most significant contribution to the cause of women's rights was its determination to ensure that women had the opportunity to pursue employment in the building industry on an equal basis with men, but the story of this remarkable campaign is the subject of the next chapter.

Nowhere is the stereotyping of new social movement analysis more inappropriate than in the case of the NSWBLF, which initiated its campaigns on behalf of oppressed others at a moment in time (the early to mid-1970s) when new social movement theorists were already putting pen to paper to condemn the old social movement for its lack of concern over such matters. This union of unskilled and semi-skilled male blue-collar workers confounds the hackneyed image dear to new social movement analysis, in which the old social movement of labour adopts socially conservative positions and ignores broader issues of social change and social equality to focus exclusively on concerns of direct material benefit only to its own membership. On the contrary, as the strong supporting the weak on issues affecting so many, the NSWBLF provided a foretaste of the social-movement unionism that is now in the 1990s proving to be labour's most effective form of mobilisation and reply to those who doubted its transformative potential.

FEMINISM AND MACHISMO:
WOMEN AS BUILDERS LABOURERS

The NSWBLF was the only exclusively male manual union ever to promote seriously the right of women to work in the industry. The union leadership was ideologically committed to the women's liberation struggle and actively supported the women's cause in significant ways; yet it did so in one of the most traditionally 'macho' of all industries. This obvious contraillction gave rise to many bizarre incidents and hitherto unencountered problems in the realm of union politics, workplace organisation and industrial relations. At the same time as Australian builders labourers were insisting on absolute equality of employment terms for its increasing number of female members, in Britain UCATT still had a 'working rule agreement' that gave the 'right' for women workers to receive 85 per cent of the relevant male rate for the same work and, in adhering strictly to this differential, withstood any move towards equal pay for equal work. Moreover, the women concerned were never employed as builders labourers and it was not until 1974 that UCATT's annual conference passed a motion that supported the principle of 'equal pay for women operatives'.[1]

The NSWBLF leadership's espousal of women's rights stemmed from its belief that the 'division between trade unions and the rest of the community is a bad thing' and that trade unionists should contest exploitation 'not just in their workplace but everywhere'.[2] Identifying women as the exploited sex, the union embarked upon practical attempts to counteract that exploitation, against the immediate economic interests of builders labourers as members of an exclusively male union, and against their wider social interests as members of the dominant sex. As harbinger of social-movement unionism, it sought from within the all-male bastion of the Australian building industry to overcome the fragmentation of the working class along gender lines.

At the time of the NSWBLF's extraordinary endeavours little had been written about the experience of women within the Australian union movement. Much has been written since; research that has been inspired by the same social forces to which the union was responding in making its remarkable gestures towards women's liberation. This scholarship reveals a history of traditional male trade unionists' complicity with patriarchal structures that constrained women's earning capacities and restrained female union activity, a situation contested only occasionally by unusually fair-minded male unionists, and by many female unionists.[3] In the wake of these historiographical advances, industrial relations theory and research has also begun to treat gender rather more effectively than hitherto.[4]

FROM MAY QUEENS TO WOMEN'S LIBBERS

Before the 1970s the NSWBLF leadership had held the traditional view of the role of women in the union movement. It had entered candidates for the May Queen competition until 1969, and until August 1965 had opposed women working as builders labourers because 'employers were taking advantage of the situation to break down wages and working conditions'.[5] Typically, the women concerned were employed as cleaners by subcontractors on less than BLF rates, although cleaning up on building sites is builders labourers' work. Since wages and conditions would immediately have been protected if the women had been admitted as members, secretary McNamara's protestations about the threat to wages and conditions, and those of generations of male unionists before him, can be seen as the flimsiest of rationalisations. In a much-publicised press statement in June 1965, McNamara argued: 'This union is perhaps the last male stronghold, and it will stay that way in the interests of the women themselves … we will never allow our wives, sweethearts and daughters to move into this rugged industry'.[6]

Some officials, notably Mundey, insisted women should be allowed into the union, and they succeeded in having the union's position reversed in August 1965. An industrial court decision late in 1966 endorsed the union's stance on equal pay for female employees. No longer favoured by employers as a cheaper alternative, and not yet welcomed enthusiastically into the union, women momentarily faded from the industry.[7] However by the early 1970s the impact of the women's movement upon the CPA had been profound, a process aided greatly by the departure of the more puritanical, mostly older, male SPA contingent in 1971. Their absence enabled the remaining party members to embrace views about women's liberation that would have been unthinkable only a few years earlier, and these ideas affected CPA union officials to varying degrees.[8] Michelle Fraser, new recruit to both the party and the NSWBLF in 1974, recalled that it was obvious to her that union policies concerning women came through the party's Building Branch and that they were the direct outcome of the successful struggle that CPA women had waged within their own organisation. Yet the new party thinking on such matters enjoyed far more support among the younger members and party intellectuals than among its trade unionists. In this context the efforts of Mundey, Owens, Tom Hogan and the other NSWBLF organisers constitute a great leap into the unknown, unequalled by any similar 'giant strides' on the part of other CPA union officials.

Initially, during and in the wake of the 1970 margins strike, the union had made the characteristic gestures towards the women's movement to which an all-male union is restricted: 'wives and girl friends' were invited to important general meetings and to strike meetings.[9] Also in 1970, the union was especially generous in its assistance to a predominantly female union: substantial support was organised for the strike of Canberra's nurses, including several stoppages and a $200 donation, plus additional collections from individual building sites. It could be argued that perhaps the nurses were wholly admirable because they were sticking to a profession stereotypical for their sex, and that such actions and responses of the union – incorporating 'wives' and supporting striking nurses – were still clearly operating within traditional parameters outlining the female role in trade union activity. However by 1973 the New South Wales branch was pressing the following motion at the BLF's Federal Conference:

> This conference calls on each state to take immediate action to establish the rights of women to work in the industry. We believe that all people have right to a job in the industry of their own choosing, regardless of sex, age, colour or race.
>
> Therefore, this union should actively support and encourage women entering and participating in the union and the industry as a whole.
>
> Knowing the prejudices of this society concerning women's role in life, industrial pressure should be brought to bear on employers, both Government and private to grant women the right of employment in our industry.[10]

How this remarkable transformation occurred is a tribute both to the women who chose to enter the industry and the union that welcomed and, in many instances, encouraged them.

THE WOMEN AT WORK

In March 1971 the union became involved in its first full-scale campaign to change the role of women in the building industry to one of genuine and equal participation, although on rather more condescending terms than subsequently. A subcontractor on the Kingsgate building project hired four women to do cleaning work, claiming the 'girls' were more suited to this work than men. Mick Ross, the job delegate, reported: 'Workers on the site had no argument with this but insisted that any girls would have to become members of the Builders Labourers and as such receive the same wages and conditions'. The subcontractor tried to convince the women they would be better off if they joined another union. The women were unpersuaded and joined the BLF. Later, when the subcontractor went broke and the women's wages were not paid, the men on the job organised several stop-work meetings, and eventually a strike to guarantee the women's wages and security of employment.[11]

The job site had readily accepted these women because they were there, doing builders labourers' work from the outset. The strike developed spontaneously over a basic trade union concern, in this case the non-payment of workers, not over the issue of women's right to work in the industry. The women were seen by the men as young innocents being helped to a better understanding of unionism and subcontractors' tricks by the worldly wise and beneficent male unionists. The women were suitably grateful to their benefactors and the anticipated client relationship was established: Karlene Slattery insisted that 'the men treat us very well. They're very good and considerate to us.'[12] Their subordinate position was ensured, too, because they were engaged in cleaning work, which although being traditional builders labourers' work, was much less stereotypically masculine work than general labouring.

Later in 1971, Marjorie Olive started working at Crosstowns and reported: 'The boss tried to sack me after I had been there only five minutes. When the delegate asked him why he said, "But it's a girl, it's a girl" (I emphasise the "it's"). But I was forced upon them and they are stuck with me.'[13] Olive's friend Glenys Page became interested in working as a builders labourer and Olive got her a job by the simple procedure of turning up on a job at Randwick with four women instead of three, and informing the boss that he had an extra worker. The women, at this early stage, had to fight hard against a protective attitude towards them on the part of bosses and fellow labourers. For instance, Glenys Page was not allowed to work on the external staging of the top floor of Kingsgate, even though she was willing.[14] Thus it was harder to argue women's rights to equal employment opportunities while they could be seen to be protected from certain work.

By the end of 1971 the BLF had nine female members.[15] They were not yet seen as a real threat to the male enclave, and accepted relatively easily by the rank and file. In Glenys Page's words, they were regarded as exceptions to the rule, as 'oddities' or 'aberrations'. However, the oddities became more numerous. In 1972 several strikes occurred to force bosses to accept female labour.

In these confrontations the employers' objections were couched in terms of a threat to management prerogative: a rejection of anything that smacked of 'union hire'. Karlene Slattery's job as a nipper on an office building in North Sydney caused a 14-day stoppage. The workers were striking as much over their right to 'union hire' as over the right for a woman to work. (Nippers get the lunches, clean the change rooms, boil the billy and generally look after the site amenities.) Even the company spokesman denied the dispute was over the employment of a 'girl'; he simply denied they had agreed to take on a nipper. The employer maintained 'the right to put on its own staff'.[16] However, as the male labourers knew, the employer would not have objected if a male nipper was concerned, so the women's rights issue became inextricably linked to that of job-control. This was to be a recurring motif.

In September 1972 a similar job control/women's rights incident developed when Glenys Page was sent by the union to be the nipper on an EA Watts job in North Sydney. The company's original objection was that the position was being kept for a one-armed man, but the company then claimed it was not in a position to employ a nipper at that time even though it had advertised for one. Reflecting upon the company's response, Page believes it was primarily anxious to preserve its right to employ its own labour: 'they didn't want to be told who to employ or who not to employ'. But her sex was also an issue: 'Because I was a woman it meant changes they did not particularly want to make'. The employer ordered her off the site and she was escorted from the job by police, who could not charge her because she was a minor. Workers from her job and others in the area stopped work and went down to support her at the police station, where police were harassing her to stay away from the site. The next day the job was closed and a two-week lock-out ensued, during which bans occurred on other EA Watts jobs. The union argued successfully in court that she was being denied employment merely because of her sex, and she eventually started work on the job, where she remained for two years.[17]

A short time later Carmen Rose, a Maltese woman married to another builders labourer, was sacked from a Lend Lease job in Kogarah for, among other things, refusing to work with non-unionists. Builders labourers at other Lend Lease jobs stopped work in solidarity and she was reinstated. Once again, a traditional union issue such as 'scabbing' was inextricably linked with the women's issue. In November 1972 a dispute occurred in Newcastle over a female nipper. The employer took out a summons to prevent June Philpott being on the Civic Centre site 'without reasonable cause'; the union took the matter to the industrial court.[18]

Another confrontation occurred when Wendy Stringer applied for a job as a safety officer at a Crow Industries job in Hoxton Park. Although she had not applied through the union office, she was qualified for the job and the men on the site decided to work her in. As she described it: 'we were working in mud so we had to wear gumboots and as I'm more shortlegged than anyone else the mud used to run into them'. Eventually the mud issue (warranting a site allowance) and the woman issue became intertwined and after working in for a week, the job went on strike because the labourers had been sacked for doing so. The strike lasted 16 weeks and Stringer became involved in collecting strike levies from other city jobs and began attending union meetings. Although the entire gang of about fifteen labourers were never allowed to return to the site, the last laugh was at the boss's expense: convinced he had finally rid himself of the dreadful Stringer, he hired a new gang that happened to contain her twin sister, Robyn Williams. The boss refused to believe she was not Stringer until both of them turned up to persuade him.[19]

Stringer's next job was similarly eventful. The subcontractor who had hired her was told to fire her instead. He refused, and was fired himself. Then the man who hired the subcontractor was also fired and, after a bewildering series of events in which Stringer won her case in the courts three times, she was eventually kept on at the site. When Robyn Williams applied for her next job, she was only accepted when the union told the employer he had to have her or he would not have a workforce at all.[20]

The fact that Stringer and Williams had applied for jobs in the outer western suburbs and without any previous contact with the union indicated the way in which the union was becoming publicly identified with the women's struggle. Many of the previous incidents had received press coverage and it was becoming widely known that builders labouring was a new option open to women with a taste for outdoor life – who did not wish to be 'cooped up in an office', as many female builders labourers explained it – and one that paid better wages than women generally received for manual labour.

Unfortunately for the women anxious to take up this new employment opportunity made possible by the union, media coverage of the serious 'women's rights' strikes was sexist. Invariably the women were described as 'attractive', 'pert', 'bright-eyed'; normally, they were asked whether they had burnt their bras (an obsession in media speculation about feminists at this time). Moreover, the serious industrial issues involved in some of the disputes were mostly ignored by the press, which preferred to dwell upon trivial details: 'Joan Cox recently caused a storm when she was refused the daily beer ration given to men when she was working on a brewery site' or 'hard work won't ruin a woman's looks or figure, said Mrs Denise Bishop'.[21]

Presumably the media portrayals to some extent moulded the expectations of the male builders labourers, who therefore found themselves unprepared for the new breed of feminists who started entering the industry during 1973. In June, 17 women enrolled for a hoist drivers' course at Sydney Technical College. Around this time, Janne Reed, an outspoken working-class feminist from Wollongong with extensive union experience, applied for a nipper's job on the North Shore hospital site:

> When I went for the job, there'd just been a six-week strike over grievances including the right to have a nipper. So when I rolled up as a woman, the company, instead of saying 'we won't employ a woman, we'll put a man on instead', just said 'no job'. I think if they'd just said 'no woman', the men whose consciousness was not very good at the time would have just copped it.

A stop-work meeting was called immediately, which Reed attended and, after more approaches were made to the company a work-in was declared, and later a strike. By then, the issue had become a women's issue and Reed believes about 90 per cent of the men were prepared to support it on those grounds: 'they were very good – the old boilermakers were really brilliant'. When she reprimanded the boss for threatening to call the police and have her arrested, the men on the job stood and cheered.[22] Such was a typical response on the part of male builders labourers: although they might disapprove of female builders labourers in the abstract, once they had met one, heard her arguments and saw the employer discriminate against her, they became more accepting and often supportive. Eventually this particular dispute was resolved in Reed's favour and she became actively involved both on the job, where she was elected delegate, and within the union.

Lyn Syme, another woman who later became prominent in the union, entered the industry at the end of 1973. She says the men on her job suspected one of the women who had completed the hoist drivers' course was going to turn up, because the area organiser, Tony Hadfield, had insisted that the company hire a ticketed hoist driver and that the union would have one on the job by Monday. She describes the men's reactions as 'quite good really'. Hadfield had just succeeded in achieving proper pay rates for the labourers on the job, so the union was in good favour at the time. The men's reaction protected her from the boss's displeasure when he first encountered her after she had already been working the hoist for several hours: 'he freaked at first, but I was there, I'd met everybody – there was nothing he could do'.

During 1974 the union announced it had 80 female members, although there were probably no more than 20 women working at any one time. Some jobs had three or four women on the one site: this bunching occurred because union hire (in this case forcing employers to hire women) could only be implemented on already militant jobs. These included Crystals in Surry Hills, Dillingham in Clarence Street and Canns, an extension to a bridal salon in Market Street. From the Canns site, Rhonda Ellis recounts the experience of herself and Lesley Mason, a fellow female builders labourer:

> … we spent time trying to communicate with women in the lifts on their way up to buy bridal gowns. Picture Lesley and I in our overalls and big boots, wearing our helmets and not looking at all like them … We'd tell them how good our wages and conditions were and face them with an alternative to getting married and being the suburban dream. I don't know whether we actually won any but they certainly used to look at us.

Builders labourers on the International Women's Day march in 1974 (left to right: Glenys Page, Lyn Syme, Rhonda Ellis, unidentified, Michelle Fraser, Janne Reed, Caroline Graham).

However, employers were still repeatedly refusing women work. When Michelle Fraser applied for a job in Glebe, she was 'just laughed at'. When she returned to the site with an organiser, who happened to be Lyn Syme, the boss became intimidated. (Like most NSWBLF organisers, Syme had a forceful personality.) Under pressure from the men on the job, he capitulated, but not before offering Fraser a month's pay 'to leave him alone'. Later at the Dillingham site in Clarence Street, the boss refused to employ Fraser, but the workers advised her to 'hang around' and attend their strike meeting. Although she performed no work at all, at the end of the day her pay was waiting for her.[23]

Likewise Ros Harrison was refused employment as a first aid officer on the Eastments Angus and Coote development project in George Street, despite the fact that she was a doctor, a graduate of University of Queensland's medical school. Instead, the company appointed a less qualified man and denied that Harrison was rejected because she was a woman. After a month's strike, a strange compromise was reached whereby Harrison started work as a labourer and was to relieve the first aid officer when he was off duty. The *Hobart Mercury* reported: 'Dark-haired Dr Roslyn Harrison, who has exchanged a cosy consulting room and $300 a week for a wind-swept Sydney building site and laborer's wage of $120, said yesterday: "I am quite content. Money doesn't interest me."' In this interview after her first day's work, coating raw timber beams with wood preservative on the 15-storey project, she paid tribute to the union that had made her bizarre career choice possible: 'The guys in the Builders Laborers' Federation have accepted me completely'.[24]

Dillingham's was the scene of the biggest dispute over women. In February 1974 an inspector from the Department of Labour and Industry approved the labourers' demands for a safety officer. Philippa Pieters duly arrived on site but was refused employment because she was a woman. The men decided to work her in but the following day the employer called in police, who ordered the builders labourers off the site under threat of arrest. A three-week strike ensued-the first building site dispute in which the women's movement became actively involved. The Dillingham workers and the BLF Women's Collective organised demonstrations at which women's liberation groups, the Women's Electoral Lobby, Women's Trade Union Action and public service women were represented. The women's movement paper *Mabel* published an attack on Dillingham, and the BLF Women's Collective produced a leaflet. Eventually the strike was won and Pieters remained on the job.[25]

The women who worked as builders labourers could be classified roughly

A sign of the times! A protest at the Eastments' Angus & Coote project in George Street, June 1974, where Dr Ros Harrison was refused employment as a first aid officer.

into two groups: those from working-class backgrounds, attracted to the work because of the wage levels or its outdoor nature; and those who were already politically involved, inspired by what the union was doing in other areas and who wished to be part of such an exciting organisation. From both groups, many of the women stayed long periods on their various jobs: stints ranging from six months to three years were quite common, long periods for an industry in which the builders labourer turnover is estimated to be 50 per cent each year. Having won the battle to get on to a job, the women felt less inclined to leave of their own accord than the average male worker.

Moreover, as banner-holders for women in the industry, they possibly tried extra hard not to get sacked for minor misdemeanours.

The union had changed dramatically in less than a decade. In 1974 a male builders labourer discovered in the office an old press clipping of Mick McNa-mara's 1965 announcement that the union would never allow wives, sweet-hearts and daughters to move into 'this rugged industry'. So great had been the sea change in the men's thinking on this matter over the intervening nine years that when this archival gem was rediscovered and pinned to the office notice-board, it caused considerable merriment among the organisers, now confident in their new-found anti-sexism. In the NSWBLF, 'girls' were now, officially at least, 'women' and to be accepted as fellow workers and treated strictly as equals. In Britain by comparison the practice of calling women 'girls' persisted, as did the kind of condescension typically practised by male trade unionists, who continued to believe they were entitled to higher rates of pay for perform-ing the same work as the small numbers of women working with them.[26]

The NSWBLF leadership's support for women in the industry was shown in many ways. It actively encouraged women to take official union posi-tions. For instance, the Rank and File Committee pre-selected Denise Bishop to stand for the executive in 1973. And many of the posters advertising the Owens-Pringle-Mundey team featured large pictures of Denise Bishop with slogans such as 'Vote for a Woman'. (While the NSWBLF journal's photo-graphic portrayals of women incited men to support them as organisers and vote for one as a member of the union executive, the British builders labourers' union journal was still publishing pin-up girls in this period.) Bishop topped the ballot, as a result of extensive campaigning. She was also appointed as a temporary organiser in 1974, as were Lyn Syme and Rhonda Ellis. Moreover, and contrary to the ways in which trade union bureaucracies normally rein-force a woman's feeling of powerlessness, the union encouraged all members, including women, to participate in all decisions and activities. The women responded accordingly: the percentage of activists among the female members of the union was even higher than among the male members.[27]

There were countless examples of leadership support for the right of women to work in the building industry. The New South Wales branch's agenda items for the 1973 Federal Conference called on each state to 'take immediate action to establish the rights of women to work in the industry'. By 1974, its agenda items included abortion leave as well as paternity and maternity leave. Also during 1974 the branch sought to insert a claim in the National Award log 'that the right of women to work in the building industry be recognised without discrimination'. The 1973 Rank and File Committee's election policy statement demanded 'not only the right of women to work as builders labourers but giving maximum assistance to women's struggle for complete political and social liberation in our society'. As an issue of *On Site*, published by Trotskyist building workers, noted: 'The Builders Labourers Federation has taken a principled stand on the question of women in the building industry. Bitter struggles have been fought by rank and file workers to get women on job sites, and they are an example to all.'[28]

Despite the building industry's tendency to encourage machismo in the workplace, the union leadership's commitment to gender equality did influence the membership, greatly encouraging acceptance of the women by the male labourers. Generally the women reported good experiences of support from the labourers and many were made delegates or co-delegates. All the women recounted individual acts of kindness and support: men who taught them how to lift things more easily and safely, strip wood, use jackhammers and so on; and men who argued with their fellows in support of women labourers. The strikes and work-ins already recounted, which confronted the employers' sexist forms of discrimination, were a true indication of the genuinely egalitarian atmosphere generated within the union.

THE LIMITS OF MACHO FEMINISM

Despite the strong support the union and its members gave for their right to work in the industry, some female builders labourers believed nonetheless that certain officials lacked the desire to 'go down and fight it out on the job', to adopt the kind of pugnacious attitude that characterised the leadership's struggles over other issues. This milder mannered approach on sexual equality may have indicated either a reluctance to push too heavily a somewhat contentious issue, or the lingering sexism of some of the officials, or both. As an anonymous female builders labourer stated, there was 'doubt about whether the verbal support of some organisers is genuine'.[29]

Wendy Stringer admitted there were 'those officials who genuinely were concerned about women's rights but there were others who only supported women because it was a popular wave'. Denise Bishop interpreted her original preselection thus: 'they wanted to say "look how we're treating women as equals – this is a free-thinking union and it gives the union a better image"'. As it turned out, she believes that her unique position as Australia's first female building union official was much more difficult for the men to handle than it was for her. Stella Nord thought that the union's policy on women:

actually forced some of the officials to declare themselves, in the sense that they were either for it or against it, and those who were for it, they went out onto meetings and actually promoted the idea of women in the industry and encouraged strikes, as against some others who while they said they supported it would not have been so active.

The limits of the men's support for feminism were eventually felt by the BLF Women's Collective. This had long existed in an informal way, since women had first trickled into the industry. In 1973 it had produced a 'Questions and Answers' document, which attacked most of the common arguments against women in the industry. However, by 1974 when the collective became more formally organised, many of the male officials, according to the women, felt threatened and claimed they were 'working as a clique'. Since such a clique was considered to be in opposition to the official union policy of 'openness at all levels', the women were pressured to 'expand' – or as they saw it, to 'disband' – the collective. The women agreed to turn the collective into an anti-discrimination or right-to-work group. Two men came to the first open meeting, and then no more. By this time, Intervention was distracting the union and the collective never functioned properly in its new guise.[30]

While the female builders labourers remained quiet and grateful, the male leaders' real feelings were obscured. It was when the women began speaking out and demanding conditions and rights relevant to women that the men began to feel threatened. Lyn Syme thought that she, as an outspoken activist, was resented: the male prerogative always to be the speaker was under attack. Wendy Bacon believes the male builders labourers were especially wary of Janne Reed, because she saw herself as an industrial equal. Reed herself feels the men objected more to her feminism than her femaleness, and this response was especially marked on the part of the men who knew only about her feminist background and were unaware of her previous union activities.

These women, who dared to rebuke the men in the pub for their sexist language, were very different to the early female labourers or to the women from the resident action groups, who were cast inevitably into a grateful client status by their dependence upon the green bans. Many male labourers, who may have been prepared to accept women as fellow labourers on male terms – as honorary blokes – were simply not prepared to countenance any transformations to the industry that in any way constituted feminisation of it. This resistance to feminisation of the industry was paralleled in the leadership's aversion to any feminisation of its own otherwise radically democratic union practices.

Janne Reed and Brian Rix (either side of the dog box) help replenish supplies during a crane occupation at the Institute of Technology site in George Street, late in 1974.

As in the wider women's movement of the time, the women promoted discussion about more collectivist forms of leadership; and the male leaders accordingly felt rejected, because they felt the women's discussions constituted attacks on them personally. Lyn Syme believes the men also felt menaced because such ideas would threaten their positions as the elected officials of the union. Since the leadership, with good reason, considered themselves to be the harbingers and leading proponents within the trade union movement of true internal democracy, they naturally felt somewhat offended that their definition of democracy was being queried by apparently more radical, feminist ideas. It was the women who saw and comprehended best the informal power structures operating within the union, for only the women, out of the 46 builders labourers interviewed, understood properly the questions about informal or personal power: Rhonda Ellis noted 'charisma overriding collective decision making'; Michelle Fraser and Paula Rix observed 'power positions'; and many referred to the existence of 'pecking orders'.

Such pecking orders existed even among the women involved in the union.

Nor were the female builders labourers immune to some of the elitist errors of the men: during a strike of the office staff in 1974 over the absorption of an award increase, none of the female labourers came to talk to the clerks about the issue. The male leadership clearly distinguished between the female builders labourers and the female office staff, and the female builders labourers, for all their democratic feminist ideals, absorbed this distinction, even as they took the formally egalitarian position of incorporating the office staff in the women's collective. The clerks – Robyn Cockayne, Carol Kalafates, Paula Rix and Jenny Healey – felt that all the builders labourers, the women included, considered them inferior because they were not part of the builders labourers' camaraderie, the fellowship forged by a shared participation in rough, tough and dangerous manual labour. Pat Fiske personally experienced the two main 'power positions' of the women by occupying both: during Intervention, she used to return to the union rooms each afternoon where male officials would clap her on the shoulder and say 'goodday', greeting her as a fellow builders labourer; but one day, when helping with the typing, 'not a soul said hullo, not a male even noticed I was there'.

There was confusion in the minds of the men, according to the clerks, about their role. Were they clerks or were they builders labourers? Often they were expected to behave like builders labourers and put the union's interests before their own, even though they were only paid as clerks. The men did not like the women pointing out that clerks were paid much less, 'even though we're highly trained and you aren't'. When the union, to its credit, abolished the iniquitous junior clerk positions that received even less pay than senior clerks, Paula Rix felt the men were nonetheless 'giving things on their terms, they were the great benefactors'. And given that they saw themselves as the 'ice-breakers' on questions such as feminism, the office strike of late 1974, though amicably settled, was 'like the dog biting the hand that feeds it'. Moreover, when the clerks, inspired by the union's own ideas about self-management, decided to apply these principles to re-organise their working lives by rotating office co-ordinators, sharing boring tasks and so on, the officials were not amused.

Under attack from all quarters, the leadership saw incidents such as the office strike and the formation of the Women's Collective as 'disloyalty'. Some of the men admitted in due course they had made mistakes with the way they treated the women in the office. Owens, for instance, said 'when it came to the crunch we acted like bosses'. In an earlier interview, also, he conceded that 'we were so unselfish in some ways and so selfish in others, like in our personal relationships'.[31] In the sense that no man is a hero to his valet, it was the clerks who saw the union's leaders at their worst. Yet their worst compared well with the best practice of traditional unions: the clerks remained intensely loyal to the union and, like the female builders labourers, felt they had participated in an interesting and exciting period.

The leadership's reservations about feminism in its own backyard was not only mirrored at membership level but magnified. Many of the rank and file were not even committed to the idea of female equality. However, as Michelle Fraser put it, in individual cases at the job level 'where there was support for you, it was much more genuine or they wouldn't have accepted you at all'. More than the officials, the builders labourers working in a rugged and largely unskilled industry invested their egos in their raw strength and not at all in their skill or managerial ability. The labourers' physical strength and their ability to face danger were the means by which these men measured their superiority over women.[32] The builders labourers shared this kind of ego-investment with miners and other workers in heavy, dangerous occupations: 'It contributes to their sense of maleness', Stella Nord observed, 'They even regard themselves as superior to other men who are not working in that kind of industry. So think how much higher they would regard themselves compared to women.' Whereas male students or academics have usually been obliged to acknowledge that a woman has beaten them in an examination or written a better book, these labourers had never had to pit their strength and daring against women or even admit that women were capable of doing the work they proudly and self-consciously performed as men. Women in their industry thus posed a much greater threat to their self-image than they would have in a less rugged, and therefore less overtly macho, industry. Stella Nord relates her unusual encounter with a spontaneously reflective and self-aware builders labourer who saw her driving a hoist:

> He said 'Jesus Christ what's this?' as though I'd come from another planet. I said 'What's wrong, haven't you ever seen women doing this before?' 'No, it makes me feel so inadequate, it makes me feel as if my job is not what I think it is – sheilas can do the work I'm doing!'

Considering the women with whom they worked as exceptional was an obvious way in which the male labourers could maintain the feeling of superiority over women in general. For Lyn Syme, therefore, 'it was a bit like becoming one of the boys in a really despicable way'. Yet the mistakes of one woman tended to be generalised and all women blamed.[33] Most women reported a feeling of being tested. Michelle Fraser described these ordeals: 'They'd tell you to do something and if you couldn't do it, it was because you were a woman; not because no one had ever shown you, evidently the men had been born knowing how to do it'.

The sexism expressed by male builders labourers was usually submerged or furtive, because it lacked official union sanction. Stella Nord describes men attacking women in the industry 'behind your back, never to your face', so she used to argue it out with such offenders 'boots and all'. Most women experienced wolf-whistling and sexual comments, particularly on the larger jobs. They reported other remarks such as 'you're a bunch of bloody lesbians' and attempts to ridicule women's liberation. Rhonda Ellis felt she was being treated by the men as 'some sort of a joke'. In a less offensive, but nonetheless tedious way, Lyn Syme reports the inevitable response: 'what's-a-nice-girl-like-you-doing-in-a-place-like-this' and 'it-might-be-OK-for-you-but-not-for-my-wife'. That the men were unsettled by the intrusion of women was evident in linguistic codes and practices: some men reacted by swearing excessively, even more than usually; other men apologised for swearing in front of them; others were disgusted when the women themselves swore.[34]

A common reaction the women had to overcome was the assumption that, because they were female, they could not pull their weight and that the men would therefore have to do extra work. It appears that, in practice, these prejudices were not difficult to dispel. Women labourers reported that the men were pleasantly surprised after working alongside them and subsequently treated them better. Some women such as Robyn Williams even felt that after a while the other labourers 'didn't even notice I wasn't a man'. In Janne Reed's words this 'person to person contact' and 'forcing the men to look at your individual position' were crucial in the successful acceptance of women. Small job sites were obviously best for this, as Pat Fiske observed: 'You could get to them and talk to them better'. However, the great advantage of big job sites over smaller ones was that they were generally more militant and therefore supportive of leadership policy. The women felt they had the union behind them on these jobs. All the women found it easier to 'get through' to the younger men and, especially, to immigrants. Indeed the nexus between exploited immigrant and oppressed woman worker was frequently mentioned during interviews. For, despite efforts by the leadership, immigrants still encountered discrimination on many building sites. Often this meant that it was the women (in the process of being tested either by the boss or the other labourers) and the immigrants – regularly assigned to such work – who ended up working together on the hardest tasks. Janne Reed reported that it was the immigrants who realised most promptly she was enduring discrimination because they also were struggling on the biggest jackhammers. Just as many women mentioned Kevin Cook, the Aboriginal organiser, as one of the most sympathetic to them, the immigrant workers were in a position to recognise and understand discrimination as a general issue.[35] The women were predictably herded into the more stereotypically female roles within the industry: nipper (cook), first aid officer (nurse) and cleaner (housewife). These roles better fitted the notion in the men's minds of 'correct' work for women; and in performing these roles they were kept more physically segregated from the other builders labourers. All the women agreed that the male labourers saw a distinction between women working in these positions and as a general labourer. It was in attempting to depart from these roles that the women most obviously tested the limits of their acceptance by the men.

Even nippers' work was too good for women, according to some of the men, who argued that the women were taking nippers' jobs from old builders labourers, who having served the industry well should enjoy the easy nippers' jobs in old age. This argument, according to Janne Reed, was deliberately peddled by the small number of Maoist supporters within the union, who were vehemently opposed to the intrusion of women into the industry. Stella Nord conducted a brief survey and discovered it was hard to find a male nipper over 25 – with the advent of multi-storey buildings, the nipper's job was no longer the comparatively easy one it used to be. Likewise when the women started to move into hoist drivers' positions, they were attacked for taking away the jobs of qualified men. As a hoist driver Nord believed: 'It wouldn't have mattered what we did, those opposed to women in the industry would have made an excuse about it'.

The women believe that their acceptance as individuals depended on different factors. Showing an interest in the overall struggle of the workers was considered important. A working-class background was generally a help, but a middle-class background was not necessarily a hindrance. Sekai Holland found that her fellow labourers were suspicious about her motives for becoming a builders labourer instead of finishing her law course, but were more sympathetic when they were persuaded that she really needed the money.[36] Janne Reed found that her working-class background, combined with the fact that she had 'two kids to feed on her own', was decidedly in her favour when the men discussed it among themselves. The key factor, however, seems to have been personality and the extent to which the individual women were able to express their feminism with guts and humour – through stereotypically masculine characteristics.

THE BROADER IMPACT

The experience of women within this unusually enlightened male union kindled debate within the women's movement about female participation in male-dominated structures, of which the trade union movement was a classic example. The more positive aspects of the female builders labourers' experience provided practical evidence to support the views of those within the women's movement who believed that activism in trade unions was both capable of securing meaningful changes and important to the feminist project. Against those feminists who evinced a strong antipathy towards unions, others such as Ros Harrison, who worked as a builders labourer, could argue in *Gay Liberation Press*: 'You can't turn your back on the working class movement and say "Stuff it, it's male dominated". That just sets you apart on a little island in society rather than trying to bring about some very fundamental changes in that society.' To which Janne Reed could add: 'You realise that short of annihilating the whole male race, what are you going to do?'[37]

However the women's experience during Intervention could be taken as evidence to confirm the position that conservative patriarchal trade union structures could never be altered permanently. The women featured prominently in the fight against this takeover which, apart from its other significant aspects, represented a return to masculinist trade union norms. The federally appointed state secretary, Les Robinson, expressed the views of the Gallagher team on the subject of women in the industry, when he maintained:

> I wouldn't like it to become like Asian countries where women work in the building industry – because it's hard work and I don't agree that women should come in and take the job that the old timer should have. I wouldn't like to see women in concrete – it's not sexism I just don't think they should be doing that sort of work.

Many female labourers were sacked for refusing to accept 'Gallagher tickets'. They knew full well that the federal branch would never support their right to work in the industry. By the same token, because of the support they had received from the state leadership over the years, they rendered that leadership considerable support and loyalty during Intervention. Their fears were well founded: all the women lost their jobs after the federal takeover; and three women figured among the 25 prominent militants black-listed – refused union tickets so they could not work – by Gallagher. After Intervention there were no women working in the building industry. There was a return to normal, to work as usual.

Although the NSWBLF leadership was committed to the right of women to work in the industry and actively supported these beliefs, it did so in an industry that was one of the most macho there is. Reflecting upon the conservatism of the other building industry unions and the strength of Australian male chauvinism, Lyn Syme concluded: 'I don't think it was a reality at any time, getting women accepted into that sort of industry'. Given the rapid reversal of policy after Intervention and the absence of any equivalent effort on the part of any similar union over the succeeding two decades, it appears the union's bizarre attempt to integrate women into the building industry on equal terms with the men had a much greater impact on the women themselves than on 'this rugged industry'. All the women who had been involved were adamant that their involvement in the NSWBLF had been rewarding and politically formative. They stressed in particular the benefits to them of such lessons as 'gaining a class perspective' and 'realising the power of unified workers' and, above all, the exhilarating experience of 'being able to participate in a near-perfect democracy'.

PART 3

PREVENTING THE PLUNDER

DEFENDING THE OPEN SPACES

By the time the Battlers for Kelly's Bush approached the union in mid-1971, the leadership's interest in the environment and town planning was well established, as was shown in Chapter Three. Thus, with the union's considerable disquiet about development, and the inclinations of builders labourers to care about the great outdoors, Mundey and many others in the union leadership were easily persuaded that, in the face of outright employer and government resistance to any degree of social and political control over the development process, the union had to use its strategic industrial power to thwart this ecologically irresponsible project. This chapter discusses bans such as Kelly's Bush that aimed to protect the natural environment. Chapters Ten and Eleven examine the bans in defence of urban habitat and heritage.

KELLY'S BUSH (JUNE 1971)

In 1892 Mr TH Kelly had bought 20 acres (8.3 hectares) on the Hunters Hill waterfront, part of which he used for a smelting works, while designating the remaining 12.1 acres (4.9 hectares) – 'Kelly's Bush' – for citizens to enjoy in perpetuity. The threat to Kelly's Bush nearly eighty years later was the catalyst that prompted the builders labourers' latent environmentalism to express itself so dramatically. Tom Hogan described the executive meeting that recommended the implementation of a ban:

> We can't truly say that eleven great people sat down and decided what
> we were going to do. It was thrust on us in the first place. I think it was
> picked up very well. I mean, we were the same people that destroyed that

city. We had all those ideas in our heads but not till something came up was anything done. There is no doubt that Kelly's Bush was the start of the Union going outside of the traditional union role.

Hogan considered Kelly's Bush was 'what started to make us into a humane union-interested in people and interested in the environment'. He recalled that Bob Pringle was the one who wanted the union to make contact with the Battlers; who insisted 'this has got to be supported'. Thus the executive minutes record an historic but, at the time, unremarkable resolution: 'Moved Bro. Owens, seconded Bro. T Hogan that R Pringle investigate a report next Tuesday on Kelly [sic] Bush'.[1]

Pringle visited the bush, accompanied by the entire 13-strong committee of the Battlers for Kelly's Bush. The committee had been formed in September 1970 at a meeting of concerned residents after local people had been aroused by the publication of Betty James's article, 'The Battle to Save Kelly's Bush', in the *Sydney Morning Herald*. It was deliberately representative of a range of political parties, churches and other organisations, but it could not help but reflect the generally high socio-economic status of residents of the

The secretariat of the Battlers for Kelly's Bush were (from left to right) Monica Sheehan, Kath Lehany, Betty James, Christena Dawson. (Marion Marrison/VISCOPY Ltd)

Hunters Hill area. These 'housewives' (whom Kylie Tennant described as 'the descendants of the first white settlers turning out to defend the last of the green foreshores') eloquently pleaded their case for conservation. That the Battlers were all female was not surprising: they both lived and worked in the area and had some flexibility in their working hours. Betty James recalls the influence upon the Battlers of Mary Campbell of the National Trust: 'Mary impressed on us how important it was for us as housewives to be concerned about the environment. She believed we could do more about the fight for the environment because we were there all day.'[2]

To those in the Hunters Hill area, especially the local councillors, who supported AV Jennings' desire to build 25 luxury houses on the 4.9 hectares of Kelly's Bush, it was 'a tick-infested rubbish dump'; to the estate agents and developers, 'Kelly's Bush was nothing more than a spot on the map for which they had no regard, except to see dollar signs'; to the Battlers for Kelly's Bush and the thousands who supported them it was pristine bushland relatively untouched by two centuries of European intrusions. Moreover, the alleged rubbish dump was an Aboriginal midden dating back to 1200 AD.[3]

Green Bans activists demonstrating in support of the Mundey/Owens/Pringle leadership outside The Master Builders Head Office March 1975. Left to right: unknown, Meredith Burgmann, Jean Pender, Pat Fiske

Well-known environmentalist Vincent Serventy visited the bush in June 1971 and recorded his favourable opinion of the area in a letter to Betty James:

> This little primitive area was surprisingly little affected by the deteriorating effects of nearby 'progress'. The Banksias, Sheoaks, Geebungs, Grevilleas, Kunzeas were growing splendidly … No wonder the native animals such as the Ringtail Possums, continue to find a haven here, as well as the birds. I was especially pleased to see the Aboriginal rockhold, with the carvings, and the intact midden nearby. What a splendid relic of past social history we have in your midst.

He hoped the bush would escape the calamity of being 'developed'. The president of the Australian Wildlife Preservation Society stressed 'there has been an increasing recognition that science teaching on the environment becomes meaningless unless there are bushland areas which can be used as educational laboratories', and the presence of honeyeaters and blue wrens in home gardens depended on a web of bushland spread over the metropolitan area. That the children of Hunters Hill already appreciated Kelly's Bush was borne out by their independent direct action in defence of the bush: they removed the surveyor's pegs and string put there at the behest of Jennings. For Kath Lehany, whose children were complicit in this activity, it expressed 'children's frustration at destruction of their environment'.[4] For many years the Hunters Hill Council also valued Kelly's Bush, decreed 'Open Space' by the State Government in the County of Cumberland planning scheme of 1948. In 1966 the town clerk had written to the State Planning Authority: 'It would seem most important that the whole of this area should be acquired for posterity.' In 1968 AV Jennings (then the 77th largest company in Australia, with a market value of $57 million) had bought the 4.9 hectares for $400,000. It applied to the council for suspension of zoning orders, but the council refused the application in uncompromising terms: 'Council is unanimously and emphatically opposed to any alteration in the zoning of that part of the land'. Jennings' original idea was to build a couple of hundred high-rise units on the land; but in response to protest from the Hunters Hill Trust, the Minister for Local Government decided the State Planning Authority should allow only single dwellings on the site and purchase 2.3 hectares for waterfront reserve, so AV Jennings aimed to use the remaining 2.6 hectares for the construction of 25 luxury homes and began to line up support for this scheme among its State Government friends. The council agreed to this project in a 5 to 4 vote in November 1970. The majority in favour of the development warned of exorbitant rates if the bush were retained and claimed that the unsewered homes in the area would not be connected to sewerage unless Jennings built their houses (although the Water Board had already scheduled the sewerage connection and was insistent it would take place regardless of the development, as indeed it did).[5]

The previously strong community opposition to the development was diluted somewhat by the compromise plan proposed. 'Many locals were also very pro-development in those days – it was thought to be beneficial for the community', Miriam Hamilton concedes. But for the Battlers and their supporters, the scheme still violated both the bush itself and the principle of pu blic access to the foreshore. The 2.3 hectares saved as public reserve were the steeply sloping fore shore cliffs, useless for recreation; it was the 2.6 hectares of the bush actively used by the neighbourhood that were to become luxury housing for a few individuals. Joan Croll maintained:

> Open space in Hunters Hill was very limited and already many areas had been encroached upon by greedy developers. Foreshore land was stolen from the public by people moving in and 'acquiring' waterfront access by building seawalls and retaining walls, some destroying mangrove swamps which had been there for centuries. But this is progress?

The Battlers were motivated by the thought: if this housing development is unnecessary and proceeding despite violent opposition, what rights do people have? 'Kelly's Bush Now – What Next?' proclaimed a headline from a Battlers' brochure.[6]

Those with a strong financial incentive to utilise remaining open spaces for personal gain, invariably wealthy men, were mobilising their supporters in high places. Betty James observed: 'Now our Government was encouraging an invasion of developers. Our politicians were no longer statesmen planning wisely for the future'. The Battlers made a number of attempts to see Pat Morton, Minister for Local Government, but he was otherwise engaged. Premier Askin, while studiously polite to a Battlers' deputation, was duplicitous in the extreme. On the eve of the state election in February 1971 he sent the Battlers a telegram: 'Very hopeful of a helpful decision on your problems and will advise within 24 hours. RW Askin, Premier'. The electorate of Hunters Hill was held precariously by the Liberal Party's Peter Coleman, who had endeavoured not to antagonise the Battlers while doing nothing to aid their cause. He was narrowly returned at the poll. The Battlers responded to the Premier: 'Still awaiting your solution …' But there was no reply. Monica Sheehan noted: 'He won the election but we heard nothing'. The women were learning the hard way. Betty James describes their education:

We were inexperienced in the ways of business and politics but we learned week by week as one step led to another. We found out quickly that politicians had a language of their own; that decisions were made behind closed doors; that power and money came first and that people's wishes came second, if considered at all.

Christena Dawson was shaken by the experience. 'Before the Battle for Kelly's Bush, being politically naive, I had infinite faith in the democratic process. My faith is no longer infinite.'[7]

Kath Lehany was especially alert to the invidious treatment the women received by dint of their sex. The Hunters Hill mayor told an acquaintance, 'they're just thirteen bloody housewives – I've investigated!' The abrasive treatment of Betty James and Kath Lehany by Nigel Ashton of the State Planning Authority and his offsider was remarked upon by Sid Vaughan of the BTG of Labor Council, who attended a meeting at which these men had attempted to present the bush as 'unimportant regrowth' that had been bare ten years previously and were displeased to have their allegations disproved by the documents – the County of Cumberland map and council minutes – produced by the women. Lehany recalls: 'Jennings were always polite to us, like patient adults humouring nuisance children'. Media commentary encouraged this paternalistic treatment, as Peter Manning noted, by stressing 'the irony of the teacup matrons of Hunters' Hill playing politics with heavies like the State Government and AV Jennings'.[8]

In May 1971 the council signed its agreement to the Jennings development; it was now up to Local Government Minister Morton to sign the necessary documents. It was as 'a last resort', in Mundey's words, that the women turned to the labour movement: 'they gave us to understand that we were their last and only hope'. Such a move was not one that came naturally or easily to them. But they had exhausted every move of the democratic process: writing individual letters to every member of the New South Wales Parliament; collecting signatures for petitions; lobbying councillors, politicians, public servants and businesspeople; writing letters to newspapers; producing publicity material about the bush; contacting conservation groups, professional associations and other residents' groups; and organising 'Boil the Billy' functions to encourage appreciation of the bush. Rod Cavalier, a Labor Party activist and student radical who aided the Battlers in various ways, had telephoned them and suggested the unions might help. On 3 June Morton signed the rezoning order, but the Battlers were now busy writing and hand-delivering letters to FEDFA and the Miscellaneous Workers Union, which were tabled at the meeting of Labor Council on 3 June by Jack Cambourn of FEDFA (the BLF being temporarily suspended). When the Battlers heard of the council's unanimous decision to support their cause, they were 'overjoyed'. FEDFA's support for the Battlers, though overshadowed ultimately by the publicity accorded the BLF's role, was crucial as its members were involved in bulldozing, grading and land clearing work.[9]

According to Judith Taplin it was at this stage that the Battlers had decided – though by no means unanimously – to ask for help from the 'aggressive and militant Builders Labourers Federation'.[10] This was an immensely difficult decision, breaching not only a deep class divide but a gender one as well; while middle-class men frequently in the course of their working lives mix, though not normally with great ease, with working-class men, middle-class women rarely do. Indeed, historically it has been the wives of middle-class men who have policed the class boundaries, enabling middle-class men to associate with 'the lower orders' in the course of doing business, while maintaining a social distance precisely through their wives' lack of contact with such men or their wives. There were also serious tactical considerations to weigh up: 'The Hunters Hill Trust wouldn't have anything to do with unions', explains Kath Lehany, 'so we lost their help the minute we began to contact labour unions, because it feared the community support it had would quickly fade away if it associated itself with groups like the BLF'. So the Battlers pondered the matter long and hard, discussing it with their husbands – scientists, doctors, lawyers and so on who had codes of professional responsibility. 'Why shouldn't working men have their own codes?' they asked each other. 'Why shouldn't the construction site worker be able to question the ethics of his helping to knock down an historic old building or bulldoze some bushland?'[11]

Mundey's account is that the Battlers contacted the union in response to its recently published statement arguing the concept of the social responsibility of labour. 'They came to us and said that the time had come for us to put our theory in practice.' It was the day after the Labor Council resolution that the special executive meeting decided to send Pringle to investigate. When Pringle phoned the Battlers, they were pleased yet alarmed. (They had all seen pictures of hi m sawing down the goalposts at the Sydney Cricket Ground to prevent the South African rugby team playing.) Opting for safety in numbers, the full 13-woman committee received Pringle at Betty James' house in Prince Edward Parade and questioned him closely over several hours. They asked him how the union might help. 'We can put a black ban on it', he replied. The women stressed: 'We want to do our own picketing if the bulldozers come. There mustn't be any violence.' Pringle agreed. 'How would the workers react?' the women enquired. Pringle made it clear he would have to put it to meetings of builders labourers, that he couldn't authorise it, but he could put the idea forward.[12]

After Pringle's favourable report back to the executive, a delegation from the Battlers came to meet the executive at Trades Hall and impressed the executive with their determination to save this last bit of bush on those reaches of the Parramatta River. After the middle-class women of the suburbs departed, the working-class men of the labour movement discussed their cause. Mundey recalls that, although the 11 members had come through the struggle to democratise the union, this was an issue that divided them:

> Some opined that since Builders Labourers couldn't afford to live in Hunters Hill, and none of us lived there, we should not become involved. Others argued that, if we were to be consistent, we should apply the same criteria, regardless of the wealth of an area. It was a question of the quality of life.

The executive decided after spirited debate, which Jennings' historian described as 'a struggle with their collective class consciences', that the bush should be saved. In Mundey's opinion, 'If we let that piece of parkland go, other neighbourhoods would go, too'. The union focussed its objections on Jennings:

> A millionaire developer, hell-bent on building luxury homes and apartments for the fortunate few at the expense of the many who would lose a natural outdoor space of beauty and recreational value. Just one instance of a nice business deal taking precedence over any other consideration.[13]

One important condition was attached to the union's support, which was to constitute an important feature of all the subsequent bans: a ban could only be imposed after there had been an enthusiastic public meeting by the people concerned, for the union neither set itself up as the arbiter of taste nor attempted to impose bans that lacked local support. So the union stipulated that the Battlers call a public meeting in Hunters Hill, 'to determine that they enjoyed widespread public support in the area, and that it was not just a handful of residents concerned with their immediate amenity'. Over 600 people attended the meeting, which formally requested a ban, to which the NSWBLF executive agreed. The following week, on 17 June, a branch meeting of a couple of hundred delegates and active members endorsed the ban; an historic era had begun. For Monica Sheehan: 'We gratefully accepted – a handshake and the beginning of a close friendship'.[14]

If the women had impressed the men, the reverse had also occurred. For Miriam Hamilton the men of the NSWBLF were very different from the men of the local council, estate agencies and companies, who were capable of seeing only short-term gain but not long-term disadvantages: 'The men from the BLF had more vision'. Unlike the developers and their accomplices, the unionists' order of priorities placed their own financial interests after those of society in general. As Mundey pointed out, the workers in the NSWBLF were not imposing the bans in their own economic interests. 'Indeed, in the short term, the workers were denying themselves work. In the long run, the workers could see that such a ban to save open parkland was in the interests of the entire community.' Of Pringle's initial meeting with the Battlers, Kath Lehany remembers: 'A lot of us were pretty wary of a unionist but we came to trust these men. The whole committee was very impressed by Bob Pringle's open approach and sincerity.' Monica Sheehan was deeply appreciative of Mundey, 'a colossus who inspired the loyalty of his union', and of Pringle and Owens, who with Mundey 'declared they would build always with the future generation in mind' and were responsible for their union leading the battle for environmental awareness. Joan Croll, whose conservative Methodist and Liberal Party upbringing had prompted her to drop out of the campaign in alarm at the involvement with Communist union leaders, was drawn back to the movement after listening to Pringle and Mundey 'and hearing their articulate and reasoned approach'.[15]

There were other differences between the two sets of men with whom the Battlers had to deal. For Kath Lehany, who had so acutely observed the sexist treatment meted out to the Battlers by the men on the other side of the dispute: 'The unionists we met were gentlemen – they treated us with great respect'. Mundey believes the important changes that had taken place within the union, including the limited tenure rule that combated entrenched bureaucracy in its leadership and the fact that it was the first construction union in the world to win women the right to work as building workers, facilitated the 'unlikely alliance' that developed.

> The union had civilized a rough industry, winning dignity and respect for the workers, and making the work much safer. The openness of the NSWBLF ensured that the 'Battlers for Kelly's Bush' found a fresh and responsive executive committee when they arrived to seek support.[16]

It was not simply that the NSWBLF pledged itself not to provide labour for the destruction of Kelly's Bush; its industrial power and its preparedness to use that power deterred the developer from even attempting to find other labour for that purpose. When Jennings reacted initially to the union ban by declaring it would build on Kelly's Bush using non-union labour, builders labourers on a Jennings office project in North Sydney sent a telegram to Jennings' head office: 'If you attempt to build on Kelly's Bush, even if there is the loss of one tree, this half-completed building will remain so forever, as a monument to Kelly's Bush'. The union executive assured Jennings that any attempt to violate Kelly's Bush would indeed result in the withdrawal of BLF members from all Jennings building sites. This 'firm action' had 'a sobering influence' on AV Jennings. The Battlers could see that the union's decision 'frightened the previously tough developers', who 'were accustomed to buying what they wanted'. Premier Askin, who had sweet-talked the Battlers, now condemned the unionists, who had kept their promises.

Although the women were 'just housewives' and the men 'mere builders' labourers', in the words of editorial writers echoing the premier, Jennings was nonetheless obliged to fly senior executives in from Melbourne to discuss matters with these mere builders labourers. By August, according to Jennings' historian, Jennings had 'wisely dropped' the idea of developing Kelly's Bush and publicly announced this decision. 'The Kelly's Bush episode really started something,' explained Pete Thomas. 'Environmentalists everywhere, and others who had felt powerless to halt destruction, realised that there did exist an organised strength in the trade unions whose help they could invoke to bring effective force to their cause.'[17]

EASTLAKES (NOVEMBER 1971)

Another open space threatened by the rapacity of developers was on the Eastlakes housing estate in the inner south-eastern suburbs. The former Rosebery Racecourse of 56 acres (22.7 hectares) had been bought in the 1960s for $450,000 by Parkes Development for a high-density housing estate. As individual buyers purchased each home unit, Parkes' agents promised them that 3.5 acres (1.4 hectares) in the centre would be retained as a park, and some buyers were shown maps with the area marked in green; but the company subsequently denied this land was offered as a park.[18]

In November 1971 there were ominous signs of building preparations on the disputed area: bricks were delivered and trenches dug. A Botany Councillor, Mrs MD Kelly, maintained: 'We are already far too overdeveloped here'. After considering submissions by Parkes, the State Planning Authority and the Botany Council, Local Government Minister Morton concluded the area should be retained for recreation, because there was a lack of open space in the locality.

However, to compensate Parkes, the Minister gave his approval for Parkes to construct much higher unit blocks, a total of 165 units, in part of the area allowed for development. Morton thought the erection of these additional units was 'a reasonable solution to the problem'; but it was a problem born of the developer's attempt not to honour its commitment to retain the open space.[19]

A public meeting of concerned residents on 7 November, attended by Mundey and Pringle, formally requested that the union ban any further work on the Eastlakes estate. Building stopped on the planned $1.5 million block of home units. Dean Barber explained that his personal support for this particular ban was informed by indignation that the people had been 'hoodwinked' by developers, that they had bought the units on the strength of a plan they had been shown, then 'the developer had reneged on the deal'. Mundey admits it was considerably easier to secure his fellow unionists' instant support over Eastlakes than over Kelly's Bush, because the people of Eastlakes were less affluent than those of Hunters Hill. Informing the BTG of the union's decision to ban the Eastlakes development, Mundey explained:

> Residents of the area, particularly residents of units nearby, have complained bitterly about the encroachment of this last remaining green area where their children could play in safety. Parkes Development have duped the residents, who purchased units by assuring them the parkland would remain and eventually a swimming pool would be built within the park. Many residents paid up to $1500 to $2000 per unit extra because of the adjacent parkland and swimming pool.

In calling for the support of the BTG, Mundey added: 'It is becoming more imperative for all conscious organisations and individuals to speak up on issues that have a direct bearing on our environment'.[20] The ban was backed by an undertaking that if any attempt was made to build on the site, builders labourers would stop construction on all the other work done by Parkes Development. At that time, the Parkes group, headed by Sir Paul Strasser, was perhaps the biggest developer in Sydney, with properties in the inner city, suburban homes and home units and masses of land still undeveloped on the outskirts. The company was obliged to negotiate with the union and the residents, the local council and the State Government. Strasser invited Mundey to lunch with the vain hope of persuading him to 'understand his problems'. When a meeting of residents on 13 August 1972 reiterated opposition to the erection of further home units in the municipality, Mundey reaffirmed the union's position:

... that whilst we appreciate the fact that a City of three million people cannot be housed in individual homes and that the construction of home units and flats are necessary, we state emphatically that no units or flats should be erected unless there is adequate provision for sufficient green area around such flats or units.[21]

On 14 February 1973 Botany Municipal Council unanimously approved a new plan by Parkes Development for four eight-storey home unit blocks, totalling 176 units, to be constructed in the carpark area of the Eastlakes shopping centre, in return for establishing the park in the vacant lot. At a meeting held on the vacant lot, residents reaffirmed their determination to have the promised park, but insisted 'the price is too high'. While Councillor Kelly urged residents to approve the plan as 'the best deal we can get', the meeting voted to reject the council's decision and instead seek an enlargement of the union's ban to cover any home unit development in the Eastlakes area.[22]

The NSWBLF agreed to impose a ban on any additional unit development in Eastlakes. Tony Hadfield said the union supported local residents' desire to oppose the four eight-storey units and believed the vacant area should immediately be resumed as a park. He confirmed that the ban meant no building could take place until further negotiations took place between the union, local residents, the Minister for Local Government (now Sir Charles Cutler), Botany Council and Parkes Development. With the ban continuing to ensure the additional building could not take place, in mid-1974 an agreement between the council and the developer confirmed that the park would indeed remain.[23]

THE BOTANIC GARDENS (MARCH 1972)

The most farcical example of poor planning in this period was the attempt by the State Government to locate the carpark, which had been 'forgotten' in the plans for the Opera House, under the part of the Royal Botanic Gardens poised on the cliff-face overlooking the site. The proposed carpark would interfere with the root system of splendid and ancient Moreton Bay fig trees and cause the loss of at least three, and pose a danger to all the nearby vegetation and people's health from exhaust fumes. Conservationists had complained bitterly about the destruction of the fig trees; architects and engineers had expressed concern that ventilation plans for the underground carpark were inadequate. With government authorities dismissing their concerns, these groups had turned to the NSWBLF for support. On 22 March 1972 the union announced its members would refuse to work on the $4 million carpark until guarantees could be given that the three fig trees would not be destroyed and that there would be no excessive pollution from the carpark.[24]

The union received hundreds of telegrams and telephone calls in support. 'It is magnificent that so many people think, like the Builders Labourers' Federation, that the environment must be protected at all costs', declared Mundey, as he announced his intentions to discuss the matter with the Minister for Public Works, Davis Hughes. If Hughes' response was not 'satisfactory', the union, which had 'a duty to the public', would 'go to other unions for support in doing what has to be done'. But to the company contracted by the government to construct the carpark, altering the plans to save trees was not good accounting: 'It does not seem economically viable, or practical, to spend another $500,000 to save … three trees'. The union upped its demands. In addition to its original objections, it now wanted assurances that the 'undulating contours' of the garden would not be changed nor the cliff face destroyed by openings in the carpark.[25]

The New South Wales Chapter of the Australian Institute of Architects also maintained its opposition to the planned carpark. Hughes dismissed its objection to the alienation of park land as unimportant compared with the need to provide parking facilities for the Opera House. Newspapers were unusually supportive of the ban: 'plausible reasons can always be found', a *Sun-Herald* editorial warned, 'for filching bits of the public estate and assurances that the land invaded will be restored to its original condition are not worth a rap'. While this editorial insisted unions should not normally block developments of which they or their officials disapprove, it acknowledged that manual workers 'can have sincerely held beliefs and possibly be more ready to make sacrifices for them'. Although the *National Times* made sarcastic reference to 'the proletarian town planning institute (known in some circles as the Builders Labourers Federation)', the principal object of its derision was the planning process: the carpark fiasco was 'an object lesson in how not to solve' the major problems of city planning.[26]

By August, a frustrated Hughes had authorised the Opera House architects to plan completion of the forecourt without providing for an underground carpark; he had been 'forced to this action' because attempts to have the ban lifted had failed. In October he conceded in parliament there was 'a complete stalemate' on the carpark because no company would sign a contract to build it under the Botanic Gardens while the ban remained. To the Australian the whole episode represented 'a thorough-going indictment of the planning system in the whole of Australia'. Sydney was deemed a particularly bad example of the power exerted by self-perpetuating, self-appointed bodies; of innumerable bureaucratic institutions making planning decisions without public input. 'If there is one outstanding lesson from the Opera House car park affair it is not that the builders laborers are particularly wrong, but that the processes of city planning need to be reorganised radically.' The preferences of the people who live and work in the city, and whose contributions maintain it, should at least be heard at a decision-making level, 'instead of being represented in a diluted and unsatisfactory way through the unions and professional organisations'.[27]

The ingenuity and bad taste of developers attempting to devise alternatives for a carpark became evident by the end of the year when one proposed a five-storey carpark jutting out over Sydney Harbour and running the full length of Circular Quay. Naturally, the opinion of the NSWBLF was sought; and Mundey reaffirmed his union's opposition 'in principle' to any proposals for carparks that encroached on water, gardens or parkland, and suggested the best position would be underneath the Opera House forecourt, which had been approved then abandoned without satisfactory explanation by the State Government.

Enthusiastic amateurs now flooded the newspapers with suggestions: a miniature railway, with carriages 'of open construction and gay appearance', running through a tunnel from the Domain carpark; a carpark beneath the harbour; a moving footway from the Domain carpark; a monorail across the Botanic Gardens from the Domain carpark; a fleet of battery-powered mini-buses to operate from the city's 30 carparks; a garden-topped carpark jutting on to Farm Cove jammed against the Bennelong Point cliff face, topped with turf and plants to merge with the gardens. The union was invariably consulted on each scheme. And, whenever asked about a carpark under the Botanic Gardens, Mundey maintained the union 's position: 'We're not going to desecrate this area now purely for the sake of present-day expediency'. It was not simply a matter of three fig trees, because the construction of the carpark under the gardens would mean 'the defacing of the whole area'.[28]

With the Queen's official opening of the Opera House timed for October 1973, the State Government announced on 26 December 1972 it would hold Jack Mundey 'publicly accountable' for any chaos over parking. It stressed that, because of the union's bans on the only two 'practical propositions', there was no prospect of completing either by the official opening. Hughes deflected public criticism of the government for its failure to provide a carpark by presenting the union's position as obstructionist and unrepresentative of public opinion:

'The whole community is being frustrated by the actions of Mr Mundey and his group … It is not the Government that Mr Mundey is holding to ransom – it is the community at large.' Mundey replied that 'successive Governments completely forgot the need for a car park', that the forecourt option should be reconsidered or the Planning Institute's suggestion that professional planners be called on to arrange 'the best possible car park without any destruction of the environment'.[29]

The Farm Cove proposal did not meet these conditions. When the Sydney City Council, controlled by the Civic Reform Association (a 'front' for the Liberal Party), decided to investigate this option, which involved reclamation of eight hectares of foreshore for a two-storey underground carpark, the union indicated a ban would eventuate if the proposal was approved. Pringle said the union had received advice from architects and town planners that the Farm Cove carpark would destroy the view and the contours of the harbour, and would adversely affect trees and shrubs: 'For this reason we must declare the project black because we believe a city is for the people and not a place in which cars are stacked at all costs'. The harbour foreshore 'must be kept at its best for the benefit of future generations'. Pringle, too, insisted the 'sanest' solution was to build the carpark in the forecourt 'where it was originally planned'.[30]

Otherwise the union favoured the solution of battery-powered mini-buses running between existing carparks and the Opera House. Tom Hogan said the union would be 'delighted' to see greater use of public transport, which 'would fit in nicely with our interests in fighting air pollution'. The controversy focussed attention on such issues. Christopher Jay argued in the *National Times* that the area was well served by various forms of existing public transport; that it was impossible to handle large inner city crowds coming to one venue if one relied primarily on private transport; that opera patrons in the great cities of Europe saw nothing incongruous in relying on buses, trams, trains or taxis; and that any carpark would encourage further congestion of the Quay area because it would be available not merely in the evening for opera patrons but also, to ensure financial viability, during the day for other users.[31]

When the Queen finally arrived to open the Opera House, the union was, predictably, blamed for the parking 'problem'. And in an ironic twist to the saga it was another union, Actors Equity, that threatened strike action – on the part of the performers drenched trying to reach the Opera House in the rain – because the performers were dissatisfied with parking arrangements, dressing-room facilities and general conditions at the Opera House. The short-term solution utilised the Domain carpark and shuttle buses, unfortunately not electric. In 1975 the State Government announced it would build an underground parking station for 500 cars beneath the street adjacent to the Botanic Gardens and Opera House. The fig trees were saved.[32]

CENTENNIAL PARK–MOORE PARK (JUNE 1972)

During his governorship in the early nineteenth century, Lachlan Macquarie set aside 1000 acres (402 hectares) of land known as the Sydney Common 'for the benefit of the present and all succeeding inhabitants of Sydney'. Part of this common became Centennial Park, established in 1888 and re-dedicated by Lord Carrington 'to the enjoyment of the people of New South Wales for ever'. It was planted and reclaimed from that time in a style which adopted some of the best principles of English landscape gardening. In 1901 the official inauguration ceremony of Federation was held there, and a plaque erected to mark the site. By 1972 its plantings were reaching a splendid maturity.[33]

To the residents of the area and conservation-minded Sydneysiders generally, the park was '400 acres of ponds, lawns and wilderness where we and our children can relax in peace and quiet', 'Sydney's most beautiful and natural unspoilt parkland, where birds are breeding in peaceful surroundings, undisturbed by man', 'a gift of unique peacefulness and tranquillity in an increasingly noisy city', and 'a precious heritage'. The neighbouring Moore Park area, too, was greatly appreciated by thousands of Sydneysiders who regularly used its facilities for amateur sporting events: tennis courts, basketball fields, cricket and softball fields and a golf course.[34]

On 15 March 1972 the Minister for Lands, Mr Lewis, presented to Cabinet a proposal for a $76 million State Sports Centre in Moore Park, including construction of an 80,000-capacity concrete stadium. In part of Centennial Park, there was to be an accompanying swimming pool with seating for 10,000 and an entertainment complex compromising:

> Facilities for picnics and barbecues, small courts and light game equipment rentals, wading pools, miniature golf, outdoor restaurants ... A terraced earth entertainment bowl capable of seating five to six thou sand persons with a stage and suitable public address system ... Also, a cycle trail ...

Other parts of Centennial Park would be turned into 'a gigantic parking lot' for patrons attending events at the new Sports Centre. It was presented by the State Government as a project that would enhance a possible bid by Sydney to host the 1988 Olympics. The chairman of the Olympic

Committee strongly supported the idea, stressing that it would have 'a tremendous beneficial effect on commerce and industry'.[35]

A storm of protest erupted immediately, objecting not merely to the location but to the process by which this decision was made. 'A Failure in Consultation' was the title for an address on the matter by Dr Neil Runcie, Professor of Economics at the University of New South Wales, president of the Save the Parks Campaign and secretary of the Centennial Park Residents Association. In another address Runcie suggested the proposed Moore Park Sports Complex had 'exposed serious weaknesses in the appraisal of large public investment projects in New South Wales'. It was widely judged a very poor example of the planning process, the outcome of minds who could only think in terms of the area near the showground and the cricket ground as a venue for Sydney's sporting activities. Yet objections to the site were 'manifold and obvious'. This 'lazy solution' or 'planned stupidity' was considered 'indicative of the lack of proper planning by the Government' and 'the type of planning we have come to expect'.[36]

A non-expert committee within the Department of Lands had commissioned consultants for a cost of $70,000 to prepare a feasibility study of locating such a facility in the area. Its terms of reference were narrow; it was not instructed to consider how large numbers of people would be transported or the impact of traffic congestion on the local area or possible damage to the environment. There had been no consultation with planning and traffic experts, local resident associations or those who used the Moore Park facilities . Sporting clubs had not been asked for their ideas. Representatives of the Royal Agricultural Society (proprietors of the showground) and the Sydney Cricket Ground were 'most unhappy' with the proposal. It had also ignored the findings of expert investigations in the previous five years, which had all concluded the most suitable locations were in the western suburbs. Adequately based estimates of the total cost were not made available for public discussion, and as many critics pointed out, proper feasibility studies logically required consideration of various alternatives and not simply 'a priori selection' of the one location; the process involved had been 'putting the cart before the horse'.[37]

The principal objection raised was the chosen location: it was far from the geographic centre of the metropolitan area; the existing road system and parking facilities were inadequate, 'traffic congestion was already chaotic … and the scheme would compound it'; there was no railway facility; the proposal to provide extra roads into the area was at variance with modern principles of inner-city traffic development; it was contrary to government policy on the decentralisation of facilities and equitable distribution of facilities (indicative of the government's 'neglect of the Western Suburbs'); it involved duplication, not rationalisation, of existing facilities in the area; it involved drastic changes in the parkland dedication of Centennial Park and adverse effects on the open playing fields of Moore Park; the birds and other wildlife in Centennial Park would be disturbed; in short, it would involve 'environmental mayhem'.[38]

Some sporting bodies were inclined to jump at any offer of state-funded new facilities, wherever located. The chairman of the Amateur Swimming Association blithely stated: 'With expressways planned for the future I don't think it matters very much on this complex's locality'. Other sporting bodies disagreed, pointing out that the area's lack of rail transport and paucity of feeder roads was a serious drawback. The president of the New South Wales Rugby League argued that experience from overseas showed clearly that rail transport was by far the best way to shift large crowds; the complex should therefore be at St Peters, serviced by three lines and accessible to residents of the western suburbs, which were areas with a strong following of rugby league. The Rugby Union championed Homebush Bay as a desirable alternative location, because of its geographic centrality, underdeveloped nature, and accessibility by rail, road and water – a view shared by several contributors to the debate, including Mundey. The sporting community generally felt that a stadium larger than the one that could be built on such a circumscribed location as Moore Park was required to cater for the needs of a growing sports-watching population: Richie Benaud for one deemed it 'absurdly small'.[39]

Even John Laws, an habitual supporter of Coalition governments, declared it a brilliant idea in the wrong place. Newspaper editorials politely criticised the location. The *Sydney Morning Herald* described the proposal as 'ambitious and exciting' but observed that a 'serious drawback to Moore Park as a site for crowd-generating fixtures is its lack of rail public transport' and acknowledged its 'inadequate roads system' was 'unsatisfactory' even for its current traffic needs. Moreover, as the president of the Paddington Society insisted, it was best to build a sporting complex 'where ugliness and neglect could be redeemed', not where beautiful houses and parkland would be destroyed. The western suburbs, increasingly the centre of Sydney's population, were poorly provided with sporting venues and the new project could redress this paucity. The Professor of Highway Engineering at the University of New South Wales agreed: apart from strongly opposing the scheme as a traffic engineer, he also argued that 'It will serve to downgrade an existing amenable area whereas, if such a large sum of money is going to be spent, the object should be to upgrade a less amenable area'.[40]

The plans for the area required compulsory acquisition and demolition of 54 houses in Martin and Lang roads overlooking the park, 'one of the most sought after' residential areas in Sydney, which just happened to house both Patrick White and Pat Hills, Leader of the Opposition Labor Party in the New South Wales Parliament. When a *Daily Telegraph* editorial maintained resumptions 'are often necessary for progress', opponents pointed out that these 'old and beautiful homes', 'the finest stand of Edwardian dwelling construction in Sydney', included rare examples of the genius of Waterhouse and Burley Griffin; and asked whether such a project really was 'progress' and wondered where such progress would lead.[41]

Even without the prospect of having his house bulldozed, Hills opposed the scheme on the grounds that it would cost considerably more than the amount estimated. Patrick White, patron of the Centennial Park Preservation Society, described it as 'a gigantic political lurk for the glorification of shaky politicians'. In his first-ever television interview, the 'normally retiring' White vented his anger and that of his fellow residents: '*We* are fighting against the great god sport'. If he lost the battle, he would move to Adelaide, 'which is a civilised city'. With an 'aesthetically execrable elevated roadway along Anzac Parade' (also part of the planners' design) George Molnar, a professor of architecture and cartoonist for the *Sydney Morning Herald*, was determined to prevent this desecration, because the Parade, 'with its beautiful Moreton Bay figs, straight flow and generous scale, is the only roadway Sydney has that is worthy of a metropolis'. To whom did Molnar turn? 'It's about time', he concluded, 'that the conservationists, ecologists and building labourers united to preserve not just a house or tree, but an entire avenue'.[42]

The obvious complicity of the State Government in putting forward the proposal suggested an alignment of the priorities of government departments with those of developers. The Planning for People Campaign, headed by Peter Gamble and Andrew Jakubowicz, asked concerned Sydneysiders: 'Will you join us in battling to preserve the environment, and keeping it safe from pollution by developers and bureaucrats?' Faith in government as the representative of all, as the disinterested arbiter who would judge the claims of partial interests in the interests of the collectivity, was clearly shaken by the experience of the Centennial Park–Moore Park proposal. 'Are we to repeat all the Opera House errors of inadequate investigation again?' enquired Professor Runcie. The *Paddington Journal* stressed: 'Nobody stands to benefit from the above proposals but the developers who get the building contracts and generations of people will be deprived if the proposals eventuate'.[43]

Under the slogans of 'DECENTRALISATION, NOT DESTRUCTION' AND 'CONSULTATION, NOT COERCION', Runcie urged his fellow citizens to 'use the existing crisis as an opportunity … to get valuable reforms that will be of lasting benefit – and an opportunity to demand enlightened Ministerial and Town Hall leadership', for 'It is our money and our achievements as a community that are being affected'. Two large protest meetings were held, with speakers as diverse as Patrick White, Harry M Miller, Kylie Tennant, Vincent Serventy, Jack Mundey and Anna Katzmann, captain of Sydney Girls' High School. Cardinal Gilroy sent his apologies, due to ill health, and his support. In June, the NSWBLF placed a ban on the project: the trees and the wildlife of Centennial Park, the splendour of Anzac Parade, and the Edwardian houses were now safe from the disastrous effects of poor planning. As Roddewig noted, the Centennial Park green ban had the desired effect: 'Development of the Olympic complex never got past the planning stage'.[44] (Roddewig should have termed it the 'lack of planning stage'.)

MERRYLANDS (AUGUST 1973)

Lack of planning was also apparent in Merrylands, where a factory, greatly desired elsewhere, was proposed for an area where it was not wanted. In West Merrylands, known unofficially as Greystones, in western suburban Sydney, the local council gave approval to Fowler Ware Industries to turn 6 hectares of forest into a factory for making vitreous china bathroom items. Initially residents thought the council were employing the workers to turn part of the forest into a park; as they started excavating it was naively assumed a swimming pool was being provided. When the nature of the development became known, a citizens' action group protested strongly with petitions, demonstrations and arguments at council meetings.[45]

When work nonetheless proceeded on the factory, the residents turned to the NSWBLF in August, which accordingly withdrew all workers from the Merrylands construction site. The residents argued that they wanted the forest to remain as it was or be turned into a park, and they did not want any more industrial sites in their developing residential area. They requested Fowler and the Minister for Decentralisation to build the proposed factory in the Mudgee-Gulgong area, where the clays for the china were extracted. While discussions continued between the NSWBLF and Fowler, and the Total Environment Centre carried out an 'in depth study' of the environmental effects of the proposed factory, the Resident Action Group in Mudgee asked the Mudgee Municipal Council to take action to attract the industry to the area. This council expressed its surprise that the Minister for Decentralisation had not proposed the Mudgee area as a site for the factory in the first place and agreed with the Resident Action Group that strong efforts should be made to gain the industry, which would employ 300 to 400 people.[46]

Because the union had persuaded Fowler to carry out an environmental impact study and had suggested the Total Environment Centre as one of two appropriate consultants, this event was twisted beyond recognition by a Liberal MLA in parliament. In a curious sophistication of traditional anti-Communism, Mr Barraclough declared the NSWBLF, under 'Trotskyite' leadership, was blackmailing companies by placing bans on building projects and then extorting money from the companies on behalf of the Environment Centre: 'People are paying out in fear to avoid BLF black bans'. The union replied with a press statement, explaining that when the company involved had indicated that it was willing to modify its proposals and commission an environmental impact study, the union had told the company it was for the residents to decide whether the amended propositions were satisfactory: 'At no time and in no discussion with us have the company or ourselves made any mention of payment of any money'. The union called for an inquiry into the building industry which should 'thoroughly probe the facts ... including the commercial rampages by developers while community needs go neglected'. Mundey said Barraclough's remarks, which he had declined to repeat outside parliament, were the sort of false allegations made time and again against the union, 'ever since we have been applying our industrial strength to help environmentalists and other community groups'.[47]

By October 1973 Cudgegong Shire Council in the Mudgee area announced it would very much like the prospect of having Merrylands' unwanted $5 million industry in its back yard, and resolved to offer Fowler a range of inducements – cheap land, water, sealed roads, electricity and housing – to transfer the factory to the area.[48] The company decided not to build its factory in Merrylands.[49]

RILEY'S ISLAND, GOSFORD (SEPTEMBER 1973)

Having observed the effects on St Hubert's Island of development that transformed the Brisbane Water island into 700 allotments, a public meeting in Gosford in September 1973 attended by 500 people unanimously called for a halt to similar development of nearby Riley's Island. Hooker-Rex Estates had purchased the 19-hectare island in 1969 and caused a general outcry early in 1973 when it announced its intentions to build 300 home sites on it, development that would denude the vegetation and cause irreparable eco-logical damage. Environmentalists, biologists, the Littoral Society, fishermen and nature lovers protested strongly; and (in an unusual stance for a local council) the Gosford Shire Council came to a unanimous decision to ask the State Government to buy the island from the developer. Explaining the council's viewpoint and that of the locals who wanted to see the island kept as a nature reserve, Councillor Jim Laurenson said the proposed develop-ment would destroy the natural fish nursery around the island, threaten the bird life and destroy the aesthetic qualities of the island; development of the island would mean 'a tragic loss not only to the shire but to the whole State'.[50]

However, with the company insisting development would proceed and with bulldozer work starting on the island, the concerned locals who had formed into the Central Coast Environmental Protection Society realised, as a local paper put it, that passing motions and talking at public meetings was useless. So they asked the builders labourers for help. Tony O'Beirne, district organiser, and Bill Holley, an executive member, visited the mangrove island with members of the society and reported back to the executive, which put a green ban on Riley's Island. As the *Builders Labourer* warned, Riley's Island not only performed the 'important aesthetic role of a visual buffer between areas of heavy development activity' but was ecologically the most significant area in the Brisbane Water, the development of which could cause the whole system to degrade rapidly. The motivating force of the Hooker-Rex Corporation was profit. 'Is the Community prepared to take the risk?': the union was not.[51]

THE TOMAREE PENINSULA, PORT STEPHENS (JANUARY 1974)

By 1974 many residents in the Port Stephens area on the New South Wales central coast were becoming increasingly opposed to 'indiscriminate high rise, especially on the foreshores'. They argued the existing sewerage system could not cope with so much additional population and that the high-rise buildings seriously detracted from the beauty of the area. They had become disenchanted with the behaviour over several years of their local council, which 'has amply demonstrated that it leans toward the developer', ignores 'the opinion of the local people' and disregarded the need of industrial and office workers in New-castle and Cessnock for recreational facilities 'free from pollution'. In this sit-uation, locals felt justified in turning to the NSWBLF, 'which is playing such an important part in conserving some of our national heritage'. In response to a request from the Port Stephens Conservation Society and the Tomaree

Peninsula Council of Progress Associations, the union placed a 'holding ban' on the construction of buildings of more than four levels in the Port Stephens area, specifically on Tomaree Peninsula, including Nelson Bay, Shoal Bay and Fingal Bay. An agitated *Port Stephens Pictorial* editorial (after acknowledging that the NSWBLF 'merits credit for past action on environmental preservation') asked did the local initiators of the green ban 'fully consider the implications and possible effects of involving a militant trade union in an area with a history of industrial peace?'[52]

This aversion to militant unionism notwithstanding, the Port Stephens Shire Council felt obliged to arrange a meeting with NSWBLF officials to discuss high-rise development and attempt to defend the council's planning regulations. Some councillors felt green bans would have 'an explosive effect on the area', because the building industry was the biggest in the area; another councillor conceded the council had not 'applied common sense to some buildings permitted', which had spoilt the landscape and lifestyle of existing residents. In justifying the council's position, Councillor Everitt reported receiving threatening calls from speculators because of the severity of the existing code on height limitation. In the meantime, pending this meeting on 1 February, the building unions affiliated to the Newcastle Trades Hall Council endorsed the holding ban imposed on 'high-rise buildings for which development approval has been granted by the council, but against which protests have been lodged by residents'. After the meeting, Tony O'Beirne announced the ban would continue 'until such time as the matter is resolved to the satisfaction of the people'.[53]

Against those who argued the protesters should consult experts, they responded: 'we do not have to be experts to see that high rise detracts from the Peninsula's natural beauty'. Against the stock criticism that the protesters should utilise democratic processes and not resort to union power, the resident activists explained in great detail the extent to which they had already pursued those avenues, with petitions signed by 1700 local residents, submissions and objections, to no avail and usually without any reply from the council: 'Quite simply we are using the last weapons possible in a fight in which the tranquil future of the Peninsula will be won or lost'. Any developer, it was pointed out, who is dissatisfied with the local council's treatment of its development application could appeal to a higher body; 'not so the private individual' who had, necessarily, to resort to 'drastic action' to have their say on local development:

> ... and this seems to be the situation not only in Port Stephens, but right
> throughout NSW and the actions by the resident groups and at their request,

the Builders Labourers Federation, in imposing green bans have served a useful purpose and put a stop to the indiscriminate destruction of our environment. Action by the local people has gone by the board, hence the assistance of the BLF which is playing such an important part in conserving some of our national heritage.[54]

Among the various high-rise projects prevented by the ban was the construction of an eight-storey block of flats in Magnus Street, Nelson Bay. However, a 17-person syndicate building its own four-storey block of flats in Laman Street, Nelson Bay, in an area that the Tomaree High Rise Environmental Action Group's 'people's building code' marked as a 20 feet zone, broke the union ban by working on it themselves. The president of the Newcastle Trades Hall Council pointed out that the members of the syndicate were relatives or employees of a firm attached to one of the biggest developers in Australia and were being used as 'guinea pigs in a test case'. Possibly tiring of manual labour, the syndicate members came to an agreement with the union after a few weeks, that if BLF members were allowed to resume the work, construction would not proceed beyond the first floor, pending the outcome of the big public meeting called by the local council on 19 May to discuss the high-rise issue, prompted by that particular ban.[55]

The meeting was a setback for the local environmentalists, in that it voted 450 to 50 to support the shire council's residential flat code, but it was an achievement in the sense that the council defended its position by insisting it did not favour high-rise development throughout the peninsula and, under directions from the State Planning Authority, was preparing a new code. This Interim Development Order 23, developed in response to the green bans, only permitted flats of more than four levels on conditions 'so hard to comply with' that the council did 'not believe development of more than four storeys will take place'. The Tomaree High Rise Environmental Action Council, while remaining critical of the council, decided nonetheless to request the union to lift the green ban out of respect for the decision of the public meeting, but only on buildings that conformed to the new, stricter code; those in violation of it remained banned. The president of the Port Stephens Conservation Society claimed in retrospect that the turn to the BLF was 'an historic decision' that triggered off 'a new dimension for conservation in this area'; but it was only one of the skirmishes in the bigger battle that will surely come, during which it would be necessary 'continually to point out to people what the spoilers are doing with the environment'.[56]

There were more bans and even more rumours of bans as concerned residents increasingly turned to those who could prevent the various threats hanging over the open spaces of their local areas. In February 1973 the NSWBLF placed a ban on any buildings Ryde Council might try to erect at Dunbar Park, because local residents had told the union they were afraid the council was intending to use the park as a rubbish tip. In August 1974 the NSWBLF and FEDFA, supported by the Central Coast Trades and Labour Council, banned construction of a sewerage treatment works in the Wyong Valley. A series of 'possible' or 'threatened' bans were placed at residents' requests on additions to a block of flats overlooking Kendall's Beach at Kiama on the south coast; on Sydney's projected second airport at Galston on the outskirts of Sydney's 'green belt'; on sand mining at Ebenezer near Windsor; and on any future building development in the Narrabeen Lagoon area.[57]

These rumours and threats, as much as the actual bans, indicated the extent to which recourse to the union's power was becoming an expected response on the part of anxious residents. The next two chapters examine the green bans placed in defence of the built environment, that distinctive aspect of green ban activity that was even more imaginative than bans to protect the natural environment.

PRESERVING THE BUILT ENVIRONMENT

Whereas the bans discussed in the previous chapter were imposed to protect open spaces, the majority of green bans were aimed at protecting the built environment from the perils of 'redevelopment'. Mundey emphasised the importance of urban environmental issues, not simply because most people live in cities but because urban environmental campaigns were especially meaningful to working-class people. Certainly these bans were supported enthusiastically by rank-and-file builders labourers precisely because they were predominantly concerned with the defence of working-class communities.

In places such as The Rocks, Woolloomooloo, Victoria Street, Waterloo, Surry Hills, Glebe, Ultimo and Newcastle's East End, the builders labourers could identify easily with the people affected. Ian Makin and Bob Baker noted that they were saving the homes of workers who had 'struggled' to buy them or who had rented them for years, so there was good support, 'about 80 per cent', for these bans among builders labourers. These bans were especially popular with the many European builders labourers who, according to Owens, had a particularly strong sense of community, so 'there was no way they were going to destroy historical Australian Working Class areas like The Rocks or Woolloomooloo'.[1] The *Victoria Street Rag* announced: 'For too long we, the people of the inner city, have stood passively by while the developers were wrecking once viable communities and replacing them with a soulless wilderness of motels, office blocks, car parks and apartment houses for the rich'.[2] When the people decided to fight back, they formed resident action groups; and their ultimate weapon was the NSWBLF green ban.

Present-day Sydney, as well as regional centres, owe much of what is valuable and valued in their built environment to green bans, for these bans halted some of the destruction that developers, business men whom Gavin Souter described as 'those who have turned the city in to a continually chang- ing chaos of hoardings, excavations, lorries, noise and dust'[3], had in mind. The story of these bans is a tale of conflict, of people versus profits, of com- munities against an individual or institution, of labour confronting capital.

THE ROCKS (NOVEMBER 1971)

The third green ban, after those on Kelly's Bush and at Eastlakes, was the first to protect a working-class neighbourhood, and the first in which the direct oppo- nent was the State Government rather than a private developer. As Roddewig argued, The Rocks green ban involved more fundamental issues than did Kelly's Bush: 'It was a challenge to the very nature of Australian urban planning and development, and the support it enjoyed evidenced more clearly the wide dis- illusion with a political process that gave some interest groups no chance to be heard'. On the western side of Sydney Cove, the birthplace of white settlement and the environment that had produced the characters exemplified in Henry Lawson's ode to 'The Captain of The Push', The Rocks had become a centre of government attention during the 1960s. The area was almost completely in public ownership: the Maritime Services Board acted as landlord to the sailors, wharfies, pensioners and other low-income earners, such as cleaners and shop assistants servicing the CBD, who had lived in The Rocks for generations. Now the government was anxious to capitalise on its proximity to the CBD during the commercial office boom."

A series of plans in the 1960s, culminating in the creation of the Sydney Cove Redevelopment Authority (SCRA) in January 1970, all favoured massive demolitions and high-rise development. Rushed through to meet a State Gov- ernment deadline, concerned as the government was to have a 'cash flow' as soon as possible, the planning process undertaken by the SCRA did not include consultation with the residents concerned. 'The people on SCRA's board had no familiarity with planning,' one of the planners recalled. 'They told us to forget about public participation by the residents of the area, since including it would mean we wouldn't make the deadline'. The plans for the $500 million, 21.5-hectare scheme were unveiled at a champagne press conference at the State Planning Authority office in February 1971, without even the usual period of public exhibition and comment that every other public plan in the state had been required to allow. 'The authority thought the residents of the area had no rights in the matter anyway, since they were only tenants of the state.'[5]

The rights of these working-class tenants were certainly not counted among those of 'the people of NSW', for the benefit of whom SCRA executive director, Colonel Owen Magee, claimed the redevelopment scheme was being carried out. Kay Anderson and Jane Jacobs draw attention to the contrast with Kelly's Bush: in The Rocks, private rights were eroded to such an extent that its residents were not even secure in their dwellings; by contrast, the home owners of Hunters Hill were not only secure in their shelter, but were able to enlarge the ground of their privacy claims to include control over the additional space of Kelly's Bush. Private rights in working-class areas like The Rocks were presumed by the state and capital to be negotiable, even dispensable, and the rights of The Rocks' residents were compromised further by their status as public housing tenants. 'Their houses were unquestionably available for redevelopment, in what was dubbed the "public interest".'[6]

The residents had become aware of the moves afoot to displace them, because the SCRA that had replaced the Maritime Services Board as their landlord had been reluctant to repair their houses, and had raised rents 200 to 300 per cent. Nita McRae, mother of three, who had lived in the area for 42 years, like her parents and grandparents before her, described the SCRA's attitude: 'If you don't like it, move out, 'cause we're just going to throw you out in due time, anyhow'. After voicing their protests through the usual channels, and discovering their local member had not even participated when the *Sydney Cove Redevelopment Authority Act (1968)* had been discussed in parliament, The Rocks Resident Action Group quickly sprang into life with about 200 members. It turned to the NSWBLF in desperation in November 1971.[7]

Demolition was due to commence in January 1972 for two 105-metre skyscraper buildings as Phase One of the SCRA plan: a luxurious hotel above a major department store, and an office block, at a total cost of about $60 million. But the union responded to the residents' plea and announced on 6 November 1971 it would not move a single brick until the 416 residents forced to move had been satisfactorily rehoused; it stressed that these residents had not even been given undertakings that they would be rehoused. Ralph Kelly described his feelings about their situation: 'They were people who, unlike the people of Hunters Hill who wanted a nature strip – they just said, this is our home this is where we've always lived. You blokes know what we feel like – what we want – they touched me very deeply.' As action group secretary Nita McRae observed: 'Our whole lives have been spent here and now we are expected to get up and go just like that'. One family of five in the threatened area had approached the Housing Commission about alternative accommodation and been told they would be put on the end of the 40,000-person waiting list.[8]

With the Askin Government's recent amendments to the *Landlord and Tenant Act*, there was no adequate protection of tenants' rights. Previously, the landlord had an obligation to the tenant to pay compensation or to adequately rehouse people being displaced; since the amendments, the landlord had no responsibility to the tenant and the tenant had no legal claim on the landlord. Pringle and Owens objected to these changes in a statement defending the ban: 'We believe that these amendments are contrary to the rights and needs of the people. Progress should be for all the people and not be detrimental to some for the benefit of others.' Having lived in the area for decades, paying rent to different state authorities over the years, probably paying for their homes several times over, Pringle and Owens insisted these people had 'a right to dignified consideration'.[9]

The union was concerned not merely about the invidious treatment meted out to the residents but also about the threat to the historic buildings of the area: it halted the project 'because the scheme destroys the character of this historic area and ignores the position of the people affected'. Although the plan envisaged that a limited part of The Rocks, around the 1814 Cadman's Cottage (Sydney's oldest surviving house), would be renovated and maintained as an 'historic precinct', it was a tiny part of the overall plan and would be overwhelmed visually by neighbouring high-rise buildings. Neville Gruzman, an architect and town planner critical of the scheme, commented: 'To restore isolated "historic" buildings and sandwich them in with glass and concrete offices is to make a shallow mockery of our heritage'. On this matter, the union therefore parted company with the National Trust with whom it formed a productive partnership in many other bans, for the Trust had finally endorsed the SCRA plans. But the union felt the proportion of historic buildings preserved in the plan was inadequate and agreed with Nita McRae that 'the uniqueness of The Rocks area is the people who live in the historic buildings with all their past generations of ancestors who lived and died here'. Mundey defended the ban against the inevitable charges that it was 'politically motivated': 'Everyone should be interested when Sydney's history and beauty is going to be torn down, and when people in the way of this so-called progress are regarded as minor inconveniences'. He announced that a conference was being arranged between architects, local resident action group leaders and union officials to discuss ways of saving the historic areas as well as getting a better deal for displaced residents.[10]

The first of the 'minor inconveniences', the 85 tenants affected by Phase One, had been told they must leave by midnight on 14 January, but 31 had defied this instruction. The SCRA insisted excavation would start within a few days and remaining tenants would be issued with summonses. The union confirmed it would not provide labour, except for restoration of historic buildings, and FEDFA instructed its members not to operate bulldozers without action group consent; and the group continued with public meetings and other forms of protest. A few days later, with only 15 tenants remaining, the SCRA threatened they would face legal action. Local Government Minister Morton announced: 'Tenants who will be displaced by the redevelopment must obey the law and move out'. The *Sydney Cove Redevelopment Authority Act* had empowered the SCRA to terminate tenancies. But Mundey, for the union, declared that the environmental interests of three million Sydney people could not be left to developers and building employers whose main concern was profit-making. His men preferred to build 'urgently required hospitals, schools, other public utilities, high quality flats, units and houses, provided they are designed with adequate concern for the environment, rather than to build ugly, unimaginative, architecturally bankrupt blocks of concrete and glass offices'.[11]

In defiance of a State Industrial Commission ruling that the ban on The Rocks redevelopment be lifted, the union maintained its stance, even attempting, unsuccessfully, to have the premier, the Minister for Local Government, representatives of the Housing Commission and the SCRA summoned before the commission on the grounds that the matter was a political and social one and not an industrial issue. The executive voted in March to continue the ban. In one of its leaflets, The Rocks Resident Action Group noted that, 'once again, in the face of the usual apathy, inaction and favoritism of the Askin Government', it had been left to unionists 'to show leadership in protecting our citizens and their historic buildings'.[12]

Colonel Magee commenced correspondence with The Rocks Resident Action Group, hoping it would thereby gain 'a clearer picture of the Authority's task'. He also wrote to Labor Council acting secretary John Ducker, describing the SCRA's undertakings in relation to the rehousing of displaced tenants. Conceding these had been 'roundly attacked' by the NSWBLF, who had demanded instead that the SCRA undertake to rehouse all residents to their 'absolute and total satisfaction', Magee pleaded with Ducker that the NSWBLF's requirements 'seem impossible' and begged for his assistance in resolving the issue. Ducker's effort to persuade the NSWBLF and FEDFA, now joined by the AMWU, to lift the ban was to no avail, and his suggestion that the BTG should set up an organisation to assist people to move out of The Rocks was treated with contempt.[13] In June 1972 the Royal Australian Planning Institute reported that The Rocks plan 'left much to be desired' and stressed the area was not privately owned real estate to be exploited in the most profitable way, but was controlled by the government on behalf of the people as part of the national heritage, so should be used in a way that would bring the greatest benefit to the greatest number. On 30 October 1972 the resident action group announced its intention to commission a 'people's plan' for The Rocks in opposition to that proposed by the SCRA, one that would liaise directly with Rocks residents and, according to Nita McRae at the public meeting that launched the scheme, take into account 'the new mood of public concern for the environment'. Neville Gruzman, agreeing to work with other architects on the 'people's plan', stressed that overseas experience showed it was vital that people remain living in the inner city.[14]

The 'people's plan' published in April 1973 specified that the future planning of The Rocks should involve as fully as possible, to the point of veto, those who lived and worked there. It embodied the residents' desire that their neighbourhood be retained as a residential and historic area, separated from the CBD. Its recommendations were worded in terms such as 'long-term social benefit', 'old residential precincts', 'existing community' and 'irreplaceable historic environments'. It recommended, in short, that the area be revitalised through a return of residents, an injection of cultural and entertainment centres and an extensive program of historic preservation.[15]

Magee insisted the SCRA envisaged 'an increasing residential clement' and many cultural pursuits in the area, and boasted about the restoration of ten terrace houses, but was adamant that construction of high-rise buildings was necessary to finance such projects. The new Minister for Local Government, Charles Cutler, accused the NSWBLF and Mundey in particular of being 'traitors to this country which gives them protection, and traitors to their fellow citizens', because the ban was 'bringing business interests to financial ruin'. The union's treachery had already resulted in the restoration program, exempted from the ban, proceeding ahead of schedule, and the opening of the Old Spaghetti Factory, an 1890s-style restaurant which offered much cheaper meals than those provided at the more up-market Argyle Tavern. In general, during 1973 the SCRA modified its plans to extend the designation of 'New Residential Areas' at the expense of commercial areas, added more to the 'Historic Retention Areas', and dropped one of the hotel proposals, which did not go un noticed by those whose protests had prompted the improvement.[16]

Moreover, in place of the initial plans for high-rise residential blocks, in August 1973 the SCRA put forward plans 'to boost the population of The Rocks from 200 to 2500': a five-storey block of terraced apartments 'available to all socio-economic levels' in Playfair Street opposite newly renovated terrace houses, designed to merge with the old buildings in the surrounding streets. Mundey admitted it was 'gratifying to see the authority coming up with low-rise residential developments, something definitely not in the original plan', but said the plans conflicted nonetheless with the 'people's plan', so he could not direct builders labourers to work on the development, which was 'a sop' designed to get the green ban lifted so developers could proceed with high-rise construction. 'My federation will lift its ban when the residents are satisfied with what is being put forward by the authority.' The SCRA was patently annoyed with the union's response to the sop in question. Sir Charles Cutler 'foamed at the mouth'.[17]

After a concerted effort in October 1973 to break the green ban (which is related in Chapter Twelve) by the beginning of 1974 the SCRA had started to emphasise how much restoration work had been done on buildings of historic and architectural value, and agreed that the 107 families still in the area could stay at Housing Commission rents. Profit and loss calculations on the part of the State Government meant a backdown was imminent, because a union ban in the building trade was 'the equivalent of the Black Death'. It was paying $2 million per year in interest to service the $22 million loan to pay for land resumptions, and without having concluded 'one firm deal for a building'. It started to see the benefits of foregoing some of the estimated $10 million a year by 1980 from rentals it had been hoping to receive due to the high proportion of office space and low proportion of residential space in the original scheme. In March 1974 the SCRA sent the redevelopment plans back to the Melbourne architect who had devised them, to reconsider them in the light of the ban. 'It has taken the Government and the big development companies quite a time,' wrote a Melbourne reporter, 'to accustom themselves to the idea that, in terms of site-to-site decisions at least, the most powerful town planning agency operating within NSW at the moment is the BLF'. The State Government had been 'shot down in full flight on its way to making 10 million a year'. However by May 1974, under a headline 'Green Ban Helps Rocks Exploit its Past', the *Daily Mirror* was observing that, prevented from moving into the future, The Rocks was 'profiting from its colorful past', and the SCRA was 'going ahead with plans to bring back the past'. By this stage 70 old buildings had been restored, and art galleries, restaurants and craft centres established – with the help of BLF Labour – but the ban on demolition and high-rise constructions, Owens explained, was as solid as ever.[18]

In this situation, as Max Kelly describes it, the SCRA 'recognising that heritage was not only important, but was also commercially attractive, decided that history still had a role to play'. The new plans eliminated the high-rise buildings in conformity with the 'people's plan', the residents were reasonably satisfied and the ban was accordingly lifted in 1975. From the side of Sydney buses came the message: 'The Rocks – where history is alive and kicking'. In 1993, as Rocks historian Grace Karskens notes, the word 'redevelopment' was 'quietly dropped' from the Sydney Cove Authority's title. In 1995 estate agents revealed that leasing space in the historic sections of The Rocks was so popular it was difficult to obtain, with 'the kind of people who liked exposed beams' such as architects paying premium rents and the whole area enjoying a vacancy rate considerably lower than in the CBD it had wanted to emulate in the original plan. The Ministry for Planning acknowledged that as it turned out the redevelopment had been 'an overwhelming success', reflected in the high number of visitors to the area. While the green ban purists complain the area has too few residents and has become too attractive to visitors – with 4000 restaurant seats and a late-night atmosphere as lively as Kings Cross – they concede that the outcome is a considerable improvement on the fate from which it was rescued, of becoming an extension of the CBD.[19]

WOOLLOOMOOLOO (FEBRUARY 1973)

Redevelopment plans for Woolloomooloo approved in 1971 envisaged that about 55 per cent of its buildings would be high-rise office blocks, supplemented by three skyscraper hotels with 2000 rooms, large retail, recreational, exhibition and convention centres, and parking for 3400 cars. This high-rise jungle of office and hotel blocks would be segmented into two halves by the projected Eastern Expressway. There was no provision for residential development, because the development consortium headed by Askin's friend, Sydney Londish, considered this 'hot little basin' unsuitable for housing.[20]

The residents thought otherwise. Woolloomooloo, or 'the Loo' as it was popularly known, on the north-eastern edge of the city, where it slopes down into Woolloomooloo Bay, was traditionally home to maritime workers and fishermen. Many had been forced by rising rents and prices to move out of the area to distant suburbs:

> Before I even knew it, we were shifted to Mt Druitt,
> And the planners never gave me any say, boys.

Now it really makes me weep I am just at home to sleep
For it takes me hours to get to work each day, boys.

But many were determined to stay. Mrs Honora Wilkinson, who had been born and raised in the area, explained: 'I've flatly refused to take what seems to me to be a fortune for my terrace house. I feel that my soul and memories are not for sale.' Since 1968 when the State Planning Authority's Sydney Region Outline Plan changed plot ratios in Woolloomooloo to favour high-rise development, residents had watched houses being demolished for an office tower that remained empty for 18 months, and houses resumed by the Department of Main Roads left to rot and decay while the Housing Commission 's waiting list stood at 40,000. Their opponents were a formidable threesome: the Federal Coalition Government, which aimed to use its 2.2 hectares of Commonwealth land in the area to build a $15 million 'complex of Commonwealth office buildings'; the New South Wales Department of Main Roads, which by late 1972 had already displaced 600 residents to make way for the Eastern Expressway; and private developers, who planned to demolish another 4.5 hectares for the $400 million commercial redevelopment already described. A street meeting of Woolloomooloo residents in October 1972, organised by federal and state Labor members of parliament for the area concerned that population decline would threaten this Labor

Residents Nellie Leonard (back) and Gerry Leonard (with hat)
study plans for Woolloomooloo.

stronghold, formed the Woolloomooloo Resident Action Group, which collected 1500 signatures for a petition urging that the area remain residential. Important amongst these Woolloomooloo resident activists were Gerry and Nellie Leonard and Father Ed Campion – local Catholic priest, historian and journalist.[21]

Shortly before Labor won the federal election in December 1972, Tom Uren, as Labor spokesperson on urban affairs, indicated an incoming Labor government would aspire to prevent both The Rocks and Woolloomooloo redevelopment schemes, as 'bad planning' that also cut across Labor's commitment to decentralisation. Shortly after the accession of the Whitlam Government, the NSWBLF announced on 14 February 1973 that, at the request of local residents, no demolition or construction would take place in Woolloomooloo, in the area bounded by Victoria, William and Macleay streets and the Sydney Domain. 'These people have called for the preservation of the area as residential', Mundey explained. Residents wanted the 2.2 hectares of Commonwealth land released for the New South Wales Housing Commission to build terrace-style homes for low-income earners. 'The 'Loo traditionally is a place for homes. People living in the area want to keep it this way.' For Owens, the ban on Woolloomooloo was the best: not only was the area very obviously working class, there were quite a few builders labourers living in the area, so the union felt directly involved.[22]

Within a week of the ban being placed, Londish announced the $400 million redevelopment scheme would be replaced by a mere $80 million residential and community commercial-centre project in the area bounded by Plunkett, Bourke and Forbes streets and Junction Lane. The amount of office space in the modified project was 'only a small fraction of the amount originally proposed', there was provision of residential units for about 8000 people and there was 'planned retention of a few of the old buildings'. A *Sydney Morning Herald* editorial argued the BLF ban was 'now redundant', implying this had not previously been the case. Moreover, this editorial recommended other bodies 'review their thoughts' on Woolloomooloo: the Department of Main Roads should postpone work on the expressway until the Sydney Area Transportation Study was completed, and the Railways Department should take up the residents' suggestion for trees and lawns under the Eastern Suburbs Railway viaduct in place of the projected carpark.[23]

On the ground the union was busy preventing Londish's attempt to break the ban by using scab labour to demolish six terrace houses. About a hundred builders labourers converged on Woolloomooloo within 20 minutes to stop demolition work, ably assisted by pickets of local residents. 'When we get here to work at six in the morning', one of the scabs complained, 'there are already women in dressing gowns here before us, standing on the footpath or sitting on the demolition rubble'. The union and Londish finally agreed the demolition would cease, pending a report from Uren's department, and that union labour could be used for removing the existing rubble. Just in case, the union guarded the houses over the weekend and Owens warned: 'We are better organised now and within an hour we could have a picket line of at least 500 members at Woolloomooloo to stop demolition work'. As developers, residents and unionists awaited the Federal Government's response, activists from the resident action group patrolled the area.[24]

At a conference held by the action group to discuss Londish's new plan, Mundey reiterated the union's determination not to take part in any redevelopment of which the local residents did not approve. He challenged Sir Robert Askin, Sir Charles Cutler and Colonel Magee to a public debate on the various development plans in the inner city areas. 'We are not setting ourselves up as the town-planning authority,' he explained, 'We are merely supporting progressive architects and planners'. The resident action group decided it needed more time to work with sympathetic professionals on an alternative plan for the area and to see what the Federal Government had in mind. Meanwhile, Londish was losing $4000 a day from the 8 per cent interest payments on money borrowed to buy 3.6 hectares of Woolloomooloo. Asked whether this made it hard to sleep at night, he replied: 'Not really ... the "Loo" is appreciating at 20 to 25 per cent'. Nonetheless he offered Canberra this 3.6 hectares at cost price plus holding charges, and with bridging finance. 'He's bought himself a pup,' Uren commented, 'and he's trying to find a way out'.[25]

By October 1973 it was reported that the green ban on Woolloomooloo had been responsible for Londish's Regional Landholdings' $296,803 loss for the previous financial year. In April 1974, Londish declared he was 'sick and tired' of waiting for the new Sydney City Council plan for the area commissioned late in 1973 by the Federal and State governments, who had at last agreed to formulate a fundamentally different scheme for the area: 'My company has lost $5 million in interest rates since 1971'. A few days later the Federal Government indicated it would buy out Londish, and the promised new plan was released. This proposed that the suburb become an open area of parks and gardens with no streets, the only through traffic to be the proposed Eastern Suburbs Expressway; the predominantly residential nature of the area maintained by town houses and low-rise home units; the preservation of all existing hotels; the New South Wales Housing Commission to provide home units limited to six storeys; some office and retail blocks limited to 17 storeys along William Street only and widely separated allowing pedestrians to walk through them into the residential section; and at least 6 of the 36 hectares to be parklands and playgrounds. Alderman Briger said every effort would be made to retain 'the colourful character of Woolloomooloo, which included Italian fishermen, who daily strung their nets to dry in the streets outside their homes'. After public display for three weeks, the 1500 residents still in the area would be asked to vote for acceptance of the scheme.[26]

The New South Wales Institute of Urban Development urged the NSWBLF to lift its ban, because it 'had succeeded in its reasons for placing the ban': the union and resident action group had caused the three tiers of government 'to involve the community in planning the suburb's redevelopment', with even the State Government showing a willingness to collaborate and acknowledge 'the necessity for community participation in redevelopment projects'. Private development plans for Woolloomooloo had been scrapped and low-income earners assured of homes. 'A sense of responsibility is being shown by others, so the federation should ensure the Woolloomooloo scheme's success by assuring the Governments that its ban would be lifted.'[27] With confirmation of a Federal Government grant of $17 million for the proposed New South Wales Housing Commission plans for the area, the ban on the public housing area was lifted early in 1975 with the residents' approval. With the signing on 27 June 1975 of an agreement between the Prime Minister, the Premier and the Lord Mayor, *Now & Again* reported that at last 'the die has been cast to keep the 'Loo predominantly low-income residential'. Indeed 65 per cent of Woolloomooloo housing was to be retained by the Housing Commission for low-income earners. Instead of becoming a district of empty canyons of redundant office space, the green ban led ultimately to a development with a genuine socio-economic mix of residents living in medium-density buildings with many trees and landscaped surroundings. Acclaimed by anthropologist Margaret Mead and inspected by town planners from the USA, Germany and Singapore, the Woolloomooloo project was awarded six separate architectural awards in 1980. Ed Campion observed that the green ban had been the single most important feature of resident action history: 'Certainly, without that green ban, the Woolloomooloo group wouldn't have had a feather to fly with'.[28]

The Whitlam Government announces it would fund low-income housing in Woolloomooloo, 27 June 1975 (from left: Tom Uren, John Mulvena (back to camera), Nellie Leonard, Gough Whitlam, Gerry Leonard, Col James).

VICTORIA STREET (APRIL 1973)

'Victoria Street was for people on low-incomes, a place where they could live according to their own means. We are the people who love and need Victoria Street.'[29] Described as one of the most elegant and attractive areas of Kings Cross, the street was not just interesting for its architecture; most of the terrace houses and tenement buildings, many converted internally into separate flats, were rooming-houses for transient low-income earners, such as wharfies, artists, labourers, city workers, 'as well as a few old men and women of character and note'.[30] In February 1971 the National Trust advised the Sydney City Council to give the Victoria Street terraces and streetscape first priority for preservation under the council's strategic plan, but this advice was ignored.[31]

The National Trust had reason for concern. From the late 1960s most of Victoria Street was being bought by developers. It was the properties acquired between March 1970 and June 1971 between numbers 55 and 115 Victoria Street by Victoria Point Pty Ltd, under Frank Theeman, that became the object of the most fiercely contested green ban of all, where the developer employed armed thugs to vandalise the buildings and terrorise the residents, where one resident disappeared and returned too frightened to say what had happened to him, and where one activist disappeared forever. Theeman's links with criminal elements such as Abe Saffron and James Anderson, and discredited detective Fred Krahe, whom he hired to assist his plans for Victoria Street, are well documented. Those who survived Theeman's machinations recall the 'violence, tear and terror'.[32]

Theeman's first redevelopment plan, three 45-storey towers and carpark, was approved by Sydney City Council (dominated by the Civic Reform Group, for the Liberal Party) but rejected by the State Planning Authority as 'one of the worst cases of visual pollution' it had seen. A second scheme, which provided for a 20-storey tower set on a 3-storey podium with stepped development and a 6-storey carpark, was approved by the council on 16 April 1973, though Labor Alderman Gerard Draper indicated he would move a notice of rescission against the application on 21 May. The same day, the National Trust began its deliberations to decide whether the streetscape to be demolished to make way for the $70 million high-rise redevelopment was of 'architectural importance'.[33]

The NSWBLF, in this instance, did not wait for the Trust's decision, because events in Victoria Street warranted immediate action. The developer was clearly determined to inflict as much devastation, possibly complete demolition upon the area, before the Trust had time to classify the street or the council debate the rescission motion. While the Trust still lacked statutory powers, its classifications had 'gained real force', according to *Now & Then*, due to the support given its judgements by the union. It was precisely this combination Theeman wished to thwart, so he employed a 'real estate troubleshooter', Fred Fletcher, 'to get everybody out, within the week if possible, and start to "work" on the buildings'.[34]

On 3 April eviction notices were sent asking the 300 tenants to quit within the week, or agents, visited telling tenants to move. By the end of that week about half the tenants had left. To 'encourage' the more resistant to leave, they were offered amounts ranging from $20 to $2000; told the buildings had been condemned and the utilities would be disconnected; or forcibly removed, including an 84-year-old man who had lived in his flat for more than 40 years. At the same time, locks were removed, doors kicked down, wrought iron and stained glass removed, and bricks hurled through windows at night. Agents refused to accept the rent of tenants unwilling to move. Residents informed the press they were 'scared stiff'. The NSWBLF declared a ban on demolition in the area. Resident activists were 'very glad to see a few people there who were going to be prepared to be very strong and stand up to it', and acknowledged 'it was an extremely difficult thing for the BLs to take on'. A meeting on 6 April between residents, the NSWBLF and the developer extracted a 'promise' from Theeman that no further evictions would take place until the National Trust meeting on 16 April; but the evictions and vandalism continued. Clearly the developer hoped that empty houses would make council's approval more likely; demolition might be able to proceed before the National Trust met; and prompt evictions would render resistance less likely.[35]

The tactic almost succeeded, but a group of about 40 tenants became determined to resist not only the evictions but the whole redevelopment of the street. They held a street meeting on 8 April, which formed the Victoria Street Action Group (VSAG), and organised patrols to ward off the vandals and arranged a larger meeting for 11 April at the Wayside Chapel, which declared itself overwhelmingly against the redevelopment of the street and the tactics of the company. Leading this resistance was Arthur King, who had lived for many years in Number 97, had been around the libertarians of the Sydney Push for about ten years and had made the contact with the NSWBLF that prompted the ban.

In the early hours of Saturday 14 April, King was abducted from this home. On Sunday 15 April, with mounting concern about his whereabouts and thugs driving down the street yelling out 'we're going to get you and you'll be gone', the NSWBLF confirmed its ban on the demolition of Victoria Street. Mundey admitted to fears for King's safety and that of others, said it was 'the sort of thing that's going to happen if we keep confronting capital' and remarked presciently: 'I wouldn't be surprised to see actual death in the struggle to see which way the inner city goes'. He promised NSWBLF support for the residents, whatever the National Trust decided.[36]

On 16 April King reappeared, packed his belongings and left his home, and never again involved himself in the defence of Victoria Street: he had spent several days blindfolded in a motel room and locked in the boot of a car. About 2 am on 18 April a man carrying a wrench, torch and gunnysack was intercepted by resident activists who saw him entering several houses and removing taps, without turning off the mains so water cascaded into the street, but he escaped before police could apprehend him. Around this time, too, Theeman employed Joe Meissner, a karate expert, and he and other Theeman employees patrolled the street and entered buildings carrying sticks and crowbars. By this stage only about 14 tenants remained; the older tenants regretfully told VSAG they were too frightened to stay. Then Mick Fowler, a seaman devoted to his home in Victoria Street, returned from sea to find all his belongings had been thrown out of his flat at Number US. He attempted to take repossession of his flat on 30 April, but the agent's guards physically prevented him. In a move described by an *Australian* headline as 'Laborers Defy Karate Experts in Bid to Save Old Home', about 50 NSWBLF officials and members assisted Fowler to re-occupy his own home on 3 May, by storming the house and turning out three security guards, including Meissner, and fortified by members of the Seamen's Union of Australia, declared they would stop any attempt by the guards to re-enter the building.[37]

The previous day the National Trust had placed Victoria Street on its Classified List, 'because it possesses a combination of environmental qualities which make it a boulevarde unique to Sydney': topographical interest; beauty and scale of streetscape, including the trees; quiet and peaceful atmosphere; a blending of architectural types in the terrace houses and other buildings; and historical associations, particularly with people notable to Australian literature and art. Trust Director RN Walker said: 'It could be described as the Montmartre of Sydney'. The classification was the first made under the Trust's new system that replaced the A to C gradings with two – a Classified List (essential to heritage, must be preserved) and a Recorded List (contributes to heritage, preservation should be encouraged). The Trust conceded some buildings in the street were of little significance, that there was scope for some changes to take place provided any new development was sympathetic in scale, form and texture, but otherwise the classification was unusually broad in scope. Moreover, under the new system, being placed on the Classified List meant not just buildings but 'all other parts of the physical environment' must be preserved.[38]

Theeman exploded: 'Suddenly after years of doing nothing about the area the National Trust decides it is an area of national importance'. In a statement that implicitly criticised the council for approving his scheme despite the Trust's opinion of Victoria Street, he asked: 'why has the Trust suddenly with breakneck speed decided to declare the whole of Victoria Street a national heritage …?' VSAG believed the Trust 'became bolder' precisely because of the green bans, which were at last 'giving teeth' to the Trust – never before had it classified an entire street.[39]

With every week's delay costing him $14,000 in interest, a frustrated Theeman employed Ken Woolley, a prize-winning architect on the Historic Buildings Committee of the National Trust, to develop a third plan for the redevelopment that would preserve the essential characteristics of Victoria Street, involving restoration of the terraces and construction of a development behind them that would harmonise with the surrounding environment. Woolley agreed with VSAG's judgement on the Trust: 'it has been presented with an extremely effective implementing force by the policy of the Builders Labourers' Federation'. But when asked whether the Trust should be condemned now for its haste because of previous slowness and ineffectual action, he conceded that the Trust could and should have classified the street on several earlier occasions and that its failure to do so had been 'disastrous' for Mr Theeman.[40]

'Now it seems', Theeman admitted, 'that we can only build what the BLF wants. If they approve the new ideas, we will build them.' So desperate was Theeman that he announced he would consider constructing low-cost workers' homes on the site and, in conference with the NSWBLF and the VSAG, agreed to their demands that, while Woolley was working on an alternative scheme, all evictions and harassment cease, that facilities would be restored for Fowler, that Meissner would be sacked and other guards removed. But the following week mattresses were found smouldering in houses and one tenant's plumbing was ripped out and his basement flooded.[41]

The National Trust endorsed the Woolley plan on 4 June 1973. This third plan, costing a mere $20 million, retained a row of 22 terrace houses previously marked for demolition and proposed that rising behind them to about ten storeys would be a series of stepped town-house apartments, shopping arcades and pedestrian plazas, with frontages in Brougham Street. In the place of several old buildings in the street deemed to have no architectural merit there would be low-rise buildings designed to fit in with the existing terrace houses, occupying one-third of the total site frontage in the street. 'I will provide as much low-cost accommodation as is humanly possible in my new scheme,' Theeman promised; but VSAG vowed to continue its opposition because the plans did not ensure Victoria Street would remain a low-cost rental area. Alderman Draper indicated he would oppose the plan because it entailed buildings of nine storeys and the Trust had expressed its concern that the view of the Victoria Street escarpment from the city and Woolloomooloo should be unaltered.[42] With council and State Planning Authority approval almost certain, attention was now focussed on the union. Would it lift the ban? Owens observed that 'the developer is consulting us because we are the "muscle" in this dispute. But the muscle is being guided by a brain and the residents are the brain.' To reconsider its ban in light of the Trust's turnaround, the NSWBLF organised a conference for 21 June to be attended by Theeman, Woolley, a Trust representative and members of VSAG.[43] Beleaguered on a number of other fronts, the union was concerned about maintaining a ban that lacked Trust endorsement. Clearly, the emphasis of the ban had shifted away from aesthetic concerns and towards the more expressly political demand for low-income housing in this increasingly desirable area.

For a few weeks VSAG feared the ban might not be maintained. In this desperate mood, with only 12 residents remaining and fires mysteriously breaking out in the empty houses, the squatting started. It was organised to a large extent by the libertarians of the Push such as Wendy Bacon, Liz Fell, Ian Milliss, Roelof Smilde, Sasha Soldatow and Darcy Waters, who saw the direct confrontation method as consistent with libertarianism. About sixty people occupied some of the empty buildings, 'to keep Victoria Street available for low-rent housing'. The NSWBLF admitted it was caught between two sides it traditionally supported, being the resident action groups and the National Trust, and that the Woolley plan was 'a substantial improvement' on the original scheme. Even so, it announced the union would only lift the ban if the Woolley plan was approved by the residents of Woolloomooloo, Darlinghurst and Victoria Street at a meeting being arranged within a month: 'This Union, expressing its social consciousness, has consistently supported residents' and community groups which wish to help plan and protect their environment'. In the meantime the squatters, many of them pensioners, low-income workers and single women with children, began repairing the houses, planting vegetable gardens and lawns, and paid rent calculated at a quarter of their incomes to a maximum of $10 a week into a Theeman company account, something which Theeman considered 'outrageous' activity on the part of 'trespassers'.[44]

Theeman's main concern now was not to evict the 'trespassers' but to persuade the union to lift its ban via a concerted media campaign. He had already hired Neilson McCarthy as press agents, to bud the Woolley scheme and depict himself as an innocent victim of 'harassment', 'lawlessness' and 'anarchy'. This was a battle for hearts and minds that could run to a full-page advertisement in the *Sydney Morning Herald* of 8 November 1973 (ANARCHY REIGNS!!) during Askin's 'law-and-order' state election. With the resources at Theeman's disposal it was difficult for VSAG members to have their point of view expressed in the press, for he flooded the papers with his own copy about Victoria Street. 'It must now be clear to all thinking people,' Theeman insisted, 'that "green bans" are a communist tool to bring into difficulties developers who have to pay hundreds of millions of dollars yearly in interest on frozen properties'. He also proceeded with prosecutions for trespass against the squatters, whose numbers were growing and who had successfully established 'non-profit, low-rent co-operative housing' with communal eating and child-care arrangements. He succeeded in establishing the illegality of squatting, a few days after a meeting on 14 December with the Minister for Justice and Police.[45]

On Thursday 3 January, beginning at 7 am, over eighty people were forcibly evicted from the houses. ('The Siege of Victoria Street' is described in Chapter Twelve.) With most squatters ejected, the hired thugs went systematically through every house and removed wiring and doors, making them uninhabitable. Before being released on bail the 53 arrested squatters and supporters had to sign undertakings not to return to Theeman's properties. The NSWBLF and FEDFA reaffirmed the green ban and other unions expressed their opposition to 'the use of thugs as scab labour and to the eviction of the squatters'. The *Victoria Street Rag* concluded the government's obvious complicity in Theeman's action revealed its priorities as being private profit before public utility: 'The pretexts of law and order and protection of the rights of an individual conceal the real injustices against which we took our "lawless" stand in Victoria Street and the human costs of the alliance of political power and profiteers'. Taking comfort from the fact that the squatting had been a seven-month long victory for co-operative living, and 'we have brought low-rent housing in the inner city into the political arena as a major issue for the first time', the *Rag* acknowledged: 'None of this would have been possible without the support of the BLF and their Green Ban on the street'.[46]

Whereas the squatters of outback Australia erected wire-fences to keep out rabbits, Theeman now placed wire-fencing in front of the emptied terrace houses to keep out squatters. But the wiring stopped short of the last of the 22 houses – Number 115 – for Mick Fowler was still a legal tenant.[47] However, early in April 1974 Mr Justice Begg refused to overturn a magistrate's decision ordering his eviction. With 5 May 1976 eventually set down for his eviction, a section of the May Day March on Sunday 2 May 1976, that had marched under the Victoria Street banner to the music of Uncle Bob's Band (Bob Pringle) and the Fowl-House Five (Mick Fowler), adjourned to Victoria Street for a wake. A coffin signifying 'the rights of the low income earners' was ceremoniously buried in Fowler's front yard.[48]

Gallagher's first action after Intervention against the NSWBLF in October 1974 was the lifting of the green ban on Victoria Street, an action that did not surprise those people who had direct evidence of the liaison that had developed between Gallagher and Theeman. With the ban lifted the BTG entered into negotiations with Theeman, extracting a stay of demolition promise from him while attempting ineffectually to persuade him to allocate 10 per cent of the development to low-income housing. On 4 July 1975 Juanita Nielsen, publisher of *Now*, who had been actively campaigning against redevelopment in the street, disappeared – forever. (Her murderers were never brought to justice but, with a recent alleged confession, the case was reopened in 1998.)[49] Early in 1976 the BTG, with plaudits from Gallagher, approved Theeman's project, modified yet again to conform with the height restrictions imposed by the Woolloomooloo Redevelopment Plan of June 1975 that had arisen from the ban there. Accepting that allocation of the 10 per cent to low-income earners was too complex, the BTG instead took a cash settlement to build a club in the western suburbs.[50]

Protesters on chimneys and scabs outside Mick Fowler's rooms in Victoria Street, January 1974. (Courtesy *The Australian*)

Preserving the built environment | 213

When Theeman's units went on the market in 1978 they sold quickly at prices from $29,000 to $175,000. 'There are no more rooms for $5 a week in this development', the *Sydney Morning Herald* reported in 1979, 'Victoria Street is increasingly the home of the middle and upper income earners. Low-income earners have had to go elsewhere.' The restoration of the terrace houses catered for a similar high-income market, the auction notices boasting of Victorian terrace-style 'executive' apartments in what is 'now billed as the Paris Boulevard of Sydney'.[51] In marked contrast to the pat tern of middle-class flight from American inner-city areas, the remorseless trend towards gentrification of the equivalent parts of Australian cities placed the long-standing low-income residents of such convenient locations in an increasingly precarious position.

Mick Fowler died in Western Australia in August 1979 and was given a traditional street funeral in Victoria Street, with jazz musicians playing him off the street. NSWBLF officials gave speeches and read lines from *Such is Life*. The cortege paused outside his old home, resplendent with new paint-work, and the procession ended where Juanita Nielsen once lived.[52]

> Victoria Street used to have charm. It was a leafy, quiet place, sheltered from the bustle of the Cross. The buildings were old, solid, elegant. They had a slight air of decadent dishevelment about them, but they were houses of a fine vintage and they created a street with character. The people who lived there had character, too ... Today, much of that charm is gone. The restored terraces look impressive, but homogeneous. The patina of age has been stripped away. Details such as carriage lamps and aluminium lace make the effect too calculated, too strained ... The people are different too.[53]

Because the ban was broken at a crucial stage, the ultimate beneficiaries of the attractive streetscape saved by the ban were the 'yuppies', the middle-class gentrifiers of the inner city.

NEWCASTLE'S EAST END (MAY 1973)

Green bans hit Newcastle early in 1973. Until then, according to Tony O'Beirne, there hadn't been much 'real understanding' of the issues involved, but when Newcastle East residents turned to the local builders labourers for help and their situation was discussed at stop work meetings, 'they understood it alright – they marched off jobs all over the place'. It was the historic and traditionally working-class area east of Watt Street, the 'East End', that was becoming the object of high-rise office building and motel redevelopment, and residents had not been consulted; it was simply happening, bit by bit, without any coherent plan being devised and discussed. O'Beirne announced on 21 February that the union was concerned about the redevelopment, especially where high-rise buildings were proposed, and that it was seeking to confer directly with Newcastle City Council and developers. 'Our members are engaged on these buildings and they should have some say in their construction.'[54]

A columnist for the *Newcastle Sun*, Mat Hayes, found the union's position deeply offensive and threatening. 'Can you imagine what is going to happen if the union acts to prevent approved development in Newcastle East on this ground?' 'Yet while lambasting the union for its effrontery, his answer to his own question conceded the extent of support for green bans. 'It will be inundated with requests for similar action from other home-owners, and perhaps office dwellers.' When the resident action group in the endangered area did indeed request a ban in May, the union obliged; the residents informed the union no work should be carried out until the council had presented a redevelopment plan approved by the local residents. The first building saved from imminent demolition was a pub. Alerted to its impending fate by local residents, O'Beirne informed the press the Golden Sands Hotel 'serves a community need', that several pubs had been knocked down recently and if the Sands went, the residents would have nowhere to drink. A few months later, in October, another attempted demolition of a house in Ocean Street was discontinued when officials intervened to enforce the ban and to criticise the Newcastle City Council for awarding a contract for demolition while a green ban was on the area.[55]

Now well-organised as the Newcastle East Residents' Group (NERG), the locals organised a large public meeting on 27 July to 'reinforce the claim by "east enders" for a say in the development of their area', which they invited Mundey to address, along with Mark Harris of CRAG, environmentalist Zula Nittem, Dr John Turner of Newcastle University and several local politicians. Press coverage of the plans for the meeting stressed NERG was anxious to forestall demolition in the East End before proper planning had taken place. NERG president Bruce Chisholm explained of the green ban: 'some sort of brake' had to be applied in the meantime to Newcastle City Council. Mundey suggested to this meeting that residents draw up a plan of what they wanted for Newcastle East and that, until this was done and approved, the NSWBLF would retain its ban on the area. Of the unanimous resolutions passed, the first declared support for the builders labourers' green ban on demolition and development east of Watt Street until an overall plan for the area was formulated, with public participation at all stages. A few months later, in October

1973, a meeting of the Hunter Valley Coalition of Resident Action Groups (HVCRAG), representing 23 resident action groups in the area, expressed unanimous support for the union's 'green ban policy' and its actions to stop redevelopment in areas such as The Rocks in Sydney and the East End in Newcastle. In December 1973 the council approved, in principle, that planning consultants should be appointed to present a redevelopment plan acceptable to the residents.[56]

Despite the clear position of Newcastle resident activists, and the obvious efficacy of the green ban, in December 1973 Mat Hayes' column in the *Newcastle Sun* warned readers that the NSWBLF was directed largely by the CPA, which was 'looking for a revolutionised system of society', and that communist infiltration of action groups was becoming a serious problem. HVCRAG president Mr H George took issue with the column. Another resident activist, whose personal involvement had made him 'particularly aware of the amount of help' the builders labourers were giving to 'the residents of this country', wrote to the *Newcastle Morning Herald* objecting to the way the NSWBLF was 'the butt of a lot of criticism' when the union was 'the only people accepting some moral responsibility … for the welfare of ordinary people'.[57] As secretary of NERG, Jean Perrett wrote warmly about the effect of the NSWBLF's ban:

> … a long overdue halt has been called to the unplanned, piecemeal development which in recent years has been allowed to so adversely affect the amenity of living in the area … This green ban has been invaluable in providing the necessary breathing space and time for proper planning for the area and must be as much appreciated by sincere planners as it is by the residents.[58]

Mat Hayes next blamed the union for placing Royal Newcastle Hospital night-duty nurses at serious risk of sexual assault as they had to park in nearby streets, because the demolition of buildings for a hospital carpark was delayed by the ban. This theme was also stressed in a formal letter from the hospital to the union: that its action was endangering 'these girls' who were obliged to park 'in areas frequented by undesirable characters'. Although a NERG public meeting on 25 March 1974, addressed by Pringle, reaffirmed the community's support for the green ban and publicly endorsed and adopted the 'People's Plan for Newcastle East', the union was criticised for creating a public health and fire hazard by delaying the demolition of derelict buildings resumed by the council for an extension to Pacific Park. This extension was included in the People's Plan, but the ban on demolition was serving the important purpose of halting development until the principles contained in the People's Plan were incorporated in the scheme being devised by the council's planning consultants. However, after union officials and NERG representatives inspected the buildings with the council's chief health inspector, it was agreed that they were a hazard and that the ban should be lifted in this instance in return for the council's agreement that no construction work in the area would proceed until the development plan for the East End was ready in October and approved.[59]

Paradoxically the most resounding justification for the ban on Newcastle's East End was sounded by Mat Hayes in his denunciation of the union the day before it lifted the ban on demolition of the hazardous buildings: there could no longer be any excuse for delaying demolition of these properties, because the green ban had already served its purpose. 'It jarred a complacent City Council and aloof planning authorities into recognition of the right of East End residents to a voice in the future redevelopment of their area.' There was no longer dispute, Hayes claimed, about the need for an overall plan for the area and moves towards that were well under way. 'The green ban undoubtedly provided the spur; and the planners may well need to feel the whip again if they slacken their pace.'[60]

HALTING EXPRESSWAYS

For those concerned about the detrimental effects of increased private car usage and expressway building in this period, the union's environmental consciousness was most welcome. The NSWBLF officials were quite consistent in their stance against relentless freeway construction and the consequent diversion of resources and funding away from public transport. Neither Mundey, Owens nor Pringle owned cars, and Mundey in particular preached against the 'god car' mentality. The union even switched from cars to light motor bikes for the city organisers in 1972, a move which gained great publicity and ruffled a few union feathers when Dave Thomason, one of the newly equipped organisers, announced that cars provided by unions for their officials were 'perks' and inefficient for city work. However, this environmentalist gesture was abandoned when Owens fell off his bike and broke his ribs.[61]

The areas affected by the projected freeways were predominantly inner-city working-class residential areas, two-thirds of whose adult residents did not own cars: housing in Ultimo, Pyrmont, Glebe, Annandale, Rozelle and Leichhardt was threatened by the Northwestern Expressway; housing in Darlinghurst and Woolloomooloo by the Eastern Expressway. The Department of Main Roads had adopted the policy of securing vacant possession of houses in these routes, then internally wrecking and sealing the houses to prevent occupation of squatters at a time of housing shortage, but five years prior to construction commencing. 'The DMR appears to have followed a policy of guerilla warfare in which the residents of the areas slated for highways are dealt with individually, bought out in a slow process, and their houses torn down leaving ugly and structurally dangerous gaps in rows of terrace housing.'[62]

> Where is me house, me little terrace house,
> It's all gone for profit and for plunder,
> For the wreckers of the town just came up and knocked it down
> Now across the Western Suburbs we must wander.

The department ignored the regular motions of democratic protest organised by the Anti-Urban Radial Expressway Committee which was formed in 1971 with the support of Leichhardt Council. In desperation, therefore, in April 1972 a group of residents in the Darghan Street area of Glebe called on the builders labourers to prevent further demolition in their area. In July 1972 the Save Lyndhurst Committee requested and received a ban on Lyndhurst, the historic 1833–35 building in Darghan Street, to protect it from demolition planned by the department. Although the State Government had carefully re-drawn the expressway route to miss the nearby Wentworth Park dog racing track, the building that was subsequently classified by the National Trust as 'essential to the heritage of Australia' was only preserved by a union ban.

In August 1972 four people from a counter-cultural group moved into an empty house in Glebe before the Department of Main Roads could wreck it; they repaired and cleaned it. On 18 August, at the instigation of the department, they were arrested and charged with trespass, and the department started demolishing the house. The NSWBLF bailed out the four and provided a barrister for their court appearance on 7 September. In the meantime the anti-expressway activists of Glebe and Leichhardt organised a rally and march on 19 August, at which Mundey spoke and conveyed the union's support in imposing a ban on all further demolition work connected with the expressway. The Department of Main Roads responded by hiring private contractors – who attempted to terminate their contracts when they found they required police assistance to carry out their work. The union then extracted a promise from the department that no further demolition work would be carried out.[63]

An organisation called Ecology Action, together with 35 community organisations, held a large meeting in Sydney Town Hall on 11 December, to discuss the effects of freeways on city living and natural environments and how they could be stopped, announcing: 'Only union black bans appear to be preventing extensive demolition programmes'. Mundey and WR Blunden, a professor of traffic engineering at the University of New South Wales, were speakers at the meeting. On 2 April 1973, 11 inner-city resident action groups called on the State Government to stop the evictions from houses resumed by the Department of Main Roads for expressway construction. The Federal Whitlam Government, it was noted, had embarked upon a full study of the matter.[64]

On 3 April, following a request from the Darlinghurst Resident Action Group, the union announced a ban on demolition work for the $500 million East Sydney redevelopment scheme and in the process all demolition for the proposed Eastern Expressway running from Woolloomooloo to Bondi. The area banned was bounded by College Street, Oxford Street, St Vincent's Hospital and William Street, supplementing the area covered by the Woolloomooloo ban on the other side of William Street. The ban would remain in force until town planners and architects, selected by the residents, made counter-proposals for medium-rise development acceptable to the local residents.[65]

The following month attention shifted north ward, when Newcastle City Council gave its approval for Motorway 23 to go through Blackbutt Reserve: the State Government had threatened that the money allocated 'could be spent elsewhere if Newcastle did not want it'. The decision was opposed by civic, conservation and progress associations from Newcastle, Lake Macquarie and Port Stephens, who described it as 'despicable', 'cowardly' and 'undemocratic', taken as it was in the absence of six aldermen, and without any environmental impact study being undertaken by the Department of Main Roads or any alternative routes proposed. Newcastle unions were generally more supportive of the CPA, and the nine other unions whose members could be working on the project supported this ban, in line with Newcastle Trades Hall Council policy that opposed any highway through Blackbutt, and in consideration of the intense public opposition to the routing of the expressway. The president of one of the preservation societies observed: 'We are working our way toward the situation where the only hope is for the unions to preserve the environment because the council does not want to'.[66] With the Northwestern Expressway halted by bans to prevent demolition of houses in Glebe, Ultimo, Balmain, Annandale and Summer Hill, and the Eastern Expressway stopped by bans on demolition in Woolloomooloo, Darlinghurst and Bondi Junction, the union announced additional expressway-related bans on 28 March 1974. At a stopwork meeting in Paddington Town Hall the builders labourers voted unanimously to extend their green bans to cover any demolition of houses to make way for inner-city expressways proposed by the recently released plan to update Sydney's transport system over 25 years, which allocated the bulk of the projected $6000 million to road works rather than public transport. Mundey pointed out that international experience had shown expressways would not solve Sydney's transport problems and that more money should be spent on trains, trolley-buses and trams. At a subsequent symposium on freeways and the environment, Mundey insisted workers had a responsibility to ensure their work was 'for social good' and the green bans had successfully prevented projects that would have proved harmful to the environment. Unions had not yet done enough in such matters, but they had a responsibility to act: 'We've got to use shock tactics'. Only by such means would governments be persuaded to do something about the appalling state of public transport.[67]

Anti-expressway sentiment was mounting in Sydney by this stage. A wide range of resident action groups and organisations formed expressly to oppose the projected freeways were marshalling convincing arguments on economic, social and environmental grounds, and mobilising public opinion against the Department of Main Roads' outdated plans, which had been drawn up as far back as 1948. The planned expressways would uproot the homes of 115,000 people; divide suburbs; encourage car use and thereby increase traffic, noise, parking and pollution problems; would not provide efficient peak-hour movement of people, which could only be achieved by mass transit systems; and the Northwestern Expressway was costing $1000 an inch to build. The Australian Conservation Foundation, in opposing the projected freeways, pointed out that Sydney's carbon monoxide levels had exceeded the standards set by the World Health Organisation on 220 days the previous year and that motor vehicles had produced 60 per cent of that pollution. The *National Times* had earlier publicised the conclusion of a confidential internal report on government transport priorities prepared in Victoria: 'The cost of a mile of freeway could alternatively provide 95 miles of double tram track, 23 modern trains, 250 modern trams or no fewer than 640 modern buses'.[68]

However, the Department of Main Roads, which enjoyed the wholehearted support of the Askin Government, was not deterred and it made a concerted attempt late in September 1974 to break the green ban impeding the Northwestern Expressway by demolishing houses in Fig Street, Ultimo, using labour from the Australian Workers Union. The Macquarie University

Students' Council Anti-Expressway Committee concluded this proved 'that the NSW Liberal Govt. is a repressive, capitalist mismanaged, un-coordinated bureaucracy that is "influenced" by the vested interests of Big Business and that lacks any Social responsibility in Planning and Decision-making'. Resident activists from Glebe and the surrounding area fought hard against the demolition work, assessing the situation as a 'last ditch' attempt to stop the expressway. There was no other way, local residents felt, to stop the North-western Expressway 'except by a war … against the DMR and the NSW State Govt, and consequently the Police Force and Courts'. 'The Battle of Fig Street' (described in Chapter Twelve) in defence of the green ban succeeded ultimately in halting the demolition work. The Northwestern Expressway was subsequently re-routed and in 1978 the Wran Labor Government decided to abandon much of the projected inner-urban expressway network, to avoid destruction of domestic housing.[69]

THE HIGH-RISE LOW-RISE BATTLE

The extent and increasing height of high-rise buildings had also been a matter of increasing concern since at least November 1971, when Earlwood residents had mobilised considerable local opposition to the construction of three- to seven-storey units in Homer Street, in an area zoned residential and thereby limited to three-storey units. By 1973 the issues were debated extensively in the letters columns of newspapers, the *Sydney Morning Herald* commenting that the 'high-rise low-rise battle' was getting hotter and 'more emotional'. Its columnist felt it was important to point out that town planning, unlike politics, was not an amateur's field, that people who made town planning decisions 'need to be thoroughly trained and informed about many facts, details and figures'.[70] The implication of such obeisance to technical rationality was that people were wrong to favour medium-density housing and to prefer not to live in or near high-rise developments.

Mundey joined the fray, arguing for the 'advantage of cluster-type housing, town house terrace-style buildings with concern for retention of a green area and a general aesthetic consideration over highrise living'. The high cost of land was not a good reason for going 'up and up', rather it was time for governments and municipal authorities to face up to their responsibility of ensuring that urban dwellers pay reasonable amounts in rent for decent housing:

> The shameful speculation of so-called property developers and a lack of
> courage on the part of government to tackle the "sole right" of the developer,

is the reason why ordinary people are being driven out of the residential areas of the inner part of our cities, particularly Sydney.

The community plans drawn up for The Rocks, Woolloomooloo, Darling-hurst and Kings Cross were testimony that people were determined to pro-pose their own ideas about their residential communities and were no longer relying on government instrumentalities 'which have failed to display any genuine concern for sky-rocketing rents and increasing prices of u nits and houses'. The NSWBLF, he promised, would use its green bans always 'in support of those most urgently in need of quality housing'.[71]

The union's bans on specific high-rise projects, at the request of residents, raised the heat on this 'high-rise low-rise battle'. On 19 July 1973 the union announced a green ban on all future demolitions and construction in Cook Road near Centennial Park, following an angry meeting of local residents opposed to Hooker's erection of five multi storeyed home unit blocks. The ban prevented work on all except the almost completed first block. When the dis-pute between the MBA and the NSWBLF over this development reached the Commonwealth Arbitration Court, Mr Justice Aird admitted he was uncer-tain whether he should treat the dispute solely on its industrial merits, since a much broader environmental issue existed in New South Wales and had for some time. 'A vacuum apparently existed which the union has occupied. I don't know whether it is appropriate for the union to occupy that vacuum.' After Intervention, when bulldozers started to arrive at this site, the NSWBLF green ban was replaced by a combined ban imposed by several unions.[72]

Occasionally the union shared Aird's reservations. In the case of the South Sydney redevelopment scheme – which aimed to build six 30-storey blocks, scattered among three-storey blocks, on a 13-hectare block at Waterloo, with two of the tower blocks to consist of flats for elderly Housing Commission tenants who wished to remain living in the inner-city – the union's aversion to high-rise developments was counteracted by its commitment to comply with the wishes of the residents concerned. Initially, in February 1973, the union had placed a 'temporary green ban' on the proposed development which was opposed by the South Sydney Resident Action Group on the grounds that planning for the redevelopment had been 'undemocratic'; more than 80 per cent of the residents did not approve of the commission's intentions; pension-ers would be moved into high-rise housing against their will; the commission was taking advantage of migrants who did not speak English; and 79 per cent of residents in the 504 homes affected did not want to move.[73]

To ascertain whether the pensioners wished the union to proceed with constructing the two blocks, the NSWBLF organised an open meeting in Trades Hall in July to give those concerned an opportunity to air their views and committed itself to respect the outcome. At the meeting Pringle alerted the pensioners to a recent conference in Kiev where the 3000 delegates were firmly of the opinion that it was not in the best interest of pensioners to be housed in high-rise buildings and pointed out there were hundreds of vacant houses in the inner city that could be renovated to provide houses for old age pensioners. When the pensioners, under pressure from the Housing Commission, expressed their desire for the development to proceed, the union agreed to lift the ban and allow its members to supply labour for the construction of the two blocks. Ian Makin of the NSWBLF and a local resident admit ted he was 'very surprised' at the request to lift the ban. However, the union made clear that the remainder of the development, involving the other high-rise blocks, was still subject to a green ban, which was also supported by the FEDFA.[74]

A few weeks later federal Housing Minister Les Johnson urged the State Government to reconsider the remainder of the development, in the light of reports from overseas about a decided retreat from high-rise housing and the fact that locally residents in high-rise flats suffered three times the suicide rate of those in low-rise accommodation. Given the extent of 'high-rise phobia' he regretted that, although the projects were being built with Commonwealth Housing Agreement money, the Federal Government had no power to prevent high-rise projects. On 21 November 1973 South Sydney Council decided to seek 'drastic alterations' to the housing scheme, in line with the wishes of the Federal Government, resident action groups and the NSWBLF. The secretary of the Housing Commission conceded that the council's decision might lead to the 'complete abandonment of the project'.[75]

In March 1975 the Housing Commission began preparing an evaluation of nine alternative schemes for Waterloo. Local residents, including Ian Makin of the NSWBLF and 'high-rise mothers', became increasingly active in opposition to the construction of any further 'suicide towers'. The times had changed since 1972, as an inner Sydney resident action group's series of press releases in September 1975 pointed out: more information was available about the deleterious psychological effects of high-rise living and the correlation with increased suicide rates; residents have not been thrown out of other inner-city areas on the scale predicted in 1972; other inner-city lands were available; rehabilitation of existing housing stock had proved itself a very real alternative to comprehensive redevelopment, since two homes could be purchased and rehabilitated for the price of one high-rise unit and in a much shorter time span, thus producing income and reducing inflation of building costs. The inner Sydney group pointed especially to the success of the Glebe project of housing stock rehabilitation carried out by the federal Department of Urban and Regional Development. By October the resident activists were claiming it was 'obvious that the Minister has backed-down'.[76]

So strong were the feelings against high-rise living that the NSWBLF and other building unions were frequently requested by resident activists to save their neighbourhood from the blight. The entire BTG, including the NSWBLF, imposed an indefinite ban on all new high-rise development in Bankstown in September 1973 after an appeal from local resident groups. A month later, the Eastern Hills Resident Action Group in Manly voted 230 to 20 at a meeting attended by Mundey to ask the union to ban buildings more than 8 metres high in their area. Specifically residents were opposed to a 21-storey Hooker development; but the 16-storey block already commenced would be allowed to continue. However, the 18 BLF members working on the 16-storey block and anticipating employment on the banned 21-storey block disagreed among themselves about the ban. The media gave more generous coverage to those who opposed it, creating the impression there was no support on site for the ban: 'A ban would mean throwing us out of work and we have work here for another two years', was the typical coverage. However, after considerable debate and discussion with executive members, the men on site retained the ban 'with reservations' and, after an agreed three-month review period, again endorsed the ban. With the first tower block completed in mid-1974, the fate of the second one was still uncertain, with a green ban still placed on the second stage of this Hooker project.[77]

In Newcastle, a remarkably short and successful green ban was placed early in 1974, at residents' request, on a projected home-unit development set back on the hill above King Street. The ban, announced by Jim Clark as president of the Northern Area Committee of the NSWBLF, was endorsed by the Newcastle Trades Hall Council. Residents explained the development would obstruct their views and interfere with access to properties of about 25 residents off Church Street, some of whom lived in a row of four cottages more than 100 years old and classified by the National Trust. The green ban prompted a conference, described by Trades Hall Secretary Keith Wilson as 'the first of its kind', between representatives of the MBA, the residents, the NSWBLF, the BWIU, the painters' union and the Trades Hall, which resolved that the builder, architect and owner alter the plans to eliminate the problems to which residents objected. The compromise plan, which lowered the building by 5.5 metres to one floor only and shifted the units' boundary 1.5 metres northward for improved access, was accepted by the residents, who accordingly resolved that the ban should be lifted 'because the developer had acceded to their claims'. To safeguard their future interests, and to ensure the building remained one-storey, the residents drew up a legal document, which the developer agreed to sign.[78]

In Sydney other bans were imposed on high-rise schemes in Mascot and South Sydney and on two- and three-storey home units in Matraville, because local residents maintained the project contravened State Planning Authority specifications for the development of the land in question.[79] Otherwise, as we have seen in the previous chapter, the high-rise battle was waged with particular intensity beyond Sydney during 1974 in areas hitherto open spaces.

SURRY HILLS (AUGUST 1973)

In the inner-city suburb of Surry Hills, locals of this predominantly lower-income residential area were concerned about the demolition of terrace houses, and the conversion of old factories and construction of large buildings for offices or expensive high-rise residential accommodation. They formed the Planning for People campaign to give residents a voice in the planning of their area; to improve amenities, such as parks and playgrounds; to keep out high-rise buildings; control traffic and reduce pollution; and protect the rights of tenants. At a meeting on 14 August 1973 over 200 Surry Hills residents resolved to hold open hearings on developments proposed for Surry Hills and voted for a green ban from the NSWBLF 'to support this idea and prevent development or demolition not acceptable to residents'. In particular, residents wished to prevent all development not in keeping with the principles of the action plan for the area drawn up by the Sydney City Council's town planners, which provided for: the retention of the area as a mixed-income residential one; a stop to the intrusion of commercial interests; and a rezoning of West Surry Hills back to residential. 'The ban was called for', Planning for People explained, 'because the City Council cannot stop demolition of buildings, or people being evicted from their homes'. Such problems, it pointed out, were occurring frequently in Surry Hills, and the residents now wanted to have their voice heard. The union agreed to place the entire area under a green ban so that residents had to agree to any new development before it was allowed to proceed.[80]

One site affected by the green ban became, in the absence of building activity, an adventure playground for the local children, who in an area with few trees especially enjoyed the large climbing tree saved by the ban. Another ban that was part of the invaluable support the union gave the Planning for People campaign occurred in February 1974, when the union refused to demolish a kindergarten in Surry Hills until alternative facilities were found for the mothers and children. This was described colourfully by the *Sunday Mirror*: 'The rough, tough Builders' Laborers Federation this week joined forces with the kindergarten set ... to stop demolition of a Sydney nursery. Their hearts were touched when they heard of the plight of unmarried and deserted mums.' Joe Owens explained the closure of the centre, because it was considered old and inadequate, prior to the opening of an alternative kindergarten, would be a great hardship on many 'working mums' and suggested both the State and Federal governments should step in with financial assistance for the City Council to build a new centre immediately.[81]

NORTH NEWTOWN, NORTHGATE AND OTHERS

In two separate disputes with the Education Department, the union placed one ban on the demolition of a house next to the primary school in Nicholson Street, Balmain in September 1973. In requesting the ban, the Parents and Citizens' Association were acting in support of the school principal's attempt to persuade the department to allocate the house as an after-school-care centre that could also be used for other community purposes. The department was determined to demolish the house to enlarge the school playground area, although parents and staff insisted they were satisfied with the existing space and would prefer the house for after-school-care purposes.[82] The other confrontation with the Education Department occurred over proposals to build a teachers' college in Newtown. Residents who had formed the North Newtown Action Group in March 1973 opposed the proposals on the grounds that the area had a valuable stock of housing suitable for low- and medium-income earners who worked in the city's essential services; the location of the college would add to the centralisation of Sydney's educational institutions and most prospective students lived in outer suburban areas, where land was also cheaper for such a college; Sutherland Council was anxious to have the facility built in the new town area of Menai; and the increased traffic from a complex with 3000 students would clog the already congested surrounding streets. In short the department was deemed to have displayed 'arrogant disregard of the community its plans will disrupt'. In this situation the union placed a ban in April 1974.[83]

In Newcastle, apart from the East End ban discussed above, the union also imposed bans on proposed home units in an historic area known as 'The Boltons' in February 1974, and on a projected eight-storey development between Church and Tyrell streets in July 1974. These were opposed vehemently by local residents. NSWBLF officials met with the developer, who agreed to reduce the height of the building by one storey and to make more open space available at ground level, but this compromise was rejected by the residents and the ban remained.[84]

In July 1974, the union placed a green ban on the proposed Northgate Shopping Complex at Hornsby. Local residents had barely been aware any development was planned and the Hornsby Shire Council had rushed through approval for this massive project, with councillors having insufficient time to read and understand the full implications of the reports. No independent assessment of the reports' conclusions and no shire-wide assessment of traffic implications were obtained by the council. Moreover the plans were only displayed to the public after the council's decision had already been reached, for a total of ten hours, and there were only one copy of each document and no photocopying facilities available. Existing retailers would be severely affected by the competition and the estimated extra 11,000 vehicles a day would strain the local road system, create environmental hazards and increase the cost to ratepayers for road maintenance. Concerned residents therefore fell back on 'the line of last defence', the NSWBLF with its 'ultimate weapon' of the green ban.[85]

Initially the ban and a NSWBLF-organised meeting with the developer forestalled the development by obtaining company agreement to an independent assessment of project impact studies, plus a promise not to start work in the meantime and to encourage the council to display these studies for general perusal. Ultimately the Northgate Shopping Complex was constructed in the late 1970s, any hope of its being halted dashed by federal BLF Intervention against its New South Wales branch. Dave Shaw, one of the rank-and-file builders labourers interviewed for this study, who had been attracted into the industry by the union's commitment to the principle of the social responsibility of labour, was killed while building Northgate on 20 December 1978, due to the less rigid safety standards typical of the post-Intervention period in the New South Wales building industry.[86]

SAVING THE NATIONAL ESTATE

The philistinism of developers and their political supporters was glaringly demonstrated in the plans for The Rocks, Woolloomooloo, Victoria Street and elsewhere, and the union had clearly opposed the lack of aesthetic judgement displayed. However, the bans on those areas were comprehended by the public as the defence of working-class territory. It was the bans placed purely and simply in defence of heritage, where no threat existed to working-class residential areas, that most confounded the prejudices of middle-class Australians. That the 'blue-singleted Builders Laborers Federation'.[1] was campaigning against the destruction of historically significant buildings was considered simply remarkable. Not only did the builders labourers breach accepted standards of industrial behaviour in imposing these bans, they also surprised the middle classes by failing to conform to their notions of working-class priorities and values.

This middle-class sense of the incongruity of these bans is evident in the spate of satiric attacks that greeted the union's announcement that it would not demolish National Trust classified buildings. A Molnar cartoon showed a beefy builders labourer saying 'All out! I don't like the cornice'; and Emeric depicted a similarly muscly builders labourer reading a book entitled, 'Do it Yourself, Restoration of Historic Buildings'.[2] Despite the distinctly classist nature of this raillery, it was received with good humour by the builders labourers, who accepted their position as protector of the nation's heritage, bizarre though this seemed to the public.

It was not a circumstance of the builders labourers' own choosing, but one thrust upon them by the boom-induced consequences of the cultural barbarism of the Australian ruling elites. A Melbourne correspondent to the

Age, in deploring the replacement of Collins Street's gracious old buildings with 'massive, ugly and soulless barracks which could only be conceived in the loveless greed of a society dedicated solely to the pursuit of money making to the exclusion of all aspects of beauty', made the serious point in defence of the NSWBLF that, while it could be argued that unions should not decide which buildings should or should not be erected, it was equally true that the issue should not fall within the prerogative of the company concerned either.[3]

Yet that was precisely what was happening: although companies had ownership merely of certain pieces of land and the buildings erected thereon, these constructions affected entire neigh bourhoods, and so these companies' aesthetic standards – informed by the profit motive – were inflicted upon whole communities. Considering the extent to which the green ban movement represented in part a struggle against philistinism, it appeared that Australia in the 1970s was not suffering the often-feared scourge of a convict proletariat, but rather the affliction of a convict bourgeoisie, which revealed itself as not only corrupt but devoid of either the conservative traditionalism of the British establishment or the more enlightened and philanthropic predilections of the American ruling class.

BUILDINGS OF HISTORICAL AND ARCHITECTURAL SIGNIFICANCE

Aware of the execrable taste and deplorable judgement of those with money and power, the National Trust and the Institute of Architects were concerned by the threat to heritage posed by the development boom. Impressed by the union's decision to ban demolition of The Rocks, Don Meisenhelter of the Environment Committee of the New South Wales Chapter of the Institute of Architects approached Mundey in November 1971 with a suggestion that architects, the National Trust and the building unions combine to save historically or architecturally significant buildings. Mundey said his union agreed with the principle, but added: 'I hope there aren't too many-our blokes still have to eat'. Meisenhelter felt there was no alternative but to turn to the unions: 'Anyone who owns a building is free to knock it down when and how they choose. A council can refuse a permit to build but not to demolish.' Given the bias of local councils towards developers' interests, an amendment to the *Local Government Act* was urgently needed: 'At the moment the National Trust has the means of determining which buildings should be saved, but we cannot determine which buildings will be saved.

"All out! I don't like the cornice."

Cartoonist George Molnar expressed public bewilderment at
builders labourers becoming the principal defenders of cultural heritage.
(Courtesy George Molnar and *Sydney Morning Herald*)

Until that power exists, the only way to stop demolition is for the builders
to refuse to destroy.'[4]

That the architectural profession had become concerned about development in Sydney is indicated by the invitation to Mundey to be guest speaker
at a seminar co-sponsored by the New South Wales Chapter of the institute
and the University of Sydney School of Architecture in February 1972. The
Dean of Architecture, Professor RN Johnson, spoke of proposals being considered by the institute to take disciplinary action against architects who
accepted commissions involving the destruction of historically or architecturally valuable buildings. 'There is a very strong move within the profession
to take greater account of the community's interest.'[5]

After meeting with Meisenhelter, Mundey wrote to the BTG on 8
December 1971 informing the other building unions of the architects'
approach and the NSWBLF decision to support the National Trust, because
of 'the ruthless manner in which developers have demolished many of these
historic buildings'. He urged the other unions in the group to join in the

protection of heritage, and anticipated the response:

> With growing unemployment, it could be argued that in placing bans on these
> buildings we are preventing our own members from working; our answer to
> that is that we believe there should be diversion of public money to that sector,
> such as hospitals, schools and high quality low price flats, units and houses.

The NSWBLF announced on 19 January 1972 that it would refuse to
demolish all buildings 'which the National Trust of Australia recommends
for preservation'. Mundey said that the NSWBLF had been given a Trust
list of about 1700 New South Wales buildings. 'Anyone with a conscience
has to speak up – the building industry has gone mad ... We have every
right to speak up to make ours a better industry – we don't want the next
generation to condemn us for slapping up the slums of tomorrow.' National
Trust director RN Walker referred to the bans as allowing 'a breathing space
for projects to be publicised'; in the meantime, the Trust was 'pursuing every
avenue available to it to secure the enactment of adequate legislation to protect historic buildings'.[6]

Peter Keys, a federal councillor of the Institute of Architects, wrote in late
1972 that every building of historic importance in Australia was in danger
of being demolished. He again cited the problem that governments had no
statutory power to prevent demolitions. But the crucial problem in New
South Wales was the strong suspicion that, even if the government had such
a right, it would be unlikely to exercise it against developers' interests. The
National Trust argued in its annual report in October 1972 that there was an
urgent need for the State Government to pass legislation to preserve historic
buildings, backed by funds to compensate owners for losses incurred in decisions based on consideration of national interest. 'The NSW Government,'
it noted, 'appears content to be a bystander. The vacuum created by this
stalemate has resulted in direct action by industrial unions, which thwart the
proposals of the developers by with holding labour from demolition work.
This is no way for a State to go about conserving its heritage.'[7]

Mundey commented in January 1973 that if governments enacted laws
so owners of historic buildings could be compensated and these buildings
retained for posterity, 'it will not be necessary for the Builders Labourers'
Federation to be the conscience of Sydney, and we can join those civilised
countries which do appreciate their rustory and the need for retention of
some of the best of our past'. In the meantime, and in the absence of such
legislation, 'our union will continue to ... give teeth to the National Trust's

list of buildings worthy of preservation, by our refusal to demolish such buildings'. The Trust insisted it had never sought the support of Mundey or his union, but acknowledged that 'many significant and much-loved buildings' would not still be standing if builders labourers had not withdrawn their labour from demolition work. 'The trust does not consider that this is the way historic buildings should be preserved, but absence of existing legislation has created a vacuum into which Mr Mundey has stepped.'[8]

PITT STREET CONGREGATIONAL CHURCH (FEBRUARY 1972)

Following closely upon the union's bans on the 1700 'classified' buildings, it placed a specific ban on the Pitt Street Congregational Church in February 1972, which the Trust had deemed 'a highly significant building' and strongly recommended its preservation. The church authorities intended to demolish the church, considered 'no longer functional in relation to contemporary church worship and programs', and redevelop the site as a public plaza: with a church centre, chapel, theatre and restaurant, and with church offices located underneath and a 20-storey office block backing the plaza, which would provide the 'financial sinews necessary for the church to minister to the people of Sydney'. The Reverend John Bryant insisted the redevelopment was essential to finance the mission of the church and the delay caused by the ban had 'seriously impoverished' the church; the Congregational Union of New South Wales had met every requirement of the City Council and the Height of Buildings Committee, and had the approval of the Minister for Public Works. 'The democratic processes have been followed. We should now be left unimpeded to implement the plans agreed upon in the duly constituted councils of the Church.'[9] Clearly the numbers were in favour of serving both God and Mammon.

Pete Thomas summed up the church's attitude: 'Demolition, redevelopment, money, for sacred purpose'. Opposing this attitude was communist Jack Mundey. 'Nothing personal, you understand,' a Molnar cartoon depicted him saying to Bryant, 'actually I'm an atheist'. In justifying the attempt to save the church, Mundey insisted the NSWBLF intended to have a voice in what buildings could be destroyed to make way for office blocks and the like; the National Trust could rest assured that the Pitt Street Church would not be demolished by builders labourers:

> If architects, engineers and building workers combine to preserve a little of
> our history, people in the future will be grateful for our belated action. In the

building industry, we will strive to continue to make our presence felt, not only in our members' interests but in the interest of the general public as well.

Bryant wrote to Bob Hawke (the son of a Congregational minister), declaring he was not unsympathetic to the working class, but maintaining it was ridiculous that the church should be impeded by representatives of the people 'we are seeking to serve more effectively' and appealing to the ACTU 'to be understanding of our position and to advise us in the dilemma in which we find ourselves following the action of Mr Mundey'.[10]

The dilemma was of the church's own making, and by implication prompted by sectarianism, according to Professor Freeland of the University of New South Wales Architecture Department. He revealed that nine months previously the State Planning Authority had proposed to the owners of the Congregational Church and adjacent sites an integrated redevelopment of the area that would leave the church intact but nonetheless provide it with the 'financial sinews' as strong as, if not stronger than, those afforded in the church's intended plan:

> The proposal depended on the co-operation of the property-owners involved, which included the Catholic Church and the Free Presbyterian Church.
> Mr Bryant and/or his congregation refused to participate for reasons which, in the absence of any public statement, can only be surmised.[11]

The church was preserved, while discussions continued for an alternative redevelopment scheme negotiated with the church and an adjoining land-owner by the State Planning Authority. Professional groups advised the Congregational Union that the site could be redeveloped without demolition of the church building. But Bryant was a sore loser: two years later he wrote to the *Sydney Morning Herald* regretting the return to the old church building for worship on the occasion of the Church's 141st anniversary on 2 June 1974: 'Momentarily the armchair conservationists and the atheistically and communistically led Builders Labourers' Federation have won the battle'. Against those concerned to save Sydney's historic buildings, he declaimed: 'Sydney! Who is Sydney – the National Trust, the Institute of Architects, the communists, tile Jack Mundeys or Jack (sic) Owenses, the Builders Labourers' Federation?' Saved from demolition by 'the communists', the church was subsequently protected by a Permanent Conservation Order from the New South Wales Heritage Council and listed in the Register of the National Estate by the Australian Heritage Commission.[12]

BANK AND INSURANCE BUILDINGS IN MARTIN PLACE (JULY 1972)

The three grand old bank and insurance buildings still standing on Martin Place – the ANZ Bank, the National Mutual Building and the Colonial Mutual Building – were all protected from demolition by a ban in July 1972. The National Mutual Building, built in 1892, was an especially fine example of late Victorian commercial building.

In August 1973 an acceptable alternative solution was reached in the case of the Colonial Mutual Building. Colonial Mutual had intended complete demolition, having obtained permission to erect a new building on the site because the old interior was no longer functional. However, because of the ban, an alternative plan for the building was developed in consultation with the National Trust, the City Council and the Government Architect: the building was retained with its interior renovated but its facade untouched, with some new floors above the original cornice stepped back under a mansard roof so they would not be visible from most of Martin Place. The National Trust regarded the plan as a prototype for dealing with similar problems in future. Professor Freeland, chairman of the Trust's Historic Buildings Committee, pointed out: 'If people get on to something early enough, it is quite possible to find a solution that does justice to both preservation and progress'.[13]

BUSTLE COTTAGE, WOLLONGONG (NOVEMBER 1972)

The South Coast branch of the NSWBLF firmly supported the union's environmental stance. When Wollongong City Council decided, in the words of branch organiser Don Forskitt, to 'turn its back on Wollongong's history', he announced the South Coast branch would have nothing to do with the destruction of Bustle Cottage. This cottage had been built in 1882 and was one of the ten buildings in Wollongong classified by the National Trust, but it was threatened by a Sydney company anxious to build a high-rise development on the cottage's half-hectare site at Smith's Hill. The company had the support of the eight ALP councillors, but the seven independent councillors voted in favour of acquiring the property to save it from destruction. Members of this group wished to see it turned into an arts and crafts centre. Speaking for the majority ALP eight, the Lord Mayor claimed (wrongly) that Bustle Cottage was only 70 years old and could only be 'a liability' to the council: 'I won't be enticed and council certainly won't be enticed to save the building'. However, the South Coast unions, to which many of the ALP councillors belonged, supported the ban. As secretary of the South Coast Labor Council, Merv Nixon said his body was not in favour of destroying historic buildings.

Illawarra Historical Society chairman, Mr J Maynes, also considered the City Council's decision 'regrettable' and indicated the society now feared for the future of other historic buildings in the area, such as Cormiston. Since the society was not in a financial position to buy Bustle Cottage but wished to do all it could to prevent demolition, it was 'interested in the stand taken by the Builders Laborers' Federation'.[14]

Although Bustle Cottage was permanently preserved, fears for Cormiston were well placed. The union was unable to save this 130-year-old historic homestead in Smith Street, because the owner, and his wife and children, proceeded to carry out the demolition themselves. The Student Representative Council of Wollongong University College had been agitating for some time to have the homestead, with its National Trust 'C' classification, saved from demolition by a development company. (The C classification means 'Of considerable interest: their preservation should be encouraged'.) Despite demonstrations outside the Wollongong Council meeting, the council gave its approval for the developer to build high-rise units on the site. Having exhausted all other channels, the students had sought the union's help, which in keeping with its policy of protecting classified buildings had banned its demolition. The South Coast Labor Council also banned the project. However the Wollongong businessman, who had bought the old house for $36,000 then sold it to a developer, proceeded to remove the roof and ceilings assisted by his family, because the contract stipulated the homestead be demolished first. He was unrepentant about defying the ban: 'When Westwind Holdings offered $170,000 for the land it was like winning the lottery'.[15]

HELEN KELLER HOSTEL (MARCH 1973)
Demolition of the Helen Keller Hostel for Blind Women in Waimea Avenue, Woollahra, was halted shortly after demolition commenced on 12 March 1973 when Joe Owens, alerted by an urgent phone call, hastily arrived on the site. The National Trust had awarded the hostel, as one of a group of buildings in the street, a 'C' classification and was in the process of considering the group for a 'B' classification ('highly significant, preservation strongly recommended'). A strong local protest meeting, arranged by the Queen Street and West Woollahra Association and attended by Owens on behalf of the union, had opposed destruction of the building. The developer's tin sheds were painted with the slogan 'SHAME. IS THIS PROGRESS?' The Royal Blind Society, which had used the hostel since 1949 to house 'the normal blind working woman', explained blind people had recently gained greater independence

and did not wish to be segregated in a hostel, and 'there was urgent need for the society to make use of its assets to the best advantage'.

With the ban remaining in force, the National Trust and the local association were able to commence negotiations with the Royal Blind Society, fortified by a telegram sent to the president of the association, Leo Schofield, from Federal Urban Development Minister Tom Uren and Environment Minister Moss Cass: 'Support efforts to preserve historic houses in Waimea Avenue including Helen Keller Hostel. Wish to advise Government pressing ahead with national estate fund to assist the preservation of Australia's historic houses. Please keep us informed of development.' In the meantime builders labourers tied tarpaulins over that part of the roof of the hostel the developers had already demolished. That was as far as action was necessary, for the society reversed its decision to knock down the building. As the union journal boasted: 'Swift action by the NSW builders' labourers once again saved an historic building in one of Sydney's inner suburbs from being destroyed'.[16]

DR BUSBY'S COTTAGE AND THE ROYAL AUSTRALASIAN COLLEGE OF PHYSICIANS (DECEMBER 1 973)

A 'temporary green ban' was placed on the destruction of the oldest house in Bathurst, 240 kilometres west of Sydney, on 20 December 1973. The 1836 single-storey wooden cottage in Howick Street had been erected for the then Government Medical Officer in the district, Dr George Busby. The Sydney-based company Marayong Developments had bought the home from two elderly sisters, Myrtle and Mable Kessey, still living in the cottage. Marayong planned to construct a four-storey office block with a basement carpark on the site. The ban was placed in response to opposition to this on the part of the National Trust, Department of Urban and Regional Development, Bathurst City Council, the Bathurst Historical Society and the Bathurst Action Committee to Secure Unified Planning.[17]

Back in Sydney, an 1848 building at 145 Macquarie Street, used since 1938 as the headquarters of the Royal Australasian College of Physicians, was rescued from demolition shortly before Christmas. The Sydney City Council was considering demolition of the building, almost the last of the distinguished Georgian terraces of that period, to make way for a 17-storey office block. Mundey announced on 22 December that the union, having consulted the National Trust, would ban any demolition work. The Trust then classified the building. It was subsequently extended very carefully, retaining the former elegance of the facade.[18]

To discuss the future of Dr Busby's Cottage, the NSWBLF organised a meeting in Sydney on 7 January 1974, attended by the company, the National Trust and the union, which decided to make a joint inspection on 10 January. This inspection was attended by the co-directors of the development company, the town clerk, the health surveyor, representatives of the National Trust, the convenor of the Historical Buildings Committee of Bathurst Historical Society, the secretary of the Bathurst Action Committee to Secure Unified Planning, an expert in restoration, a consulting engineer, and Joe Owens as secretary of the NSWBLF. The developers indicated they were prepared to resell the cottage without profit to the National Trust or the Federal Government, if they desired to preserve it.[19]

Following this inspection, the National Trust re-classified the cottage downwards, placing it on the 'recorded' rather than the 'classified' list, because much of the original joinery was missing. Owens agreed the building's structure was 'too far gone' to be worth saving. The Trust announced it was not able to continue an active campaign to protect a recorded but not classified building, and it formally notified the union of the reclassification. On 30 January the union considered the matter and decided to lift the ban in line with the National Trust's change of mind.[20]

Although Dr Busby's Cottage was beyond repair, an 1850s cottage in the same street benefited from the improved protection for historical buildings in the wake of the green bans. In 1981 it was fully restored by the National Trust under a scheme it established in 1974, aided initially by a Whitlam Government National Estate Programme grant, whereby a house is bought, restored and sold with the long-term protection of a covenant and a permanent conservation order under the New South Wales *Heritage Act*, the proceeds from each sale being put into a revolving fund for further purchases and restorations.[21]

CATHOLIC CHURCH PRESBYTERY (MAY 1974)

A last-minute reprieve was effected by the union on 22 May 1974 after demolition had already started on the roof of an uninhabited Edwardian mansion in Moore Park Road. This former Catholic Church Presbytery had been allowed to fall into disrepair – with white ants and dry rot affecting the back, and vandals having damaged it – prompting the local council's health department to ask the church to ensure the building was no longer a health hazard. The church responded by attempting to have it demolished. However because it was listed by Sydney City Council's preservation committee and considered 'well worth preserving' by the Centennial Park Resident

Action Group, the six builders labourers who commenced work on the site were called off by the union because the mansion was 'of historic interest'.[22]

BUILDINGS OF CULTURAL AND ARCHITECTURAL SIGNIFIC ANCE

A feature of the bans placed during 1972 was their expansion to include the 'cultural bans' placed on the Theatre Royal, Regent Theatre and the Newcastle Hotel. In 1974 there were bans placed on the State Theatre, and the Capitol Theatre in Inverell. The union's interest in the arts pre-dated these bans, especially in bringing cultural activities of political significance to the membership. In November 1971 the union sponsored a performance of ex-prisoner Jim McNeil's play 'The Chocolate Frog', based on life in Parramatta Gaol, for workers at the Opera House during their lunch-hour. The experiment was successful and received much media publicity, not simply because it was staged at the uncompleted Opera House but because manual workers were not supposed to be cultured. Commentators, with barely suppressed surprise, noted that the play was enthusiastically applauded by an audience of more than five hundred construction workers.[23]

THEATRE ROYAL (MAY 1972)

Along with FEDFA, the NSWBLF banned demolition work on the Theatre Royal in response to entreaties from Actors Equity and the Save Sydney's Theatre Royal Committee. The ban enabled the committee to enter private talks with the developer, GJ Dusseldorp of the Lend Lease Corporation, whose venture was backed by the MLC insurance giant. The issues were also debated publicly. At a meeting at Circular Quay, the committee's star-studded cast – Robin Lovejoy (director of the Old Tote Theatre), Tony Robinson (director English Prospect Theatre), Alderman Leo Port of the City Council, Peter Coleman MLA, Neville Wran (Leader of the Labor Opposition in the Legislative Council) – argued the case for preservation in front of Dusseldorp, who criticised the union for placing the ban after he had already made his investment decision. Mundey intervened at the meeting and was applauded for his insistence that Australians had a right to decide which buildings should be retained and which destroyed: 'They had seen too many buildings, declared by the National Trust to be worth preserving, fall to the jack hammer. If industrial action hadn't been taken to save the Pitt Street Congregational Church, it too would have gone.'[24]

Ultimately the developer modified his plans to incorporate in his

$70 million development project a new 1000-seat theatre, to be called the Theatre Royal and incorporating contents from the present one thought worthy of preservation, on an adjacent site. At a meeting of more than a thousand people at the Lower Town Hall, the committee agreement to this compromise plan was given a vote of approval, though a large minority wished to continue the battle to preserve the old theatre intact. Given the majority vote, Mundey applauded the compromise, saying it came as a result of concessions from both sides.[25]

REGENT THEATRE (OCTOBER 1972)

On 30 October 1972, less than a day before JC Williamson Theatres Ltd auctioned its Regent Theatre in George Street, the union placed a ban on any future demolition of the theatre at the request of Actors Equity and the Save the Regent Theatre Committee. Hal Lashwood, convenor of the committee and president of Actors Equity, informed the press: 'There must not be any further depletion of Sydney theatres'. If removal of the Regent, which dated from 1928, could not be prevented, the committee hoped to secure a replacement theatre, in much the same way that the ban on the Theatre Royal had achieved. 'We are extremely grateful for the demolition ban placed on the Regent by the Builders Laborers Federation. Without their support in the past we would not now be getting a new Theatre Royal.' Mundey explained the union was demanding the theatre be retained to reverse Sydney's rapidly dwindling cultural facilities; if the Regent could not be preserved a theatre of comparable proportions must be built on the site.[26]

Passed in at a mere $4,550,000 – well below the reserve price – the indifferent bidding was inevitably blamed on the union ban. Having been criticised for placing the ban on the Theatre Royal after its purchase, it was now lambasted for affecting the auction of the Regent because it was 'giving the: developers fair warning'. The director of the company in charge of the auction said he had few doubts as to the cause of the auction's failure: 'I'm darned certain Mr Mundey's threat affected it. He doesn't run the country yet, but he's got the big developers worried.' Other sections of the community were delighted. On 3 November Actors Equity gave '100 per cent support' to the union's campaign to save the Regent Theatre from demolition. It declared all major entertainment industry unions wanted the theatre saved, including the Musicians Union of Australia, the Theatrical and Amusement Employees Association and the Australian Writers' Guild, and admitted it had been these unions that had suggested the builders labourers be requested to ban the demolition.[27]

Fearing continuing destruction of theatres, the Save the Regent Theatre Committee merged with the Save the Theatre Royal Committee on
6 November to form a new all-purpose Save Sydney's Theatres Committee, which included Neville Wran. Although Wran wrote to Hal Lashwood
expressing reluctance to associate himself with Mundey, Lashwood's first
engagement as president of the new committee was to attend a NSWBLF
meeting 'to thank the union for its support'. JC Williamson continued to
insist the Regent had been built as a cinema, was no longer suitable for live
theatrical performances, and could not be upgraded for less than the cost of
a new theatre. The unions representing the actors and musicians who performed there maintained this argument was 'absolute nonsense': the theatre
had been granted a licence for live performances from 1932 onwards, advice
had indicated $300,000 was ample for suitable ren ovations and Williamson'
s had recently bought land at the back of the theatre for extensions to the
backstage facilities. Moreover, as press reports conceded, because of Sydney's
shortage of live theatres the Regent's facilities had been much in demand.
Among the 122 actors and musicians who publicly indicated their support
for saving the Regent were the cast of 'Jesus Christ Superstar' and musicians
from the Elizabethan Theatre Trust.[28]

A few months later, the *Australian Financial Review* announced that,
while institutional bidders for the Regent Theatre had shied away because
of the demolition ban placed on the site, a carpet manufacturer had taken a
calculated gamble on buying the building in a private, unpublicised sale. The
chairman of JC Williamson commented: 'We feel very lucky that we have
found a buyer … All of our probable buyers – mostly life insurance companies – didn't want to have anything to do with us once the demolition ban
was imposed.' However, in a remarkable deal the buyer was allowed three
months after the exchange of contracts before paying a deposit, during which
time it hoped 'the emotional outburst by the actors and the stand taken by
Mr Jack Mundey, secretary of the Builders Labourers' Federation will have
been lost in the mists of time, allowing the site to be used as a possible office
tower development'. Actors Equity and the Save Sydney's Theatres Committee reaffirmed their commitment to save the theatre in its present form or
have it rebuilt as a live performance theatre. The union ban remained in force
long enough to frustrate all demolition plans.[29]

In 1981 the Minister for Planning and Environment approved a permanent conservation order on the Regent Theatre, on the recommendation of
the New South Wales Heritage Council, which ensured the preservation of

its facade, entrance vestibule, upper foyer and grand stairway. The theatre's owners said it would remain as an entertainment and concert venue.[30]

NEWCASTLE HOTEL, GEORGE STREET (OCTOBER 1972)

The Newcastle Hotel on the lower end of George Street, with its verandah front and stone-carved rear and otherwise destined to become part of The Rocks redevelopment scheme, had an 'amber ban' placed on it, because it was 'part of Sydney's culture', and 'a well-known workers' pub where struggling artists traditionally sell their works, without fee'.[31] The impending ban was announced during a premature farewell party on 7 October 1972. Arriving at 5.30 pm, Mundey delivered a speech from the bar, the opening line of which, according to the *Bulletin*, was shouted with unconscious irony: 'This pub is a symbol of what all thinking Australians are concerned about. Builders labourers are not going to say "Thank you" to the boss and build what we are told. We will preserve the best of Sydney and we will decide which buildings will be put up and which pulled down.'[32]

As the builders labourers gathered at the Lower Town Hall for a stop-work meeting on 16 October to consider both a new two-year industrial agreement and the ban on the Newcastle, Mundey claimed that if present tendencies continued Sydney would have no hotels 'for the working class'; instead there would be a profusion of 'expensive taverns where people would have to pay 30c for a middy of beer'. Opposing its intended replacement by a Hyatt hotel block owned by a US company, Mundey insisted 'the Newcastle must stay'. The stop-work meeting agreed with the executive's recommendation that the Newcastle should remain 'as a workers' and artists' hotel'. It voted 2000 to 4 to ban demolition, a day before it was scheduled for closure to make way for yet another multi-storey giant.

> *What's happened to the pub, our little local pub*
> *Where we used to have a drink when we were dry, boys.*
> *Now we can't get in the door for there's carpets on the floor*
> *And you won't be served a beer without a tie, boys.*

Recalling some of the other traditional pubs that had gone – Pfahlert's, The Tudor, Durban Club, The Old Assembly, The Phillip, The Royal, the Balfour – Pringle explained that the Newcastle, 'a favourite watering hole' a stone's throw from Circular Quay, was one of the few left in the city with character and was 'a meeting place for labourers, seamen, wharfies, artists, journalists, airline pilots and other diverse groups'. (The meeting also accepted the two-year agreement giving pay rises from $6.78 to $8.56 a week from November, with a further rise of about $2 week in November 1973.)[33]

Heartened by the ban, the licensee applied for an extension of his licence (due to expire the following week) and patrons of the hotel arranged a protest meeting to support the ban. 'They've saved the day for us so far', the hotel manager commented approvingly of the builders labourers. Reminiscing affectionately about his own experiences of drinking at the Newcastle, Ron Saw of the *Daily Mirror* insisted the Newcastle, which was 'appallingly noisy, cramped, uncomfortable, smelly, hot, cold, ugly and absolutely marvellous', must never become some huge, American-owned hotel restaurant. 'They're trying to give us a complex where once we had the Newcastle and happiness and life and living; and only the Builders' Labourers are trying to stop them ... God bless them for their effrontery.' If a 'well-designed and tidy and super-efficient and sterile' American-influenced pub replaced it, he would not visit. 'Without discomfort and romance and noise and struggle and a touch of lust and a lot of love, who the hell wants a drink anyway.'[34]

Internationally known as a bohemian meeting place, the Newcastle had long been holding exhibitions of artists' work and was a popular meeting place for the Push, whose gatherings there are recounted by Frank Moorehouse in *Days of Wine and Rage*. 'Long before women's lib was ever heard of,' the *Daily Mirror* noted of the Newcastle, 'women mixed freely with men in all bars'. The Newcastle had become famous for its paintings, including nudes, which adorned the walls in every bar. 'Leading figures in art, literary and academic circles rubbed shoulders with wharfies, seamen, builders laborers, office workers and business executives at the Newcastle's bars ... To be seen at the Newcastle was "in".' The *Sun* conceded the 'well-known pub' was a 'colourful haunt of workmen, artists, students and intellectuals'. But the *Sun*'s sceptical columnist, Robin Ingram, did not feel Sydney's historic places quite compared with Britain's big tourist-pleasers: 'with a little help from the Builders Labourers' ban on the demolition of Jim Buckley's Newcastle Hotel, we'll be able to post "Wharfies Drank Here" plaques instead of "Shakespeare Slept Here"'. The *Mirror* cartoonist Rigby depicted a pub full of beer-gutted, beer-swilling plebeians resolving: 'The ayes have it, brothers. When the beer runs out here we preserve the next pub down the road!'[35]

And that is more or less what the builders labourers decided to do, concerned as they were at the death toll of Sydney's hotels – 48 in the inner city since 1945. 'Instead of a cosy pub they have been transformed into monolithic office blocks owned by insurance companies, banks and developers.' On 4 November the union announced a general ban on the demolition of all workers' hotels in the inner-city area if residents and regulars wanted the hotel preserved. It was estimated this stand could cost developers more than $500 million, considering the number of development projects on the Sydney City Council's register that involved hotel sites. Mundey explained the union had received petitions from hotel customers and residents about such developments. 'People don't want to lose their local, and the local is part of Sydney's history. The union does not want Sydney to become a concrete canyon-and a dry one, at that.' Also especially offensive, Mundey added, was the way in which many hotels were up-priced when updated. 'If a hotel is modernised, the hotelier seems to regard it as a legitimate excuse to slap on higher prices. A saloon bar middy could be 19 cents before the development. Then it shoots up to 25 cents and in one case we know of, 30 cents.'[36]

In the meantime, the fate of the Newcastle was being decided. Late in October Jim Buckley's licence came up for renewal and was contested in the Licensing Court by the SCRA, threatening to make the Newcastle a pub with no beer. The licence was instead transferred to the SCRA which claimed the demolition of the hotel was important to Sydney's progress, but denied there was any plan to build a huge international hotel on the site. Rather there would be an office block that would contain a Newcastle Tavern, retaining some of the old hotel's features. SCRA director Colonel Magee insisted there would be more hotels in The Rocks area when the scheme was completed than presently. After two hours legal argument in the Equity Court in January 1973, fought over Jim Buckley's attempt to have the judgement against him overturned, Buckley and the SCRA settled their differences in an out-of-court conference. The Newcastle Hotel ceased functioning as a pub in May 1973, but the building remained. The Push reconvened its drinking in the Criterion – a builders labourers' pub – and the cross-fertilisation of ideas between libertarians and unionists became, as Anne Coombs argues, an important element in the Victoria Street campaign.[37]

STATE THEATRE (JUNE 1974)
The union's significant role in protecting the grand old theatres of Sydney was acknowledged during the Sydney Film Festival in June 1974, held at the 2584-capacity State Theatre which celebrated its 45th anniversary on 7 June. With attention focussed on this theatre, which according to the president of the festival was regarded as one of the most beautiful cinemas in the

world, the NSWBLF announced a ban on its destruction. The owner, Greater Union Theatres, immediately assured the union it had no plans to demolish the theatre. It admitted, however, that it was concerned by the fact that it was paying more than $3000 a week in rates and land taxes. Emerging as a spokesperson for the arts, even for cultural proprietors in difficulties, Mundey expressed his concern about such prohibitive charges and requested Tom Uren to arrange a conference between the Federal Government, the New South Wales Government, the Sydney City Council and the owner of the theatre about its future. The magnificent State Theatre was saved for posterity.[38]

CAPITOL THEATRE, INVERELL (JULY 1974)

The union's battle to save the 47-year-old Capitol Theatre in Byron Street, Inverell, was fraught with unusual difficulties. This was due to a degree of support for its demolition from local residents, and the intervention of local council employees backed by the Municipal Officers' Association and the Electrical Trades Union, who announced they would not reconnect electricity to the building because retention of the theatre would be 'a financial burden'. Coles had bought the site – indicating it wanted 'the dirt and not the theatre' – to erect a supermarket. With local councillors enthusiastic about welcoming Coles' investment to Inverell and warning residents about increased rates if the theatre were retained, a public meeting in Inverell on 16 July had decided, against the wishes of an earlier public meeting that had resolved to save the theatre, that Coles should be 'allowed to proceed with whatever development it desired on its Byron Street site' and asked the council not to involve ratepayers in any financial obligations in connection with the Capitol Theatre. It also decided to ask the National Trust and the NSWBLF to withdraw their interest in the project. The decision of the meeting was approved by an unholy alliance of the Inverell Municipal Council, the local chamber of commerce and the Inverell branch of the ALP.[39]

The union had been one of the four parties to a meeting held the previous week to discuss the fate of the building; the others were Coles, the National Trust, and the Inverell Capitol Redevelopment Committee – the local group anxious to preserve the building. With only days left before Coles planned to commence demolition, the meeting had nonetheless agreed that no attempt would be made to demolish the theatre until the National Trust had time to consider classification, or until discussions regarding the future of the theatre had taken place with the Federal Government which had sent Department of Urban and Regional Development representatives to Inverell to inspect the building. This was not yet a 'green ban', for the union explained it had to be guided by the National Trust, but the effect of the union's 'interest' was similar. Coles' state manager conceded: 'Now that the National Trust and the Builders Labourers' Federation are showing interest in the preservation of the theatre the future development of a supermarket in Inverell must depend on the decision they reach'.[40]

When the National Trust decided the building was worthy of its highest classification, the NSWBLF instantly placed a ban on its demolition. As Mundey explained in an interview on 26 July at nearby Armidale airport, a national meeting of builders labourers in 1973 had decided any building classified by the Trust would have an 'automatic green ban' and the union was committed to that resolution. 'The builders laborers will not be part of the destruction of Australia's national heritage.' The argument that the building was not functional was a matter for the State or Federal Government to consider by way of subsidy, he insisted.

> The theatre must be retained for posterity. There should be more cultural facilities in country areas. We should use our creativity to retain the use of the theatre instead of its destruction simply to make way for a supermarket. Surely Coles is not short of land at Inverell on which to build a supermarket. Other unions should take a more far-seeing view. The Capitol theatre at Inverell will not be demolished by any member of the Builders Labourers' Federation. Any employer or client who attempts to go against the green ban is likely to have possible action taken against them anywhere in Australia. If the ban is ignored retaliatory action of stopping work on all Coles projects will certainly be considered.

Unions with 'a social conscience' had been obliged to act and over one hundred buildings in provincial towns were still standing because of green bans.[41]

However, in the face of continued local support for demolition the union agreed it would review its ban if a decision 'honestly' made at a further public meeting, convened by an independent person and with representatives from the National Trust, the union and Coles, favoured demolition. Pringle announced to the press that people attending such a meeting could either make 'a selfish decision' or 'one for the nation and the future', and suggested implicitly that the moral lead of the builders labourers, who were denying themselves employment over the matter, should guide the citizens of lnverell. 'If it is good enough for lowly builders labourers to make a decision in the interest of the overall society which has a negative effect on their personal interest, then every individual person attending the meeting we propose at Inverell should do some soul searching.' He asked the people of Inverell to ask themselves whether or not the environment was as important as profit. He also indicated that, during a meeting with Coles and the National Trust, Coles' state manager had not dismissed the possibility of an alternative site for the supermarket.[42]

Meanwhile the issue continued to rage at local level, with the community sharply divided and abusing each other through the columns of the local paper. Worse, Dr Philippa Whish, one of the campaigners on behalf of the Capitol, recalls being 'nearly run out of town'. Some supporters of the Coles development admitted they would favour retention of the Capitol if the Federal Government offered financial assistance. The Inverell Municipal Council wrote to the National Trust asking it to reconsider its decision to classify the theatre, while the Capitol Redevelopment Committee made a submission to the Department of Urban and Regional Development and commissioned three specialist advisers from the nearby University of New England (AT Yarwood, GB Pittendrigh and B Davis) to prepare a report on the building, which described the theatre as 'an excellent theatre – the sight-lines, acoustic and spatial qualities of the auditorium appear to be so good as to make it one of the best auditoria in rural NSW', and praised its 'excellent contribution to the visual quality of the town centre'. They added that, with due respect to Coles, it had nowhere demonstrated 'any ability to bring into being buildings which make equivalent contributions to their setting'. The report then suggested many ways in which this 'fine, important and irreplaceable artifact' could be adapted to become a 'multi-purpose facility' that would prove 'a valuable community asset'. Like the NSWBLF it expressed the view that Coles should simply build its supermarket elsewhere in town.[43]

A few days later the National Trust's report on the theatre was released, which deemed the interior 'an outstanding example of 1920s interior design, completely unspoilt ... in the delicate neoclassical style' with 'most gracefully curved proscenium arches' and the exterior had 'considerable townscape value' as 'a remarkably handsome beginning to the town'. All in all it was 'a fine symbol of urbanity and civilisation'. The Trust also recommended that Coles give up the building in exchange for a similar area in the less attractive part of town. This report notwithstanding, the MBA's industrial officer John Elder, offered free public advice: 'The best suggestion I could give to GJ Coles would be to engage a demolisher, tell the builders labourers to go to blazes and commence work on demolishing the buildings'. He intimated ban-breaking labour could be found in Inverell, due to rising unemployment and decline of building projects: 'it would be understandable for builders labourers who live in Inverell to question the right of their union to engage in enterprises which will deprive them of work'. He hoped Inverell would not be subjected to 'intimidation, sabotage and mob violence by "the unfortunate decision of some people who invited this union to involve itself in the affairs of the Inverell community"'. It was 'a very dangerous situation' when a union started 'dictating terms to the people of Inverell'.[44]

On the recommendation of the Department of Urban and Regional Development, the Federal Government offered the Inverell Council $250,000 to restore the theatre on condition that the council maintain it in perpetuity. Those who had campaigned to save the theatre were unaware of this offer, which was quietly rejected by the council. With the NSWBLF no longer functioning and no longer able to protect the building, the theatre was demolished on 20 August 1975 and the Coles supermarket was erected on the site. No sooner had it been knocked down, Philippa Whish recalls, than townsfolk regretted its disappearance, wishing money had been available to save the building and unaware such Whitlam Government largesse had been offered, for there was nowhere to stage local productions and events, since the Town Hall acoustics were 'frightful'. Yvonne Ford, secretary of the Inverell Pioneer Village Auxiliary, spoke in 1997 of the remorse many local people still feel about the decision. The Inverell website, which displays a keen interest in marketing what remains of Inverell's real heritage while obliged in the main to advertise the ersatz heritage of the Pioneer Village, is testimony to the economically irrational nature of many decisions based on financial considerations.[45]

BREAKING THE BANS,
BREAKING THE UNION

The green bans attracted sustained press attention and public debate. In one week in January 1972 Mundey was quoted in both the *Sydney Morning Herald*'s 'Sayings of the Week' ('More and more we are going to determine which buildings we will build') and in the Australian's 'For the Record' ('We don't want the next generation to condemn us for slapping up the slums of tomorrow'). Leonie Sandercock noted at the time that Mundey was getting almost as much press coverage as the Prime Minister. In 12 days in August 1972 the *Sydney Morning Herald* devoted five editorials to attacking the NSWBLF leadership; in two weeks during October–November 1973 another five editorials criticised the union.[1]

TRIAL BY MEDIA

Often the green ban movement was portrayed positively in the media, not just in the letters columns where enthusiasts had their letters published alongside those who denounced the bans, but in the process of honest reporting of genuine community support for each ban. The negative portrayals of the movement emanated primarily from editorial writers and certain columnists. Dependent on commercial enterprises for advertising, there was a predictable reluctance on the part of most newspapers to criticise developers. In any case, as large-scale businesses themselves, media outlets tend spontaneously to recoil from any exercise of working-class power.[2] When blaming the union rather than the developers for the green bans, a recurring theme was fear of capital being withdrawn: 'Potential developers looking at Newcastle as a site for major office buildings will have second thoughts about investing in the city'. With this all-important consideration in mind, the *Newcastle*

Morning Herald concluded: 'there is a limit to how much the community can be expected to take from this union – and that limit has just about been reached'.[3] Another theme was the communist conspiracy:

> The federation's NSW branch has sought to disguise its communist aims and strategy under a cloak of environmental concern. Its green bans have been supported by conservationists whose blind refusal to accept the reality of communist domination of the branch has lent a wholly undeserved air of respectability to a politically motivated attempt to sabotage Sydney's construction industry and produce a 'confrontation' with employers.[4]

However, such criticism was frequently tailored to accommodate the support in many quarters for the green bans. There was greater hostility evinced towards the means employed in the movement than towards the ends to which it was directed. While this approach, which was taken by editorial writers and senior columnists, was partly tactical, it was also indicative of genuine prejudice: it mirrored the position of JD Martin as executive director of the MBA, who insisted that the point at issue was not the environment but 'who controls the decision-making process in our society', that Mundey and the NSWBLF had every right to voice their protest on such a matter, but that they should be 'the ultimate decision-makers is repugnant to the social environment'. Even *Rydge's* complaint that green bans 'have been holding up development programs to a ridiculous level' was accompanied by the concession, 'no matter how justified some of the stands may have been on environmental grounds'.[5]

A careful reading of mainstream press criticism of the movement strongly suggests it was not so much the green bans as such that really offended, rather it was the manner of their imposition. The assertion and clear demonstration of union power disturbed most commentators more than the ends to which this power was directed. Time and again the union's detractors sought to own the point of the bans while disowning those who imposed them. Commentators lauded the aims of the movement, while alerting readers to the dangers of unions getting their way and denouncing the policies and practices of the NSWBLF in particular, renowned as it was for its preparedness to challenge employer prerogatives in all manner of unorthodox ways.

For instance the *Sun* argued that while Australians were 'rightly suspicious of self-appointed public saviours', Mundey's talk of banning the demolition of historic buildings and preference for building hospitals and schools to ugly office blocks made sense: 'Unions have a right – perhaps a duty – to concern themselves with social issues that affect all of us. But,' it then insisted, 'nothing in the Federation's recent history of building site violence ... suggests its new cause will lead to anything but anarchy'. A *Sydney Morning Herald* editorial, while casting aspersions on the right of mere manual workers to make aesthetic judgements, skilfully combined the issues of violence and the environment: 'There is something highly comical in the spectacle of builders laborers, whose ideas on industrial relations do not rise above strikes, violence, intimidation and the destruction of property, setting themselves up as arbiters of taste and protectors of our national heritage'.[6]

In September 1972 an editorial in the *Australian* entitled 'Ridiculous Mr. Mundey' conceded there was 'a body of public opinion fairly clearly on his side' over Kelly's Bush, the Theatre Royal and the Opera House carpark, but disputed his authority to object to The Rocks redevelopment: 'When the vocal leader of a tiny minority in one union begins to sway public and municipal decisions on multi-million-dollar questions in which he has no expertise whatever, it is time to begin asking what has gone wrong with the process of government in this country'. (Or, one might ask, what has gone right?) Mundey replied to this 'tiny minority' allegation by asking who had voted for Rupert Murdoch or the editor of the *Australian*. Enraged by the ban on Katingal in January 1974, the *Sydney Morning Herald* editorialised: 'There would be few who would quarrel with the need to protect the environment and preserve historic buildings. But the use of industrial muscle is not the right way to pursue such objectives.'[7] Most criticisms emphasised, as the real bone of contention, the union's attack on management prerogative, whether in the course of environmental bans or some purely industrial matter.

The extent to which NSWBLF was a common target of the press, regardless of green ban activity, must not be overlooked when analysing the union's demise. The array of actively hostile forces that confronted the union, and the inaction of those who would normally have supported it, was inspired as much by the otherwise militant posture of the union as by the green bans, which rendered the NSWBLF a constant irritation to the State Government and MBA, challenged the power and influence within the union movement of the BWIU and the federal BLF, and alarmed most other union officials. The *Sydney Morning Herald* of 29 May 1970, a year before Kelly's Bush, announced that 'Mr Mundey, a leading member of the Communist Party, seems to be out to make a name for himself and his party in an extreme and adventurist manner. His union followers should consider where he is leading them before it is too late.'

Mundey observed that many traditional trade union leaders expressed the same sentiment.[8] The story of the union's downfall, therefore, is not merely one of concerted victimisation by developers but also one of supineness and even betrayal on the part of sections of the labour movement.

A WITCH-HUNT AGAINST A MILITANT UNION

Well before the green bans were under way, the MBA was attempting to rid itself of this meddlesome union, and had been threatening since 1969 to apply for its deregistration. Had the union been registered in the state, the MBA would have moved for its deregistration during the margins strike. However, as a federally registered union the employers could not attack the part without affecting the whole ABLF.[9] In this protection lay also the NSWBLF's ultimate vulnerability, for the MBA began to caution the ABLF to 'do something about the NSW Branch or face the threat of deregistration'. When the MBA executive director told Gallagher in September 1971 it intended to apply for deregistration, the *Australian's* Neal Swancott commented with uncanny prescience:

> The employers are using the Federal union as a lever against a particularly sharp thorn in their side. It is known the Federal leaders of the union are not prepared to see it deregistered on a Federal basis because of the actions of one State branch … It was widely speculated yesterday that a Federal take-over of the NSW branch is likely.[10]

Employer anxieties about the NSWBLF were vociferously expressed by the State Government, and not merely because it was haunted generally by the spectre of a loss of investment interstate or a cessation of overseas investment. Premier Askin's proximity to many of the developers who became the object of green bans ensured his tolerance threshold for militant unionism, already very low, was clearly reached over the green bans.[11] But the union's record on purely industrial matters rendered it in any case anathema to employers and the Askin Government. In the case of the NSWBLF, the usurpatory power of organised labour had increased beyond the point that was fully consistent with working-class subordination.[12] Pringle described the atmosphere: 'I reckoned in 1971 we'd pushed things industrially to the point where we had to be attacked – and we were'.[13]

Askin called for a police probe into alleged industrial blackmail by the NSWBLF, and the New South Wales Minister for Labour and Industry, Hewitt called a press conference and appealed to people 'subjected. to threats of violence or black banning' by the NSWBLF to provide details. On

19 September 1971 the MBA called for a Royal Commission to investigate 'the atmosphere of violence and bashings associated with the NSW branch of the BLF'.[14] At this stage the union leadership displayed the tactical ingenuity that often enabled it to avoid or postpone conservative reactions to its militant activities: the officials called a press conference to 'welcome the proposed Royal Commission on condition that the terms of reference be broadened to include all aspects of the building industry' and offered to cooperate to demonstrate to the public the nature of this industry:

> The 'concrete jungle' is the best way to describe the building industry today. In every major city, particularly where high rise buildings have been erected, scandals have abounded around re-zoning, the rape of the little remaining 'green' areas, where developers and builders have plundered much of the natural bushland in a most ruthless manner.
>
> The terms of reference should be broad enough to allow the Minister for Local Government to testify, also Sir Albert Jennings on the Kelly's Bush issue, and countless other controversial issues involving practically every Municipal Council in NSW Metropolitan areas.
>
> This type of thorough commission will be applauded by the thousands and in fact, hundreds of thousands, that have been duped by 'land sharks', 'developers' and so-called 'builders'.[15]

The statement had its desired effect: Hewitt, who had favoured a Royal Commission, changed his mind; and Askin refused the MBA's request for what he now termed 'an expensive long-drawn-out Royal Commission'. Although Askin created some more law-and-order headlines by offering police protection to witnesses giving evidence 'into alleged blackmail in the building industry', the union's call for a broadened Royal Commission had diverted the employer-government offensive. When the police visited Mundey in his office over the invented allegations of industrial blackmail, Mundey handed the officers a prepared statement which detailed for the constabulary the 'scandalous state of the whole building industry', the mismanagement of the government, the industrial neglect of 'callous employers', the scandals around re-zoning, 'the rape of the little remaining "green" areas', and the 'notorious' accident rate in the industry.[16] Not being interested in the 'whole industry', the police soon left.

Police harassment became a common feature of the concerted offensive against the NSWBLF. The New South Wales *Summary Offences Act*, from its proclamation in 1970, was used consistently by employers in industrial disputes, but the Act's main target was undoubtedly the NSWBLF, which therefore spearheaded the campaign to have it revoked. During 1972, police were regularly called to jobs by employers and occasionally arrested NSWBLF organisers under the provisions of the Act. In this climate of blatant police interference on the side of employers, there was an increasing number of physical attacks on organisers and delegates by employers. Organisers provoked assault, not by offering physical violence themselves but by their industrial attitudes and their refusal to 'treat bosses as bosses'. While there is no newspaper or MBA evidence of NSWBLF organisers offering personal violence, over a dozen physical attacks on organisers and delegates occurred during 1972. In one case Pringle was 'viciously king hit by an employer after the job decided to go on strike over wages and amenities'. His nose was broken and he was hospitalised for three days. While the union's opponents were attempting to implicate its membership in acts of violence, Mundey and Pringle issued a press statement which noted that 'our president was in Sydney Hospital undergoing a facial operation following an assault by an employer' and, after outlining the MBA's poor record on enforcement of safety conditions, repeated its call for a Royal Commission into the industry. 'This would serve the public far better than the employers conducting a witch hunt against a militant union.'[17]

Askin maintained the pressure: referring to the ban on the Regent Theatre in November 1972 he condemned 'Mundey's latest example of irresponsibility' and claimed 'responsible NSW people have had a gutful of this self-avowed Communist'. The following day Hewitt urged employers and individuals to take action against 'union violence and intimidation'. He considered the formation of vigilante groups 'a very disturbing innovation to the strike pattern', expressed concern that such activity could spread, and applauded the actions of 'responsible' union leaders such as John Ducker. Askin followed this with an extraordinary press release: 'Mr Mundey and his musclemen have created a reign of fear within the Builders Laborers Federation itself and the building industry generally'. It was because of this 'fear complex which surrounds the building industry' that police had been unable to procure any evidence linking the union leadership with industrial blackmail.[18]

Undeterred by lack of evidence the Legislative Assembly began debating Peter Coleman 's private member's motion, which called for an investigation of 'industrial anarchy and politically motivated violence instigated by militant union leaders'. Most government speakers referred to vigilante action during the recent plumbers' strike and blamed this on the dangerous example of the NSWBLF. Clearly the government feared its style was spreading to other unions. And to add significant insult to considerable industrial injury there were the green bans: Minister for Education Eric Willis accused the union of wanting to 'impose its will on the community rather than let people responsible do as they had planned'. He concluded: 'If Mr Mundey had been on the scene during the past 10 years, Sydney may not have had many major commercial and retail developments. Indeed if he is around for much longer it will be a very sad thing indeed.'[19]

The Liberal Party's attack was not just pre-election union bashing. The bans were seriously threatening development activity in the state, and so naturally the Askin Government wished to discredit the union and its leaders and eliminate the bans. The *Sydney Morning Herald* commented at the onset of the offensive: 'So far the Government has found no tactic to counter the situation, which has been causing it increasing concern'. Reporting to organisers and delegates at the beginning of 1973, Mundey noted that during 1972 there had been 'many vocal and hysterical attacks on the NSW branch', because the union had 'intervened in social and political issues of great concern to all Australians but issues which, in the past, have been ignored or neglected by the Union movement'. The attacks were testimony to the efficacy of the green bans:

> Because of our criticism of the Government and the way in which it has
> favoured so-called developers, because we have imposed environmental bans at
> the request of residents and other professional groups, we have caused the wrath
> of those powerful and vested financial interests, thus the attacks on this union.[20]

THE LONELINESS OF THE LEFT-WING ADVENTURISTS

Although George Petersen, MLA for Illawarra, argued strongly that the NSWBLF 'must not be left alone', most Labor members of the Legislative Assembly in New South Wales made no attempt to defend the union when their Coalition counterparts regularly sought to defame it in parliament; Sid Einfeld even referred to Mundey as 'an enemy of the workers and an enemy of the people'.[21] Such responses from the right-dominated state Labor Party were to be expected. It was the union's lack of allies within the industrial wing of the labour movement, and especially in the BWIU and the ABLF's Federal Management Committee, that brought it to grief. The increasingly poor relations with both these bodies form an important part of the narrative of defeat. In effect, the NSWBLF became the victim of the serious industrial consequences of the three-way split within the CPA.

BWIU resentment and federal BLF disapproval were expressed spatially. After the margins strike, the BWIU informed the NSWBLF its northern organiser could no longer use the BWIU room in Newcastle 'because of overcrowding', so it was obliged to procure an office in Newcastle Trades

Hall. In Sydney in April 1971 the NSWBLF abruptly moved out of the BWIU's Vine House and in to Trades Hall. Ralph Kelly claims 'we were given 24 hours to get out'. On 10 September 1971 a NSWBLF mass meeting in the course of a strike resolved that the absence of Gallagher and Clancy be noted and both invited to the next meeting. When neither attended, two chairs were nonetheless set out for them. Pringle recalls: 'Jack's theatrics with the two empty chairs on the stage really hit the spot on the day. It was really lonely up there on the stage – just me and Jack. Normally officials from other unions are queuing up to be invited to stopwork meetings.' According to *Tribune*: 'Mr. Clancy stayed away because he said he didn't agree with the tactics of continuing the strike; Mr. Gallagher just stayed away.'[22]

The BWIU was anxious that the NSWBLF tactics not be pursued in the case of the building industry strike of May 1971. BWIU officialdom not only disapproved strongly of industrial sabotage, but deplored the way in which it was organised. What the NSWBLF viewed as democratic participation of the rank and file, the BWIU saw as an unorganised rabble. 'Our style,' Mundey explained, 'was to encourage rank and filers to show their initiative while at the same time remembering that unity was important. *We* didn't pose one argument against the other. You want unity at the top *but more importantly you want action by workers down below.*' To the BWIU such action constituted 'efforts by ultra-left elements to establish a duality of leadership'. Mundey saw the situation as more complex, encompassing important questions about democratic practice: 'We were allowing shop committees and area strike committees to be set up … to make decisions affecting their own area. The BWIU saw anything like this as a challenge to their own centralised leadership.' BWIU antipathy towards the NSWBLF was crucial in isolating it. Mundey acknowledged of the BWIU: 'they were successful to some degree in painting us as "Left-wing adventurists"'.[23]

The 'Labor Council brawl' in May 1971 revealed how quick most other unions, like the press whose prejudices they echoed, were to blame NSWBLF officials. None of the nine culprits who started the fight in the gallery were NSWBLF leaders: in fact, four were well-known opponents of the union leadership,[24] but accusations and allegations about the NSWBLF's 'thug tactics' and 'violence towards fellow unionists' continued to be nude, whenever its militancy annoyed a union official. It was a feature of the co-operation that was emerging among conservative union leaders and the anti-Aarons faction within the CPA to isolate the pro-Aarons unions, particularly the NSWBLF. For instance, in mid-1972 Bob Hawke supported disciplinary measures against 'the damaging of private property during strikes', a comment directed at the NSWBLF as the only union to uphold its right to destroy non-union work; and the SPA endorsed this view by criticising the 'ultra-left' tactic of 'smashing scab-constructed plumbing'.[25]

The crucial importance of trade union solidarity became apparent in March 1972 when the New South Wales MBA moved to deregister the ABLF 'in an endeavour to protect itself … from the high incidence of strikes in the building industry'. Gallagher stood by his New South Wales branch, but for the last time, threatening a national strike and complaining the state MBA was attempting 'to put pressure on the federation to discipline the NSW Branch'.[26] This branch was not yet as isolated as it was to become and the New South Wales MBA did not yet have the full support of other MBA state branches. But the most important factor in explaining Gallagher's support was the booming condition of the industry in New South Wales in 1972, which greatly strengthened the state branch's position in relation to the federal body. Gallagher's time was not yet ripe. The deregistration moves had produced unity within the federation; MBA actions had backfired, but employers had learnt a lesson that would be invaluable in 1974.

THE 1973 BRANCH ELECTIONS, THE BATTLE OF THE ROCKS, AND THE OCTOBER LOCKOUT

MBA and State Government hopes now centred on the union's triennial elections due in October 1973. The logic of their position was to hope for victory for the Maoist, pro-Gallagher opposition forces within the New South Wales branch, led by John McNamara, Ron Donoghue and Joe Ferguson, whose platform criticised many of the green bans. The media pinpointed the real issue in the election: the bans. 'The middle-class "greenies" have an unusual stake in the elections … among the … builders labourers in NSW.'[27] All newspapers carried reports such as 'green bans imposed on building projects valued at $3000 million would be reviewed' if the opposition won. The Bulletin remarked succinctly: 'The developers must certainly have an interest in the election'. The MBA made it perfectly clear where its support lay. In the middle of the balloting period, it inserted full-page advertisements in the daily papers, 'To all Building Workers: A Message of Concern'. It criticised the NSWBLF for disregarding agreements, ignoring the arbitration authorities and orders to return to work; and for failing to turn up for court hearings. It concluded with a warning that, 'if the current situation continues – then the MBA will be forced to take action to protect its members',[28] implying that if the membership voted again for the existing leadership, the MBA would force another lockout. This is precisely what happened.

On 8 October, three days after the convincing election win for the leadership team, with Owens as secretary and Pringle as president, five builders labourers were arrested under the Summary Offences Act. These arrests were the overture to the employers' increasingly confrontationist strategy. On 16 October, Silverton Ltd broke The Rocks green ban by commencing demolition of old garages at the Playfairs site opposite the Argyle Terrace. Immediately, more than 100 builders labourers stopped work in protest and Pringle and two others were arrested for refusing to leave the site. Tom Hogan recalls: 'I picked up the megaphone and said … "We'll show you. We'll stop the City." But I was too late, it had stopped of its own accord. There wasn't one job left working in the city when I walked through it to the Trades Hall.' The *Sydney Morning Herald* reported that 4000 labourers walked off the job, then smashed open a double gate and occupied the site until the SCRA agreed to halt demolition. The following Monday another clash occurred when resi-

Builders labourers prevent scabs from entering the Playfair Street site in The Rocks and breaking the green ban, 23 October 1973. (Courtesy *Sydney Morning Herald*)

Breaking the bans, breaking the union | 257

dent activists and builders labourers occupied the site. This time, 58 people were arrested, including Mundey, Owens, Denise Bishop and about twenty Victoria Street squatters. Two demonstrators climbed a tree and 'Elvis', an ABC technician who according to Wendy Bacon 'had run into Victoria Street on one of his long-distance runs and never ran out again', clung to a branch 15 metres up for 14 hours.[29]

'The Battle of The Rocks' received massive publicity and Mundey claimed in court that the State Government was manufacturing a crisis 'to suit its law-and-order election campaign'. The MBA applied yet again to have the union deregistered and cited The Rocks dispute as part of its argument, and announced a ban on weekend overtime. A stop-work meeting of Sydney builders labourers was called, but Gallagher declined to support the New South Wales branch 'in such a parochial matter'. About five hundred builders labourers and resident activists demonstrated outside the Commonwealth Arbitration Court where the union was called to a compulsory conference with the MBA. 'We won't be dictated to by courts or anyone else,' Mundey insisted. 'This is a new dimension, a social issue, and goes past the bounds of a conciliation commission.' Meetings were held on university campuses and the union organised a rally at Circular Quay, attended by residents, students and other supporters. Many 'city workers' including waterside workers, metal workers and plumbers, stopped work to attend the rally. Jack Cambourn of FEDFA and Frank Bellins of the Australian Metal Workers' Union were among those who spoke in support of the NSWBLF and The Rocks green ban. Later 2000 supporters marched up Pitt Street and surged across Macquarie Street shouting 'Green Bans in – Askin out'. Pringle and 20 others were arrested. The evening papers predictably headlined the events as 'Union Riot' and 'Mob Scenes'. The union held another mass meeting and decided to stay on strike.[30] Gallagher criticised the New South Wales bans publicly and severely, calling some 'unjustified and stupid' and indicating he wanted 'some if not all' lifted. At Federal Management Committee meetings federal officials argued that the ABLF could maintain its federal registration only if the state branch lifted its green bans. Gallagher announced the federation would instruct New South Wales to lift some of its bans else 'action will have to be taken against the Branch'. He complained, 'we can't carry the whole conservation movement on our backs'. Despite these obvious warning signals the branch remained adamant. 'We have a commitment to the people of NSW,' Bud Cook announced, 'and we are not prepared to hand that over'. Owens claimed Gallagher was 'falling' for the attacks by the MBA and the

Askin Government on the New South Wales branch.[31]

In the face of Gallagher's obvious intentions the state branch took precautions. It withdrew its funds from the bank in what Mundey called the branch's 'fight for survival', while instructing members throughout New South Wales to remain on strike indefinitely 'until all scab labour is removed from the Rocks area'. A meeting of 1200 labourers telegrammed Gallagher to stop attacking the branch. Resident activists and other supporters held meetings and travelled to Melbourne to demonstrate outside the Federal Management Committee meeting that was to decide the branch's fate. Melbourne resident activists also held a meeting and joined the pro-New South Wales branch protest. Gallagher labelled these moves 'disruptive tactics' and Mundey replied, perhaps undiplomatically in the circumstances, that Gallagher 'talks more like a merchant banker than a unionist'. Mundey announced to the crowd of banner-waving residents outside the federal committee meeting that the state branch would 'stand firm on every single green ban we have'.[32]

The Federal Management Committee made an ambivalent decision. In

Jack Mundey arrested during 'The Battle for the Rocks', 23 October 1973.

the face of growing support for the green bans, and the state branch's intransigence, the federal officials affirmed 'complete support' for the bans on The Rocks, Kelly's Bush, National Trust classifications, inner-city housing and threatened parklands; announced all other bans would be reviewed by the Federal Council; and resolved by ten votes to three to uphold 'a balanced campaign on conservation issues'.[33] Mundey claimed the decision was a 'moral victory', while expressing disappointment that the green bans did not get unequivocal support. Insisting the branch leadership attend a Commonwealth Arbitration Commission conference to investigate the New South Wales branch's handling of industrial disputes, Gallagher warned Mundey: 'The NSW leadership is not yet out of the woods. If they refuse to attend today's conference we will take appropriate action against them.' Mundey maintained the green bans were not a matter for discussion by any industrial tribunal, since they were a social rather than an industrial matter. The branch officials attended the conference, but Mundey announced: 'Not one of our green bans will be lifted and others will be imposed'. At a mass meeting, the builders labourers voted 450 to 227 to return to work on several conditions, including: a total ban on Silverton Constructions until it dismissed 'scab' labour; Federal Management Committee endorsement for all the New South Wales green bans; no recriminations against union members or Rocks residents; and the Arbitration Court to accept that it had no authority over green bans.[34]

As part of the MBA–Askin strategy to isolate the union, the MBA now decided to close down its high-rise projects in Sydney. A CRAG rally in defence of the union called on the MBA to have discussions with Labor Council and resident groups about environmental protection in the state, criticised the state Liberal and Labor parties for not proposing 'well thought out plans of environmental protection', and called on them 'to guarantee … every citizen's right to participate in planning his own environment'. Far from guaranteeing such rights, Askin announced in his election policy speech he would introduce 'drastic anti-strike legislation soon'. Owens commented: 'It simply proves what so many people have thought for a long time – that Sir Robert has one of the finest minds of the nineteenth century'.[35]

Despite efforts by the BTG, the lockout continued with over 10,000 building workers stood down. The MBA imposed conditions for its termination so demanding – including the lifting of all green bans on MBA sites – that no union would have consented to them, let alone the NSWBLF. Apart from applying for deregistration of the MBA, the builders labourers used other tactics such as 'work ins', but the tradesmen would not participate in these and attacked the NSWBLF's 'go-it-alone' policy. By this stage Justice Aird had urged employers to allow work to start on all but the green ban sites. The MBA insisted green bans should not be decided by 'self-appointed dictators' and its advertising became increasingly sensational. On 11 November the MBA announced:

> This dispute is about anarchy and the destruction of democratic processes. We believe an element of the BLF is engaged in anarchy. This is the Communist way – issues come and go but the eventual goal of communism is to destroy the existing political system. Green bans are just a political tool to create anarchy.

The final comment was a fitting tribute to the BWIU's role: 'We applaud the initiative, restraint and moderation of the Building Trades Group'. In settling the dispute on 14 November, the MBA agreed in part to the tradesmen 's demand for stand-down pay and consented to re-open all jobs except those covered by green bans. Owens called it 'the most unsuccessful expensive experiment' the MBA had ever undertaken.[36]

However, it was obvious from Gallagher's remarks that more was expected of the New South Wales branch than was agreed to at the settlement. He advised the branch to 'quieten down' and added 'we are sick and tired of having the NSW Branch involve this Union in irresponsible acts'. He instructed the branch to restrict green bans to projects that ran contrary to National Trust recommendations and announced the forthcoming ABLF conference would 'review' the Sydney green bans. The *Manufacturers' Monthly* saw the long term implications: 'The Jack Mundey led builders labourers in NSW are slowly being encircled, with the noose getting tighter. With the MBA prepared to close down "indefinitely", other unions have moved against the BLF with at least tacit support from the ACTU.' Mundey recalled: 'The pressure was really on – but what could we do? To do what Gallagher and Clancy wanted would have meant the end of the green bans.' The officials saw the bans as a matter of principle, not political expediency. As Owens remarked, 'we made plenty of wrong decisions but we never made an unprincipled one'.[37] Mick Curtin described the feelings of the rank and file: 'The three weeks lockout was a trying period. I thought we'd really had it then. The bluntness and frankness of the elected leadership helped us to survive. We fully supported them.' Owens and Pringle expressed their appreciation:

> On behalf of the Executive we take this opportunity to pay tribute to the manner in which builders' labourers have conducted themselves against the persistent, unrelenting attacks of the employers. There is no doubt that if it

was not for the strong social conscience so vigorously expressed by builders labourers in NSW the people of this state would have suffered under the ravages of the developers and their friends, the Askin government. In the years ahead, the actions that the builders labourers took in 1972 and 1973 will become a proud part of Australian History.[38]

Much to the state branch's surprise, the ABLF conference in Hobart in November 1973 passed its resolution expressing 'concern at the failure to preserve historic buildings … which are part of our cultural and historic development' and calling for 'more effective legislation' to protect them. Although this resolution carried no policy instructions, delegates at the meeting saw it as encouragement for other branches of the BLF to impose green bans on projects endangering buildings of historic interest, just as the conservative Tasmanian branch had agreed to the ban on the whole Battery Point area. Media commentary interpreted the resolution as 'a national green ban … placed on the demolition of all historic buildings and historic precincts'. For the New South Wales branch it signified that 'the green bans … are here to stay'.[39] These interpretations were unduly optimistic, yet the decision was more favourable to the green bans than expected.

Gallagher was keenly aware of the amount of public support generated by the state branch and he did not, as yet, want to be seen as the man who killed the green bans. On the contrary he was still claiming responsibility for the militant environmental policies of the union and capitalising on the green bans' popularity in ABLF publications.[40] Gallagher was also mindful of the rank-and-file support the New South Wales branch officials enjoyed, for his own team in the branch elections had been swamped by them two to one. Since it was obvious this branch would not concede any ground on the green bans, Gallagher was wary of becoming embroiled in what would become a contentious affair while there was still hope of retaining registration: after deregistration in 1974 he had nothing to lose.

THE SIEGE OF VICTORIA STREET, DEREGISTRATION AND THE BATTLE OF FIG STREET

During 1974 the major building companies moved to break several green bans, with violent physical confrontations occurring in January at Victoria Street and in September at Ultimo. On 3 January 1974, during a period when builders labourers traditionally take holidays to coincide with the industry close-down between Christmas and New Year, Frank Theeman's Victoria Point Pty Ltd resorted to outright confrontation to rid itself of the squatters in Victoria Street. With the aid of 250 police, 30 men employed by Theeman led the assault wielding axes, sledge hammers and crowbars. Reinforced by builders labourers who rushed to the scene, squatters barricaded themselves in the buildings, climbed onto roofs and two clung precariously to chimneys for 17 hours. In a siege that lasted two days and attracted an estimated crowd of 400 green ban supporters, 53 demonstrators and builders labourers were arrested, including Owens.[41]

Theeman was testing the new secretary's adherence to the green ban policy, but as Wendy Bacon commented 'Joe was as committed and militant about the ban as Jack was'. Although the squatters were physically eliminated from the scene, the ban remained solid and VSAG continued its publicity campaign, producing with the union's assistance a poster featuring photographs of Theeman's 'security' employees entitled: 'Not WANTED in Victoria Street or anywhere, THEEMAN'S SCARS'. VSAG also produced the lively *Victoria Street Rag*, which, in popular press-style, included boxed weather reports such as 'Forecast: There might be trouble but there will be no demolition' and 'Forecast: Victoria Street will be saved. Low-cost cooperative housing will triumph'. Popular green ban slogans such as 'People before Profits' and 'Green

Joe Owens negotiates with Superintendent Ray Hutchings at the Siege of Victoria Street, in January 1974. (Courtesy *Sydney Morning Herald*)

Breaking the bans, breaking the union | 263

Bans Forever' were used and the hopeful subtitle 'We'll go on forever' of one edition was changed to 'We'll go on forever and forever' in the next. Confrontations of a minor nature continued for several weeks and mass meetings were organised by the squatters. The union eventually extracted an agreement from Theeman whereby 'he will not demolish, he will withdraw the thugs from the Street, and no development will take place until it has been endorsed by the residents'. Owens thanked all the builders labourers 'who assisted in Victoria Street with pickets etc. during the confrontation'.[42] Although Theeman's thugs continued to patrol the street, no further demolition occurred until Gallagher gained control of the branch.

It was the Victoria Street evictions that alerted the resident action groups, particularly VSAG, to the strain on the union. Wendy Bacon wrote: 'the pressure ... has been on the BLF membership and leadership for months ... For the green bans to survive ... mass action by residents will be needed.' Support activities began to be organised. One particularly imaginative demonstration occurred when Theeman held a party at his luxurious Bellevue Hill house, at which Askin was present. A group of resident activists and builders labourers 'disguised' as high society guests infiltrated the proceedings, distributing small cards which informed guests that 'Under Concrete and Glass Sydney's Disappearing Fast' or 'The person next to you may be a demonstrator' and placing propaganda leaflets under plates and in bathrooms. Eventually, they were noisily ejected. A fashion reporter for one of the daily papers later told demonstrators she had 'spotted' a dinner-suited Joe Owens with powdered grey hair and was about to award him best-dressed male of the occasion when he was summarily eliminated from the proceedings. During the boisterous demonstration of several hundred green ban supporters outside the house, police made arrests, including Pringle and Lyn Syme.[43]

While resident activists were busy supporting the NSWBLF, Labor Council officialdom criticised it. In May 1974 John Ducker pilloried the NSWBLF, for 'tactics that often precipitated violence' and being 'far too undiscriminating in their selection of targets', and later the same month deplored its approach of 'slapping green bans on Willy Nilly'. He argued for 'official' rather than 'unilateral' union action, ignoring the fact that 'official' union action had been noticeably lacking.[44]

In June 1974 the MBA, 'desperate to find a way to get around the green bans', succeeded at long last in securing the deregistration of the ABLF. George Hurchalla observes that most developers and contractors were 'perplexed' with the refusal of the union to negotiate over the bans, having become accustomed to solving disputes with unions by coming to an 'arrangement' of some sort that benefited either officials or membership. With Mundey persistently declining Swiss bank accounts, penthouse apartments and extravagant gifts, 'Steamrolling the ABLF seemed to be the only option left for the MBA to get their projects moving again'. Gallagher did not oppose deregistration.[45] Dismissing it with Maoist bravado as a 'Foreign Bosses' Plot' (sentiments echoed in the Maoist press[46]) his real reason for staying calm was that deregistration was not aimed at the federal or Victorian bodies but at the New South Wales branch. 'The sole aim of the MBA in seeking deregistration,' an MBA leaflet made clear, 'was because the industry has been brought to the brink of chaos by the irresponsible actions of BLF leaders in NSW'. In May 1974 three major developers had announced they would switch their operations to other states 'because of building industry unrest in NSW' and predicted other construction companies would follow suit. Hewitt announced that this 'crisis' in New South Wales was because 'extremist groups such as the BLF hold employers to ransom'.[47] Ray Rocher from the MBA explained the employers' tactics:

> There was no way that the Industry could work with the Mundey, Owens, Pringle Group, and so the deregistration … was to get rid of those people from our industry … Our only defence was deregistration, in fact it was the only way the saneness could be brought in from the other states. Eventually it … forced Federal intervention with a consequent resolution of our problem.

However, deregistration alone did not solve the 'problem' for employers, because, as Rocher observed the union was still 'out of control' and 'green bans were still rolling': 'After preliminary discussions with Gallagher, we realised we could work out our problems with him'.[48] The true value of deregistration to the employers lay in the promise of re-registration. With Gallagher anxious to achieve re-registration as part of his industrial power-play with Clancy's BWIU, the employers had a willing instrument. Gallagher became their solution to the problem of green bans.

With pressure mounting on Gallagher due to deregistration, he wanted to demonstrate to the employers his ability to deal with the state branch. Rocher made this quite clear: 'He couldn't stay out of it like he attempted to … he was being hurt. He couldn't control [the branch] so we took him out of the ballpark as well.' Building industry employers could sense Gallagher was no Mundey. 'Gallagher knows when we can't take too much more, he really only pushes so far,' commented Bruce Shaw, industrial relations manager of the Victorian MBA. 'He knows what the limit is and he backs off if the industry is about to collapse.' When Rocher was questioned whether the BLF would have achieved re-registration while the New South Wales leadership remained, he was emphatic: 'we would have continued opposing … re-registration. Had there been no change in the structure or the people involved in NSW there wouldn't have been a chance that we would accept an agreement or promises made by them.'

Reregistration was achieved in October 1976, unopposed by the MBA, because Gallagher's destruction of the New South Wales branch enabled the ABLF to promise, and be believed, that it would resort to conciliation and arbitration 'rather than direct action' and that employers need no longer expect 'acts of destruction of property, interruption of concrete pours, interrupting the unloading of vehicles and the use of selective bans on vertical transport machinery'.[49]

The employers were also assisted by the inaction of the BWIU; as Owens observed, 'the MBA knew they could count on Clancy not defending us, because although he hated Gallagher he hated us worse'. As a step towards 'unity', the BWIU state conference in August 1974 called for an end to 'some of the green bans that are holding up building and demolition work worth $3000 million in NSW'. Just as the SPA had opposed union bans on war materials being sent to Vietnam – 'the decision to withdraw the troops must be made by a government and not by some queer form of workers' control' – so the BWIU opposed most green bans as an invalid form of class struggle. When asked whether the enmity was industrial or ideological, Mundey replied 'how can you differentiate?'[50]

Worse than BWIU lack of support was the AWU's overt role in attempting to break the ban on the Northwestern Expressway on Saturday 28 September 1974. Taking advantage of ABLF deregistration, the Department of Main Roads began demolishing houses in Fig Street, Ultimo, using AWU bulldozer drivers and labourers. Although such demolition was clearly BLF not AWU work-and the AWU conceded this – the AWU did have coverage both for road-building and earth-moving equipment not involved on construction sites, so it was now presuming to use such equipment to demolish houses preparatory to road-building. In the words of state secretary Charlie Oliver, as he defended the AWU's action, 'We build roads, and if there is anything in the way – rocks, trees or anything – we push it out of the way'.[51]

After the unannounced destruction of the Sunderland Arms Hotel, hundreds of resident activists and builders labourers arrived on the scene, but the department officers, 'with massive police assistance smashed their way into some of the houses'.[52] Ten demonstrators were arrested and the violent confrontation brought work to a halt. Tom Uren and federal Transport Minister Charlie Jones condemned the demolition, declared it was in defiance of the federal *Roads Grants Act* that required consultation with the Federal Government on all urban arterial projects, and threatened to cut off all road grants to New South Wales if the expressway project proceeded. Further large-scale demonstrations eventually halted the demolition work. 'The Battle of Fig Street' was fought hard, with demonstrators being physically and often violently 'worked over', for the resident activists were fighting not merely to stop the expressway but to contest a serious threat to the power of the NSWBLF.[53] With the green ban movement bloodied but unbroken, Gallagher's moment was approaching.

INTERVENTION

Sectarian considerations weighed heavily in Gallagher's ultimate decision to move against the New South Wales branch. From his CPA (M-L) perspective, he was plagued by a state branch aligned to the CPA, and by October 1974 deregistration was seriously hampering him in his power play with Clancy's SPA-dominated BWIU. For a union such as the BLF, whose scope was largely covered also by other unions – BWIU, AWU, FEDFA, Federated Ironworkers' Association, Amalgamated Metal Workers' Union and Plumbers and Gasfitters Employees' Union of Australia – deregistration constituted a serious problem if any of these other unions were inclined to body-snatch, as the BWIU clearly was. As Owens noted, the ideological gap between Clancy and Gallagher had industrial consequences: 'With the Sino-Soviet dispute, every time the tanks moved up to the border, you could rely on a demarcation dispute in Pitt Street or Flinders Street'.[54] Not just coverage but domination of the building industry unions was at stake. Association over the years with smaller craft unions such as the stonemasons, the plasterers and the glaziers, had led to the BWIU emerging as the leading union in the building industry, and Clancy was now discussing amalgamation with such unions. The BWIU was also dominating the negotiations for the national paid rates award, discussions which in their official stages excluded Gallagher as a consequence of deregistration. Although Gallagher had won the building industry seat on the ACTU executive with right-wing support in 1973, he could not rely on pulling off such a deal at the next ACTU congress in 1975. He had to regain registration to take the limelight away from Clancy in the national arena.[55]

Another problem for Gallagher was his own standing within the ABLF. Although he dominated the Federal Management Committee and was untouchable while the election of general secretary remained a collegiate vote, a proposed change to the *Conciliation and Arbitration Act* to provide for popular election of federal union officials – which the New South Wales branch naturally supported – was a serious threat to his position. In a popular election, nearly half the votes would come from New South Wales, giving that branch's candidate, presumably Mundey, a very good chance of defeating the lesser-known candidate from the less populous state, Gallagher. While Gallagher was virtually unknown outside Victoria, Mundey was a national celebrity and as a rank-and-file labourer was still receiving more press coverage than Gallagher, which the Victorian clearly resented. Gallagher's desire for attention had him consent to publicity acts that would have made Mundey blush: riding a camel through the streets of Carlton, or entering court wearing a ball and chain. Gallagher's grandstanding during Intervention revealed a liking for media publicity that even his supporters have never denied. The importance of this factor cannot be disregarded in analysing Gallagher's animosity towards Mundey. As some disenchanted Maoists observed of their one-time hero: 'He undermines and continues to undermine anyone who stands on his own two feet, or who shows ability and could possibly over-shadow him'.[56]

Another factor that weighed heavily in Gallagher's calculations was the economic situation in the building industry. The boom which had come to Sydney in the late 1960s was beginning to wane there, whereas Melbourne, which had taken off at a later date, was still at peak activity. This situation was propitious for Gallagher because a booming industry and full employment in his home state provided a strong base for Intervention in New South Wales; and a declining industry and some unemployment in that state provided perfect conditions for a raid on the Sydney branch membership. With employer support Gallagher could enforce the policy of 'federal tickets only' with the alternative being unemployment for most builders labourers.

Although re-registration was desired by Gallagher, he undoubtedly benefited in the short-term from deregistration (so long as employers supported wage rises and flow-ons for his members – which they did) because of the absence of legal restraints on him in his attack on the New South Wales branch. Since the ABLF no longer had any legal standing, Gallagher did not have to obey its rules and was under no obligation to hold monthly branch meetings, stop-work meetings or even elections; and when the branch officials were expelled they had no recourse to industrial courts as an avenue of appeal.[57] Gallagher's bragging that he was free of the shackles of registration was true in the most sinister of senses.

Declaring the New South Wales branch 'had been irresponsible and had gone too far on green bans', Gallagher arrived in Sydney on 12 October and set up temporary headquarters on a whole floor of the Hyde Park Plaza Hotel at $600 week. He announced he was in town to 'take over the NSW Branch' and informed the puzzled Sydney press, unused to his florid style, that he would have 'green ban soup' for breakfast. He appointed 22 federal organisers, six of whom had been unsuccessfol candidates in the 1973 branch election. Confident of Gallagher's obliging policy on bans, an MBA circular advised members that the MBA 'actively encourages commencement of work on projects subject to illegal bans'.[58]

On his arrival Gallagher was met by a noisy demonstration of 200 resident activists chanting 'Go Home Gallagher' and a petition requesting he leave the state branch alone. The Australian Conservation Foundation expressed concern that the green bans, which have been 'a major, effective weapon', would be the first casualty of Gallagher's move and cautioned Gallagher that the only people who would gain from lifting the bans would be the New South Wales Government, the MBA and developers; Gallagher told Dr Richard Jones of the Conservation Foundation to 'keep his nose out of BLF business'. Gallagher also criticised the resident action groups, saying they 'have deprived our members of their jobs. We will make our own decisions in the future.'[59] A mass meeting of 1500 builders labourers voted unanimously to reject Gallagher's takeover and reiterated support for the state leadership. Gallagher was invited to address the meeting but refused, saying it was stacked with 'residents and poofters'.[60] Intervention was timed to coincide with the annual dues renewal period, but in the first three weeks the NSWBLF signed up 7000 members while Gallagher netted less than 1000. Rank-and-file builders labourers raised money to fight Intervention by raffling a prize greyhound donated by a loyal mem ber, with a guessing competition to fill in missing letters: 'Gallagher is a T- -D'. They also brought out three issues of *The Rank and File Rag*. As Hurchalla notes, blind rage prevailed and Gallagher could not understand 'the anger of people who were seeing the destruction of the revolution in trade unionism that they had participated in'.[61] The resident activists held two fundraising dances, a Green and Black Ball and a Green Ban Ball, four fundraising parties and organised various demonstrations of support, including an occupation of MBA head-

Seaman Mick Fowler entertains the crowd with his famous 'banjalalee' and kazoo, at a demonstration outside the Hyde Park Motel where Gallagher and his interstate organisers were in residence, October 1974.

quarters and a rally where over a thousand 'residents, blacks, prisoners, women, homosexuals, environmentalists and students' marched from Martin Plaza to the head office of Concrete Constructions.[62]

Thirty-four federal Labor Members of Parliament signed a press statement: 'We have no doubt that the Builders Labourers' policy on green bans is being attacked in order to accommodate the interests of those most responsible for the insensitive destruction of mainly working class areas'.[63] However, in an intimation of the future direction of the ALP under Hawke, the ACTU declined to assist the beleaguered NSWBLF. Hawke publicly supported Gallagher and refused to chair a meeting between the two factions when requested by the state officials. The only unions in New South Wales that openly supported the state branch were FEDFA, the Teachers' Federation and the Australian Telecommunications Employees' Association.[64]

Mundey claims this isolation was the result of the influence of union officials, whereas much of the rank and file and some former officials of other unions 'adored us as a fighting union' and particularly approved NSWBLF practices that limited union officials' tenure and wage rates.[65] The unease felt by most 'left bureaucrats' about the ultra-democratic organisational practices of the NSWBLF, and the sectarian SPA or CPA (M-L) influence upon many of them, meant that in the NSWBLF's hour of greatest need its friends in key positions within the union movement were few and far between. 'Despite the general public support the NSWBLF had gained as a result of the green bans,' Hurchalla remarks, 'the bulk of the union movement regarded the branch as having gone far beyond the bounds of trade unionism and many welcomed the possibility of a more conventional BLF in New South Wales'. Gary Wickham observed that the majority of unions at the time regarded the NSWBLF as 'trouble makers'. The branch position, Malcolm Colless noted, was 'weakened by a lack of support from the ACTU and most other building unions'.[66]

The CPA Building Branch criticised the union movement for its inactivity: 'While this attack has gone on the trade union movement has remained silent. In the words of the BWIU "staying neutral", and thus by their non-action aiding the employers.' However, even within the CPA there was a degree of ambivalence about the NSWBLF that paralysed its capacity to organise support for the union that had markedly enhanced the party's radical reputation. As Jim McIlroy stressed in *Tribune*, the CPA bore some responsibility for the union's demise, for it failed to take up the defence of the NSWBLF 'as the single main political campaign of the period', necessary because 'key sectors of employers saw the overthrow of the NSW Builders Laborers as a vital question and a test case for the advance of militant unionism'.[67]

Aware of the extent of the state branch's following among 'residents and poofters', not to mention builders labourers, Gallagher consistently refused to speak at meetings during the entire six months of Intervention. In general the federal body refused to debate the issue with the branch leadership, or to call branch meetings or elections to 'let the membership decide', as the state officials urged. When eventually they were forced to call an election the federal officers ruled invalid every opposition nomination received, then declared the uncontested result 'a bonecrushing defeat'. In fact the illegality of Intervention was successfully substantiated by the state branch in the Equity Court and the New South Wales leadership won every case about Intervention in this court, the Industrial Commission and the Federal Court of Australia from October 1974 onwards. However, these rulings were of no value to the state branch in practice, since Gallagher simply refused to comply with them, and the branch personnel were simply not prepared to pursue the gaoling of a union official, not even Gallagher, for contempt of court.[68]

Ray Rocher of the MBA believed Intervention was inevitable, because a union in Australia cannot exist without registration. 'So we took that step knowing in the end that it was going to force some issues.'[69] However, Intervention was not simply the result of employers forcing an issue that then resolved itself, but was the result of collusion between the MBA and the federal body.[70] When questioned about the all-important green bans, Rocher commented: 'if there was a decision by Mr. Gallagher it would be far more likely to be reasonable'.[71] Gallagher was widely reported to have said that he had an 'understanding' with the employers in New South Wales.[72] Speaking of this employer collusion, Les Robinson, whom Gallagher installed in Sydney as his state secretary, admitted that: 'The boss is never neutral, the boss always plays a hand.'[73]

An important hand the bosses played was the MBA decision on 21 October 1974 to impede or prevent the entry of state officials onto building sites and to facilitate that of federal officials. 'We certainly did as much as we could to make it impossible for Mundey, Owens and Pringle to work,' admitted Rocher, for 'they were the people who had caused us all the problems over the years'.[74] As Intervention proceeded the MBA dismissed builders labourers who refused to take out federal tickets; attempted to have the metal trades margins flow-on of $9 granted only to members of the federal BLF in New South Wales; and cut the wages of crane drivers back to the award rate and banned overtime, because FEDFA crane drivers had refused to work with federal BLF ticket-holders. While the crane drivers were on strike over the pay cuts, Gallagher flew crane drivers from Victoria to Sydney to break the strike. After six weeks FEDFA conceded defeat and an agreement was signed with the MBA whereby the drivers undertook to work with federal BLF ticket-holders.[75]

Most importantly, developers financed Intervention, for the federal body could not otherwise have afforded to undertake such a large-scale operation. This became apparent during the joint Commonwealth and Victorian Royal Commission into the BLF in 1981–82, conducted to ascertain whether certain officials indulged in corrupt activities, and which exposed many instances of Gallagher accepting bribes from builders. By contrast NSWBLF officials were regularly, but obviously unsuccessfully, offered bribes to lift green bans. In one of the many fruitless attempts to bribe Mundey he was offered $20 million to allow half of a proposed development to take place.[76] With the NSWBLF incorruptible, the motivation for builders to bankroll Gallagher's Intervention is obvious. Green bans were costing some developers millions. Frank Theeman claimed three years' delay had cost him an extra $3 million in rates and taxes, $2 million in interest on loans and 'at least $3000 a day' in holding charges. One day during the Intervention period Mundey was walking down Elizabeth Street when he saw Gallagher, Robinson and Theeman in Theeman's Mercedes. 'Gallagher and Robinson ducked down when they saw me.' The first green ban to be lifted by Gallagher was that on Victoria Street.[77]

In March 1975 the employers came out openly in support of the federal body. 'We had to work fairly closely with Norm', Rocher admitted. 'We had many discussions. He would suggest certain tactical things we could help with … making provisions to allow only the federal organisers on site, while frustrating and deterring Mundey's organisers from getting on site.'[78] Their hand was forced by the resistance that the rank and file were showing. As Pringle recalled: 'When I heard the news that they were coming into NSW I thought it would be all over in six weeks, or even six days … It's a tribute to our rank and file that it took them six months.' But it was a hard dispute to fight. 'We had to convince them to stay on the job rather than go on strike because once our blokes went on strike Gallagher would send his scabs in.' Brian Boyd's *Inside the BLF* notes a 'steady trickle of interstate "conscript" workers' arrived to 'do the work of sacked pro-Mundey builders' labourers'. The Watts job was the site of the most spectacular of the many industrial actions undertaken by the rank and file in support of their ousted officials. NSWBLF members and two crane drivers occupied the two cranes hundreds of feet above Broadway and stayed there for several days, bringing the job to a virtual standstill.[79]

On 12 March 1975 Gallagher and Rocher agreed to a deal whereby the MBA was to practise systematic preference of employment for federal ticket holders; and individual employers continued to inform builders labourers they would be sacked if they did not take out federal tickets. With the rising unemployment of the period, the New South Wales branch could not avoid annihilation. The final blow came on 17 March 1975, when the branch's office in Trades Hall was broken into overnight and all the membership files stolen.[80] The branch officials pointed out the records were of no commercial value, and useful only to the federal BLF. This 'Chicago-style burglary', was designed to prevent the state branch, which had 'fought this struggle cleanly and in a principled manner, despite interference from employers and police', from functioning as a viable organisation. 'This latest provocation has no place in the Labor Movement.'[81] The loss of their records hastened the inevitable.

A week later the New South Wales officials called their final stop-work meeting. In pouring rain, 2000 builders labourers crowded into the Town Hall for an emotional finale. The officials advised members to change their state tickets to federal tickets and begin paying the federal branch, and promised to fight as rank and filers within the federal union for democratic organisation and socially responsible policies. Though still commanding the loyalty of thousands of members, the leadership stood down from office: they spoke of the importance of 'not hanging onto leadership and destroying the members in the process' and how a dual union situation 'only benefits the employers'.[82] Mundey's farewell speech observed: 'Over the past number of years, particularly since the big strike in 1970, the Master Builders and successive State Governments have used everything they know to try and smash this Union'. At the end of the meeting, Mundey, Owens and Pringle were chaired off the dais amid a tearful standing ovation which lasted ten minutes.[83]

The employers and their political representatives, and those in the ABLF who aided them, were all too aware that the NSWBLF had become 'a different sort of union'. Les Robinson, the new branch secretary, admitted three years later: 'I think we destroyed a virile organisation and it didn't do the Federation any good either'.[84] Some builders labourers and CPA members maintained Intervention could have been avoided. Judy Mundey, for instance, believed that abandoning 'just some of the green bans' would have appeased Gallagher. Owens agrees:

> There was a chance we could have avoided Intervention but in that there would have been a deep and serious danger of us having to give away certain principles which would have been unacceptable ... The price demanded by the employers would have been ... a dismantling of the State apparatus ... certain policies such as job action and the green bans. Besides the membership wouldn't have copped it.[85]

The green ban on Victoria Street was lifted within a few weeks. Gallagher dismissed as 'nothing more than a brothel' what Mundey had seen as a 'beautiful area full of nostalgia'. Gallagher announced the union would progressively review the remaining forty or so bans in Sydney, retaining only those on buildings of historical value that enjoyed both National Trust and 'general public support'.[86]

Regrouping for a fight from below, as Mundey had promised the Town Hall meeting, was obstructed by Gallagher expelling 20 officials on charges of financial impropriety, that he was never able to substantiate, and refusing to issue tickets to the more prominent militants. Gallagher persistently opposed the re-admission of the expelled branch leaders and, in a case before the Federal Court, the MBA entered the case on Gallagher's side.[87]

In as much as the new branch offered industrial resistance to employers, the anonymous employers' organisation official interviewed in 1981 described it as 'a piss in the Pacific compared to the stuff we got from Mundey, Owens and Pringle'. Indeed from Intervention onwards Gallagher had mutually co-operative relationships with builders and enjoyed close connections with employers generally. One of the complaints often aired by Gallagher's opponents within the union movement was that he indulged in 'frequent booze ups and luncheons with top executives'. Bruno Grollo described his relationship with Gallagher as the same as 'with any other business associate'.[88] Apart from the revelations of the later Royal Commission into the BLF, between 1985 and 1988 various other court cases also found Gallagher guilty of numerous corruption offences, such as receiving bribes from employers. Owens now muses that Gallagher had sowed the seeds of his own destruction. Having lined up with the bosses, he eventually found the bosses lined up against him, and with the federal BLF accordingly deregistered again in 1986, and builders labourers deserting the union in droves, the BWIU again benefited from Gallagher's machinations, because its successor, the Construction Forestry Mining and Energy Union, absorbed the remnants and secured coverage of defunct ABLF.[89]

On 20 April 1978, in response to Gallagher's allegation that the former New South Wales branch officials were 'of general bad character' and should not be re-admitted, the Federal Court concluded 'no material has been placed before us on which it could possibly be held that one of the applicants is of general bad character'. Gallagher's counsel argued, as evidence of 'bad character', that they had sworn at employers – prompting the comment from the bench that the applicants were seeking re-admission to a labourers' union, not a ladies' knitting group. The court ordered the New South Wales officials be re-admitted to the union. Despite the courts exonerating them, Gallagher continued to libel the former officials with unsigned leaflets. He also refused to re-admit the majority of expelled officials including Mundey and Pringle, despite, or perhaps because of, many job-site meetings over the years voting in favour of their re-admission.[90] Gallagher's stated desire to eliminate 'bad characters' from the union concealed his true motive: fear of the popularity and ideological ascendancy of those he had so ruthlessly and illegally ousted.

GREEN BANS FOREVER?

Green bans forever, green bans forever,
Green bans forever in Victoria Street.
We sang as I've hopped from chimney top to chimney top,
Green bans forever in Victoria Street.

This gallant green ban song notwithstanding, the NSWBLF would have been appalled at such a prospect. As requests for green bans snowballed, and the attacks from employers, police, government and media built up, the union found itself in a state of perpetual siege. Although the frenetic activity attracted support from both inside and outside the union, the imposition of green bans clearly had serious drawbacks for it. Mick Tubbs of the CPA observed the pressures on the union: 'often it wasn't so much the leadership itself pushing ideas as people inside and outside pushing them into the next step. The situation developed its own internal dynamics. It was difficult to find a period for consolidation.' Members commented about the problems for the union in its imposition of green bans. Owens remarked: 'There was too much going on but there was nothing we could do about it'.[1] Darcy Duggan observed: 'We got a dirty big world moving and it was gaining momentum. We were moving too fast for a small union and we couldn't slacken up because people were coming to us with their problems when no other trade union would help them.' As the strong supporting the weak on the one issue that truly affected everybody – a union protecting society generally from environmental vandalism – the green ban movement was the ultimate way in which the NSWBLF in this period can be seen as a prototype of social-movement unionism.

THE UNION VIEW OF THE BANS

The union did not see green bans as a permanent solution, stunningly effective though they were. It would agree with Bob Carr's assessment that the most important effect of the green bans was to hold the developers at bay while community attitudes caught up. The metaphors employed by the union to describe its green ban activity – 'holding operation', 'thinking time', 'breathing space' – evoked a temporary state of affairs, an industrial equivalent to a legal injunction. Of the Kelly's Bush ban, Mundey wrote:

> We looked on this ban as a holding operation. The residents would now be able to speak from a position of strength. They could go back to the bureaucracies, like the local council, the State Planning Authority, or the Premier, and try to make gains. Negotiations were now a possibility.
> We didn't expect the ban to last forever and a day.

In exhorting Brisbane unionists in July 1973 to save the buildings in that city near the Botanical Gardens, he spoke of the value of the Sydney bans: 'The main thing achieved by the bans was "thinking time". Once the buildings have gone you cannot hold post-mortems. It's too late. Save them first and then say what they can be used for. A use can be found for them.' In general, Mundey insisted: 'We didn't set ourselves up as arbiters. We were merely intervening on the side of the residents to give them a little breathing space. We wanted their case to be heard, and not just that of the building bosses.'[2]

The union was aware, and proud, of this power. 'When they were confronted with our demands', Mundey observes of the Kelly's Bush ban, 'Jennings quickly changed their minds about the use of scab labour. They now began to talk to the Battlers ... the ban ensured an almost certain victory for the Battlers.' Speaking in Inverell at the time of the Capitol Theatre ban, Pringle described the union's role in preserving buildings of architectural or historical significance as action 'to support the National Trust which has no teeth'.[3] This metaphor of a toothless trust was repeatedly invoked, which conjured up images of a positively saber-toothed union.

Although Mundey, Owens, Pringle and the rest of the NSWBLF leadership would not have acknowledged nor even recognised the term 'syndicalist', this is undoubtedly the most accurate way of categorising the NSWBLF's 'theory' and practice; they were adamant that unions, as combinations of those whose location within production gave them extraordinary power, were the organisations within capitalist society best placed to secure either reforms or more fundamental transformation. When Mundey stepped down from office and went back to the job he spoke to the bevy of reporters obstructing his first day's work of his plans to influence more trade unions to take direct action on ecological issues, because 'intellectuals and academics, while important, do not have the muscle to change developers' minds'. Owens hinted at an even wider significance for the demonstration of working-class power shown by the bans: 'Too many people have regarded their position in life as immutable. Then came our green bans and now they realize they can fight the developers and all the other exploiters.'[4]

Unlike the BWIU, which justified its inaction on environmental matters by arguing that capitalism inevitably spoilt the environment, the NSWBLF was attempting to alleviate the effects of capitalism's excesses, and to encourage more socially responsive and ecologically responsible planning than would otherwise prevail. Yet the union was not inclined to over-estimate the impact of its bans on the larger scheme of environmental vandalism. On the contrary Mundey emphasised the extent of the destruction in which developers were constantly engaged. In noting that the union had saved 11 historic buildings in Sydney in the previous two years, he stressed that in the same time 41 had been razed. Pringle also pointed out that while some buildings had been saved 'because the BLF has accepted the responsibility', many were destroyed because no law had been provided to give any elected body the authority to stop demolition. 'Some of the most beautiful buildings have now been smashed because of this.'[5]

Therefore, apart from the important immediate effect of bans in saving individual buildings, localities or spaces, the union clearly hoped the longer-term and more general impact of the green bans would be to provoke the state into responding to the assertion of industrial muscle and indications of public support. Mundey threw down the challenge: 'We have had support from all sections of the community. The Government should bring down legislation so that it will not be necessary for us to take this action.'[6]

THE EFFECTS OF THE BANS

In July 1973 the Australian reported that 'Mr Mundey and builders labourers saved the inner city residentials and stopped buildings and freeways worth $3000 million in two years'. Later in 1973 a submission from the Department of Urban and Regional Development to the Inquiry into the National Estate referred to the impact of the NSWBLF:

> This body has unexpectedly, and somewhat to the embarrassment of the more conservative and 'establishment' members of the trusts, provided teeth for the

preservationists' cause. Where pleas and reasonable requests could be ignored or summarily dismissed by government, and especially by private developers, the threat of direct strike action by workmen on the site is a matter of immediate concern and negotiation.

An *Australian* editorial on 25 March 1975, by way of a funeral oration on the NSWBLF, acknowledged that every green ban had 'brought the issue of the quality of life squarely back to the public arena'. The task now was to develop a planning structure that was flexible, environmentally oriented and human, for the lack of such had prompted the green bans. The NSWBLF had forcibly reminded people 'that the human consequences of build, build, build cannot be ignored'. Around this time, Hugh Stretton argued that the green bans were intelligently chosen to do more good for the city than its planners had ever been allowed to get away with. Alluding to Askin and his accomplices, he added: 'If you love any of Sydney's old buildings or poor people, don't ever forget who first stopped that government, and the class and party that put it there, from the injury they tried to do to all of us and all our heirs'.[7]

In 1976 the Australian Conservation Foundation published its tribute to the NSWBLF, 'to a group that has achieved more for urban conservation Australia than many a government', claiming that the combination of resident action and worker power had revolutionised Australian planning, borne out in the extent to which planning journals, official reports, consultants' briefs, academics' papers all reeked of the 'planning is people' syndrome. An American researcher concluded in 1977 that, in the four years from 1971, green bans were responsible for the modification, postponement or cancellation of over 40 construction projects valued at over $4 billion Australian dollars; that the concept given life by the green ban movement was continuing to give pause to the development spree that characterised Sydney in the 1960s; and in the neighbourhoods and landmarks that remain 'the people of Sydney possess permanent reminders of that crusade'.[8]

These were early judgements. The longer-term achievements of the bans lay in the extent to which governments accepted Mundey's challenge to obviate the need for bans. As the environmentalist Vincent Serventy stressed during Askin's union-bashing election campaign in November 1973, there was a very simple solution to the 'problem 'of green bans: legislative protection for threatened areas until enquiries were held. It was only in 'the present state of lack of appropriate legislation' that conservationists necessarily welcomed 'the interest taken by trade unions in the environment'.[9]

Taking issue with Serventy, the New South Wales Minister for Environment Control insisted late in 1973 that green bans were unnecessary because there was adequate power to protect the environment in the existing *Pollution Control Commission Act*. However, he then added that this Act (which he had insisted did not need reinforcement) was being strengthened by a new Environment Protection Bill shortly to be placed before Parliament.[10] Clearly the government had been forced to respond to the green bans, reluctant though it was to admit that the much feared and despised 'industrial muscle' of 'mere builders labourers' had prompted its new initiatives.

This influence of bans upon the planning process was, paradoxically, encouraged by developers. Because of the green bans' obvious popularity with the general public, a significant section of developers began to adopt a more subtle approach that aimed to deflect criticism away from developers and onto the government. Prominent as spokesman for these developers was Bruce McDonald, senior vice-president of the Institute of Real Estate Development (subsequently the national Urban Development Institute of Australia), which was formed by representatives of most of the major development companies to counter the problems faced by the industry at a time when green bans were 'becoming the fashion'. McDonald clearly saw his role in the green ban debate as 'a catalyst for the vested interests involved'.[11] Accordingly he approached various government bodies in an effort to upgrade state and federal planning laws. He portrayed the villains as the government, not the developers, and did not directly attack the green bans or NSWBLF: 'State and Federal governments have until recently, appeared to lack understanding and imagination on social planning issues. Much blame could be directed towards them for the social and planning failures which manifest themselves in green bans and other confrontations'.[12]

McDonald subsequently conceded that 'the builders labourers had caused us to stand still and look at things, and to realise that things weren't right'. But this admission was used to direct blame once again at the government and thereby deflect it away from the developers themselves: 'The government hasn't responded so we've got to go to the government and let it know what's happening out in the streets'. Allan Vogan, the president of the same institute, was also careful not to adopt what could be interpreted as an anti-green ban stance. He conceded that 'the unions certainly have a point – maybe they have done Sydney a service'.[13]

The Whitlam Government, long sensitive to the issues raised in the green ban movement, had sponsored important initiatives to protect the environment, heritage and working-class residences. According to Roddewig, this sensitivity was 'a direct response to the green ban movement and the new politics of the environment'. In May 1973 the Whitlam Government established a Committee of Inquiry into the National Estate. In 1974 this committee's report prompted the far-reaching national estate program to identify and preserve sites of 'aesthetic, historical, scientific, social, cultural, ecological or other special value'. This program became a joint effort of the Department of Urban and Regional Development and the newly created Department of the Environment. Under Dr Moss Cass as Minister for the Environment, this Department also protected natural heritage via the *Environmental Protection (Impact of Proposals) Act 1974* and the expansion of federal government powers to declare national park areas, even in the face of state government resistance, as in the case of the Great Barrier Reef Marine Park.[14]

At state level, submission to green ban pressure was considerably less magnanimous, but the Askin Government did abolish the much-maligned State Planning Authority and replace it with a New South Wales Planning and Environment Commission. Sir John Fuller, in announcing this change, admitted to a grudging respect for the NSWBLF and acknowledged: 'The Government realises that communities are looking for opportunities to participate in planning and we are looking to make this possible'. The *Financial Review* pin-pointed the reason for this policy change:

> This is an obvious reaction by the Government to the rising power base being cemented by the increasing number of resident action groups. The Government has been embarrassed into recognising them following their alliance with the BLF which has become their muscle arm in imposing green bans.[15]

Even Liberal politicians espoused the now popular environmentalist viewpoint, while pillorying the NSWBLF and its leaders. Indeed, anxiety to provide better means for ensuring that environmental concerns were enshrined in planning processes was clearly motivated by fear of the union's continuing influence and popularity in the absence of such measures. For instance the state Liberal member for Burwood, Mr Jackett, argued in parliament 'the need for legislation for some practical means of providing incentives to ensure the preservation of historical buildings'. When Kevin Stewart interjected 'You have Jack Mundey', Jackett's reply was: 'God forbid that we should ever have to rely on Jack Mundey ... The formulation of such a means of protecting valuable historical buildings should not be handed over to persons who have an axe to grind or to the self-appointed judges of what should be preserved.'[16]

With the Askin Government at last defeated at the polls, the Wran Labor Government from 1976 embarked upon significant legislation to protect heritage more adequately. In its first year it announced the preparation of laws under which developers would risk six months gaol plus $10,000 fines for demolishing historical buildings, and if a developer did damage an historical site the government would have the power to ban all development on that site for ten years. Companies and individuals who found themselves forced to preserve their buildings would be given rate and tax relief and, if hardship could be proved, the government would consider acquiring the property or pay for repairs. While awaiting the new legislation the government prepared a comprehensive list of historic buildings. In 1978 this *New South Wales Heritage Act*, which covered public and private buildings made it possible, as Bob Carr noted, for a protective order to be nailed to the door of a property even while the bulldozers were trundling in its direction. In 1979 the Wran Government also enacted the *Environment Planning and Assessment Act, the Legal Aid Commission Act* and the *Land and Environment Court Act*, passed into law with substantial bipartisan support: all three promoted public involvement in environmental decision-making and the provision of legal aid made it possible for the public to exercise their rights. The Land and Environment Court was given the exclusive jurisdiction to judicially review and enforce nominated environmental laws.[17]

Alan Gilpin considered in 1980 that green bans not only 'reduced the scale and rate of social displacement in the inner city area of Sydney' but had encouraged this review in New South Wales of planning procedures generally. In 1981 Neil Runcie observed that large cities tended, through expansion, to destroy their inner city residential district, but in Sydney 'largely as a result of the green bans' there was a policy to retain inner-city living and a proportion of it for low-income earners. Referring to the 1979 acts, Professor David Yencken, president of the Conservation Foundation, maintained in 1993 that the green bans had led indirectly to these most significant pieces of environmental legislation.[18]

While the union itself did not over-estimate the effect of the bans, others have been more effusive. In November 1997, Professor PN Troy, director of the Urban Research Unit at the Australian National University and who had been an adviser to the Department of Urban and Regional Development during the green bans period, stated quite simply that it would be 'hard to over-estimate the importance of the bans' because of their 'subtle influence' in transforming the culture of urban planning in ways that now evince greater sensitivity to

environmental concerns, better appreciation of heritage, the need to publicise proposed developments well in advance and to seek approval from the
people affected. He also spoke of the way the ideas embodied in the movement
were 'picked up internationally'. Yencken attributed significant imponderables
to the green bans: 'the environment was on the political agenda, and public
involvement and people power were taken seriously, due to a great extent to
the moral and economic force of Green Bans'. Craig McGregor wrote about
the way the green ban movement cut right across the old 'develop at all costs'
ethic and alluded to the architectural prescience of many of the ideas in that
movement: the way in which Australian housing authorities by the late 1970s
were 'coming around to the idea of medium-density housing' and admitting
that high-rise developments were a mistake; and the tendency for the spaces
between the skyscrapers of American cities to become no man's land, owned
and loved by nobody. With so much high-rise office space still vacant in Sydney,
Bob Carr argued in 1981 that a major effect of green bans was not only to halt
over-construction but also to save expansion-mad developers from going bust,
for social movements often have unintended effects. Academic commentators
such as Michael Berry have also stressed that although the green bans were
crucial, the collapse of the office building boom clearly facilitated outcomes
like the Woolloomooloo project.[19]

While wary of claiming too much indirect influence, Mundey is prepared
to boast about the green bans' more direct achievements. 'Most Sydneysiders
would agree we have been well and truly vindicated by our overall stand.
Sydney is a better place because of those community-trade union actions.'[20]
Woolloomooloo became for Mundey 'a prototype for attractive and useful
inner-city re-development'; for the *Sydney Morning Herald*'s civic reporter
it succeeded in 'setting world standards in town planning'. With more than
350,000 tourists visiting The Rocks each year, Mundey can be excused for
bragging 'Would anyone bother to go if it had been $500 million dollars
worth of concrete and glass, as the developers had wanted?' Likewise Yencken
refers to The Rocks as 'the jewel of Sydney's CBD, thanks to Jack and his
union'; and on 8 December 1996 a plaque was unveiled in The Rocks by
the Carr Government's Minister for Planning, Craig Knowles, to commem-
orate the area's preservation as 'a world-class example of urban conservation'
and 'the courage and vision of all who worked to save this precious part of
Sydney's heritage'. Who would now dare consider turning Centennial Park
into 'a concrete sports stadium' to facilitate a bid for the Olympics, Mundey
asked.[21] 'Nobody', is the answer recently given in the choice of Homebush

Bay for such a purpose – a choice Mundey and others had urged at the time.

The Wran Government also purchased Kelly's Bush in 1983 and dedicated it as an open public reserve. Wran's press statement stressed the area was for the use of all Sydneysiders, not just the locals, and announced: 'It represents a victory for environmentalists generally'. In 1984 the Department of Planning and Environment established a Management Committee for Kelly's Bush, to investigate the regeneration of natural bushland and removal of refuse and contamination, which spent over $850,000 on extensive rehabilitation. On 30 December 1993 control of the bush was handed over to Hunters Hill Council and a plaque unveiled commemorating the Battle for Kelly's Bush, for it created a precedent: 'It became known internationally as the urban area that was saved by the first Green Ban, thanks to Jack Mundey and the Unions'.[22]

With both Paul Ehrlich and Petra Kelly arguing the Australian green bans gave the environmental movement a new and wider dimension and opened up the possibility of involving a much broader strata of the population in ecological actions, environmental groups the world over expressed interest in the green bans movement.[23] In 1975 the Centre for Environmental Studies in London invited Mundey to lecture for six months to environment, union and community groups throughout Britain. During this visit, he addressed the Labour Party Conference and at Spike Milligan's instigation was instrumental in persuading construction workers to prevent demolition of Birmingham Post Office by striking to 'keep Britain beautiful'. Impressed by the success of the Australian green ban movement, Birmingham unionists also formed a Green Ban Committee to promote the 'social responsibility of labour'. In 1976 Mundey was the only Australian among the '24 world thinkers' invited to address the first United Nations conference on the built environment in Vancouver: 'the platform awash with PhDs and there was the rumpled, corduroy-jacketed Mundey who does not own a tie'.[24] The following year he was invited to the World Wild Life Congress in San Francisco in 1977. In the late 1970s and 1980s he addressed trade union, anti-nuclear and environment conferences in Europe, Japan, Canada and the USA. In 1990 he was invited to the Third World Conference on the Environment and Development in Nicaragua and in 1992 to the New Zealand Trade Union Conference. In 1998 both the University of New South Wales and the University of Western Sydney presented Mundey with honorary doctorates in acknowledgment of his 'eminent and vital service to society' (in the words of Professor John Niland, quoted in the *Sydney Morning Herald*, 12 May 1998).

Yet the advances made must not be exaggerated. There is considerable evidence that the union was correct in stressing the connection between capitalism and environmental problems. Yencken regretted recently that rescission now means that many of the old environmental battles must be fought again.

> Many bad projects are being put forward and accepted in the name of finding
> jobs for increasing numbers of people. We need to think again about the
> sacrifices made by the old BLF unionists in foregoing jobs for the social good.
> Maybe it was easier then when there were more jobs to go to. Nevertheless,
> they did it.[25]

Mundey also admits the new planning processes prompted by the bans flourished all too briefly and that by the late 1980s large developments were being taken out of public scrutiny and control vested in ministers who did secret deals with developers; and in 1987 the Unsworth Labor Government sacked the Sydney City Council, because the Community Independent council members, Mundey among them, were partially successful in thwarting developers.[26] (Mundey had thus been sacked twice for upholding environ mental standards.)

Costello and Dunn reveal how the ability of resident activists to contest development has been restricted during the 1990s. In response to a new spate of resident activity during the 1980s, the State Government moved to curb severely the planning powers of local government, because it is that tier of the state on which resident activism is usually focused. These measures included a reversal of some of the legislative reforms attendant upon the green bans activity. In mid-1991 the Legal Aid Commission revised its guidelines on providing funding for public interest environmental matters, because the government had been embarrassed by recent court decisions in favour of community groups. Local government and community groups were thereby disempowered in the planning process through restricted access to financial assistance for cases in the Land and Environment Court. In March 1992 the New South Wales Premier stated his government was reversing its former policy of non-interference in local government, particularly with regard to major job-creating projects; in mid-1992 the government announced it would appropriate planning powers for all major projects due to a recent trend that had seen potential developments located out of New South Wales, due to delays, high costs and uncertainty.[27]

Such regressive actions have clearly been facilitated by an absence of working-class resistance. As early as 1976 the *Bulletin* noted that the left was attempting to reconvene the coalition of workers, middle-class conservationists and intellectuals that had proved so effective in the green ban movement. Tim Bonyhady's recent study of environmental politics reveals the essential weakness of a green movement that cannot rely on trade union co-operation.[28] The withdrawal, or threat of the withdrawal, of labour, remains the ultimate deterrent to environmental vandalism on the part of employers, as the green bans vividly illustrated. Organisations such as the Australian Conservation Foundation and resident activists are still to this day systematically challenging environmental irresponsibility and poor planning, yet visibly they lack the much-vaunted 'teeth' they once had.

Mundey was one of the first to see the significance of the alliance between 'trendies' and workers: 'the importance of the more enlightened middle class and the more enlightened working class coming together'. The great success of the green bans movement was the way in which it forged 'a winning alliance between enlightened middle-class people in the environmental movement and enlightened trade unionists in the NSWBLF'. Too frequently middle-class activists 'fail to understand the importance of involving the working class in the movement'; and too frequently unions have merely fought for better wages and conditions. 'Trade unions must become involved with environmental issues, and environmentalists must become more concerned with the importance of promoting trade union struggles for socially useful production and consumption. Too few people question the products we make.'[29]

THE ALTERNATIVE PUBLIC SPHERE

On Australia Day 1974, Australian of the Year Patrick White said he wanted to use the opportunity to salute Jack Mundey: 'the first citizen of our increasingly benighted, shark-infested city of Sydney who succeeded effectively in calling the bluff of those who have begun tearing us to bits, ostensibly in the name of progress, but in fact for their own aggrandisement, with little regard for human need'. In grappling with the problem of how to encompass this quixotic gesture of Australia's Nobel Laureate, the Australian editorial conceded Mundey had 'forced Australians to look at themselves and their values'.[30]

The extent to which Mundey and the NSWBLF had prompted public political debate is apparent in the extensive programme of speaking engagements undertaken by Mundey. Community, institutional, student and environmental groups across Australia were anxious to hear from the union's best-known spokesperson, especially after his voluntary 'release of power' placed him in a position to accept such appointments. His return to the job as a pick-and-shovel labourer had not removed him from public exposure;

like TE Lawrence during his 'Ross' days, Mundey had a genius for backing into the lime-light. He was mostly received with great enthusiasm, his message of the social responsibility of labour finding receptive audiences. The Students' Council of Wollongong University even directed the students to vote for Mundey in the 1974 Senate elections.[31]

Mundey, as the foremost representative of the NSWBLF, loomed so large in the public mind that his speeches were capable of causing controversy before they were even made. Invited to speak at a meeting organised by the Narrabeen Lagoon Regional Park Association, local federal member Michael MacKellar hotly opposed the invitation, describing Mundey's acolytes in colourful terms: 'The people who support and encourage him remind me of rabbits mesmerised by snakes – only as they lie twitching do they realise the extent of their foolishness'. Likewise Lismore City Council objected to the Regional Library Committee's invitation to Mundey to address a public meeting during Library Week. The council directed that the invitation be withdrawn and a heated debate about free speech took place in the area. In a sermon preached in St Andrew's Anglican Cathedral, Rev Alan Nichols deplored that 'trade union leaders like Jack Mundey, an avowed Communist, should be making decisions on moral and social issues on behalf of the Australian public', because 'builders' labourers have no special right to dictate policy on such matters as the preservation of historic buildings'. He was particularly distressed by those who had made 'unionism another religion'.[32]

The polarisation of the community, consequent upon the way in which the union forced Australians to look at themselves and their values, had carved out a significant body of support for the union and its radical political and social agenda. Although lambasted by those whose power it most obviously contested, and defeated ultimately by those within the union movement most clearly threatened by its 'new concept of unionism', the NSWBLF had changed public opinion for the more radical. An alternative public sphere, determined upon green principles and policies, and impressed to a large degree with other aspects of the 'new concept of unionism', was clearly interacting with the wider public sphere. Sydney journalist Peter Manning concluded:

> The Mundeys and the Pringles and the Owens and the rest of the builders labourers' leadership and the rank-and-file have effected one of those rare shifts in public thinking that occurs only a few times in a life-time. Maybe they were madhatters and larrikins – a true Australian tradition – but, by God, there's many a Sydney resident who will remember them with love.[33]

That the officials had the majority support of the rank and file in imposing bans cannot be doubted. Each ban was approved by full branch meetings and, in August 1972, in the face of concerted attacks, a stop-work meeting of about a thousand builders labourers 'unanimously and enthusiastically re-endorsed the union's policy of action on environmental issues'. Stop-work meetings in other New South Wales centres also endorsed the bans policy. Members were also prepared to down tools and physically defend bans under threat. Explaining the leadership's remarkable resilience during this hectic period, Pringle commented: 'We always had the members to fall back on. They were solid and that was our strength. See, someone like Jimmy [Staples] has to fight on his pat [own]. He's got no one to pull him into line or to back him up. We always had the rank and file.' The loyalty of the rank and file, which enabled the union to stage the green bans so effectively, also facilitated the way in which the boundary between union and radical public was blurred. Owens believed the union's major achievement was in 'breaking down the false distinction between us and the public ... extending the union to the community'. Pringle described the NSWBLF as 'more a movement than just a union', because it 'extended well beyond the realms of the usual field of industrial relations' and took 'an interest in how labor affects the community'.[34]

In raising the principle of the social responsibility of labour in such an effective and dramatic way, the union had succeeded in creating around it a subaltern counterpublic that was unusually determined and active. The introduction to the book on the green bans produced by the Australian Conservation Foundation gives some indication of how those who experienced that period felt: 'We hope it reflects some of the elan and excitement that pervaded this uniquely Australian phenomenon'.[35] A truly counter-hegemonic struggle, the green ban movement had a style and spirit of optimism essential for the success of great missions. One of the union's great achievements was that, despite an often unsympathetic media, it managed to communicate what the green ban movement was about. This was partly because of the ability and 'star quality' of the leaders but also because, unlike other officials whose media stance is mostly geared towards either their membership or the employer, they were genuinely concerned with enlightening the public. And their message came across. Adherents wore 'BLF Supporter' badges and carried bumper stickers proclaiming 'Green Bans Forever' and 'BLF supports green bans – We support the BLF'. Victoria Street publications declared: 'The BLF supports people, people support the BLF'. The clincher according to Wendy Bacon was the union's ability to provide positive direct action solutions, which appealed to both idealists and activists among the Sydney left. 'With the Rocks and Victoria Street, when hundreds of police were brought out and the BLF still won – that's pretty exciting stuff for most left-wingers.'[36]

The Glebe Society (left to right: Prof Bernard Smith, Joye Wallace (behind), Jeanette Knox, Kate Smith, Jan Potter) demonstrates in Darghan Street, Glebe, against the Northwestern Expressway, in 1972. (Courtesy *Sydney Morning Herald*)

But support for the BLF extended far beyond the self-consciously left-wing. Many of those, such as the Battlers for Kelly's Bush, who had cause to be grateful to the union but were otherwise distant from the left sub-culture, rallied to its defence, demonstrating angrily against Gallagher's Intervention. Patrick White's public support for the union was frequent and eloquent. Many other prominent and respectable people with no direct self-interest in the green ban movement sang the praises of the union. The distinguished art critic Bernard Smith attended green ban demonstrations and organised the Glebe Society to oppose the Northwestern Expressway. Margaret Mead, the famous anthropologist, who visited Sydney in 1973 as a guest of the state Housing Commission, applauded the union for its refusal to pull down elegant old houses and replace them with high-rise office blocks: 'I'm very impressed that they have taken up the cause of humanity'. Whitlam Government ministers – especially Cameron, Uren, Johnson and Cass – gave verbal and sometimes practical assistance. Leading architect Neville Gruzman regretted that so many of his profession had contributed to the destruction of cities, and the erection of what Sir Paul Hasluck rightly described as 'monstrosities'; and he enumerated the many worthwhile places that would have been razed to the ground by insensitive developers were it not for the breathing space provided by the actions of the NSWBLF.[37]

When the *Australian* canvassed its readers' suggestions for Australian of the Year in 1973, a Rockhampton correspondent nominated the members of the NSWBLF because they 'risked their security for a cause which, if allowed to come to fruition, will ensure that Australian cities will always be places for the people rather than centres for financial speculation'. There were countless similar letters to the papers, from across the country: for example, from Melbourne expressing gratitude to the builders labourers for being prepared to fight to protect the environment 'while the rest of us are led down the garden path by our legislators'; from Adelaide arguing that the 'little man' was left only with the hope of a green ban, admitting that 'much as one dislikes union intervention … I feel sympathy for the unions'; and from Queensland congratulating the builders labourers on 'their magnificent stand'. Ian Turner's 1978 history of Australian unions described the green bans as doing 'more than anything else to improve the image of Australian trade unionism in recent years'.[38]

The MBA's lockout of the builders labourers late in 1973 caused the swell of public support for the New South Wales branch to increase dramatically. Resident action groups wrote letters to the newspapers, as did sympathetic architects, environmentalists and doctors. Institutions as different as the University of New England Students' Council and the Newcastle Trades Hall moved motions of support. The Department of Urban and Regional Development gave the green bans its seal of approval ('Endorsing Sabotage', as the *Sydney Morning Herald* saw it).[39] Patrick White wrote to the media:

> It is a sad reflection on our so-called civilization that residents of Sydney ... are forced time and again to turn to the BLF ... It is a rare thing to find a union with so advanced a social conscience. But how much longer can the citizens of Sydney ask these men to endure the responsibility for protecting a citizen's right to live comfortably and without anxiety.

White's letter was read out at a rally of several hundred BLF supporters in Centennial Park organised by CRAG in protest at the lockout.[40]

However important such wide-ranging support for the union was, the shock troops of the subaltern counterpublic were undoubtedly from among the self-consciously left-wing, both working-class and middle-class, in Sydney. Here the radicalised public responded with a degree of devotion never before displayed towards an Australian union. The counter-culture media wrote admiring articles.[41] A group of supporters produced *The Little Green Book*, which detailed the 40 green bans to date and defended the union with gusto. Support campaigns – which included posters, pamphlets, graffiti, balloons, sit-ins, picnics, demonstrations, green ban balls, crane occupations and a host of other imaginative tactics – displayed inventiveness, humour and vigour. And as the union became increasingly beleaguered by its opponents these supporters became frenetically active in its support.

One public meeting in support of the union, in this case over its demand for permanency of employment for builders labourers, was organised by VSAG in May 1973. The leaflet that advertised the meeting explained: 'The other building industry unions have refused support for the builders' labourers and have, in fact, asked them to shelve their demands. This makes it even more urgent for the public to make it clear it supports the BLF – the union that cares about people.' About three hundred people from many different organisations attended the meeting in the Trades Hall and made speeches from the floor in appreciation of the BLF. The radical newsletter, *Scrounge*, described it as the 'BLF Love In' and noted representation from the following groups and unions: plumbers rank and file; black community in Redfern; metal workers unions; Centre for Workers Control; CRAG; Women Workers; VSAG; Teachers' Federation; Painters and Dockers Union; and The Rocks, Newcastle and Woolloomooloo resident action groups. *Scrounge*

A Green Ban Supporters demonstration in Martin Place, March 1 975 (front left to right: Janne Reed, Pat Fiske (with camera), Glenys Page (partly obscured), Stella Nord, unknown, Aileen Beaver (hand to ear), Roelof Smilde (obscured), unknown, Liz Fell, John Cox, Meredith Burgmann (partly obscured), Seamus Gill (back to camera), Richard Walsham; seated: Julie McCrossin, Linda Young, unknown, Irene Bruninghausen).

also recorded the formation of a committee to continue active support for the NSWBLF.[42]

While the mainstream labour movement, as represented by the right-dominated Labor Council, largely stood back and allowed the union to be annihilated, other unions and unionists, such as those who attended such meetings, were affected by the NSWBLF vision. Barry Egan of the conservative Shop Distributive and Allied Employees Association argued in December 1973, in a statement with which many other left unionists agreed, that the green bans were simply doing the state's job, that in the absence of environmental safeguards in the building industry it was unfair to criticise the NSWBLF. Echoing NSWBLF sentiments, Egan declared trade unions would and should expand their responsibilities. 'In modern society the trade union must play a really meaningful role in all industrial, political and social matters affecting employees.' However, as Bob Carr argued, when it came to influencing the behaviour of the rest of the union movement in any longer-term sense, 'the green bans proved an isolated, one-off phenomenon'.[43] Bearing this uniqueness in mind, it is therefore necessary to examine the dynamics within the union that sustained such a unique phenomenon.

As far as the members were concerned, the new concept of unionism worked exceedingly well for them as both unionists and workers. The ultra-democratic organisational practices of the union endeared the leadership to the membership and the militant industrial relations strategies brought significant material rewards, such as substantial real wage rises, accident pay, paid public holidays, improved safety and amenities and the near eradication of subcontractors who failed to pay their workers. For such improvements, the membership was prepared to listen sympathetically to the leaders' other ideas and, as it turned out, act upon them. As Clyde Cameron observed at the time, Mundey, with his undoubted 'charisma', was the kind of unionist who stuck to his ideals and won his members' respect.[44]

Mundey and the other NSWBLF ideologues and agitators possessed an important agitational attribute: they were never dull. They were all competent and even accomplished speakers. They were honest in their approach to fellow workers; able to admit ignorance or even error, a quality much admired by Australian workers. Without the binding dogma of a vanguard party to impede them they found, like generations of syndicalists before them, that their philosophy was sufficiently vague and flexible to allow a good deal of doctrinal variation, enabling them to maintain a decentralised organic unity with a minimal tendency to fragment.[45] In fact a description of archetypal syndicalist Tom Mann could just as easily fit Jack Mundey: 'Enthusiasm, rhetoric and ceaseless energy; an unsectarian unsystematic, eclectic thinker capable of an extraordinary range of responses; above all else an agitator'.[46]

Although Mundey and Owens were members of the CPA, their refreshing lack of vanguardism, sectarianism and dogmatism – too often associated with members of left-wing political parties – was a welcome relief to the many workers in the building industry wearied by the recent upheavals of the splits within the CPA. While some of the rank and file held suspicious attitudes towards the CPA,[47] they were inclined to make exceptions in the case of Mundey and Owens. Even apart from the fact that the CPA was seen to be going through its most intensely independent phase during the early 1970s, Mundey was clearly 'one of the strongest critics of blindly following the line of any one country and defending all its works, whether the country is the Soviet Union, China, Cuba, Albania, or wherever'. This vehemently independent stance of the Mundey group was definitely to its advantage in its clashes with the Maoists. His insistence that he did not worship at the altar of either Peking or Moscow was important as an indication of the new, ecological way in which he was viewing the earth's problems, and crucial in reassuring the rank and file that he was untainted by any un-Australian tradition and that his ideology was not imported but had developed from within local union struggles.[48]

The leaders' use of commonplace terminology also set them apart from the sectarian dogmatists of previous years. Both Owens and Mundey believed that the CPA prior to the SPA split was held back by outworn and old-fashioned dogma. Owens was also critical of the way the old CPA had 'deviously projected themselves as democrats rather than communists'. Total honesty was essential, so he admitted always and readily to being both a democrat and a communist, for 'one of the biggest things is openness'. Much of their language, as well as their ideology, was derived from New Left influences: for instance, 'participatory democracy' and 'principled stands' were often mentioned. Thus NSWBLF expression of its ideology differed from Old Left practice in its reluctance to use jargon and revolutionary terminology, to which the membership would be unlikely to relate. Never once did terms such as 'hegemony' or 'surplus value' pass their lips, yet the ideas involved in these expressions were simply and effectively explained. For instance, Owens described 'class conflict' as 'a couple of friendly subbies I know around town employ me and make $2.50 an hour out of my work'.[49]

Anti-intellectualism was rampant among the leadership and struck a chord among the members. Tom Hogan, one of the few officials who ever admitted to reading Marx, described his experience thus:

> He [Jack Demsey – a BLF member of the CPA] gave me Volume I of *Capital* and he underlined what he thought was the most important part of Karl Marx. I read about forty pages of it. I thought 'Shit this is good stuff, I don't know what he's saying'. It didn't influence me at all – it just convinced me that I was a dunce … Having gone through it at party study groups later I realised that he [Jack] hadn't understood it either – he'd underlined all the most irrelevant parts.[50]

This story illustrates two points about builders labourers' anti-intellectualism. Firstly the humour and self-deprecation they displayed so often, and utilised so skilfully, is evident. Michael Schneider and Klaus Mehnert speak of the importance of humour in political education and that:

> … quite a few students who went into the factories behaved as if they were martyrs for the entire working class … This masochism for the Left by petty-bourgeois intellectuals, which banishes all humour from political work, is but the reaction of their suppressed class arrogance.[51]

Certainly the builders labourers held in benign contempt the more dogmatic and serious members of the left-wing sects that hung around their fringes. This disdain was displayed during Intervention, when a young student Maoist attempted to address a group of staunchly loyal NSWBLF members. They had physically ejected other federal organisers from their site but, with the student, they contented themselves with nailing his briefcase to the floor while he was speaking. This tale was told with great glee in the pub for weeks afterwards.

Secondly, Hogan's story about reading Marx encapsulates the builders labourers' lack of respect for knowledge and erudition. Their demeanour displayed little of the feelings of inadequacy that Sennett and Cobb found among American workers when confronted with academic interviewers. The ease with which Mundey, Owens and Pringle confronted, and in fact overwhelmed, academic audiences was obvious. This disrespect for intellectuals, 'Spittoon philosophers and blowhards' to the Industrial Workers of the World decades earlier, is a powerful strain within syndicalism.[52] The NSWBLF falls squarely within the syndicalist tradition on this count.

Syndicalist and 'ouvrierist' rather than vanguardist and elitist, the NSWBLF members also had well-formed opinions about the role, or rather lack of role, of a revolutionary party in securing change.

During a discussion on strategy, Mundey emphasised: 'No organisation can do it [achieve revolution] of itself – thus this craziness about vanguard parties having all the knowledge … Union struggles can play the biggest part.'[53] When Seamus Gill, an organiser, was asked about Lenin's view that true revolutionary consciousness had to be brought to workers by a communist party, he replied 'Bollocks'. Mick King joined the union as a 15-year-old, because he believed 'they were the people that would bring the most social change for the workers' movement'. The NSWBLF provided stunning evidence of the power of unions, if willing, to encourage the formation of an alternative public sphere, precisely because they are not alien intrusions like a vanguard party.

The fact that the NSWBLF was a union – a member of Labor Council with offices in Trades Hall and so on – was extremely important. Much that would have appeared strange and unconventional, was accepted with equanimity among the traditional and on-going union activity. Holton stresses the importance of the 'naturalness' of radical movements, noting of British syndicalism that it 'was no alien import but a highly relevant and natural response to British conditions'.[54] This insistence on working within the given social patterns to bring about change is characteristic of syndicalism worldwide. Just as the Australian Industrial Workers of the World insisted on its existence as 'part of the class', so did NSWBLF members feel it was 'their union' and that its struggles arose directly out of Australian conditions. Political philosophy which comes from among one's own, from out of the ranks, may be objectionable but it is not alien, nor does it produce isolation for those who proclaim it. Mundey believes the NSWBLF 'message' would not have 'got across', if it had been put forward by a distant organisation.

Perhaps it was significant that Manning should have referred to the leaders as 'larrikins'. What is more Australian than a larrikin, or more within the Australian tradition than a militant labourers' union with an ex-rugby league star from outback Queensland at its helm? The NSWBLF was a very Australian organisation, and the idea of 'green bans' and union activity around environmental issues was a truly home-grown concept. Opponents could never trade upon xenophobic suspicions of alien creeds. The union was, in the eyes of its members, a fair dinkum outfit, with values and attitudes, perhaps a little more honed than the average union, but certainly a product of the Australian class struggle and not a learned response from another country. This fact was vitally important in the way the membership responded to the increasingly radical ideas put before them by the leadership.

Another significant attribute the union had in abundance was a belief in its own destiny and in working-class power. Georges Sorel described this phenomenon as the power of the myth in politics: myths 'are not descriptions of things ... but expressions of will'. James Joll noted that 'the mystical belief in the ultimate triumph of one's cause, one's will to victory' was kept alive within the workers' movement of the twentieth century by the militant syndicalists.[55] Certainly, it would be no exaggeration to claim that in Australia of the early 1970s it was the NSWBLF that kept alive the 'myth' of the ultimate power of working-class struggle, restoring to militant workers a belief in the power of struggle at the point of production at a time when social democratic and reformist ideology was saturating the labour movement as a whole. The 1972 Labor Party electoral success and the economic boom being experienced in the early 1970s had lulled many previously militant workers into quiescence. Only the NSWBLF's explorations of new trade union territory and its insistence upon control over the social product of workers' labour was a foretaste of further seizure of power for the class.

Sorel's theory, that those organisations inspired by an irrational belief in their own destiny and mission are the causes that triumph,[56] is vindicated to a degree in the way the union succeeded beyond the expectations of the most optimistic cadres of revolutionary organisations. Judy Mundey recalled that the fear that 'this time they had gone too far' was often expressed by supporters, even within the ranks of the CPA. The NSWBLF's vision of a better world, to be brought about largely by its own actions, in particular the green bans, meant that it often triumphed in tactically desperate situations. The fact that its belief was irrational and its chance of success minimal in a non-revolutionary situation was irrelevant both to itself and the thousands of workers it inspired to believe in its dreams. Its message was almost its own victory. 'What went on in the workers' minds was a revolution in itself 'argued Pringle.[57]

The union's actions should therefore be evaluated on two levels: the threat posed to capital, and its mobilising effect. Of the wide range of tactics employed, the activities of the union most threatening to the employers were: encroachment strategies, such as union hire and work-ins; demands for workers' control; demands for permanency; attempts to regulate the industry through the monitoring of safety procedures; election of safety officers and foremen; the pre-meditated destruction of non-union construction by vigilante gangs; the use of guerrilla tactics such as the breaking of concrete pours; and the refusal to abide by industrial court decisions. However, the most important and most obviously transformative action taken by the union was to impose the green bans and to defend them physically. Here the employers' prerogative was not being encroached upon, it was being totally denied. And the force of the ruling class response indicates the extent of the threat to capital posed by the union.

The capacity of the union to mobilise its membership was spectacular. Besides comfortable election wins for the leadership group throughout the 1960s and in 1970 and 1973, the union won every major confrontation with the employers from the 1970 strike until Intervention. For the rank and file the policies which encouraged their participation in the decision-making process elicited a remarkable response, as important in securing their support as the material rewards brought by militant industrial relations strategies. By organisational practices – such as limited tenure for officials, temporary organisers, non-payment of officials during strikes, tying officials' wages to BLF awards, and democratic decision-making procedures – the leaders refuted the 'iron law of oligarchy'. By refusing to fraternise with employers, to dress differently from the membership, to accept 'respectability' or the 'perks' of office, they avoided co-option. By vigorously opposing demarcation disputes, they negated much of the force of sectionalism. And by raising the consciousness of members on issues unrelated to their own employment, they broke free of restricting 'economism'. Continually, mass meetings of builders labourers voted to impose green bans in support of environmentalist objectives or to aid some oppressed group, such as women, prisoners, Aborigines, homosexuals and migrants. They denied themselves work opportunities in pursuit of these policies. Not even during the recession of late 1974 or under the pressure of intervention did mass meetings vote to lift green bans.

This rank-and-file support for the bans was partly a result of respect for the leadership, but it also reflected the leadership's success in encouraging members to respond critically towards matters such as environmental irresponsibility, sexism and racism. There was a broad strategy of opposing conservative ideology on all levels. Economic demands were being supplemented by political demands. For the union's supporters in the wider public it had become a rallying point, a symbol of working-class radical potential in the period before new social movement theorists began to persuade these radicals that the workers' movement was characterised by economism, lack of concern for forms of oppression other than class, and disrespect for environmental imperatives. It was a true foretaste of the ability of social-movement unionism to arouse broad constituencies to radical action. The union could either draw back from its principled position lift the bans – and become like the rest of the trade union movement, or it could be annihilated. The union refused to alter its green ban philosophy even under extreme pressure from the employers, the State Government, the police, the established trade union movement, the other building unions and the federal body of its own union. It was therefore destroyed. The union consciously chose the course it did: it could have given in under pressure just as other unions have done in order to retain its organisation intact. Many at the time argued that radical organisations had a duty to survive, but the NSWBLF believed there was no point in survival if principle had been deserted and only structure remained.

Without a structure, and now unemployed and unemployable as a result of their principled stand, Jack Mundey and Joe Owens gave the following message on recycled paper to the Radical Ecology Conference at Easter 1975:

> More and more workers must increase the demand that workers' labor should be used in a manner which is socially useful and beneficial to the community at large, for the common good, not for rapacious profiteers. Within the widening and worsening capitalist economic and political crisis, the resources crisis, the population crisis, it is essential that workers' consciousness and workers' action be enriched if the ecological crisis has any chance of solution.[58]

ENDNOTES

THE WORLD'S FIRST GREEN BANS

1   *Sun*, 26/10/1973, 8/11/1973; Bonyhady, *Places Worth Keeping*, p 39.
2   Allaby (ed), *Macmillan Dictionary*, p 234; Ransom (ed), *Australian National Dictionary*, p 289.
3   J Mundey to V Burgmann, 1/3/1998.
4   Gindin, *The Canadian Auto Workers*, p 268; Moody, 'Towards an International Social-Movement Unionism', pp 60, 71.
5   E Mackie, *Oh To Be Aussie*, quoted in Ransom (ed), *Australian National Dictionary*, p 290.
6   Habermas, *Structural Transformation of the Public Sphere*, pp xvii–xviii, 27.
7   Fraser, 'Rethinking the Public Sphere', pp 122, 124.
8   Anderson and Jacobs, 'Geographies of Publicity and Privacy', pp 3, 22, 24.
9   ibid, p 20.
10   Mundey, *Green Bans & Beyond*, p 105; Mundey, 'Preventing the plunder', p 177; Colless, 'Carrying the can for the "Greenies"'; Jack Mundey, 3/4/1978; Joan Croll, in Kalajzich (ed), *The Battlers for Kelly's Bush*, p 57; Turner (ed), Union Power, p 22.
11   *Age*, 1/11/1973.
12   Advertisement, *Australian*, 26/10/1973, authorised by director, SCRA; Advertisement, *Daily Telegraph*, 1/11/1973, authorised by J Martin, MBA.
13   Mundey, 'Meeting "The Battlers"', p 7; Mundey and Owens, 'Green Bans'.
14   Mundey, 'Preventing the plunder', p 180.
15   NSWBLF, 'Minutes', Executive Meeting, 12/5/1970.

THE PRECONDITIONS FOR RADICAL UNIONISM

1   Jakubowicz, 'The green ban movement', pp 149–66.
2   Hill and Thurley, 'Sociology and industrial relations', p 160; Hyman, 'Industrial conflict and the political economy', p 110; CBCS and ABS, *Labour Reports, Industrial Disputes*, cited in Rawson, *Unions and Unionists in Australia*, p 131; Bentley, 'Australian Trade Unionism', p 250; Davis, 'The Theory of Union Growth', p 218.
3   Mundey, 'Towards new union militancy', pp 2–5; Mundey, 'Interview', p 10.
4   *Rydge's*, July 1973, p 25; CBCS, 'Building and Construction 1970–71', p 31; *SMH*, 13/11/72.
5   *Newcastle Sun*, 2/11/72.
6   BWIU, 'Meeting re: Gunnedah Dispute'; *Northern Star* (Lismore), 17/5/74, 22/5/74; *Coffs Harbour Advocate*, 9/8/74, 26/8/74; *Grafton Examiner*, 26/8/74, 27/8/74.
7   *SMH*, 11/11/71; *Construction*, 2/12/71.

8   BWIU, 'Some Notes on the Building Industry', pp 1–2; Comm. Bureau of Census & Statistics, 'Building and Construction 1970–71', p 130.
9   Marx and Engels, *Manifesto of the Communist Party*, p 53.
10 Gardiner, 'Union Power and Developers'; *SMH*, 26/2/72; Dean Barber, 18/12/76; Comm. Bureau of Census & Statistics, 'Building and Construction 1970–71', p 127; see also Mandel and Novak, *Marxist Theory of Alienation*, p 7.
11 Shaw, 'Crisis in the Concrete Jungle', p 15; Comm. Bureau of Census & Statistics, 'Building and Construction 1970–71', p 127; *Builders' Labourer*, 25/10/74, p 4; Hutton, *Building and Construction in Australia*, pp 1, 46–47; Minutes: 1968–71; Ralph Kelly, 'She's all in Mate', pp 43, 45; Bud Cook, 'Time for a Clean-up', p 43.
12 *Fin. Rev.*, 8/11/73; *SMH*, 25/5/73; Frenkel and Coolican, 'Competition, Instability and Industrial Struggle', pp 28–29.
13 *Construction*, 4, 11, 1/11/71, p 1.
14 Rawson, *Handbook of Australian Trade Unions*, pp 2–3; Jack Cabourn, 1/2/79.
15 Mundey, 'Towards new union militancy', p 3; Dick Whitehead, 8/6/80; *Construction*, 11/11/71; *SMH*, 18/11/71.
16 Lorne Webster, (Dept. Labour & Industry) with Pat Fiske, 1980; Joe Owens, speech, 2/11/75.
17 Building Industry Branch of the SPA, *Six Turbulent Years*, pp 8, 28.
18 Braverman, *Labor and Monopoly Capital*, p 136; Goodrich, *Frontier of Control*, foreword.
19 NSWBLF, 'An Urgent Call from Builders Laborers to all Workers', pamphlet, 1971.
20 Rawson, *Unions and Unionists in Australia*, p 36; Jack Mundey, 3/4/78, estimated the percentage of builders labourers on a construction site rose from 20 to 35 per cent because of new building methods.
21 Frenkel and Coolican, 'Competition, Instability and Industrial Struggle', esp. p 57, underrates ideological considerations to the point where a union's specific 'mode of production' and position within the industry is almost exclusively responsible for the way in which a union operates.
22 Joe Owens, 4/4/78, 24/1/78.
23 CPA, *Australia and the Way Forward*, 1967; JB Mundey to the Editor, Correspondance *Outlook*, 30 October 1968; Laurie Aarons, 28/12/77; Aarons, 'As I Saw the 1960s', p 68.
24 *Tribune*, 12/8/70.
25 Jack Cambourn, 1/2/79.
26 Hyman, 'British Trade Unionism', p 69; Moorehouse, *Days of Wine and Rage*.
27 Horne, *Time of Hope*, p 84.
28 Mundey, 'Towards new union militancy', p 2.
29 Robert Drew in the Australian, quoted in Coombs, *Sex and Anarchy*, p 280.
30 Tarbuck, 'Students and Trade Unions', p 105; Joe Owens, speech, 2/11/75.
31 Joe Owens, 4/4/78.
32 Higgins, 'Reconstructing Australian Communism', p 172; M Brugman, 'A New Concept of Unionism', p 390; Viri Press, 30/11/76; Dave Shaw, 7/8/77.
33 For a detailed discussion of the earlier history, see M Burgman, 'A New Concept of Unionism', Appendices A, B, pp i–lii; True, *Tales of the BLF*.
34 Jack Mundey, 13/8/75; Lester, As Unions Mature.
35 *Builders' Labourer*, July 1970, p 7.
36 David, 'The Theory of Growth', p 211.
37 *SMH*, 8/10/74; Jack Mundey, 13/8/75.
38 Michels, *Political Panic*, Lester, *As Unions Mature*, p 22.
39 Builders 'Labourer, July/August 1966, p 11; NSWBLF, 'Minutes', Executive Meeting, 16/6/70; Jack Mundey, 13/8/75.
40 Jack Mundey, 3/4/78.
41 *Telegraph* (Brisbane), 3/4/73; *Daily Mirror*, 3/4/73; *Daily Telegraph*, 4/4/73, 20/4/73; 28/5/73; *Melbourne Herald*, 3/4/73; R Pringle to R Jones, (n.d); *Newcastle Morning Herald*, 28/5/73.
42 *Newcastle Morning Herald*, 15/11/73.
43 Quoted in Minogue, 'Portrait of Militant'.
44 Labor Council of NSW BTG 'Submissions to the Premier of NSW, 22 June 1967', p 1.
45 Curtin, 'Permanency', p 33.

46   Evatt, 'Interim Report', pp 14–18.
47   'Minutes', Federal Conference, November 1968, p 47; Gardiner, 'Union Power and Developers'.
48   *Rydge's*, July 1973, p 25; Hutton, *Building and Construction in Australia*, p 211.

THE GREENING OF THE UNION

1   *Armidale Express*, 23/7/73.
2   Quoted in Minogue, 'Portrait of a Militant'.
3   Eyers, 'The Sydney Property Boom'.
4   Mundey, 'Preventing the Plunder', p 175.
5   *Builders' Labourer*, April/May 1967, p 11; Gavin Souter, 'The Glut in Skyscrapers', *SMH*, 7/9/71, 2/10/71, 15/10/71; *Australian*, 1/10/71, 19/10/71.
6   *Fin. Rev.*, 28/11/73; ABLF, 'Agenda Items Federal Conference, 1968', NSW Item (8) Housing.
7   Thomas, *Taming the Concrete Jungle*, p 5. The book was an official publication of the union and Thomas was recording the views of the leadership, who continually expounded exactly these issues.
8   Written and composed by Dennis Kevans and Seamus Gill.
9   *Armidale Express*, 23/7/73.
10   Mundey, 'Preventing the Plunder', p 175; *Lithgow Mercury*, 22/1/73; *Daily Mirror*, 15/3/74; Joachim, 'It makes some, breaks some'; Mitchell, 'Home ... in never-never land'; ABCE&BLF, 'Why Green Bans', poster authorised by Bob Pringle, n.d. [1973]; *Fin. Rev.*, 3/8/73; Eyers, 'The Sydney Property Boom'.
11   Foster, *Class Struggle and the Industrial Revolution*.
12   *Now*, no 131, 8/4/75, p 3.
13   McNamara Papers: unidentified newsclippings [c. July 1962, c. August 1964].
14   *Builders' Labourer*, July/August 1966, p 9, September/October 1966, p 11, April/May 1967, p 3; NSWBLF, 'Minutes', Delegates' Conference, 18/6/67, p 3; Cook, 'A Real (Estate) Scandal', p 15; *Builders' Labourer*, December 1969, p 33; Pringle, 'War on Pollution', pp 11, 13.
15   Speech reprinted in BLF, 'Statement by NSWBLF', 22/5/73, 2pp.
16   *Age*, 23/5/74; Mundey, speech, ACF, 1975; Campbell, 'Meeting Attracts Union Support'.
17   NSWBLF, 'Federal Conference Agenda Items', November 1971.
18   Pringle, Mundey & Owens, 'Submissions to Habitat Australia', p 30. Mundey takes up this theme in 'Urbanisation', pp 7–12; and in 'Ecology, Capitalism, Communism', pp 30–34.
19   *Australian*, 13/7/74, 10/5/74; *Sunday Mail*, 16/9/73; *SMH*, 11/5/74; *Murwillumbah Daily News*, 11/5/74.
20   *SMH*, 6/12/73; *Illawarra Mercury*, 11/1/74, 17/1/74; *Newcastle Morning Herald*, 14/5/74, 31/5/74.
21   *SMH*, 6/7/74; *Australian*, 8/7/74; *Sun*, 5/7/74.
22   Mundey, *Green Bans & Beyond*, pp 6, 15–17.
23   Minogue, 'Portrait of a Militant'; Interview with Mundey, quoted in Roddewig, *Green Bans*, p 11.
24   *Sunday Mail*, 23/1/72; Tom Hogan, 28/10/77; *SMH*, 9/2/74; *Melbourne Herald*, 9/2/74; Badge, 'No Crown Land Auctions, Nationalize Land Now'; Document, 'That There Be a Referendum to Give the Federal Government Power to Nationalise Land on the Following Basis', n.d., 1p; M Burgmann, 'Unionist led green bans'.
25   Jack Mundey, 3/4/78; Joe Owens (with Verity Burgmann), 30/3/98.
26   Mundey, 'Preventing the Plunder', p 174.
27   See, for example, *Sunday Observer*, 11/8/74.
28   Goodin, *Green Political Theory*, esp. pp 26–27, 39, 42–45, 50, 53.
29   Minogue, 'Portrait of a Militant'.
30   Thomas, *Taming the Concrete Jungle*, p 63.
31   *Canberra News*, 31/5/73.
32   Troy, A Fair Price, esp. pp. 94, 285–88; Hickie, *The Prince and the Premier*; Coombs, *Sex and Anarchy*, p 292; Mundey, 'Preventing the Plunder', p 175; Don McPhee, 9/12/77.

33   Roddewig, *Green Bans*, pp. 39–45, 55; NSWBLF, 'Statement by N.S.W. Branch of the Builders Laborers' Federation at Hearing before Commissioner R. Watson in Sydney on 14th October, 1971', 1p.
34   Mundey, *Green Bans & Beyond*, p 83.
35   Mundey, 13/8/75.
36   Roddewig, *Green Bans*, p 35.
37   *SMH*, 1/8/73.
38   ABCE&BLF, 'Why Green Bans', poster authorised by Bob Pringle, n.d. [1973].
39   Dr CA Runcie to *SMH*, 3/12/73.
40   *Daily Telegraph*, 18/12/73; *Australian*, 18/12/73; *SMH*, 18/12/73; *Newcastle Morning Herald*, 18/12/73; Interview with Hugh Stretton, cited in Roddewig, *Green Bans*, pp 34–35.
41   Roddewig, *Green Bans*, p 33.
42   Gallagher even claimed the Victorian union had placed an environmental ban as far back as 1949, but did not provide details of this alleged incident (*Australian*, 11/12/76).
43   Roddewig, *Green Bans*, pp 33–34.
44   Hurchalla, 'Industrial Crimes', p 9. See also *Age*, 25/7/74.
45   NSWBLF, 'Minutes', Executive Meeting, 15/12/70, 8/12/70; Jack Mundey, 3/4/78; Joe Owens, 4/4/78; Bob Pringle, 8/3/78.
46   ABC BLF, *Builders' Laborers Defend the People's Heritage*.
47   *SMH*, 16/11/72.
48   *Unity*, 16, 2, May 1973, pp 7, 14; *Age*, 1/12/73; *Adelaide News*, 5/12/73; *Melbourne Herald*, 7/12/72, 19/9/73; *Melbourne Sun-News Pictorial*, 19/9/73, 20/9/73.
49   *Age*, 4/12/73, 7/12/73, 8/4/74; *Australian*, 4/12/73; *Melbourne Sun-News Pictorial*, 8/4/74; *Sunday Observer*, 11/8/74.
50   *Age*, 7/6/74; *Melbourne Sun-News Pictorial*, 8/6/74; *Melbourne Sunday Press*, 9/6/74.
51   *Age*, 26/1/74.
52   *SMH*, 17/11/72; *Australian*, 4/12/73.
53   *Melbourne Herald*, 7/12/72; *Melbourne Sunday Press*, 3/3/74.
54   *Age*, 19/12/73.
55   *Melbourne Herald*, 13/12/73; *Age*, 14/12/73; *Australian*, 14/12/73.
56   *Age*, 30/11/73.
57   *Melbourne Sun-News Pictorial*, 9/10/73.
58   *Age*, 14/9/73; *Melbourne Herald*, 17/9/73; *Telegraph* (Brisbane), 17/9/73; *Adelaide News*, 18/9/73.
59   *Age*, 18/8/73.
60   *Melbourne Sun-News Pictorial*, 13/8/73.
61   *Melbourne Sun-News Pictorial*, 30/7/73.
62   *Age*, 5/7/73; *Melbourne Sun*, 5/7/73.
63   *Melbourne Herald*, 8/6/73; *Age*, 9/6/73.
64   Thomas, *Taming the Concrete Jungle*, pp 54–56; Hurchalla, 'Industrial Crimes', p 9.
65   *Fin. Rev.*, 17/12/73.
66   *Melbourne Sun-News Pictorial*, 25/10/73.
67   *Melbourne Sun-News Pictorial*, 16/8/74, 17/8/74; *Melbourne Herald*, 16/8/73; *Fin. Rev.*, 16/8/74; *Age*, 16/8/74; *SMH*, 16/8/74; *Australian*, 17/8/74.
68   *Age*, 21/8/74.
69   *Melbourne Herald*, 24/8/74.
70   *SMH*, 29/6/73; *Courier-Mail*, 29/6/73; *Canberra Times*, 29/6/73.
71   NL Gallagher, gen. sec. ABCE&BLF to Dear Sir/Madam, 'Re: "Green Ban" Gallery', 2 pp, n.d. [1974]; *Sunday Observer*, 11/8/74; ABCE&BLF, *Builders' Laborers Defend the People's Heritage*.
72   *Adelaide Advertiser*, 13/12/73, 14/12/73, 15/12/73; ABCE&BLF, *Builders' Laborers Defend the People's Heritage*.
73   *Adelaide Advertiser*, 14/12/73, 15/12/73.
74   *Canberra Courier*, 11/10/73; *Canberra Times*, 12/6/74, 13/6/74, 17/12/73, 18/12/73, 19/12/73; *Canberra News*, 19/6/74.
75   *Canberra News*, 20/9/73; *Canberra Times*, 24/9/73, 25/9/73; *Age*, 25/9/73. On the original ban, see *Canberra Times*, 27/1/73, 4/1/73, 23/5/73, 24/5/73, 25/5/73, 31/5/73, 5/6/73, 26/6/73; *Canberra News*, 22/5/73, 23/5/73, 25/5/73, 28/5/73, 31/5/73, 1/6/73, 4/6/73; *Australian*, 23/5/73; *SMH*, 23/5/73, 7/6/73; *Sun*, 1/6/73; Hancock, *The Battle of Black Mountain*, pp 16, 46.

76   *Fin. Rev.*, 25/1/74; *Australian*, 28/6/78.
77   Roddewig, *Green Bans*, p 34.
78   ABCE&BLF, *Builders' Laborers Defend the People's Heritage.*
79   Australian, 27/7/73; Courier-Mail, 27/7/73, 31/7/73; *Telegraph* (Brisbane), 2/8/73; ABCE&BLF, *Builders' Laborers Defend the People's Heritage.*
80   Australian, 27/7/73.
81   Quoted in *Canberra Times*, 2/3/73.
82   Jack Mundey quoted in *SMH*, 1/8/73.
83   Mundey, 'Meeting "The Battlers"', p 6; Mundey, *Green Bans Forever*, p 82.
84   *Armidale Express*, 23/7/73. Mundey elaborates on this theme in 'From grey to green', p 19.
85   Haskell, 'Green Bans', p 205; Sandercock, *Cities For Sale*, p 211; Sandercock, 'The BLF', p 295.
86   McIntyre, 'The Narcissism of Minor Differences', p 99.
87   *Daily Mirror*, 1/11/73; ABCE&BLF, 'Victorian Builders' Labourers Win $9 Flow On', n.d., 1p.
88   Sandercock, 'Green Bans', p 18; *Inverell Times*, 31/7/74.
89   Most notably, Cox, 'The politics of turf', pp 61–90.
90   Sandercock, 'Citizen participation', pp 117–32; Jakubowicz, 'The city game', pp 329–344; Costello and Dunn, 'Resident Action Groups in Sydney', p 63.
91   Yencken, 'Honorary Life Membership', p 3.
92   Quoted in Hanaghan, 'State secrecy'.
93   Sandercock, 'Citizen participation', p 123.
94   Castells, 'Theoretical propositions', pp 147–73, esp. p 151; Castells, *The Urban Question*, p 325; Castells, *The City and the Grass Roots.*
95   Hanaghan, 'State secrecy'; Evan Whitton, 'Battle for Kelly's Bush', *Daily Telegraph*, 10/1/73; *Age*, 14/9/73.
96   Hanaghan, 'State secrecy'.
97   Mundey, 'The Bans Enjoy Wide Support', p 27.
98   Hanaghan, 'State secrecy'.
99   PN Troy, 21/11/97.
100   Kalajzich (ed), *The Battlers for Kelly's Bush*, p 10; Hardman and Manning, *Green Bans*, Mundey, 'The Bans Enjoy Wide Support', p 27.
101   Bacon, 'Crusader of the Cross'; Inner Core of Sydney RAGs, *Low Cost Housing*, 1973; Save the Public Transport Committee, *The Commuter*, (produced by concerned unionists, residents, students and commuters); *The Rapier*, (produced by the concerned residents of the inner city of Sydney) n.d. [late 1973]; Robert W. Bellear (ed), *Black Housing Book*; Foundation Day *Tharunka*, 2/8/73.
102   Jakubowicz, 'The Green Ban Movement', pp 155, 160.
103   NSWBLF, 'NSW Branch Agenda Items', Federal Conference Nov 1971, 2pp.

ORGANISATIONAL PRINCIPLES AND PRACTICES

1   NSWBLF, 'Minutes', Exec Meeting, 3/3/70; Special Exec Meeting, 20/4/70; Rawson, *Unions and Unionists in Australia*, p 36.
2   NSWBLF, 'Minutes', Gen Meeting, 11/6/68.
3   NSWBLF, 'Minutes', Exec Meeting, 25/8/70, 1/9/70, 27/1/70, 17/2/70, 31/3/70, 7/4/70, 4/8/70, 28/7/70, 25/8/70, 1/9/70, 15/9/70, 24/3/70, 10/11/70, 17/11/70; Special Exec Meeting, 3/2/70, 20/4/70.
4   NSWBLF, 'Minutes', Exec Meeting, 9/6/70, 22/9/70, 13/10/70; Gen Meeting, 9/6/70
5   NSWBLF, 'Minutes', Exec Meeting, 7/7/70, 16/6/70, 22/9/70, 6/10/70, 13/10/70, 27/10/70; Gen Meeting, 6/10/70.
6   NSWBLF, 'Minutes', Exec Meeting, 29/9/70, 22/10/70, 3/11/70, 10/11/70; Gen Meeting, 3/11/70. Sporadic disputes continued over employers' occasional attempts to use non-union labour, e.g. Newcastle's Civic Centre site was in turmoil over this issue for the last two months of 1972 (*Newcastle Morning Herald*, 31/10/72, 2/11/72, 8/11/72, 15/11/72, 16/11/72, 21/12/72; *Newcastle Sun*, 1/11/72, 2/11/72, 8/11/72, 9/11/72, 10/11/72, 15/11/72, 27/11/72, 29/11/72).
7   NSWBLF, 'Minutes', Exec Meeting, 3/3/70, 31/3/70, 9/6/70; BWIU, 'Meeting Held

B.W.J.U 5th June 1974 between B.W.I.U., A.B.L.F, and Mathew Hall and Company re: Gunnedah Dispute', 1p; *Northern Star* (Lismore), 17/5/74, 22/5/74; *Coffs Harbour Advocate*, 9/8/74, 26/8/74; *Grafton Examiner*, 26/8/74, 27/8/74.

8   Michels, *Political Parties*, esp. pp 70, 93–97; Gouldner, 'Metaphysical Pathos and the Theory of Bureaucracy', pp 493–507.

9   Coull, 'The Builders' Labourers' Federation of Australia', p 253.

10   Carol Kalafates, 25/1/78. All the secretarial staff who had worked in other union offices remarked upon this fact.

11   Hearn, 'Migrant Participation in Trade Union Leadership', p 117.

12   Ralph Kelly, 13/12/77, recalls the difficulty he had in extracting promised articles for the journal from officials. He actually blames much of the lack of communication during Intervention on the failure of the *Builders Labourer* to appear regularly during the 1970s.

13   Riach and Howard, *Productivity Agreements and Australian Wage Determination*, p 85.

14   Quoted in *Newcastle Morning Herald*, 6/9/73.

15   Mundey, 'Towards new union militancy', pp 6, 2; *SMH*, 9/5/70, 11/5/70, 14/5/70, 30/5/70, 7/6/70.

16   NSWBLF, 'Minutes', Exec Meeting, 5/5/70; Mundey, 'Towards new union militancy', p 2; Jack Mundey, 13/8/75.

17   Jack Mundey, 13/8/75; NSWBLF, 'Minutes', Exec Meeting, 16/6/70.

18   *SMH*, 29/5/70; *Builders' Labourer*, July 1970, p 3; Thomas, 'Brothers, sisters and the kids', p 10.

19   Mundey, 'Our strike proves they fear workers' action most', p 3.

20   Joe Owens, 24/1/78.

21   Lipset, Trow and Coleman, *Union Democracy*, p 410.

22   Wright Mills, 'The Labor Leaders and the Power Elite', p 146.

23   Bob Pringle, 8/3/78. The room next to the NSWBLF in Trades Hall, occupied by the Felt Hatters Union, was always totally deserted whereas Room 28 was always overflowing. Myths were created about what went on in Room 27 and inspired one of BLF organiser/entertainer Seamus Gill's best songs 'For the felt Hatters Union Had a Very Good Year'.

24   The BWIU regularly recruited graduates to act as research officers, industrial officers etc, who also acted as organisers. The federal BLF recruitment patterns at this time were different from the other building unions. Although many federal BLF officials had university educations, they were normally selected from among Maoist student groups and spent a statutory few months as a builders labourer to qualify as a 'real worker'. Some officials to whom this situation applied were Dan Hillier (assistant federal secretary), Peter Galvin (NSW assistant secretary) and Jim Dixon (NSW official). In the circumstances it is ironic that one of Gallagher's attacks on the NSW branch was that it had become middle class.

25   NSWBLF, 'Minutes', Exec Meeting, 17/2/70, 31/3/70, 16/6/70; Gen Meeting, 4/8/70; Bob Pringle and Joe Owens, 'Rank and File Decision-making in the Builders' Labourers', n.d [1974], 3pp.

26   Jack Mundey, 3/4/78.

27   Jack Mundey on 'Monday Conference', September 1971, reported in *Tribune*, 6/10/71.

28   *Construction*, 30/9/71; *Daily Telegraph*, 28/9/71.

29   Williams, 'Politics a pivotal force'; *Australian*, 2/2/74; *Daily Mirror*, 5/2/74; *SMH*, 5/2/74

30   J Mundey to V Burghmann, 25/2/98.

31   Building Industry Branch of the SPA, *Six Turbulent Years*, pp 8, 24–25.

32   Owens, 'SPA "Analysis"'.

33   Bruce McFarlane even suggested forms of limited tenure for politicians and public servants: see McFarlane, 'Challenging the Control of the Australian Economic System', p 120.

34   CPA, *The Left Challenge for the '70s*, p 28.

35   NSWBLF, 'Minutes', Exec Meeting, 27/8/68; Gen Meeting, 3/9/68.

36   The only other participants were the rank-and-file plumbers. One of these, Peter Lane, described the Building Branch as 'just an addendum to the BLF. I criticised them for that. They really only discussed BLF business.' Janne Reed also criticised this aspect of the Building Branch: 'Sometimes the Plumbers wanted to say something about their struggle and it just got drowned out'.

37   Joe Owens, 4/4/78.

38   Gouldner, 'Metaphysical Pathos and the Theory of Bureaucracy', p 500.

39   *News Weekly*, 11/10/72, p 5.
40   For more details of this election, see M Burgmann , 'A New Concept of Unionism', pp 99–100.
41   Bud Cook, 5/3/78; Bob Pringle and Joe Owens, 'Rank and File Decision-Making in the Builders' Labourers', n.d [mid-1973], 3pp; Tony O'Beirne, 2/3/78; Kevin Cook, 1/12/76
42   Poster, 'Hoist: Builders Labourers Rank and File Candidates', n.d (mid-1973), authorised by Noel Olive; *Builders Labourer*, Aug 1973, p 11.
43   BLF, '1973 Triennial Election: Returning Officers Declaration', 9/10/73.
44   NSWBLF, 'Minutes', Special Exec Meeting, 23/4/70; ABLF, 'Minutes', Fed Man Cmtee, 1/6/70, p 8; N Gallagher to J Mundey, 20/8/70; NSWBLF, 'Minutes', Exec Meeting, 19/1/71, 30/3/71; *Brisbane Telegraph*, 26/11/71.
45   NSWBLF, 'Disputes Book', 28/7/72, 3/8/72, 22/8/72.
46   George Crawford, 20/1/81; NSWBLF, 'Disputes Book', 31/7/72, 2/8/72.
47   *Newcastle Morning Herald*, 23/8/74; 'US Giant Attacks Aust. Workers', 24/5/74, 2pp, authorised by Clarence Street Building Workers & BLF.
48   For examples in 1970 alone see NSWBLF, 'Minutes', Exec Meeting, 13/1/70, 20/1/70, 27/1/70, 24/3/70, 31/3/70, 7/4/70, 25/6/70, 29/6/70, 7/7/70, 14/7/70, 28/7/70, 1/12/70; Gen Meeting, 4/8/70.
49   *Builders' Labourer*, March 1970, p 47, July 1970, p 27; NSWBLF, 'Minutes', Exec Meeting, 4/8/70, 20/5/70.
50   NSWBLF, 'Minutes', Exec Meeting, 20/1/70, 27/1/70, 17/2/70, 31/3/70; Gen Meeting, 3/11/70; Mick Curtin, 29/2/76.
51   For a detailed discussion of the expulsion and the circumstances surrounding it, see M Burgmann, 'A New Concept of Unionism', pp 133–45.
52   ABLF, 'Minutes', Fed Man Cmtee, 2/6/71, p 5; NSWBLF, 'Minutes', Exec Meeting, 8/6/71, 15/6/71; Bud Cook, 30/3/78.
53   *National Times*, 7/12/80, 30/11/80; NSWBLF, 'Disputes Book', 3/7/72, 7/7/72, 10/7/72, 12/7/72.
54   NSWBLF, 'Resolutions from Organisers' Meeting', 20/10/71, 1p; NSWBLF, 'Minutes', Exec Meeting, 26/10/71, 16/11/71, 24/11/71, 7/12/71; Gen Meeting, 2/11/71; J Mundey to P Clancy, 12/11/71.
55   'Preview Construction Dispute, Carrington Street, City', 28/10/71, 1p; 'Preview Const Dispute: Advanced Roofing', 29/10/71, 1p; *SMH*, 29/10/71; 'Preview Const Advanced Roofing Dispute: Labor Council Meeting', 1/11/71, 3 pp, p 1; 'Recommendation from a Meeting of Unions in the Building Industry, Convened by the Labor Council on 1st November 1971', 1p; 'AWU Demarcation Dispute', 1/11/71, 1p; CT Oliver to J Mundey, 1/11/71; *Australian*, 30/10/7, 2/11/71.
56   NSWBLF, 'Minutes', Exec Meeting, 2/11/71; Gen Meeting, 2/11/71; J Mundey to L McKay, 2/11/71; 'AWU Demarc. Dispute', 2/11/71, 1p.
57   ABCE&BLF (NSW Branch), *Know Your Rights*, p 3.

INDUSTRIAL RELATIONS STRATEGIES

1   Jack Mundey, 30/3/78.
2   NSWBLF, 'Minutes', Gen Meeting, 3/3/70; Owens, 'Does Arbitration Have any Future?', p 41.
3   Mundey, 'Towards new union militancy', pp 3, 4–5.
4   Thomas, *Taming the Concrete Jungle*, p 18.
5   NSWBLF, 'Minutes', Gen Meeting, 6/10/70; Exec Meeting, 24/11/70; Thomas, *Taming the Concrete Jungle*, p 18.
6   Mundey, 'Job Activity the Key', p 7.
7   Hinton and Hyman, *Trade Unions and Revolution*, p 18; Bentley, 'Australian Trade Unionism', p 248.
8   Pickette, 'Rank and File Organisation'; *Power, A Communist publication*, June 1973; CPA, *Modern Unionism and the Workers' Movement*, p 6.
9   Mundey, 'Great strike proved our fighting ability', p 1; Mundey, 'Interview', p 11; Mick McNamara (with Pat Fiske), 1976.
10   Pete Thomas, 25/6/80; NSWBLF, 'Press Statement', 2/12/71, 1p; NSWBLF, 'Minutes', Exec Meeting, 1/12/70, 15/12/70; Spec Exec Meeting, 24/12/70.

11 *Daily Telegraph*, 28/9/71; *SMH*, 28/9/71. Robert Moore thanked Mundey profusely for 'making it such a good programme for us'. (Handwritten addition to formal thankyou letter, Robert Moore to J Mundey, 28/9/71.)

12 Mundey, 'Interview', p 8.

13 NSWBLF, 'Circular to All Job Organisers', 26/72, 17/11/72; Jack Mundey, 3/4/78; *SMH*, 11/12/72.

14 Joe Owens, 24/1/78; 'NSW Report to the Federal Council', *Builders' Labourer*, Dec. 1969, p 39; *Tribune*, 25/3/70, p 10.

15 *Tribune*, 25/3/70, p 10.

16 Niland, *Collective Bargaining*, p 63.

17 NSWBLF , 'Results of 259 Companies 1970–71', 1p.

18 Parkin, *Marxism and Class Theory*, pp 74, 77, 80.

19 Hyman, *Marxism and the Sociology of Trade Unionism*, pp 52–53.

20 *Builders' Labourer*, Dec. 1969, p 3.

21 Mundey, 'Interview', p 13.

22 Building Industry Branch of the SPA, *Six Turbulent Years*, p 5.

23 Mundey, 'Towards new union militancy', p 4.

24 NSWBLF, 'Minutes', Exec Meeting, 20/5/70.

25 Joe Owens, 24/1/78; Tom Hogan (with Pat Fiske) 1979; Joe Owens, 4/4/78; Jack Mundey, 3/4/78; Bob Pringle, 8/3/78.

26 Mundey, 'Towards new union militancy', p 6.

27 ABLF, 'Minutes', Fed Man Cmtee, 1/6/70, pp 3, 7; *Tribune*, 17/6/70, p 10; Ralph Kelly, 13/12/77.

28 NSWBLF, 'Circular to All Job Delegates', 20/71, 12/10/71, 1p; NSWBLF, 'Letter to NSW Builders' Laborers', 14/10/71, 1p; *Journal of the UCATT*, July 1974, 2, p 65; NSWBLF, 'Minutes', Exec Meeting, 5/10/71.

29 *Builders' Labourer*, March 1970, p 1; NSWBLF, 'Minutes', Gen Meeting, 3/3/70; Exec Meeting, 4/8/70, 15/9/70.

30 NSWBLF, 'Minutes', Exec Meeting, 10/9/70, 15/9/70, 22/9/70, 29/9/70, 22/10/70, 24/11/70, 1/12/70; Gen Meeting, 6/10/70, 3/11/70, 1/12/70; Duncan Williams, 25/2/76; CCAC, 'Dillingham Constructions Pry Ltd, (QANTAS Project) and the Australian Builders' Labourers' Federation', 30/11/70 [C no.2067 of 1970].

31 NSWBLF, 'Minutes', Spec Exec Meeting, 20/4/70; Exec Meeting, 17/11/70, 29/9/70.

32 NSWBLF, 'Minutes', Exec Meeting, 22/10/70, 27/10/70, 10/11/70, 8/12/70.

33 *Builders' Labourer*, March 1970, p 9; NSWBLF, 'Minutes', Spec Exec Meeting, 20/4/79; Exec Meeting, 17/2/70, 24/2/70, 3/3/70, 15/12/70.

34 Hurchalla, 'Industrial Crimes', p 19.

35 Thomas, *Taming the Concrete Jungle*, pp 17–18.

36 *Australian*, 6/8/74; *Tribune*, 13/8/74; *Sunday Observer* (Melbourne), 25/8/74.

37 Correspondence: J Mundey to R Hawke, 7/10/71.

38 Gardiner, 'The rise of Jack Mundey's trendy union'; Bob Pringle, 8/3/78; Joe Owens, 24/1/78; Mick McNamara (with Pat Fiske), 1976; Minutes: SEM, 20/9/71.

39 Tom Hogan (with Pat Fiske), 1979; NSWBLF, 'Minutes', Exec Meeting, 20/5/70; Jack Mundey, 13/8/75; Bob Pringle, 8/3/78; NSWBLF, 'Minutes', Exec Meeting, 9/6/70; Mundey, 'Towards new union militancy', p 6.

40 Tom Hogan, 28/10/77; Tom Hogan (with Pat Fiske), 1979.

41 Tom Hogan (with Pat Fiske), 1979; Mundey, 'Towards new union militancy', p 6.

42 Bob Pringle, 8/3/78; Mick Ross, 29/7/77; Mick Curtin, 29/2/76; Bob Baker, 16/5/80; Bud Cook, 5/3/78.

43 Mundey, 'Australia', p 31.

44 Tom Hogan (with Pat Fiske), 1979.

45 Bud Cook, 5/3/78; Joe Owens, 24/1/78; *Builders' Labourer*, July 1970, p 33.

46 *Passing Show*, 10/10/78, p 11.

47 ABC Television, 'Monday Conference', September 1971; Peter Barton, 5/3/78 confirms that although 50 vigilantes rushed on to the site, as soon as 'these characters' produced shotguns, rifles and tomahawks, the vigilantes all rushed out of the job-site.

48 *Daily Mirror*, 19/5/70, 20/5/70; *SMH*, 28/5/70.

49 *SMH*, 30/5/70; *Sun*, 27/5/70; *Daily Mirror*, 28/5/70.

50 *SMH*, 16/5/70, 29/5/70, 20/5/71; CH Monk (president), report to Annual Meeting of Employers' Federation, reported in *SMH*, 7/11/70; *Australian*, 20/5/71.

51 Anderson, 'The Builders Labourers' Federation of NSW', p 53; Owens, 'Some highlights of a strike that made history', pp 21, 23, 25, 27, 48.

52 Building Industry Branch of the SPA, *Six Turbulent Years*, p 28; Mundey, 'Interview', p 8; SPA, 'Ultra Leftism', pp 2–3.

53 For example, Mick Curtin, 29/2/76.

54 Tom Hogan (with Pat Fiske), 1980; Joe Owens, 24/1/78; Jack Mundey, 13/8/75.

55 'Improved organisation flows from the strike', *Builders' Labourer*, July 1970, p 7; NSWBLF, 'Minutes', Spec Gen Meeting, 25/8/70; Gen Meeting, 1/9/70, 2/3/71.

56 Mundey, 'Australia', p 31; *Builders' Labourer*, July 1970, pp 5, 11.

57 *Tribune*, 22/9/71.

58 NSWBLF, 'Disputes Book', 1/12/72; JD Martin, Executive Director MBA to the Deputy Industrial Registrar, CCAC, 19/9/73; JD Martin, Executive Director MBA to the Industrial Registrar [NSW], 'Notification under Section 25A of the Industrial Arbitration Act 1940 As Amended', 14/7/72.

59 CPA, *The Left Challenge for the 70s*, pp 2, 4.

60 SPA, *The Socialist Program*, p 32.

61 Angus McIntyre, 'Australia', p 390.

62 Thomas, *Taming the Concrete Jungle*, p 133.

63 On other workers' control activities, see Thomas, *The Nymboida Story*; Caldwell and Tubbs, *The Harco Work-In*; J. Mundey to George Marks, 3/12/71; Wallace and Owens, *Workers Call the Tune at Opera House*; Moss, *Industrial Relations or Workers Control*.

64 ABC Television, 'Lateline', interviews with Jack Mundey and Jimmy Reid, 20/5/75.

65 NSWBLF, 'Agenda Items for Federal Conference, 1973'.

66 *The Employers' Review*, April 1972, p 1.

67 A detailed analysis of the union 'Disputes Book' for 1972 reveals that more than half, perhaps 60 per cent, of disputes were either directly or indirectly linked to such encroachment strategies.

68 *SMH*, 17/10/72.

69 NSWBLF, 'Minutes', Spec Gen Meeting, 25/8/70; Exec Meeting, 11/8/70, 22/9/70, 22/10/70; 'U.S. Giant Attacks Aust. Workers', 24/5/74, 2 pp, authorised by Clarence Street Building Workers and BLF; NSWBLF, 'Disputes Book', 16/6/72, 19/6/72, 11/8/72, 17/8/72; Tom Hogan (with Pat Fiske), 1979.

70 JD Martin, executive director MBA, to the Industrial Registrar, CCAC, 17/8/72.

71 NSWBLF, 'Disputes Book', 24/11/72.

72 *Newcastle Morning Herald*, 16/11/72, 17/11/72, 23/11/72; *Newcastle Sun*, 21/11/72, 9/11/72.

73 *Australian*, 10/1/73; NSWBLF, 'Longspan Uses Police to Sack Workers', n.d. [c. Sept. 1974], 1p.

74 Hogan, 'Sackings Didn't Stop Them'.

75 Tom Hogan (with Pat Fiske), 1979.

76 Joe Owens, 4/4/78.

77 Tom Hogan (with Pat Fiske), 1979.

78 NSWBLF, 'Disputes Book', 11/12/72.

79 Wallace and Owens, *Workers Call the Tune at Opera House*, 1973.

80 'National Workers Control Conference, Newcastle, Easter 1973', 4 pp, authorised by John Wallace for the NWCC; Souter, 'Sacking the Boss'; *Builders' Labourer*, June 1973, p 19.

81 *Newcastle Morning Herald*, 12/4/73; *Armidale Express*, 13/7/73; *Northern Daily Leader*, 23/7/73.

82 Liberal Party, 'Workers' Participation or Workers' Control'.

83 *Bulletin*, 24/3/73.

84 Joe Owens, 24/1/78.

85 Ray Rocher (with Pat Fiske), 1979; 'The anatomy of a political strike', *Rydge's*, July 1973, p 24.

86 BLF, 'Builders Labourers Under Attack', n.d [c. May 1973], 1p.

87 *Fin. Rev.*, 11/5/73.

88 NSWBLF, 'Minutes', Exec Meeting, 23/4/68, 12/11/68, 24/6/69, 13/10/70; Spec Exec Meeting, 20/4/70; Gen Meeting, 6/10/70; Bob Pringle, 8/3/78.

89   Ray Rocher (with Pat Fiske), 1979; J Martin to S Vaughan, 20/2/73.
90   *Sun-Herald*, 6/5/73, 20/5/73; Advertisement authorised by John Martin, MBA, *Australian*,
      9/5/73, 11/5/73; *SMH*, 21/5/73, 19/5/73; *Newcastle Sun*, 24/5/73; NSWBLF, 'Circular
      to All Job Organisers', 10/73, 23/5/73; *Australian*, 25/5/73; *Newcastle Morning Herald*,
      25/5/73; *Illawarra Mercury*, 25/5/73; *Adelaide News*, 25/5/73
91   Advertisement, *Daily Mirror*, 25/5/73, authorised by J Martin, MBA.
92   CCAC, C. no. 983 of 1973; *SMH*, 31/5/73; BLF, 'Agreements Made in Canberra and
      Melbourne May 29 & 31, Between the Master Builders and the Builders Labourers'; BLF,
      'Lockout Beaten: Moving Up for Permanency', n.d., [c. June 1973], 2 pp; J Mundey to
      L Johnson, 4/6/73; M Burgmann, 'A New Concept of Unionism', pp 222, 273–75; *Tribune*,
      18/3/75; Evan, 'Interim Report'.
93   *Daily Mirror*, 7/11/73; *Sun*, 7/11/73; BLF, Collection Sheet, 13/11/73; Jim Staples, 26/7/75;
      Fin. Rev., 8/11/73.
94   'Building Workers Demand the Right to Work', n.d [c May 1974], 2 pp, authorised by the
      locked-out workers from Miruzzi South Seas.
95   All Sydney and Newcasde morning and afternoon daily newspapers, 3/5/74, carried photos
      and stories. Most did follow-up stories too.
96   'Why Wyong Workers Work-In', poster authorised by Joe Owens and Bob Pringle on behalf
      of the NSWBLF, FEDFA, Central Coast Labor Council; *Scrounge*, 31/5–14/6/74, pp 9–12;
      FED News, Supplement 17/5/74, 1p, authorised by Jack Cambourn, Secretary FEDFA.
97   *Tribune*, 2/7/74.

CIVILISING THE INDUSTRY

1   *Builders' Labourer*, July 1970, pp 1, 3; NSWBLF, 'Minutes', Exec Meeting, 1/9/70, 10/9/70;
      Gen Meeting, 1/9/70.
2   *Builders' Labourer*, July 1970, p 1; Mundey, 'Our strike proves they fear workers' action
      most', p 3; NSWBLF, 'Statement by N.S.W. Branch of the Builders Laborers' Federation at
      Hearing before Commissioner R. Watson in Sydney on 14th October, 1971', 1p.
3   *Builders' Labourer*, March 1970, p 17; Ray Rocher (with Pat Fiske), 1980.
4   *Daily Mirror*, 20/11/71; Cook, 'Time for a clean-up', p 43.
5   Thomas, *Taming the Concrete Jungle*, p 12; NSWBLF, 'Ciera: Warringah Mall', 13/3/73,
      3 pp; Mundey, 'Our strike proves they fear workers' action most', p 3.
6   *Australian*, 28/6/78; NSWBLF, 'Minutes', Gen Meeting, 1/12/70.
7   *Broken Hill Miner*, 6/2/73; Joe Owens, 11/12/96.
8   BLF, 'Disputes Book', 1/11/72; M Burgmann, 'A New Concept of Unionism', pp 78, 87, 89,
      169, 271; Joe Owens, 11/12/96.
9   Cited in Thomas, *Taming the Concrete Jungle*, pp 124–25.
10   Cook, 'Time for a clean-up', p 43; NSWBLF, 'Minutes', Gen Meeting, 4/8/70.
11   Mundey, 'Our strike proves they fear workers' action most', p 3.
12   *Tribune*, 4/3/70, p 10.
13   *Tribune*, 4/3/70, p 10; NSWBLF, 'Minutes', Exec Meeting, 17/2/70, 24/11/70, 15/12/70;
      JD Martin, executive director MBA to the Industrial Registrar (NSW), 21/7/72; NSWBLF,
      'Disputes Book', 26/7/72, 4/8/72.
14   MBA, 'Report of Proceedings of a Meeting with a Representative of the A.B.L.F. to Discuss
      the Problem Concerning Dogmen – Held on 15 June 1972', p 1; 'Violence is a bosses'
      weapon', *Builders Labourer*, n.d. [c. mid-1972].
15   Mr Justice Sheehy to the secretary, ABLF, 11/8/72; BLF, 'Disputes Book', 26/7/72, 4/8/72;
      M Burgmann, 'A New Concept of Unionism', p 174.
16   *Australian*, 19/4/73; NSWBLF, 'Statement on Excavation for Press Release', n.d. [c. April
      1973]; Age, 4/5/73.
17   *Builders' Labourer*, June 1973, pp 41 (Italian) and 45 (Greek); *Rydge's*, August 1974.
18   'Dillinghams Discriminate Against Women', n.d. [c. Feb. 1974], 1p, authorised by the
      BLF Women's Collective; 'Dillingham Clarence Street Dispute', 5/2/74, 1p, authorised by
      Tom Hogan on behalf of the NSWBLF. Also Don Crotty to R Cram, secretary Miners'
      Federation, 18/2/74.
19   BLF, 'Disputes Book', 10/11/72.
20   JD Martin, executive director MBA to the Industrial Registrar (NSW), 13/7/72; BLF,

'Disputes Book', 14, 20, 21/7/72; NSWBLF, 'Builders Labourers Under Attack', n.d [c. May 1973], 1p; Jack Mundey, 13/8/75; *SMH*, 18/3/72; *Sunday Australian*, 23/4/72.

21　J D Martin, executive director MBA to the Industrial Registrar (NSW), 14/7/72; NSWBLF, 'Disputes Book', 14/7/72, 20/7/72, 21/7/72; 'Sacked but worked on', *Tribune*, 25–31/7/72; JD Martin, executive director MBA to the Deputy Industrial Registrar, CCAC, 3/8/72.

22　*SMH*, 6/3/73.

23　BLF, 'Builders Labourers Under Attack', n.d [c. May 1973], 1p.

24　M Burgmann, 'A New Concept of Unionism', pp 123–24; *Builders' Labourer*, March 1970, p 9.

25　NSWBLF, 'Recommendation: Mass Meeting 4 February'; NSWBLF, 'Strike Actions – Demonstrations: Intensified Struggle for $6 and Accident Pay', n.d. [March 1971], 2pp.

26　'Resolution: Meeting of Striking Building Workers Employed in the Building Construction Industry, Wentworth Park, Thursday May 13', 1p, unauthorised.

27　*SMH*, 14/5/71; *Australian*, 13/5/71; *SMH*, 13/5/71, 26/5/71.

28　ABLF, 'Minutes', Fed Man Cmtee, 2/6/71, p 4; Ralph Kelly, 13/12/77; Bud Cook, 5/3/78

29　NSWBLF, 'All Workers Will Gain If … Building Industry Workers Unite!', n.d. [June 1971], 4 pp, p 3.

30　*Tribune*, 26/5/71, p 4; *Daily Telegraph*, 21/5/71; *Construction*, 24/5/71, p 1; Bud Cook, 5/3/78.

31　*SMH*, 22/5/71; Industrial Commission of NSW, no. 251 of 1971, 'Building Trades Dispute re Pay of Injured Workers', 22/10/71; CCAC, C. no. 1902 of 1971, 6/12/71.

32　Joe Owens (with Pat Fiske), 1980; Bob Petty (with Pat Fiske), 1980; NSW MBA, 'Circular No. 36/1971, Accident Pay', 14/7/71, 3pp.

33　*SMH*, 25/5/71; *Australian*, 19/5/71, 18/5/71; *Fin. Rev.*, 21/5/71; *Sunday Telegraph*, 16/5/71; Dick, 'Full pay for accidents?'; Digby Young, 1/3/79.

34　Civil & Civic Pty Ltd., 'Labour Relations in the Future', p 7.

35　Dubovsky, *We Shall Be All*, p 56; John Dunne, *Delano*, pp 22–23.

36　Jack Mundey, 3/4/78; Owens, speech, 2/11/75.

37　NSWBLF, 'Minutes', Gen Meeting, 6/10/70; Tom Hogan (with Pat Fiske), 1980; Thomas, *Taming the Concrete Jungle*, p 21.

38　NSWBLF, 'Minutes', Exec Meeting, 22/10/70; Gen Meeting, 3/11/70.

39　*Builders' Labourer*, March 1970, pp 5, 9; NSWBLF, 'Minutes', Exec Meeting, 27/10/70, 10/11/70, 17/11/70; ABLF (NSW branch) 'Circular', 24/11/70.

40　NSWBLF, 'Minutes', Gen Meeting, 3/11/70, 1/12/70.

41　*Newcastle Sun*, 8/11/72; *Newcastle Morning Herald*, 7/10/72.

42　*Newcastle Morning Herald*, 7/10/72.

43　NSWBLF, 'Attention: Notice to All N.S.W. Builders', n.d., 1p; NSWBLF, 'Handy Guide for State and Job Organisers', 7/6/74, 2pp.

44　Lenin, 'Can the Bolsheviks Retain State Power?' (1917), cited in Hyman, *Marxism and the Sociology of Trade Unionism*, p 51.

45　Lenin, *What Is To Be Done?*, p 56.

PIONEERING SOCIAL MOVEMENT UNIONISM

1　Touraine, *The Post-Industrial Society*, esp. pp 9, 11, 17, 61, 73, 75–76; Touraine, *The Voice and the Eye*, esp. p 13; Habermas, 'New Social Movements', pp 33–35. See also Offe, 'Work', esp. pp 133–36, 141, 148; Laclau and Mouffe, 'Post-Marxism without apologies', pp 103, 106; Laclau and Mouffe, *Hegemony and Socialist Strategy*, p 183.

2　For example, Brandt, 'New social movements as a metapolitical challenge', pp 60–68; Inglehart, *The Silent Revolution*; Inglehart, *Culture Shift*, esp. pp 371–92; Melucci, *Nomads of the Present*, pp 11–12.

3　Moody, 'Towards an International Social-Movement Unionism', p 59.

4　Kelley, 'Looking Forward'; Gindin, *The Canadian Auto Workers*; Seidman, *Manufacturing Militance*.

5　Coombs, *Sex and Anarchy*, p 292.

6　NSWBLF, 'Minutes', Exec Meeting, 20/1/70, 27/1/70, 22/10/70, 10/11/70, 17/11/70, 24/11/70, 1/12/70, 29/6/70.

7　M McNamara to secretary BTG, Trades Hall, 8/3/67; JA Mulvihill, Senate to M McNamara,

4/4/67; L Bury, Minister for Labour and National Service to JA Mulvihill, 3/4/67; J Mundey to F Maros, 'Re: Alfons Thiry', 16/4/68; 'Statement by Zvonimire Cabraja', 2pp; Numerous items of correspondence between Parkes (Columbia) Pry Ltd, Strasser, Geraghry & Partners and Tribe & Strasser, 13/6/74–15/7/74, with enclosures; NSWBLF, 'Agenda Items for Federal Conference, 1973', Item 27; NSWBLF, 'Circular to All Job Delegates & Activists', (5/74), 19/8/74, p2.

8   *On Site*, n.d. [1974], 2pp.
9   'US Giant Attacks Aust. Workers', 24/5/74, authorised by Clarence Street Building Workers and BLF; 'Workers Struggle Against Dillingham 's Continues', n.d., 1p, unauthorised.
10 Blake, 'Frail Old Men Shake Leichhardt'; *Scope*, 125, 25/10/73.
11 Miliband, *Divided Societies*, p 96, 110.
12 NSWBLF, 'Circular to All Job Organisers', 1/73, 24/1/72.
13 Fraser, 'Rethinking the Public Sphere', p 124.
14 On the Push, see Coombs, *Sex and Anarchy* Beilharz.
15 Roelof Smilde, 11/3/78.
16 Wendy Bacon, 16/1/78.
17 CPA, *Modern Unionism and the Workers'Movement*, CPA, *The Left Challenge for the '70s*, pp 4, 28.
18 CPA, 'Vote Red for a Green Australia', n.d. [1974], 4pp.
19 *SMH*, 24/12/71
20 *Builders' Labourer*, n.d. [c. mid-1972], p 1.
21 ABLF, 'Federal Council Agenda Items', submitted from NSW Branch Meeting, 15/8/67, p 538; NSWBLF, 'Minutes', Gen Meeting, 3/3/70, 9/6/70; Exec Meeting, 20/1/70, 27/1/70, 22/9/70, 22/10/70, 10/11/70, 17/11/70, 24/11/70, 1/12/70; ABLF, 'Minutes', Fed Man Cmtee, 5/370, p 9.
22 NSWBLF, 'Minutes', Exec Meeting, 28/4/70; 'End the War in Vietnam and End Conscription 'in 'Agenda Items, Federal Conference, 1971', p 1.
23 Review, 27/11/71–3/12/71, p 206; NSWBLF, 'Minutes', Exec Meeting, 5/1/71, 12/1/71, 19/1/71, 26/1/71, 16/3/71; ABLF, 'Minutes', Fed Man Cmtee, 24/3/71, pp 12–13.
24 'End the War in Vietnam and End Conscription' in 'Agenda Items, Federal Conference, 1971', p 1.
25 *Tribune*, 25–31/7/72, p 10.
26 *Sun*, 15/7/72; *Daily Mirror*, 15/7/72; *Sun-Herald*, 16/7/72; *Sunday Telegraph*, 16/7/72; *Australian*, 18/7/72; *Daily Telegraph*, 31/5/73.
27 *Daily Mirror*, 3/1/73; *Sun-Herald*, 31/12/72.
28 JB Mundey to JP Ducker, Trades Hall, Sydney, 26/9/68.
29 ABLF, 'Minutes', Fed Man Cmtee, 24/3/71, p 14; *Australian*, 3/7/71.
30 'Unionists Join the Mass Rally … 10th July', n.d. [1971], 4 pp, authorised by Tas Bull, WWF; R Pringle, BLF; B Childs, PKJU; *Sun*, 17/8/71, 2/12/71; *SMH*, 2/12/71.
31 *Tribune*, 1/9/71, 8/9/71; 'The Right to Work' in NSW Branch, 'Agenda Item for Federal Conference, November 1971', 2pp.
32 *SMH*, 23/8/72; *Australian*, 23/8/72; *Daily Mirror*, 23/8/72; *Sun*, 23/8/72. This sentence was overthrown by Justices Kerr, Jacobs and Meares in the Court of Appeal, which angered the Askin Government. (*Australian*, 27/9/73.)
33 *SMH*, 24/8/72; 'Transcript of Interview: Annexure B to Affidavit', 14/9/72, 3pp.
34 *SMH*, 25/8/72; *Australian*, 23/9/72.
35 'Jack Mundey Defence Committee', 27/9/72, 2pp; 'Askin and the Developers Want Mundey Out of The Way', n.d.; R Pringle, convenor, and Jack Mundey Defence Committee to Mr McCaw, State Attorney-General, 14/11/72; *Australian*, 10/11/72; Red Pen Publications, 'Why Can't We Question Judges", n.d., 4pp.
36 *Daily Mirror*, 12/10/72, 21/12/72; *SMH*, 13/10/1972, 16/11/72, 21/11/72; *Illawarra Mercury*, 13/10/1972; *Sun*, 20/10/ 1972; NSWBLF, 'Circular to All Job Organisers' (24/72), 13/11/72; (25/72), 15/11/72; *Australian*, 22/11/72, 22/12/72; Coper and Hayes, 'How to Hush Up a Scandal'; *Newcastle Sun*, 21/12/72; *Grafton Examiner*, 22/12/72; *Newcastle Herald*, 22/12/72; *Broken Hill Truth*, 22/12/72.
37 R Pringle, president ABLF, Sydney, leaflet/letter, 25/10/72; NSWBLF, 'Agenda Items for Federal Conference, 1973', items 20–22; SALC, Sydney to NSWBLF, 12/9/74.

38   'Aboriginal Builders' labourer to Represent Our Union', clipping, May 1962.
39   NSWBLF, '1965 Federal Conference Report', pp 38–39; NSWBLF, 'Agenda Items, 1965 Federal Conference', p 6.
40   NSWBLF, 'Report to Federal Conference', 1966, p 22.
41   ABLF, 'Federal Council Agenda Items, Submitted from NSW Branch Meeting', 15/8/67, p 537.
42   For example, H Cook, acting secretary NSWBLF to Rev WA Clint, Co-operative for Aborigines Ltd, 10/8/67; WA Clint, Co-operative for Aborigines Ltd to secretary, Building Laborers Union, 1/8/67; Charles Dixon, acting manager, Foundation for Aboriginal Affairs to secretary, Builders Labourers Union (NSW Branch), 15/6/67; 'Cooperative for Aborigines Ltd', 'Foundation for Aboriginal Affairs', 'Some Facts Concerning the Foundation for Aboriginal Affairs', 'Northern Territory Council for Aboriginal Rights (Inc.)', and 'Foundation for Aboriginal Affairs 1974 National Aboriginal Day Ball', leaflets.
43   J Mundey to the editor, *Tribune*, 19/6/68; J Mundey to JP Ducker, assistant secretary, NSW Labor Council, 20/6/68; T Supple to secretary, BLF, Sydney, 9/7/68; J Mundey to T Supple, 16/8/68; JB Mundey to R Hancock, Trades Hall, Sydney, 21/8/68.
44   *Sun*, 13/11/73, p 7.
45   *Tribune*, 20/6/72; JD Martin, exec. director, MBA to the Industrial Registrar, and various attachments, 27/6/72; Bob Pringle, 'The Black Awakening', 2pp.
46   Bob Pringle, 'The Black Awakening', 2pp.
47   NSWBLF, 'Disputes Book', June and July 1972; Pringle, 'The Black Awakening', pp 31–32; Lyn Thompson to Bob Pringle, n.d. [late 1972); 'Black Moratorium: Thousands Act For Black Rights', *Tribune*, 18–24/7/72; 'Black Embassy defenders tell story', *Tribune*, 25–31/7/72; 'Wee Waa Appeal', attached to 'Circular to Job Organisers', (1/73), 24/1/73, 2pp; Lyn Thompson to Joe Owens, 16/8/72.
48   *Illawarra Mercury*, 30/12/72; *Grafton Examiner*, 30/12/72.
49   *Daily Mirror*, 21/3/73; *Builders Labourer*, 1973, pp 33–35; Hogan, 'Strengthen that grip', p 13.
50   NSWBLF, 'Agenda Items for Federal Conference, 1973', item 25.
51   *Sun*, 13/11/73, p 7.
52   Hogan, 'Strengthen that grip', p 13.
53   Aboriginal Mission Canberra to Bob Pringle, Builders Labourers Union, (telegram), 1/11/74.
54   *SMH*, 29/10/73; *Australian*, 30/10/73.
55   *Australian*, 12/1/74, 22/1/74, 23/1/74; *SMH*, 18/1/74, 19/1/74, 22/1/74, 23/1/74; *Daily Mirror*, 18/1/74; *Melbourne Herald*, 16/1/74; *Melbourne Sun-News Pictorial*, 18/1/74.
56   *Australian*, 25/1/74; *SMH*, 25/1/74.
57   *Tamworth Leader*, 26/1/74; *Newcastle Morning Herald*, 26/1/74; *Australian*, 26/1/74.
58   *Age*, 23/5/74; *Western Advocate* (Bathurst), 3/6/74.
59   Parliament of NSW, 'Report of the Royal Commission into New South Wales Prisons', p 165.
60   *SMH*, 21/6/73; *Herald* (Melbourne), 20/6/73; *Sun* (Melbourne), 20/6/73; *Telegraph* (Brisbane), 20/6/73; *Age*, 28/6/73; *Daily Mirror*, 3/7/73. Thompson, *Flaws in the Social Fabric*, p 50.
61   Batterham & Tubbenhauer, 'Interview with Bob Pringle', p 14; Batterham & Tubbenhauer, 'Interview with Lyn Syme, Janne Reed and Ros Harrison', p 16.
62   'blf on women & gays', *Gay Liberation Press*, 3, Sept. 1974, p 13; Batterham & Tubbenhauer, 'Interview with Bob Pringle', p 14.
63   NSWBLF, 'Agenda Items for Federal Conference, 1973', Item 33; Batterham & Tubbenhauer, 'Interview with Bob Pringle', p 14; 'blf on women & gays', *Gay Liberation Press*, 3, Sept. 1974, p 13.
64   'Homosexuals Report Back Mailing List', Cross+Section Papers, cited in Willett, 'The gay and lesbian movement', p 35; *Tribune*, 26/8/75; Joe Owens, speech, 2/11/75.
65   Graham, 'Anatomy of a Revolutionary Union', p 2.
66   *Daily Telegraph*, 1/12/73; NSWBLF, 'Agenda Items for Federal Conference, 1973', item 30.
67   *Age*, 28/6/73.
68   *Grafton Examiner*, 29/6/73; Crouch, 'Some black among the BLF green'; Mundey, *Green Bans & Beyond*, p 106.

FEMINISM AND MACHISMO

1   UCATI, 'Report of Proceedings … June 1974', p 166.
2   Joe Owens, 29/9/77.
3   For example, Burton, *The Promise and the Price*; Curthoys, Spearritt & Eade (eds), *Women and Work*; Ellem, *In Women's Hands?*; Frances & Scates (eds), *Women, Work and the Labottr Movement*; Game & Pringle, *Gender at Work*; Kingston, *My Wife, My Daughter and Poor Mary Ann*; O'Donnell, *The Basis of the Bargain*, 1984; Probert, *Working Life*; Ryan & Conlon, *Gentle Invaders*, Ryan, *Two-thirds of a Man*.
4   For a useful discussion on this field, see Pocock, 'Gender', pp 1–19.
5   NSWBLF, 'Minutes', Exec Meeting, 4/5/65, 22/6/65, 17/8/65; Jack Mundey, 30/3/78; Bud Cook, 30/3/78.
6   *Sun*, 17/6/65.
7   NSWBLF, 'Minutes', Exec Meeting, 17/8/65, 15/2/66, 29/3/66, 12/11/68.
8   CPA, *The Left Challenge for the 70s*; CPA, *The Socialist Alternative*; Graham, 'Anatomy of a Revolutionary Union', p 15.
9   NSWBLF, 'Minutes', Gen Meeting, 9/6/70, 1/12/70; Exec Meeting, 30/3/71; Thomas, 'Brothers, sisters and the kids', p 10; Thomas, *Taming the Concrete Jungle*, p 70; Mundey, 'Towards new union militancy', p 8.
10 NSWBLF, 'Agenda Items for Federal Conference, 1973', item 5.
11 *Builders' Labourer*, April 1971, p 11.
12 *Builders' Labourer*, April 1971, pp 11, 12.
13 *Builders' Labourer*, 1972, p 7.
14 Glenys Page, 24/1/78; *Sun-Herald*, 19/12/71.
15 *Builders' Labourer*, 1972, p 7.
16 *Sun*, 23/5/72.
17 *Daily Telegraph*, 10/11/72; Glenys Page, 24/1/78.
18 Thomas, *Taming the Concrete Jungle*, p 73; *Newcastle Morning Herald*, 6/11/72, 11/11/72, 14/11/72.
19 Wendy Stringer, 5/3/78.
20 Robyn Williams, 20/4/78.
21 *Daily Telegraph*, 10/11/72; *Sun-Herald*, 19/12/71, 23/5/72.
22 Thomas, *Taming the Concrete Jungle*, p 73; Janne Reed, 18/4/78.
23 Michelle Fraser, 14/12/77.
24 *SMH*, 20/6/74; *Hobart Mercury*, 20/6/74.
25 'Dillinghams Discriminate Against Women', n.d. [Feb. 1974], 1p, authorised by the BLF Women's Collective; 'Dillingham Clarence Street Dispute', 5/2/74, 1p, authorised by Tom Hogan on behalf of the NSWBLF; NSWBLF, 'Dillingham Clarence St Dispute', n.d., 2pp; NSWBLF, 'Support the Right of Women to Work', n.d., 1p; Don Crotty to R Cram, secretary Miners' Federation, 18/2/74; *Helmet*, March 1974; *Mabel*, 2, n.d.
26 M Burgmann, 'A New Concept of Unionism', p 314; Journal of the UCATT, July 1973, p 5.
27 *Viewpoint*, Jan. 1972, p 10; Don Crotty, 13/3/78.
28 *Tribune*, 1/10/74; *Age*, 23/5/74; *Builders' Labourer*, Aug. 1973; *On Site*, n.d. [1974], p 2.
29 *Tribune*, 1/10/74.
30 Rhonda Ellis, 5/8/77; Michelle Fraser, 14/12/77.
31 Joe Owens, 4/4/78, 24/1/78.
32 For discussion of class influence on differing forms of masculinity, see Tolson, *The Limits of Masculinity*, Connell, *Maculinities*, p 36.
33 *Tribune*, 1/10/74.
34 Robyn Williams, 20/4/78; Denise Bishop, 11/3/78; Pat Fiske, 2/3/78.
35 Lyn Syme, 20/4/78; Stella Nord, 13/3/78.
36 *SMH*, 27/4/74.
37 *Gay Liberation Press*, 3, Sept. 1974, pp 15–16.

DEFENDING THE OPEN SPACES

1   NSWBLF, 'Minutes', Spec Exec Meeting, 4/6/71.
2   Betty James, 'The Battlers', p 16; Whitton, 'Battle for Kelly's Bush'; Kalajzich (ed), *The*

Battlers for Kelly's Bush, p 9; Tennant, 'Foreword for Battlers', p 1; Roddewig, *Green Bans*, p 7.

3   Christena Dawson in Kalajzich (ed), *The Battlers for Kelly's Bush*, p 23; Whitton, 'Battle for Kelly's Bush'; Monica Sheehan in Kalajzich (ed), *The Battlers for Kelly's Bush*, p 39.

4   Kalajzich (ed), *The Battlers for Kelly's Bush*, pp 11–12, 24, 35.

5   James, 'The Battlers', pp 15–16; *SMH*, 3/7/71; Whitton, 'Battle for Kelly's Bush'; Roddewig, *Green Bans*, p 6; Hardman and Manning, *Green Bans*; Kalajzich (ed), *The Battlers for Kelly's Bush*, pp 58, 41, 69.

6   Kalajzich (ed), *The Battlers for Kelly's Bush*, pp 70, 58; Roddewig, *Green Bans*, p 6; Hardman and Manning, Green Bans.

7   James, 'The Battlers', pp 15–16; Whitton, 'Battle for Kelly's Bush'; Kalajzich (ed), *The Battlers for Kelly's Bush*, pp 34, 41, 21.

8   Kalajzich (ed), *The Battlers for Kelly's Bush*, pp 29, 33, 36; Hardmann and Manning, *Green Bans*.

9   Hardman and Manning, *Green Bans*; Mundey, 'Preventing the plunder', p 175; Mundey, *Green Bans & Beyond*, p 81; Whitton, 'Battle for Kelly's Bush'; *Daily Telegraph*, 10/1/73; Kalajzich (ed), *The Battlers for Kelly's Bush*, pp 70, 29–39, 21, 43; James, 'The Battlers', pp 17–18; Undated press clippings [June 1971].

10   Kalajzich (ed), *The Battlers for Kelly's Bush*, pp 44, 65.

11   Kath Lehany, quoted in Roddewig, *Green Bans*, pp 9–10.

12   Mundey, *Green Bans & Beyond*, p 81; Roddewig, *Green Bans*, p 10; Hardman and Manning, *Green Bans*.

13   NSWBLF, 'Minutes', Exec Meeting, 8/6/71; Mundey, 'Meeting "The Battlers"', p 5; Mundey, *Green Bans & Beyond*, pp 81–2; Roddewig, *Green Bans*, p 11; Garden, *Builders to the Nation*, p 250; Mundey, 'Green Bans for Urban Quality', p 11.

14   Mundey, 'Meeting "The Battlers"', p 5; Mundey, 'Preventing the plunder', pp 176–77; Mundey, *Green Bans & Beyond*, p 82; Hardman and Manning, *Green Bans*; Kalajzich (ed), *The Battlers for Kelly's Bush*, p 45.

15   Mundey, 'Preventing the plunder', p 177; Hardman and Manning, Green Bans; Kajajzich (ed), *The Battlers for Kelly's Bush*, pp 70, 45, 57.

16   Mundey, 'Preventing the plunder', p 176.

17   Mundey, 'Preventing the plunder', p 177; Kalajzich (ed), *The Battlers for Kelly's Bush*, pp 32, 65, 57; Mundey, *Green Bans & Beyond*, pp 82–3; *SMH*, 3/7/71, 11/8/71; *Sun*, 5/7/71; Garden, *Builders to the Nation*, p 250; Thomas, 'Those Green Bans'.

18   Hardman and Manning, *Green Bans*; *SMH*, 31/1/72; Mundey, *Green Bans & Beyond*, p 86.

19   *SMH*, 10/11/71, 31/1/72.

20   NSWBLF, 'Minutes', Exec Meeting, 9/11/71, 16/11/71; *SMH*, 24/12/71; Jack Mundey, 13/8/75; JB Mundey, secretary NSWBLF to L Boyce, BTG, Trades Hall, Sydney, 10/11/71.

21   Mundey, Green Bans & Beyond, p 87–88; Hardman and Manning, Green Bans; *SMH*, 5/3/73; J B Mundey, secretary NSWBLF to Alderman OW Davis, Botany, 9/9/72.

22   *SMH*, 5/3/73.

23   *Sun*, 6/3/73; Hardman and Manning, *Green Bans*; Mundey, *Green Bans & Beyond*, p 88.

24   *Australian*, 22/3/73; Roddewig, *Green Bans*, p 29.

25   *SMH*, 22/3/72; *Daily Telegraph*, 23/3/72; *Review*, 9/4/72; *Sun-Herald*, 26/3/72.

26   *Sun-Herald*, 4/6/72; *National Times*, 1–6/1/73, p 28.

27   *SMH*, 22/8/72; *Daily Telegraph*, 6/10/72; *Australian*, editorial, 22/8/72.

28   *Newcastle Herald*, 20/12/72; *Daily Mirror*, 19/12/72; *Melbourne Sun-News Pictorial*, 26/12/72; *Sun-Herald*, 24/12/72, 31/12/72; *Daily Mirror*, 12/1/73; *Australian*, 13/1/73; *SMH*, 13/3/73, 27/12/72.

29   *Newcastle Morning Herald*, 27/12/72; *Wollongong Mercury*, 27/12/72; *SMH*, 27/12/72.

30   *Sun*, 4/1/73; *Daily Mirror*, 5/1/73.

31   *Australian*, 13/1/73; *Daily Mirror*, 12/1/73; *National Times*, 1–6/1/73, p 28; 'Sydney Opera House Car Parking for Patrons', attachment to *Sydney Opera House (Amendment) Bill*, 1972.

32   *Murwillumbah Daily News*, 16/10/73; Roddewig, *Green Bans*, note 70, p 157.

33   Helen Proudfoot, Paddington, letter, *SMH*, 1/4/72; Pat Shaw, Centennial Park, letter, *SMH*, 4/4/72; *Paddington Journal*, 5, 8, June 1972, p 1.

34   John J Cooney, president of the Paddington Society, *SMH*, 1/4/72; Beatrice Bligh, FRHS, National Trust Garden Committee, *SMH*, 1/4/72; Runcie, 'An Open Letter', pp 5–7; 'Onlooker', *Sun-Herald*, 9/4/72.

35 *SMH*, 16/3/72; *Daily Telegraph*, 16/3/72; Fox, 'Muddle at Moore Park', p 38; Dr C Runcie, letter, *SMH*, 4/4/72; Runcie, 'An Open Letter', p 6; Runcie, 'Central Decisions and the Local Repercussions'; Runcie, 'A Failure in Consultation', p 3; *Sun*, 16/3/72.

36 Runcie, 'A Failure in Consultation'; Runcie, 'Central Decisions and the Local Repercussions'; *Catholic Weekly*, 23/3/72; *Sun-Herald*, 26/3/72; HG Pearce, letter, *Daily Telegraph*, 28/3/72; EL Bedford, letter, *SMH*, 1/4/72; J Dorman, letter, *SMH*, 27/3/72.

37 *Sun*, 16/3/72; *Daily Telegraph*, 16/3/72; Petition to the Council of the City of Sydney; Fox, 'Muddle at Moore Park', p 38; *South Sydney Advertiser*, 5/4/72, p 2; Runcie, 'An Open Letter', pp 1–9; AJ McLardie, chairman Sydney Sporting Centre Committee, 'An Open Letter to the Premier of New South Wales The Hon. Sir Robert Askin, MLA', 18/4/72; Runcie, 'Central Decisions and the Local Repercussions'; Runcie, 'Political Miscalculation or Political Hoax', pp 4–5; Runcie, 'A Failure in Consultation', pp 1–6; Prof. N Runcie, secretary Centennial Park Residents' Association to Town Clerk, Council of the City of Sydney, 6/3/72; Gavin Souter, *SMH*, 16/5/72.

38 Petition to the Council of the City of Sydney; *SMH*, 16/3/72; Prof. N Runcie, secretary Centennial Park Residents' Association to Town Clerk, Council of the City of Sydney, 6/3/72; *Catholic Weekly*, 23/3/72; Fox, 'Muddle at Moore Park', p 38; *SMH*, 1/4/72; *South Sydney Advertiser*, 5/4/72, p 2; Senator James McClelland, letter, *SMH*, 25/4/72; Runcie, 'Political Miscalculation or Political Hoax?', p 4; Runcie, 'A Failure in Consultation', pp 1–6.

39 *Daily Mirror*, 16/3/72, 17/3/72; *Sun*, 16/3/72; Fox, 'Muddle at Moore Park', p 38; WR McManus, President, NSW Rugby Union, Letter to *Sun-Herald*, 16/4/72. See also FW Youngs, letter, *Daily Telegraph*, 21/3/72; RN Glissan, letter, SMH, 27/3/72; Sporting Editor in *Sun-Herald*, 23/4/72; Runcie, 'An Open Letter', p 3; *Australian*, 4/11/72.

40 'By Laws', *Daily Mirror*, 16/3/72; *SMH*, editorial, 17/3/72; John Cooney, letter, *SMH*, 1/4/72; Runcie, 'Central Decisions and the Local Repercussions'; Runcie, 'A Failure in Consultation', p 3; DF Orchard, letter, *Mirror*, 22/3/72.

41 *SMH*, 16/3/72; *Daily Telegraph*, 16/3/72, 28/3/72; Runcie, 'An Open Letter', p 7.

42 *SMH*, 18/3/72, 23/11/72; Runcie, 'Political Miscalculation or Political Hoax?', p 4; Fox, 'Muddle at Moore Park', p 38; George Molnar, letter, *SMH*, 24/3/72.

43 *South Sydney Advertiser*, 5/4/72, p 2; Runcie, 'Political Miscalculation or Political Hoax?', pp 6, 2; *Paddington Journal*, 5, 8, June 1972, p 1.

44 Runcie, 'A Failure in Consultation', pp 6, 3; Runcie, 'Political Miscalculation or Political Hoax?' p 2; Roddewig, *Green Bans*, p 30.

45 *Mudgee Guardian*, 21/9/73, 24/9/73.

46 *Mudgee Guardian*, 21/9/73, 24/9/73; Summers, et al, *The little green book*, p 20.

47 *SMH*, 17/8/73, 18/8/73; *Daily Telegraph*, 17/8/73; NSWBLF, 'Press Statement', 17/8/73, 2pp.

48 *Mudgee Guardian*, 3/10/73; *Orange News Pictorial*, 6/10/73.

49 Crouch, 'Some black among the BLF green'.

50 *Daily Examiner* (Grafton), 13/12/73; *Albury Mail*, 13/12/73; *Murwillumbah Daily News*, 13/12/73; ABCE&BLF, *Builders' Laborers Defend the People's Heritage*.

51 Clipping, unidentified local paper, 30/11/73; 'Island in the Sun: A Hooker-Rex Story', *Builders Labourer*, Aug. 1973, p 35.

52 *Raymond Terrace Examiner*, 13/2/74; *Maitland Mercury*, 23/1/74; *Newcastle Morning Herald*, 16/1/74; *Newcastle Sun*, 16/1/74; *Port Stephens Pictorial*, 6/2/74, 16/1/74.

53 *Newcastle Morning Herald*, 17/1/74, 16/1/74, 19/1/74; *Port Stephens Pictorial*, 6/2/74

54 Letters to *Port Stephens Pictorial*, 30/1/74; *Raymond Terrace Examiner*, 13/2/74.

55 *Telegraph* (Brisbane), 7/5/74; *Newcastle Sun*, 8/5/74; *Port Stephens Pictorial*, 17/4/74; 8/5/74; *Newcastle Morning Herald*, 8/4/74, 15/4/74, 8/5/74, 9/5/74.

56 *Newcastle Sun*, 20/5/74; *Newcastle Morning Herald*; *Taree Times*, 23/5/74; *Newcastle Morning Herald*, 21/5/74, 24/5/74, 11/7/74.

57 *Daily Telegraph*, 24/2/73; *Gosford Star*, 14/8/74; *Independent Kiama*, 10/10/73; *Dubbo Liberal*, 29/8/73; *Newcastle Sun*, 29/8/73; *Illawarra Mercury*, 30/8/73; *Daily Telegraph*, 31/8/73; *Windsor Gazette*, 10/4/74; *Manly Daily*, 1/6/74.

PRESERVING THE BUILT ENVIRONMENT

1 *Now*, 131, 8/4/75, p 3.
2 *Victoria Street Rag*, 5/1/74, p 1.
3 Souter, 'On the debit side of the green ban'.
4 Roddewig, *Green Bans*, pp 28, 16–18, 21.
5 Kelly, *Anchored in a Small Cove*, p 107; Roddewig, *Green Bans*, pp 19–20; *Sun-Herald*, 14/11/71.
6 Anderson and Jacobs, 'Geographies of Publicity and Privacy', pp 26–29.
7 *Sun-Herald*, 14/11/71; Roddewig, *Green Bans*, p 20; *Sun*, 19/1/72, 18/1/72; 'Minutes', Gen Meeting, 2/11/71.
8 *SMH*, 15/1/72; *Australian*, 6/11/71, 8/1/72; *Sun-Herald*, 14/11/71.
9 *Tribune*, 17/11/71; R Pringle president & J Owens acting secretary, ABLF, NSW Branch, letter, *SMH*, 15/1/72.
10 *Sunday Mail*, 23/1/72; *Sun*, 19/1/72; *Australian*, 20/1/72, 26/12/71; *SMH*, 31/10/72, 17/11/72; Roddewig, *Green Bans*, p 27.
11 *SMH*, 15/1/72, 18/1/72; *Daily Mirror*, 17/3/72; *Fin. Rev.*, 2/2/73; *Sunday Mail*, 23/1/72.
12 *Daily Mirror*, 17/3/72; *Daily Telegraph*, 19/3/72; Thomas, *Taming the Concrete Jungle*, p 46.
13 DO Magee, SCRA to Mrs N McCrae, Rocks Residents' Group, 10/3/72; DO Magee, SCRA to JP Ducker, acting secretary, Labor Council of NSW, 6/4/72; JP Ducker, 'Circular to Unions concerned with The Rocks Development', 10/4/72; Warwick Neilly, 21/1/78.
14 *Melbourne Herald*, 26/3/74; Thomas, *Taming the Concrete Jungle*, p 47; *SMH*, 31/10/72.
15 Kelly, *Anchored in a Small Cove*, p 108; Thomas, *Taming the Concrete Jungle*, p 47.
16 DO Magee, letter, *SMH*, 23/11/72; *SMH*, 24/11/72; *Fin. Rev.*, 2/2/73; Roddewig, *Green Bans*, p 26.
17 *SMH*, 29/8/73; *Daily Mirror*, 29/8/73; *Sun*, 30/8/73; Yeomans, 'A grand plan founders on the Rocks'.
18 *SMH*, 23/1/74, 26/1/74; *Melbourne Herald*, 26/3/74; Yeomans, 'A grand plan founders on the Rocks'; *Daily Mirror*, 31/5/74.
19 Kelly, *Anchored in a Small Cove*, pp 109–110; Karskens, *The Rocks*, p 5; *SMH*, 11/2/95; Carr, 'Now the ban's on Mundey', p 40.
20 *Australian*, 22/10/71; *SMH*, 2/4/74.
21 Hardman and Manning, *Green Ban*, *Australian*, 15/2/73; Mundey, *Green Bans & Beyond*, p 91.
22 Unidentifed press clipping, n.d. [c. Nov. 1972]; *Daily Telegraph*, 15/2/73; *Australian*, 15/2/73; *Illawarra Mercury*, 16/2/73; Joe Owens, 4/4/78.
23 *SMH*, 23/2/73, 16/4/73, 22/2/73.
24 *SMH*, 20/2/73, 21/2/73, 22/2/73, 23/2/73; *Australian*, 20/2/73, 22/2/73, 27/2/73; *Daily Telegraph*, 23/2/73, 24/2/73; *Daily Mirror*, 26/2/73.
25 *SMH*, 16/4/73; Souter, 'On the debit side of the green ban'; *Passing Show*, 10/10/78, p 10.
26 *Australian*, 27/10/73; *Daily Mirror*, 29/10/73; *SMH*, 27/10/73, 2/4/74, 14/5/74.
27 *SMH*, 29/6/74.
28 *Now*, 25/3/75, p 6; *Now & Again*, 9/10/75; Carr, 'Now the ban's on Mundey', p 39; *National Times*, 2/6/78; Mundey, 'Preventing the Plunder', p 178; Hardman and Manning, *Green Bans*.
29 JT, ex-resident, 'Communities Ravaged', *Victoria Street Rag*, 5/1/74, p 2.
30 Hardman and Manning, *Green Bans*.
31 *Fin. Rev.*, 4/5/73; *SMH*, 5/5/73.
32 Hickie, *The Prince and the Premier*, passim; *SMH*, 3/3/98; 'Victoria Street History', *Scrounge*, 1, p 5.
33 'The Fight to Prevent the Redevelopment of Victoria St', p 1; *SMH*, 14/4/73; *Now & Then*, 1, 3, 22/2/76, p 2.
34 *Now & Then*, 1, 3, 22/2/76, p 2.
35 'Victoria Street. History', *Scrounge*, 1, pp 6–7; 'The Fight to Prevent the Redevelopment of Victoria St', p 1; *SMH*, 14/3/73; Wendy Bacon, 16/1/78.

36 *Now & Then*, 1, 3, 22/2/76, p 2; Coombs, *Sex and Anarchy*, p 282; Wendy Bacon, 16/1/78.

37 *Now & Then*, 1, 3, 22/2/76, p 2; Coombs, *Sex and Anarchy*, pp 286–90; Bacon, 'Crusader of the Cross'; 'Victoria Street. History', *Scrounge*, 1, pp 7–8; *Australian*, 4/5/73; *Daily Mirror*, 3/5/73.

38 *Fin. Rev.*, 4/5/73; *SMH*, 4/5/73.

39 *SMH*, 4/5/73; 'Statement by FW Theeman for and on behalf of Victoria Point Pty Ltd', 9/5/73, 2 pp; *Now & Then*, 1, 3, 22/2/76, p 2.

40 *SMH*, 5/3/73, 10/5/73, 12/5/73; *Now & Then*, 1, 3, 22/2/76, p 3.

41 *Daily Telegraph*, 5/5/73; *SMH*, 5/5/73; 'Victoria Street. History', *Scrounge*, 1, p 9.

42 *SMH*, 26/5/73, 6/6/73, 21/6/73; *Daily Telegraph*, 6/6/73.

43 *Daily Mirror*, 6/6/73; *Australian*, 6/6/73; *SMH*, 7/6/73.

44 *SMH*, 11/6/73; 21/6/73; 5/7/73; Coombs, *Sex and Anarchy*, pp 279–99; *Builders' Labourer*, Aug. 1973, p 17.

45 *SMH*, 6/6/73, 16/6/73, 21/6/73, 5/7/73, 4/8/73, 23/8/73, 8/11/73, 20/10/73; *Australian*, 6/6/73; 'Victoria Street. History', *Scrounge*, 1, p 10; *Fin. Rev.*, 21/11/73; *Victoria Street Rag*, 5/1/74, pp 1–2.

46 *Victoria Street Rag*, 5/1/74, p 1.

47 Lapsley, 'Battle lost, no quarter given'.

48 'Victoria Street May Day March and Wake', 1p; *SMH*, 14/8/79.

49 Hickie, *The Prince and the Premier*, pp 476–521; *SMH*, 3/3/98; Bacon, 'Crusader of the Cross'.

50 *Now & Then*, 1, 3, 22/2/76, pp 3–4; Brooks, 'Lost'.

51 *SMH*, 5/7/79, 15/5/81.

52 *SMH*, 14/8/79, 18/8/79.

53 Brooks, 'Lost'.

54 *Newcastle Morning Herald*, 21/2/73.

55 *Newcastle Sun*, 23/2/73; *Newcastle Morning Herald*, 23/5/73, 5/6/73, 28/6/73, 4/10/73, 5/10/73.

56 *Newcastle Sun*, 23/7/73; *Newcastle Herald*, 27/7/73; *Newcastle Morning Herald*, 30/7/73, 31/10/73; Newcastle East Residents Group, 'Agenda Public Meeting', 25/3/74, 2pp.

57 *Newcastle Sun*, 10/12/73; Hunter Valley Fair Rates Committee, 'Newsletter', Feb. 1974, p 2; R Bollinger, letter, *Newcastle Morning Herald*, 18/2/74.

58 Letter, *Newcastle Morning Herald*, 22/2/74.

59 *Newcastle Sun*, 5/4/74; F Mather, Royal Newcastle Hospital to secretary, BLF, Sydney, 4/3/74; Jean Perrett, NERG to Bob Pringle, 14/3/74; NERG, 'Agenda Public Meeting', 25/3/74, 2 pp; *Newcastle Morning Herald*, 6/7/74, 8/7/74, 10/7/74.

60 *Newcastle Sun*, 8/7/74.

61 Mundey, 'The Role of Workers in a Modern Industrial Society', p 1; *Sun* and *Newcastle Sun*, 24/10/72; *Tribune*, 23/10/72.

62 Summers et al, *The Little Green Book*, p 15; *Tharunka*, Foundation Day 1973; 'To the Residents of Chippendale, Redfern, Alexandria and Beaconsfield', n.d. [Oct. 1974], 2pp.

63 Unidentified press clippings, n.d. (1972).

64 *Australian*, 11/12/72; *SMH*, 3/4/73.

65 *SMH*, 4/4/73; *Daily Telegraph*, 4/4/73; *Australian*, 4/4/73; *Sun*, 4/4/73.

66 *Newcastle Herald*, 8/5/73; *Newcastle Morning Herald*, 17/5/73, 18/5/73.

67 *Daily Telegraph*, 29/3/74; *Courier-Mail*, 4/6/74.

68 Inner Sydney RAG, 'Why Stop This Expressway', n.d. (Oct. 1974); 'To the Residents of Chippendale, Redfern, Alexandria and Beaconsfield', n.d. (Oct. 1974), 2pp; ACF, 'News Release', 3/10/74; *National Times*, 25/9/72.

69 Steve Mitchell, 'Anti-Expressway Campaign', unidentified newspaper clipping, n.d. [Oct. 1974); 'To the Residents of Chippendale, Redfern, Alexandria and Beaconsfield', n.d. [Oct. 1974), 2pp; 'War Notice', n.d. (Oct. 1974], 1p; McGregor, 'The urban crisis', p 33.

70 *SMH*, 22/11/71, 2/11/73.

71 JB Mundey, secretary, NSWBLF, letter, *SMH*, 23/8/73.

72 *Australian*, 20/7/73; *Daily Telegraph*, 20/7/73; *SMH*, 22/8/73; *Now*, 131, 8/4/75.

73 *SMH*, 16/10/71, 12/7/73, 2/11/73; *Australian*, 12/11/71; 'A Second Waterloo', 25/9/75, 2 pp; Jones, 'Living it up and liking it'.

74 *Daily Telegraph*, 13/7/73, 21/7/73; *SMH*, 13/7/73, 21/7/73; 'A Second Waterloo', 25/9/75, 2pp; 'To all Executive & Organisers etc', n.d. (July 1973), 1p.
75 *Sun*, 6/8/73; Tones, 'Living it up and liking it'; *Daily Mirror*, 22/11/73.
76 'A Second Waterloo', 25/9/75, 2pp; 'Whose Waterloo?', n.d. [Sept. 1975], 2pp; 'So, what's happened so far)', n.d. (Oct. 1975), 1p.
77 *Australian*, 13/9/73; *Daily Telegraph*, 8/10/73; *Manly Daily*, 12/10/73, 8/6/74; *SMH*, 17/10/73
78 *Newcastle Morning Herald*, 19/2/74, 21/2/74, 6/3/74, 30/3/74; *Newcastle Sun*, 22/3/74.
79 *SMH*, 17/6/74.
80 Planning for People, *Surry Hills News*, n.d. (c. Dec. 1973]; Summers et al, *The Little Green Book*, p 20.
81 *Daily Telegraph*, 10/1/74; *Sunday Mirror*, 3/2/74.
82 *SMH*, 25/9/73.
83 North Newtown Action Group, 'Newtown and the Teachers College'; North Newtown Action Group, 'Newtown Action', April 1974; North Newtown Action Group, 'Agenda for Meeting', 28/4/74.
84 *Newcastle Morning Herald*, 15/2/74, 12/7/74.
85 Maiden, 'Hornsby'.
86 Maiden, 'Hornsby'; Dave Shaw, 7/8/77; Hurchalla, 'Industrial Crimes', p 36.

SAVING THE NATIONAL ESTATE

1 Swancott, 'Builders will not knock history'.
2 *SMH*, 20/1/72, 26/8/72.
3 Edward Sykes, letter to *Age*, 24/1/73.
4 Swancott, 'Builders will not knock History'.
5 *SMH*, 26/2/72.
6 JB Mundey to L Boyce, 8/12/71; *Australian*, 20/1/72; Thomas, *Taming the Concrete Jungle*, p 41.
7 Thomas, *Taming the Concrete Jungle*, p 41; *SMH*, 30/10/72.
8 JB Mundey, letter to *SMH*, 16/1/73; John Morris, acting director National Trust (NSW), letter, *SMH*, 30/7/73.
9 *National Times*, undated clipping (c. Feb. 1972]; *Herald*, 2/2/72; John Bryant, letter, *SMH* 4/2/72; JF Dickinson, secretary Congregational Union of NSW Inc, letter, *SMH*, 7/2/72.
10 Thomas, *Taming the Concrete Jungle*, p 51; JB Mundey, letter, *SMH*, 1/2/72; *National Times*, undated clipping [c. Feb. 1972]; John Bryant, letter, *SMH*, 4/2/72.
11 Letter, *SMH*, 4/2/72.
12 *SMH*, 18/4/72, 6/2/95; John Bryant, letter, *SMH*, 21/5/74.
13 *SMH*, 3/8/73, 23/8/73; ABCE&BLF, *Builders' Laborers Defend the People's Heritage*.
14 *Illawarra Mercury*, 2/11/72, 3/11/72.
15 *Illawarra Mercury*, 22/6/73; *Telegraph* (Brisbane), 9/7/73; Jack Mundey (with Verity Burgmann), 31/3/98.
16 *SMH*, 13/3/73, 16/3/73; Thomas, *Taming the Concrete Jungle*, p 53; *Builders' Labourer*, n.d. (1973), p 15.
17 *Australian*, 21/12/73; *Daily Telegraph*, 22/12/73; *Murwillumbah Daily News*, 12/1/74
18 *Australian*, 23/12/73; ABCE&BLF, *Builders' Laborers Defend the People's Heritage*.
19 *Western Advocate* (Bathurst), 11/1/74.
20 *SMH*, 19/1/74.
21 *Australian*, 13/5/81.
22 *SMH*, 23/5/74.
23 *Daily Telegraph*, 16/11/71; *SMH*, 16/11/71; *Australian*, 16/11/71; *Tribune*, 24/11/71.
24 *Tribune*, 16–22/5/72; *Daily Mirror*, 12/5/72; *SMH*, 16/5/72.
25 *SMH*, 16/5/72; *Tribune*, 16–22/5/72.
26 *Daily Telegraph*, 30/10/72; *Australian*, 30/10/72, 31/10/72; *Daily Mirror*, 31/10/72, 9/11/72; *SMH*, 31/10/72.
27 *Fin. Rev.*, 1/11/72; *Daily Telegraph*, 1/11/72; *Sun*, 1/11/72; *SMH*, 3/11/72, 31/10/72; *Australian*, 1/11/72, 4/11/72.

28 *SMH*, 7/11/72; *Australian*, 9/11/72, 4/11/72; *Fin. Rev.*, 1/2/73; *Daily Mirror*, 9/11/72; Thomas, *Taming the Concrete Jungle*, p 125.
29 *Fin. Rev.*, 1/2/73.
30 *SMH*, 12/5/81.
31 *Daily Mirror*, 16/10/72; *Sun*, 18/10/72; *Tribune*, 8/11/72.
32 *SMH*, 8/10/72; *Bulletin*, 28/10/72.
33 *SMH*, 16/10/72, 17/10/72; *Sun*, 16/10/72; *Murwillumbah Daily News*, 17/10/72.
34 *Sun*, 17/10/72; *Broken Hill Truth*, 18/10/72; Saw, 'A "complex" must never replace Jim Buckley's'.
35 *Bulletin*, 28/10/72; *Tamworth Daily Leader*, 17/10/72; Moorhouse, *Days of Wine and Rage*, pp 287–99; *Daily Mirror*, 16/10/72; *Sun*, 17/10/72, 18/10/72; *Sunday Mirror*, 5/11/72.
36 *Sunday Mirror*, 5/11/72.
37 *Sun*, 18/10/72; *Daily Telegraph*, 25/ 1/73; Thomas, *Taming the Concrete Jungle*, p 51; Summers et al, *The Little Green Book*, p 15; Coombs, *Sex and Anarchy*, pp 280–81.
38 *Australian*, 8/6/74; Jack Mundey (with Verity Burgmann), 31/3/98.
39 *Inverell Times*, 12/7/74, 15/7/74, 17/7/74, 19/7/74, 26/7/74, 2/8/74; *Narrabri Courier*, 12/8/74; *Northern Daily Leader*, 18/7/74.
40 *Inverell Times*, 12/7/74, 15/7/74.
41 *Northern Daily Leader*, 27/7/74; *Inverell Times*, 26/7/74.
42 *Inverell Times*, 31/7/74.
43 *Inverell Times*, 26/8/74, 2/8/74, 5/8/74.
44 *Inverell Times*, 9/8/74, 26/8/74.
45 Http://www.bec.com.au/inverell/index.htm.

BREAKING THE BANS, BREAKING THE UNION

1   *SMH*, 22/1/72; *Sunday Australian*, 23/1/72; Thomas, *Taming the Concrete Jungle*, pp 117–118; Sandercock, *Cities For Sale*, p 207; *SMH*, 24/10/73, 1/11/73, 7/11/73, 8/11/73, 9/11/73.
2   For discussion of the relationship between the media and private enterprises around this time, see McQueen, *Australia's Media Monopolies*, esp. chs 1–2.
3   *Newcastle Morning Herald*, 2/11/72.
4   *SMH*, 9/11/73.
5   JD Martin, letter *SMH*, 9/2/72; *Rydge's*, 1/6/74, p 18.
6   *Sun*, 19/1/72; *SMH*, 14/8/72.
7   *Australian*, 5/9/72; Jack Mundey, letter, *Australian*, 7/9/72; *Nation Review*, 8/9/72; *SMH*, 21/1/74.
8   Mundey, 'Towards new union militancy', p 5.
9   Bud Cook, 5/3/78; NSWBLF, 'Minutes', Exec Meeting, 3/3/70, 10/11/70, 24/11/70; Gen Meeting, 3/3/70; Anderson, 'The Builders Labourers Federation of NSW', p 40.
10 *Australian*, 11/9/71.
11 Hickie, *The Prince and the Premier*, passim.
12 See Parkin, *Marxism and Class Theory*, p 77.
13 Bob Pringle, 8/3/78.
14 *Daily Mirror*, 17/9/71; *SMH*, 18/9/71; *Sun-Herald*, 19/9/71.
15 NSWBLF, 'Minutes', Spec Exec Meeting, 20/9/71; NSWBLF, 'Press Statement', 20/9/71, 2pp.
16 *Australian*, 20/9/71; *Sun*, 21/9/71, 20/9/71; *Daily Telegraph*, 21/9/71; *Daily Mirror*, 20/9/71; NSW13LF, 'Minutes', Exec Meeting, 5/10/71; NSWBLF, 'J Mundey's Statement to Detective Sergeant Bradbury and Detective Senior Constable Tunstall in an Interview in Room 28 Trades Hall on Tuesday 5 October 1971 in response to a police investigation into the AHLF NSW Branch at the instance of the Premier Mr Askin, the Commissioner of Police Mr Allan, and the Minister for Labour and Industry, Mr Hewitt', 1p; 'Report of Interview with Police and J Mundey', 5/10/71, 1p.
17 *Builders Labourer*, 1972, pp 25, 27; *Tribune*, 15–21/2/72, 4–10/4/72; NSWBLF, 'Disputes Book', 10/7/72, 21/7/72, 2/8/72, 7/9/72, 1/12/72; *Daily Telegraph*, 10/11/72; J Mundey to L Boyce, Secretary, BTG, 12/4/72; Tony Hadfield, 13/12/76; Thomas, *Taming the Concrete Jungle*, pp 124–25.

18   *Sun*, 2/11/72, 3/11/72; *SMH*, 3/11/72, 4/11/72; *Australian*, 4/11/72; Askin, 'Statement', 4/11/72.
19   *SMH*, 8/11/72, 9/11/72; Berry, 'Posing the housing question', p 114.
20   *SMH*, 2/11/72; NSWBLF, 'Circular to All Job Organisers', 1/73, 24/1/73.
21   *Direct Action*, 21/3/75; *Daily Mirror*, 9/11/72; *Daily Telegraph*, 24/10/73; *SMH*, 1/11/73.
22   NSWBLF, 'Minutes', Exec Meeting, 21/7/70, 13/4/71, 20/4/71; *Builders Labourer*, July 1970, p 9; Bob Pringle, 8/3/78; *Tribune*, 3/11/71.
23   *Building Worker*, May/June 1971, p 10; Tom Hogan, 28/10/77; Building Industry Branch of the SPA, *Six Turbulent Years*, p 22; Jack Mundey, 3/4/78, 30/3/78.
24   John McNamara, Dick Keenan, Kevin Gledhill and Pat McNamara. All except McNamara were appointed officials by Gallagher during Intervention.
25   *Daily Telegraph*, 28/10/71; *SMH*, 2/9/72, 23/8/72; SPA, 'Ultra-Leftism'.
26   *SMH*, 18/3/72; ABLF, 'Minutes', Fed Man Cmtee, 18–19/4/72, pp 2, 4, 11.
27   Leaflet authorised by BTG Rank and File, n.d., 1 p; Building Workers' Rank and File Committee, 'Builders' Labourers: Its Time for a Change', n.d. [c. mid-1973], 1p, authorised by J McNamara and Ron Donoghue; Armstrong, 'Rank versus File'.
28   *Sunday Telegraph*, 23/9/73; *Bulletin*, 29/9/73, p 29; Advertisement, *Sun*, 2/10/73, authorised by J Martin, MBA.
29   *Daily Mirror*, 9/10/73; Norman, 'BLF Outflanked at the Rocks'; *SMH*, 18/10/73, 19/10/73; *Australian*, 20/10/73, 25/10/73; *Daily Telegraph*, 25/10/73.
30   *SMH*, 19/10/73, 22/10/73, 24/10//3, 26/10/73; *Fin. Rev.*, 25/10/73; *Daily Telegraph*, 24/10/73; Freney, 'Builders Labourers Fight Back'; *Daily Mirror*, 25/10/73; *Sun*, 25/10/73, 26/10/73; *Newcastle Sun*, 26/10/73.
31   *Australian*, 20/10/73; *Sun*, 22/10/73; *Canberra Times*, 25/10/73; *SMH*, 27/10/73; *Daily Telegraph*, 23/10/73.
32   *Australian*, 27/10/73, 31/10/73; *Melbourne Sun-News Pictorial*, 29/10/73; *Sun*, 29/10/73; Whitton, 'The Greenies' Hero is Fighting for Survival'; *Melbourne Herald*, 30/10/73.
33   Advertisement, 'Notice to Builders' Labourers', *Daily Telegraph*, 1/11/73, authorised by N Gallagher, general secretary.
34   *Daily Telegraph*, 31/10/73; *Sun*, 31/10/73; *Fin. Rev.*, 31/10/73; *Daily Mirror*, 31/10/73, 1/11/73.
35   *Daily Telegraph*, 1/11/73; 'Draft Resolutions for Public Meeting, Centennial Park, 2.00 pm Sunday 4 November 1973', 1p; *Murwillumbah Daily News*, 3/11/73.
36   *Daily Telegraph*, 3/11/73, 7/11/73; *SMH*, 3/11/73, 6/11/73, 15/11/73; *Daily Mirror*, 5/11/73; *Australian*, 6/11/73; *Canberra Times*, 6/11/73; Advertisements in *SMH*, 7/11/73, *Sunday Telegraph*, 11/11/73 and *Sun-Herald*, 11/11/73, authorised by J Martin, MBA; *Sun*, 14/ 11/73.
37   *Melbourne Herald*, 14/11/73; *Daily Telegraph*, 16/11/73; *Sun*, 22/11/73; *Manufacturers' Monthly*, 15/12/73, p 17; Jack Mundey, 13/8/75; Joe Owens, 24/1/78.
38   NSWBLF, 'Circular to All Delegates' (24/73), 5/12/73.
39   *Fin. Rev.*, 22/11/73; *Age*, 22/11/73; *Sun*, 22/11/73; *Daily Telegraph*, 22/11/73; *Canberra Times*, 22/11/73; *Sun News-Pictorial*, 22/11/73; NSWBLF, 'Circular to all Delegates', 24/73, 5/12/73; NSWBLF, 'Circular to Job Organisers' (22/73), 19/12/73.
40   *Age*, 7/9/73; ABLF, 'Fight De-Registration – Save the Environment', n.d. [c. December 1973], 2 pp, authorised by N Gallagher.
41   *Daily Mirror*, 3/1/74, 4/1/74; *Sun*, 3/1/74.
42   'Not Wanted', poster, n.d., authorised by VSAG and BLF; *Victoria Street Rag*, 5/1/74, 10/1/74; NSWBLF, 'Circular to All Job Delegates and Activists', 1/74, 9/1/74; 2/74, 22/1/74.
43   Bacon, 'They huffed and they puffed'; *Sun*, 6/4/74; *SMH*, 15/4/74, 18/4/74.
44   *SMH*, 2/5/74; *Fin. Rev.*, 23/5/74.
45   Hurchalla, 'Industrial Crimes', pp 15–16; *Australian*, 22/6/74.
46   *Independence Voice*, 8, July 1974; ABCE&BLF, *Builders' Labourer Song Book*, pp 115–17; 'Deregistration: Foreign Bosses' Plot', n.d. [c. mid-1974], 4pp, authorised by NL Gallagher, general secretary, ABCE&BLF; 'Deregistration Means Nothing', n.d. [c. mid-1974], 2pp, authorised by NL Gallagher, general secretary, ABCE&BLF; ABCE&BLF,

'Builders' Labourers Stop Work Meeting: Tuesday 27th August', [1974], 2pp.
On the Maoist position, see McQueen, 'National Independence and Socialism',
pp 68–79.

47 'To All Building Workers', n.d. [c. mid-1974], 4pp, issued by RL Rocher, executive director, MBA NSW; *Age*, 18/5/74; *Daily Telegraph*, 18/5/74.
48 Ray Rocher (with Pat Fiske), 1980; Rocher quoted in Williams, 'Gallagher's war with Mundey'.
49 Ray Rocher (with Pat Fiske), 1980; L'Estrange, 'Make-or-Break Men'; *Australian*, 27/2/81.
50 Joe Owens, 4/4/78; *SMH*, 7/8/74; *Australian Socialist*, 2, cited in Higgins 'Reconstructing Australian Communism', p 187; Jack Mundey, 30/3/78.
51 *Tharunka*, 9/10/74, p 9; *Daily Mirror*, 1/10/74.
52 Concerned Residents of Sydney, 'The Fig Street Fiasco', 1, n.d. [c. October 1974], 2pp.
53 Anti-Urban Radial Expressway Committee, 'Demo in Support of the Fig Street Ten', n.d., 1p; Myers, 'The Fig Street Fiasco'; *Daily Telegraph*, 1/10/74; 'Expressway Stopped at Fig Street', n.d. [October 1974], 4pp; 'War Notice', n.d. (October 1974), 1p; *Tharunka*, 9/10/74, p 8; 'To the Residents of Chippendale, Redfern, Alexandria and Beaconsfield', n.d. [October 1974], 2pp.
54 Joe Owens, 24/1/78.
55 Mundey, Owens and Pringle all made these points in their interviews.
56 *SMH*, 11/5/73, 25/9/73; *Australian*, 25/9/73; 'Minutes', Federal Conference, November 1973; John Rose, 7/3/81; Anon. group of Marxist/Leninists, 'N Gallagher, Marxist/Leninist or Opportunist?', n.d. [1974–75], 2pp.
57 Jack Mundey, 23/3/81; *SMH*, 4/6/81.
58 *SMH*, 8/10/74, 14/10/74; Hurchalla, 'Industrial Crimes', p 20; FMC, 'Schedule', n.d. [October 1974], 5pp, p 4; MBA of NSW, 'All Member Circular', no 81/1974, 22/10/74.
59 *Tribune*, 22/10/74; Crouch, 'Some Black among the BLF Green'; ACF, 'News Release', 2/11/74, 1p; Colless, 'A case of the banners banned'; Haskell, 'Green Bans', p 212.
60 Mick Ross, finance officer NSWBLF to 'Dear Comrade', 11/11/74; NSWBLF, 'MBA–Gallagher Collusion', n.d. [c. April 1975], 1p; ABCE&BLF NSW Branch (under federal administration), 'Victorian Builders' Labourers Win $9.00 Flow On', n.d., 1p.
61 Hurchalla, 'Industrial Crimes', p 22.
62 'We Support NSWBLF Because They Support Us', poster signed by residents, blacks, prisoners, women, homosexuals, environmentalists and students.
63 'Unions and Green Bans', press statement signed by Adrian Bennett, John Button, G Clayton, D Everingham, A Gietzelt, Jim Keefe, D McKenzie, Joan Melzer, Justin O'Byrne, C Primmer, L Wallis, Tom Uren, W Brown, Don Cameron, John Coates, John Dawkins, Don Grimes, John Kerin, Gordon McIntosh, Peter Morris, Max Oldmeadow, Len Reynolds, P Walsh, G Bryant, Moss Cass, Ruth Coleman, K Fray, H Jenkins, Anthony Lamb, James McClelland, A Mulvihill, Gordon Poyser, R Thorburn, John Wheeldon, 24/10/74.
64 *Australian*, 12/3/75; *Daily Mirror*, 18/3/75; *Helmet*, 19/3/75; Teachers' Federation official Richard Walsham spoke at the final meeting in the Town Hall, 24 March 1975; Jack Kreger, NSW president ATEA, 25/7/80.
65 J Mundey to V Burgmann, 25/2/98, 7/3/98.
66 Hurchalla, 'Industrial Crimes', p 23; Wickham, 'The NSWBLF', p 11; Colless, 'Black day for the greenies'.
67 *Helmet*, 19/3/75; *Tribune*, 24/4/75, p 6.
68 Trades Hall information sheet; NSWBLF & NSW FEDFA, 'Who Would Trust a Union Led By This Man)', n.d. [c. December 1974], 4pp, p 3; ABCE BLF, 'Election Result', n.d.; *SMH*, 4/6/81; Carr, 'Mundey takes his case to the rank and file'.
69 Ray Rocher (with Pat Fiske), 1980.
70 *SMH*, 9/10/74.
71 *Australian*, 9/10/74.
72 NSWBLF, 'Unity of Builders Labourers NOW!', 13/10/74, 2pp.
73 Les Robinson, 20/2/78.
74 MBA of NSW, 'All Member Circular', 81/1974, 22/10/74, 1p; Ray Rocher (with Pat Fiske) 1980.
75 'EA Watts Dispute', 29/10/74, 1p, authorised by the EA Watts Strike Committee and

Joe Owens and Bob Pringle NSWBLF; Ind ustrial Commission of NSW, 'Dispute … re dismissals, etc', 74/480, 31/10/74; Industrial Commission of NSW, (74/523), 22/11/74; NSWBLF, 'NSW Branch Builders Labourers Win $9', n.d. [c. October 1974], 2pp; NSWBLF, 'M BA-Gallagher Collusion', n.d. [c. April 1975], 1p; *Tribune*, 10/12/74.

76 AB&CWF Federal Office, 'Statement of Income and Expenditure For the Half Year Ended 31st March', 1974, 1p; Winter, Pratt & Houghton to the federal president, AB&CWF, 23/7/74; NSWBLF, Federal Office audit, n.d. [c. November 1974], 3p; Wickham, 'The NSWBLF', pp 14–15; Boyd, *Inside the BLF*, pp 31–71; *Passing Show*, 10/10/78, p 10.

77 Neville Gruzman to Town Clerk, Sydney, 24/4/75; Theeman to the chief planner, John Doran, 2 July 1975; *National Times*, 15–21/2/81; *Sun*, 18/4/75; Jack Mundey, 23/3/81.

78 Quoted in Williams, 'Gallagher's war with Mundey'.

79 Bob Pringle, 8/3/78; Boyd, *Inside the BLF*, p 12; NSW Branch, ABCE&BLF, 'News Bulletin', n.d. [October 1974], 1p, authorised by NL Gallagher; *SMH*, 10/4/81; NSWBLF, 'Crane Occupation Book', n.d. [November 1974]; *SMH*, 7/11/74.

80 'The Builders Laborer: A Regular Newsheet of the Democratically Elected NSW Branch', 17/3/75, 1p, authorised by Joe Owens and Bob Pringle; Mick Curtin, 29/2/76; Ian Makin, 14/12/77; Graham Pitts, 2/5/80; Viri Pires, 30/11/76; *Daily Mirror*, 18/3/75.

81 NSWBLF, 'Press Statement re Break In of the NSW Branch of the BLF', 18/3/75; NSWBLF, '3 Hour Stop Work Meeting, All NSW Builders Labourers; Settlement of NSWBLF Dispute', n.d. [March 1975], 1p.

82 See also NSWBLF, '3 Hour Stop Work Meeting, All NSW Builders Labourers: Settlement of NSWBLF Dispute', n.d. [March 1975], 1p; NSWBLF, 'Unity of Builder Labourers NOW!', 13/10/74.

83 Mundey, speech, 24/3/75 (M Burgmann tape-recorded the final meeting).

84 Les Robinson, 20/2/78.

85 Joe Owens, 24/1/78.

86 Colless, 'A case of the banners banned'.

87 M Burgmann, 'A New Concept of Unionism', pp 302–307; Mundey, 'Beyond BLF'; Boyd, *Inside the BLF*, pp 10–11, 16.

88 'Industrial Crimes of Norman Gallagher', n.d., authorised by Builders Labourers Unity Committee [Victorian rank-and-file opposition], 1p; *National Times*, 22–28/2/81.

89 Hurchalla, 'Industrial Crimes'; Joe Owens (with Verity Burgmann), 30/3/98; Boyd, *Inside the BLF*, p 324.

90 'Owens, Mundey, Pringle Cleared', n.d. [April 1978], 1p; *SMH*, 2/6/81, 4/6/81.

GREEN BANS FOREVER?

1   Joe Owens, 26/1/81.

2   Carr, 'Now the ban's on Mundey', p 40; Mundey, *Green Bans & Beyond*, p 82–83; *Courier-Mail*, 27/7/73.

3   Mundey, *Green Bans & Beyond*, p 83; *Inverell Times*, 31/7/74.

4   *SMH*, 5/2/74; Hurchalla, 'Industrial Crimes', p 21.

5   *Courier-Mail*, 27/7/73; *Inverell Times*, 31/7/74.

6   *Australian*, 4/11/72.

7   *Australian*, 27/7/73; *Daily Telegraph*, 14/11/73; Stretton, *Ideas for Australian Cities*, pp 272–73.

8   Hardman and Manning, Green Bans, Haskell, 'Green Bans', pp 206, 212, 214.

9   *Australian*, 15/11/73.

10 Jack Beale, Letter to *Australian*, 19/11/73.

11 Harper, 'The NSW Liberal duel'; Souter, 'Steering Clear of Green Bans'.

12 *Australian*, 14/1/74.

13 Souter, 'Steering Clear of Green Bans'; *Daily Mirror*, 21/1/74.

14 Roddewig, *Green Bans*, pp 79–83.

15 *Fin. Rev.*, 1/3/74.

16 NSW, *Parliamentary Debates*, Third Series, 111, 20/8/74, p 396.

17 Carr, 'Now the ban's on Mundey', p 40; Yencken, 'Honorary Life Membership', p 4.

18 Gilpin, *The Australian Environment*, p 168; Carr, 'Now the ban's on Mundey', p 38; Yencken, 'Honorary Life Membership', p 4.

19 Yencken, 'Honorary Life Membership', p 5; McGregor, 'The urban crisis', pp 31–33; Carr, 'Now the ban's on Mundey', p 39.
20 *SMH*, 4/6/81.
21 Mundey, 'Preventing the Plunder', pp 178–79; *SMH*, 11/5/74, 11/2/95, 7/12/96; Yencken, 'Honorary Life Membership', p 3.
22 Betty James, 'The Battlers', pp 18–19; Monica Sheehan in Kalajzich (ed), *The Battlers for Kelly's Bush*, pp 49–50; Mundey, 'Preventing the Plunder', p 177.
23 Mundey, 'From grey to green', p 18.
24 J Mundey to V Burgmann, 1/3/98; Roddewig, *Green Bans*, p 153; Fotheringham, 'The unlikely little Aussie'.
25 Yencken, 'Honorary Life Membership', p 6.
26 Mundey, 'From grey to green', p 18.
27 Costello and Dunn, 'Resident Action Groups', p 73.
28 *Bulletin*, 27/11/76; Bonyhady, *Places Worth Keeping*, esp. pp 2–3, 39.
29 Jack Mundey, 3/4/78; Mundey, 'Preventing the Plunder', pp 180, 179.
30 *SMH*, 26/1/74; *Australian*, 26/1/74.
31 *Illawarra Mercury*, 8/5/74; *Australian Electronics Engineering*, August 1974; *Glen Innes Examiner*, 30/7/74; *Australian*, 23/3/74.
32 *Manly Daily*, 23/5/74, 25/5/74; *Northern Star* (Lismore), 15/8/74, 28/8/74; Gill, 'Unions Usurp Moral Right of Church'.
33 Hardman and Manning, *Green Bans*, final page.
34 Wickham, 'The NSWBLF', p 8; *Tribune*, 22/8/72; Bob Pringle, 8/3/78; Joe Owens, 4/4/78; *Newcastle Sun*, 10/12/73.
35 Hardman and Manning, *Green Bans*, front page.
36 Wendy Bacon, 16/1/78.
37 *Woman's Day*, 25/6/73; ABC Television, 'This Day Tonight', 2/11/73; *Australian*, 31/10/73; 'Statement by the Minister for Urban and Regional Development, Tom Uren MP', n.d. [October 1973]; *SMH*, 9/11/73; *Melbourne Herald*, 9/11/73; *SMH*, 7/6/73.
38 RJ McCabe, to *Australian*, 18/12/73; RH Riordan, East Brighton, to *Australian*, 28/11/73; PK Beckwith, Belair, to *Adelaide Advertiser*, 17/12/73; G Roberts, Red Hill, Qld, to *Australian*, 26/11/73; Turner, *In Union is Strength*, p 141.
39 *Daily Mirror*, 8/11/73; *SMH*, 13/11/73, 17/11/73; *Armidale Express*, 12/11/73; *Newcastle Morning Herald*, 2/11/73; *Daily Telegraph*, 14/11/73; *SMH*, 9/11/73, Editorial.
40 *SMH*, 5/11/73; *Australian*, 5/11/73.
41 A good example is Evans 'Don't Knock the Rocks'.
42 VSAG, 'Support the Builders' Labourers', n.d. [c. May 1973], 1p; *Scrounge*, 1 June 1973, p 20.
43 *Daily Mirror*, 5/12/73; Carr, 'Now the ban's on Mundey', p 40.
44 Wickham, 'The NSW BLF', p 5; *Daily Mirror*, 31/10/73.
45 Rushton, 'Revolutionary Theory', p 433.
46 Hinton, *The First Shop Stewards' Movement*, p 277.
47 Dean Barber, 18/12/76; Ian Makin, 14/12/77; Roy Bishop, 10/3/77.
48 Mundey, *Green Bans & Beyond*, p 23; NSWBLF, 'Minutes', Exec Meeting, 27/8/68; Gen Meeting, 3/9/68.
49 Jack Mundey, 20/6/78; Joe Owens, 4/4/78.
50 Tom Hogan, 28/10/77.
51 Michael Schneider, quoted in Klaus Mehnert, *Twilight of the Young*, p 108.
52 Sennett and Cobb, *The Hidden Injuries of Class*, p 37; *Direct Action*, 15/1/15; V Burgmann, *Revolutionary Industrial Unionism*, pp 4, 75–76, 140.
53 Jack Mundey, 3/4/78.
54 Holton, *British Syndicalism*, p 27.
55 Sorel, *Reflections on Violence*, p 46; Joll, *The Anarchists*, p 210.
56 Georges Sorel, *De eglise et de l'etat*, pp 31–32, cited in Joll, *The Anarchists*, p 210.
57 Bob Pringle, 8/3/78.
58 Mundey and Owens, 'Green Bans and the NSW Builders Laborers'.

SOURCES

INTERVIEWS

NSWBLF MEMBERS
Unless otherwise indicated, all interviews were conducted by Meredith Burgmann.

Bob Baker, 16/5/80
Dean Barber, 18/12/76
Peter Barton, 5/3/78
Denise Bishop, 11/3/78
Roy Bishop, 10/3/77
Harry Connell, 12/2/78, 27/6/80
Bud Cook, 5/3/78, 30/3/78
Kevin Cook, 1/12/76
Don Crotty, 7/3/78, 13/3/78
Mick Curtin, 29/2/76
Darcy Duggan, 12/7/77
Rhonda Ellis, 5/8/77
Pat Fiske, 2/3/78
Michelle Fraser, 14/12/77
Seamus Gill, 28/12/77
Tony Hadfield, 13/12/76
Tom Hogan, 28/10/77
Sekai Holland, 3/5/78
Bill Holley, 24/1/78
Ralph Kelly, 13/12/77
Karl King, 2/5/80
Mick King, 2/5/80
Ian Makin, 14/12/77
Mick McEvoy, 10/10/77
Don McPhee, 6/12/77
Khris Melmuth, 16/1/78
Jack Mundey, 13/8/75, 30/3/78, 3/4/78,
      20/6/78, 16/1/81, 23/3/81

Warwick Neilley, 21/1/78
Stella Nord, 13/3/78
Tony O'Beirne, 2/3/78
Noel Olive, 9/3/78
Joe Owens, 24/1/78, 4/4/78, 14/11/79, 24/1/81,
      11/12/96
Glenys Page, 24/1/78
Viri Pires, 30/11/76
Graham Pitts, 2/5/80
Bob Pringle, 8/3/78
Janne Reed, 18/4/78
Brian Rix, 20/12/77
Mick Ross, 29/7/77
Dave Shaw, 7/8/77
Trevor Steyne, 15/3/80
Wendy Stringer, 5/3/78
Lyn Syme, 20/4/78
Johnny Whitehouse, 15/3/80
Duncan Williams, 25/2/76
Robyn Williams, 20/4/78.

NSWBLF FEMALE OFFICE STAFF
Robyn Cockayne, 25/1/78
Jenny Healey, 25/1/78
Carol Kalafates, 25/1/78
Judy Mundey, 13/3/78
Paula Rix, 25/1/78.

OTHER BUILDING INDUSTRY UNIONISTS

Glen Batchelor (PGEUA, Sydney branch organiser), 14/12/80

Mick Boyle, (Operative Stonemasons Society of Australia secretary and BWIU organiser, and former Operative Plasterers' and Plaster Workers' Federation of Australia organiser), 29/1/81

Bob Bryant, (PGEUA, WA branch organiser), 10/7/81

Jack Cambourn, (FEDFA federal secretary), 1/2/79

George Crawford, (PGEUA Vic. secretary and general secretary), 20/1/81, 8/4/81

Peter Lane, (PGEUA Sydney branch secretary, former rank-and-file militant), 19/5/81

John Rose, (PGEUA Vic. branch organiser), 7/3/81

Dick Whitehead, (FEDFA, NSW branch organiser), 8/6/80

Digby Young, (AWU NSW branch organiser), 1/3/79, 20/6/80.

OTHERS

Anonymous (senior building industry employers' organisation official), 10/7/81

Laurie Aarons (CPA, general secretary), 28/12/77

Wendy Bacon (libertarian,VSAG), 16/1/78

Sid Davis (Sydney Trotskyist), 8/8/79

Murray Geddes (CRAG), 23/1/81

Janet Hancock (secretary to Pat Clancy, BWIU), 24/5/81

Jack Kreger (ATEA NSW branch president), 25/7/80

Rod Madgwick (barrister for NSWBLF), 21/12/77

Ian Millis (VSAG), 6/2/81

Les Robinson (ABLF, SA branch secretary, post-Intervention NSW secretary), 20/2/78

Roelof Smilde (libertarian, VSAG), 1/3/78

Jimmy Staples (barrister for NSWBLF), 26/7/75

Pete Thomas (journalist, writer, raconteur and CPA member), 25/6/80, 16/1/81

Mick Tubbs (CPA organiser), 26/10/77

INTERVIEWS CONDUCTED BY VERITY BURGMANN

Yvonne Ford (Inverell Pioneer Village), 18/12/97

Jack Mundey, 31/3/98

Joe Owens, 30/3/98 PN Troy, 21/11/97

Phillipa Whish (Inverell resident), 18/12/97

INTERVIEWS CONDUCTED BY PAT FISKE

Steve Black (NSWBLF, post-Intervention secretary), 1979

Bob Petty (NSWBLF), 1980

Bud Cook (NSWBLF), 1979

Vic Fitzgerald (FEDFA, federal assistant secretary), 1980

Tom Hogan (NSWBLF), 1979

Keith Jessop (NSWBLF returning officer), 1976

Ralph Kelly (NSWBLF), 1979

Mick McNamara (NSWBLF), 1976

Joe Owens (NSWBLF), 1980

Ray Rocher (MBA, senior official), 1980

Lorne Webster (DLI), 1979

DOCUMENTS, MINUTES AND REPORTS

ABLF, 'Minutes', Federal Council, November 1961–March 1975.

—, 'Minutes', Federal Management Committee, November 1961–March 1975.

ACTU Congress, 'Minutes', Sydney, September 1973.

Askin, RW, 'Statement on ABC News 4/11/72 at 7.10 pm'.

Civil & Civic Pty Ltd, 'Labour Relations in the Future', attachment to 'Productivity Agreement: Building Trades Unions (NSW) and the Electrical Trades Union (NSW) and Civil & Civic Pty Ltd 1970–1971'.

Commonwealth Bureau of Census and Statistics, 'Building and Construction, 1970–71', Bulletin No. 7; 'Building and Construction, Tables: Number of Persons Working by Occupational Status'.

Commonwealth Concilliation and Arbitration Court, Cyclone Scaffolding Pty Ltd and ABLF, C. No. 446 of 1969.

—, Dillingham Constructions Pty Ltd, (Qantas Project) and the ABLF, C. No. 2067 of 1970, 30 November 1970.

—, C. No. 1902 of 1971, 6 December 1971.

Evatt, The Hon Elizabeth Andreas, 'Interim Report of the Inquiry into Employment in the Building Industry', April 1975.

Industrial Commission of NSW, 'Building Trades Dispute re Pay of Injured Workers', No. 251 of 1971, 22 October 1971.

—, 'Dispute FEDFA & ors and EA Watts Pty. Ltd. re dismissals, etc', No. 74/480, 31 October 1974.

—, No. 74/523, 22 November 1974.

Labour Council of NSW, 'Findings of the Committee of Enquiry into Events Associated with the Suspension of the ABLF on May 20th 1971', n.d. [July 1971].

—, 'Rules', n.d.

Liberal Party of Australia, 'Workers' Participation or Workers' Control', Research Section, NSW Division, September 1973.

National Workers Control Conference, 'National Workers Control Conference, Newcastle, Easter 1973', authorised by John Wallace for the NWCC.

NSWBLF, assorted document in possession of the authors: broadsheets, Building Trades Group documents, BWIU circulars and statements, collection sheets, correspondence, CPA leaflets, CPA (M–L) leaflets, federal BLF circulars and other publications, financial statements, information sheets, Jack Mundey Defence Committee material, notes of meetings and phone calls, leaflets, Mick McNamara's collection of unidentified newsclippings, newsclippings collected by press services, newssheets, notices, Master Builders Association circulars to members 1971–75 and publicity material, open letters, pamphlets, posters, press releases, publications of other unions, rank-and-file publications, recommendations to meetings, reports, resident and anti-expressway action group publications, resolutions, returning officers' declarations, SPA Building Industry branch leaflets, statements, song sheets, women's collective documents.

—, 'Disputes Book'.

—, 'Minutes', Executive Meetings, January 1963–December 1971.

—, 'Minutes', General Meetings, January 1963–December 1971.

—, 'Minutes', Special Executive Meetings, January 1963–December 1971.

—, 'Minutes', Delegates Conference, 18 June 1967.

—, 'Minutes', Organisers Meeting, 25 June 1969.

Parliament of NSW, Report of the Royal Commission into New South Wales Prisons, [JF Nagle, Commissioner], Sydney, Government Printer, 1978.

—, Parliamentary Debates, 1972–74.

SPA, 'Ultra Leftism: How it Harms the Worker', n.d. [c. 1972], authorised by P Clancy, chairman, and P Symon, general secretary.

UCATT, 'Report of Proceedings of the Second National Delegate Conference held at Blackpool 17th to 21st June 1974', (University of Warwick Modern Records Centre, MSS 78/UC/4/2/2).

Uren, Tom (Minister for Urban and Regional Development), 'Statement', n.d. [c. Oct. 1973].

AUDIO-VISUAL SOURCES

ABC Radio, 'Lateline', (interviews with Jack Mundey and Jimmy Reid), 20/5/75.

—, Radio National, 'Green and Practical', 29/11/94. ABC Television, 'Monday Conference', September 1971.

—, 'This Day Tonight', 2/11/73.

Cole, Richard & Craig, Doug, Green City, documentary video, 1976.

Fiske, Pat, Rocking the Foundations, documentary video, 1985.

Hughes, Colin, 'Australian Public Figures on Tape: Jack Mundey', interview, University of Queensland Press, St Lucia, 1974.

Mundey, Jack, speech, 24 March 1975 (taped by Meredith Burgmann).
Mundey, Jack, speech, ACF seminar, 1975.
Mundey, Jack, 'Jobs for Use Not for Waste', ACF seminar, 11 Sept 1977.
Owens, Joe, speech, CPA function, 2 Nov 1975.
Pires, Viri, tape-recorded speech, October 1974.
Pringle, Bob, lecture, Macquarie University, 1975.
White, Denise, Fiske, Pat & Gailey, Peter, Woolloomooloo, documentary video, 1975.
Zubrycki, Tom, Waterloo, documentary video, 1981.

NEWSPAPERS AND PERIODICALS

NEWSPAPERS

Age, January 1970–March 1975
Australian, September 1964–July 1981
Australian Financial Review, January 1970–March 1975
Daily Mirror, September–December 1964; January 1970–March 1975
Daily Telegraph, January 1960–December 1975
Illawarra Mercury, October 1972–May 1974
Nation Review, September 1972–September 1974
National Times, July 1971–July 1981
Newcastle Morning Herald, January 1970–March 1975
Sun, September–December 1964; January 1970–March 1975
Sun-Herald, January 1960–March 1975
Sunday Telegraph, January 1960–December 1975
Sydney Morning Herald, January 1980–July 1981, 7/12/96, 3–5/3/98
Tribune, August 1961–August 1975
Vanguard, June 1971–March 1975.

The following newspapers were consulted for more restricted time periods, as appropriate for particular
    events, between 1971 and 1974:

*Adelaide Advertiser; Adelaide News; Albury Mail; Armidale Express; Brisbane Telegraph; Broken Hill
    Miner; Broken Hill Truth; Canberra Courier; Canberra News; Canberra Times; Central Western
    Daily; Champion Post* (Parkes); *Coffs Harbour Advocate; Courier* (Narrabri); *Courier-Mail; Daily
    Examiner* (Grafton); *Dubbo Liberal; Glen Innes Examiner; Gosford Star; Grafton Examiner; Hobart
    Mercury; Independent Kiama; Inverell Times; Labor Press; Launceston Examiner; Lithgow Mercury;
    Maitland Mercury; Manly Daily; Melbourne Herald; Melbourne Sunday Press; Melbourne Sun;
    Melbourne Sun-News Pictorial; Mudgee Guardian; Murwillumbah Daily News; Newcastle Herald;
    Newcastle Sun; News-Weekly; Northern Daily Leader* (Tamworth); *Northern Star* (Lismore); *Orange
    News Pictorial; Port Stephens Pictorial; Raymond Terrace Examiner; Record* (Grenfell); *South Sydney
    Advertiser; Sunday Observer* (Melbourne); *Review; Singleton Argus; Sunday Mail; Sunday Observer*
    (Melbourne); *Tamworth Leader; Taree Times; Telegraph* (Brisbane); *Tharunka; Western Advocate*
    (Bathurst); *Windsor Gazette.*

PERIODICALS

Australian Left Review, 1966–81
Builders Labourer (NSWBLF), December 1961–December 1974
Bulletin, 1972–74
Construction (NSW MBA), January 1970–March 1975 Helmet (Building Branch of CPA),
    1974–75
Journal of the UCATT, (University of Warwick Modern Records Centre MSS41TF48 D)
    February 1972–December 1974
Now, 1974–75
Now & Again, 1975

Now & Then, 1976
On Site (Building Workers of the Communist League), 1974
Paddington Journal, 1972
Power, A Communist publication, 1973
Rank and File Rag (Bulletin of the Job Delegates and Activists Association) 1974
Rydge's Construction, Civil Engineering and Mining Review, 1971–74
Scope, 1973–74
Scrounge, 1973–74
Socialist Building Worker (Building Industry Branch of the SPA), 1974
Surry Hills News (Planning for People Campaign), 1973
Unity (ABLF Victorian branch), December 1966 – March 1975
Victoria Street Rag, 5/1/74; 10/1/74
Viewpoint, Journal of the Amalgamated Society of Woodworkers, Painters & Builders (University of
    Warwick Modern Records Centre MSS41TF48D) 1971–January 1972.

The following periodicals were consulted for more restricted time periods:

Australian Elecronics Engineering; Australian Socialist; Building Worker (BWIU); *Catholic Weekly;
    Employers' Review; FED News; Gay Liberation Press, Independence Voice; Mabel; Manufacturers'
    Monthly; Passing Show; Plumbers News; Queensland Master Builder; Review; Shelter* (Australian
    Department of Housing); *Woman's Day.*

THESES AND UNPUBLISHED MANUSCRIPTS

Anderson, Geoff, 'The Builders Labourers' Federation of NSW: A Study of a Militant Union', BA
    Hons thesis, Government Dept, University of Sydney, 1971.
Anderson, Kay & Jacobs, Jane, 'Geographies of Publicity and Privacy: Residential Activism in Sydney
    in the 1970s', unpublished paper, [1997].
Burgmann, Meredith, 'A New Concept of Unionism: the New South Wales Builders Labourers'
    Federation 1970–1974', PhD thesis, Macquarie University, 1981.
Clancy, P, 'The Formation of the Socialist Party of Australia', paper, Communists and the Labour
    Movement Conference, Melbourne, August 1980.
Environmental Studies Program, Macquarie University, 'An Environmental Impact Study on Green
    Bans', 1977.
Eyers, Michael, 'The Sydney Property Boom', paper, Class Analysis Conference, Sydney, 1977.
Graham, Caroline, 'Anatomy of a Revolutionary Union: A Post Mortem on the BLF 1968–1975', BA
    Hons thesis, Government Dept, University of Sydney, 1975.
Hurchalla, George, 'Industrial Crimes. The History of the Builders' Labourers Federation',
    unpublished manuscript.
Kelley, Robin, 'Looking Forward: How the New Working Class Can Transform Urban America', paper,
    American Studies Seminar, University of Melbourne, 8/8/97.
McIntyre, Angus, 'Jack Mundey', unpublished paper, n.d.
Moss, Jim, 'Industrial Relations or Workers' Control: South Australian Experiences', unpublished
    paper, Adelaide, March 1973.
Mundey, Jack, 'The Role of Workers in a Modern Industrial Society, Social Responsibility and
    Ecology', lecture, Harrison Hot Springs, British Columbia, Canada, 25 Feb 1977.
Mundey, Jack & Owens, Joe, 'Green Bans and the NSW Builders Laborers', unpublished paper, 1975.
Oostermeyer, Ignace, 'Richard Hyman and Industrial Relations Theory: A Radical Alternative or a
    Radical Dilemma', Dept of Industrial Relations, Occasional Series No. 30, UNSW, 1978.
Pickette, Rod, 'Rank and File Organisation in the NSW Power Generation Industry: With Particular
    Reference to ECCUDO', BEc Hons thesis, University of Sydney, 1975.
Pringle, Bob; Mundey, Jack & Owens, Joe, 'Submissions to Habitat Australia: Social Displacements in
    the Inner Cities', November 1975.
Runcie, Neil, 'An Open Letter to the Premier of New South Wales The Hon. Sir Robert Askin, MLA',
    14/4/72.
—, 'The Proposed Moore Park Sporting Complex: Political Miscalculation or Political Hoax?', address

to the Paddington Society, 1/5/72.

—, 'The Proposed Moore Park Sporting Complex: A Failure in Consultation', address to the Centennial Park Residents' Association, 10/5/72.

—, 'Central Decisions and the Local Repercussions: The Case of the Proposed Moore Park Sporting Complex', paper, Reforming Local Government, (CRAG symposium), 27/5/72.

Willett, Graham, 'The gay and lesbian movement and Australian society, 1969–1978', PhD thesis, History Dept, University of Melbourne, 1998.

Yencken, David, 'Honorary Life Membership for Mr Jack Mundey', citation, ACF AGM, 27/11/93.

ARTICLES AND CHAPTERS

Aarons, Eric, 'As I Saw the Sixties', *Australian Left Review*, 27, October/November 1970.

Aarons, Laurie, 'Viewpoint', *Australian Left Review*, 37, October 1973.

Aiton, Douglas, 'The Mavericks', Age, 2/2/74.

Anderson, Perry, 'The Limits and Possibilities of Trade Union Action', in Blackburn, Robin, Cockburn & Alexander (eds), *The Incompatibles: Trade Union Militancy and the Consensus*, Penguin, Melbourne, 1967.

Anderson, Peter (president, MBA), 'Pressure Game Hits Industry', *SMH*, 25/11/71.

Anon., 'Disintegration of Communists Causing Industrial Havoc', *Rydge's*, 1/9/71.

Anon., 'Construction Unions Plan Hot Year for Employers', *Rydge's*, 1/11/71.

Anon., 'Flame Interviews Bob Pringle of the BLF', *Flame Magazine*, 2, 9, n.d. [c. 1973].

Anon., 'If You're In Trouble Ring The Union', *Foundation Day Tharunka*, August 1973.

Armstrong, David, 'Rank versus File', *Australian*, 1/10/73.

Austin, H, 'In Defence of Workers' Control', *Australian Left Review*, 6, December 1969.

Bacon, Wendy, 'They huffed and they puffed and they blew doors down', The *Living Daylights*, 8–14/1/74.

—, 'Crusader of the Cross', *SMH*, 5/3/98.

Barratt Brown, Michael, Coates, Ken & Topham, Tony, 'Workers Control versus "Revolutionary" Theory', *Socialist Register*, 1975.

Batterham, Terry & Tubbenhauer, Graeme, 'Interview with Bob Pringle', *Gay Liberation Press*, 3, Sept. 1974.

—, 'Interview with Lyn Syme, Janne Reed and Ros Harrison', *Gay Liberation Press*, 3, Sept. 1974.

Beilharz, Peter, 'John Anderson and the Syndicalist Moment', *Political Theory Newsletter*, 5, 1, April 1993.

Bentley, Philip, 'A Survey of Current Issues in Australian Industrial Relations', *Journal of Industrial Relations*, 15, 3, September 1973.

—, 'Australian Trade Unionism 1972–73', *Journal of Industrial Relations*, 15, 4, December 1973.

—, 'Australian Trade Unionism', in Mayer, Henry & Nelson, Helen (eds), *Australian Politics: A Fourth Reader*, Longman Cheshire, Melbourne, 1976.

Berry, Michael, 'Posing the housing question in Australia', in Sandercock, Leonie, & Berry, Michael, *Urban Political Economy: The Australian Case*, Allen & Unwin, Sydney, 1983.

Blake, Terry, 'Frail Old Men Shake Leichhardt', *Review*, 22/10/71.

Brandt KW, 'New social movements as a metapolitical challenge', *Thesis Eleven*, 15, 1986.

Brooks, Geraldine, 'Lost: the patina of old Victoria St', *SMH*, 5/7/79.

Burgmann, Meredith, 'Revolution and Machismo: Women in the New South Wales Builders Labourers' Federation, 1961–75', in Windschuttle, Elizabeth (ed), *Women, Class and History*, Fontana, Melbourne, 1980.

—, 'Unionist led green bans', *Australian*, 29/8/96.

Campbell, Graham, 'Meeting Attracts Union Support', *Education* (journal of the NSW Teachers' Federation), 19/6/74.

Carey, Brian T, 'Workers' Control Today and Tomorrow', *Australian Left Review*, 6, December 1969.

Carr, Bob, 'Now the ban's on Mundey', *Bulletin*, 24/2/81.

—, 'Mundey takes his case to the rank and file', *Bulletin*, 9/6/81.

Castells, Manuel, 'Theoretical propositions for an experiment study of urban social movements', in Pickervance, CE (ed) *Urban Sociology: Critical Essays*, Tavistock Publications, London, 1976.

Clancy, Pat, 'Automation and the Trade Unions', *Australian Left Review*, 4, December 1966/January 1967.

Clare, John, 'A Day in the Life of a Radical or Two', *Flame Magazine*, 2, 10, n.d. [c. 1973].

Colless, Malcolm, 'Carrying the can for the "Greenies"', *Australian*, 8/11/73.

—, 'Black day for the greenies', *Australian*, 24/3/75.

—, 'A case of the banners banned', *Australian*, 22/4/75.

Cook, Bud, 'A Real (Estate) Scandal', *Builders' Labourer*, February 1969.

—, 'Time for a Clean-Up', *Builders' Labourer*, July 1970.

Coper, Michael & Hayes, Robert, 'How to Hush Up a Scandal', *SMH*, 11/7/73.

Costello, LN & Dunn, KM, 'Resident Action Groups in Sydney: People Power or Rat-Bags?', *Australian Geographer*, 25, 1, May 1994.

Coull, Dave, 'The Builders Labourers Federation of Australia', in Mayer, Henry & Nelson, Helen (eds), *Australian Politics: A Fourth Reader*, Longman Cheshire, Sydney, 1976.

Cox, KR, 'The politics of turf and the question of class', in Wolch, J & Dear, M (eds), *The Power of Geography: How Territory Shapes Social Life*, Unwin Hyman, Boston, 1989.

Crouch, Walter, 'Some Black among the BLF Green', *SMH*, 2/11/74.

Curtin, Mick, 'Permanency and the Building Worker', *Builder's Labourer*, Aug. 1973.

Davis, HB, 'The Theory of Union Growth', in McCarthy, WEJ (ed), *Trade Unions: Selected Readings*, Penguin, Harmondsworth, 1972.

Dick, Ian, 'Full Payment for Accidents?', *SMH*, 14/5/71.

Evans, Grant, 'Don't Knock the Rocks', *The Living Daylights*, 1, 3, 30/10–5/111973.

Fletcher, Richard, 'Trade Union Democracy: Structural Factors', in Coates, Ken, Topham, Tony & Barratt Brown, Michael (eds), *Trade Union Register*, 1970.

Fotheringham, Allan, 'The unlikely little Aussie who could teach Canadian unions a thing or two', *Maclean* 28/6/76.

Fox, Nicholas, 'Muddle at Moore Park', *Bulletin*, 1/4/72.

Fraser, Nancy, 'Rethinking the Public Sphere: A Contribution to the Critique of Actually Existing Democracy', in Calhoun, Craig (ed), *Habermas and the Public Sphere*, MIT Press, Cambridge, Mass., 1992.

Freney, Denis, 'Challenging Architecture's Subordination to Profit', *Tribune*, 12/8/70.

—, 'Builders Labourers Fight Back', *Tribune*, 30/10–5/11/73.

Frenkel, S (ed), *Industrial Action: Patterns of Labour Conflict*, Allan & Unwin, Sydney, 1980.

Frenkel, Stephen & Coolican, Alice, 'Competition, Instability and Industrial Struggle in the NSW Construction Industry', in Frenkel, Stephen (ed), *Industrial Action: Patterns of Labour Conflict*, Allan & Unwin, Sydney, 1980.

Gardiner, Paul, 'Union Power and Developers (once naughty words) Beat the Bad Old Days', *APR*, 7/6/73.

—, 'The Rise of Jack Mundey's trendy Union – with Clarrie O'Shea's Help', APR, 8/6/73.

Geghorn, Geoffrey, 'The best steak is tenderised: Norm Gallagher on strikes and J Mundey', *National Times*, 10/12/73.

Gill, Alan, 'Unions Usurp Moral Right of Church', *SMH*, 23/9/72.

Gillespie, Jim, 'Theories of Urbanism: From Chicago to Paris', *Intervention*, 7, October 1976.

Gott, Ken, 'The Left Revisited', *National Times*, 25–31/5/80.

Gouldner, Alvin W, 'Metaphysical Pathos and the Theory of Bureaucracy', *American Political Science Review*, 49, 1955.

Habermas, Jurgen, 'New Social Movements', *Telos*, 49, Fall 1981.

Hadfield, Tony, 'Union Hire', *Builders Labourer*, August 1973.

Hagan, Jim, 'Clutha: The Politics of Pollution', *Politics*, 7, November 1972.

Hanaghan, Derek, 'State secrecy fuels the strange alliances of resident action groups', *APR*, 1/3/74.

Harper, Catherine, 'The NSW Liberal Duel: Dowd v. McDonald', *SMH*, 28/5/81.

Haskell, Mark, 'Green Bans: Worker Control and the Urban Environment', *Industrial Relations*, 16, 2, May 1977.

Hayler, Jeff, 'Because it's a Christian College', *Arena*, 6, 8, July 1973.

Hearn, JM, 'Migrant Participation in Trade Union Leadership', *Journal of Industrial Relations*, 18, 2, May 1976.

Higgins, Winton, 'Reconstructing Australian Communism', in Miliband, Ralph & Saville, John (eds), *Socialist Register*, 1974.

Hill, S & Thurley, K, 'Sociology and Industrial Relations', *British Journal of Industrial Relations*, 12, 2.

Hogan, Tom, 'Sackings Didn't Stop Them (It Was the Foremen Who Were Outside Looking In)', *Tribune*, 15–21/2/72.

—, 'Strengthen that grip', *Mereki*, 1, 1, 15/11/74.

Howard, WA, 'Democracy in Trade Unions', in Isaac, JE & Ford, GW (eds), *Australian Labour Relations Readings*, Sun Books, Melbourne, 1968.

—, 'Australian Trade Unions in the Context of Union Theory', *Journal of Industrial Relations*, 19, 3, September 1977.

Hurst, John, 'BLF Loses a Round at Omega', *National Times*, 8–14/2/81.

Hyman, Richard, 'Inequality, Ideology and Industrial Relations', *British Journal of Industrial Relations*, 12, 2.

—, Richard, 'Industrial Conflict and the Political Economy: Trends of the Sixties and Prospects for the Seventies', *Socialist Register*, 1973.

—, 'Workers Control and Revolutionary Theory', in Miliband & Saville (eds), *Socialist Register*, 1974.

—, 'British Trade Unionism: Post War Trends and Future Prospects', *International Socialism*, Series 2, 8, Spring 1980.

Hyman, Richard & Fryer, Bob, 'Trade Unions: Sociology and Political Economy', in McKinlay, JB (ed), *Processing People: Cases in Organisational Behaviour*, New York, 1975.

Inner Sydney RAGs, 'Save Our City', in Mayer, Henry & Nelson, Helen (eds), *Australian Politics: A Fourth Reader*, Logman Cheshire, Melbourne, 1976.

Jakubowicz, Andrew, 'The city game: urban ideology and social conflict, or Who gets the goodies and who pays the costs?', in Edgar, Don (ed), *Social Change in Australia: Readings in Sociology*, Longman Cheshire, Melbourne, 1974.

—, 'The green ban movement: urban struggle and class politics', in Halligan, John & Paris, Chris (eds), *Australian Urban Politics*, Longman Cheshire, Melbourne, 1984.

James, Betty, 'The Battlers', in Kalajzich, Pip (ed), *The Battlers for Kelly's Bush*, Cercus, Sydney, 1996.

Joachim, Kenneth, 'It makes some, breaks some', *Melbourne Herald*, 19/12/73.

Jones, Margaret, 'Living it up and liking it', *SMH*, 21/8/73.

Joreen, 'The Tyranny of Structurelessness', *Second Wave*, 2, 1, 1972.

Kelly, Ralph, 'She's all in Mate', *Builders Labourer*, March 1970.

L'Estrange, Richard, 'The Make-or-Break Men', *Australian*, 27/2/81.

Laclau, E & Mouffe, C, 'Post-Marxism without Apologies', *New Left Review*, 166, Nov./Dec. 1987.

Lapsley, John, 'Battle lost, no quarter given', *Australian*, 6/4/74.

Macdonald, Marion, 'Developers Make Him See Green', *Bulletin*, 12/5/73.

Macdougall, Jim, 'Town Talk', *DM*, 13/12/72.

Maiden, Tony, 'Hornsby: a classic strategy for the urban developer's handbook', *National Times*, 5–10/8/74.

Manning, Peter, 'Look Back in Anger', *Bulletin*, 13/7/74.

Mcfarlane, Bruce, 'Theories and Practices of Workers' Control', *Australian Left Review*, 6, December 1969.

—, 'Challenging the Control of the Australian Economic System', in Gordon, Richard (ed), *The Australian New Left: Critical Essays and Strategy*, Heinemann, Melbourne, 1970.

McGrath-Champ, Susan & Thompson, MJ, 'Industrial Reform in Australian Building and Construction', *Labour & Industry*, 8, 1, August 1997.

McGregor, Craig, 'The urban crisis', *National Times*, 1/7/78.

McIntyre, Angus, 'The Narcissism of Minor Differences: The electoral contest in Sydney between the Communist Party of Australia and the Socialist Party of Australia', in Mayer, Henry (ed), *Labor to Power*, Angus & Robertson, Sydney, 1973.

—, 'Australia', *Yearbook on International Communist Affairs 1974*, Stanford, 1974.

McQueen, Humphrey, 'National Independence and Socialism', *Melbourne Journal of Politics*, 1977, pp. 68–79.

Mills, C Wright, 'The Labor Leaders and the Power Elite', in Kornhauser, Arthur, Dubin, Robert & Ross, Arthur M. (eds), *Industrial Conflict*, McGraw Hill, New York, 1954.

Minogue, Denis, 'Portrait of a Militant', *Australian*, 5/9/72.

—, 'The Green Revolution Gets a Strong New Voice', *Age*, 8/2/74.

Mitchell, John, 'Home ... in never-never land', *Age*, 1/10/73.

Moody, Kim, 'Towards an International Social-Movement Unionism', *New Left Review*, 225, 1997.

Morris, John; Mundey, Jack & Griffin, David, 'Preservation of Old Buildings', *Current Affairs Bulletin*, 50, 7, December 1973.

Mundey, Jack, 'Fine Service from Jack and Charlie', *Builders' Labourer*, February–March 1968.

—, 'Job Activity the Key', *Builders' Labourer*, December 1968.

—, 'Demand for the 70s: Narrow the Gap', *Builders Labourer*, December 1969.

—, 'Great Strike Proved Our Fighting Ability', *Builders' Labourer*, July 1970.

—, 'Our Strike Proves they Fear Workers' Action Most', *Builders' Labourer*, July 1970.

—, 'Rattling the Employers', *Builders' Labourer*, July 1970.

—, 'Towards New Union Militancy', *Australian Left Review*, 26, August–September 1970.

—, 'Interview with Jack Mundey', *Australian Left Review*, 32, September 1971.

—, 'Strangling the Unemployment Ghost', *Shelter*, 1, 3, October 1973.

—, 'The Bans Enjoy Wide Support', *Current Affairs Bulletin*, 50, 7, December 1973.

—, 'Green Bans for Urban Quality', *Habitat*, 2, June 1974.

—, 'Ecology, Capitalism, Communism', *Australian Left Review* 51, May 1976.

—, 'Urbanisation: A Challenge to Socialism', *Australian Left Review*, 54, n.d. [c. 1976].

—, 'Beyond BLF: One Industry, One Union', *SMH*, 10/3/81.

—, 'Growthmania or sustainable economy', *Australian Left Review*, 84, Winter 1983.

—, 'Preventing the Plunder', in Burgmann, Verity & Lee, Jenny (eds), *Staining the Wattle*, McPhee Gribble/Penguin, Melbourne, 1988.

—, 'From grey to green', *Australian Left Review*, 108, Dec. 1988/Jan. 1989.

—, 'Meeting "The Battlers"', in Kalajzich, Pip (ed), *The Battlers for Kelly's Bush*, Cercus, Sydney, 1996.

Mundey, JB, 'Australia: Progress and Difficulties of the Trade Union Movement', *World Federation of Trade Unions Journal*, October 1971.

Myers, Stephen, 'The Fig Street Fiasco', *Tharunka*, 9 Sept 1974.

Nelson, Roy, 'Cities for the Future', *Australian Left Review*, 4, Dec 1966/Jan 1967.

Nittim, Zula, 'The Coalition of Resident Action Groups', in Roe, Jill (ed), *Twentieth Century Sydney: Studies in Urban & Social History*, Hale & Iremonger, Sydney, 1980.

Norman, Lance, 'BLF Outflanked at the Rocks-forward defences crumbling', *APR*, 18/10/73.

Offe, Claus, 'Work: the Key Sociological Category', in Offe, Claus *Disorganised Capitalism*, Polity Press, Cambridge, 1985.

Owens, Joe, 'Does Arbitration Have any Future?', *Builders' Labourer*, March 1970.

—, 'Some Highlights of a Strike that Made History', *Builders' Labourer*, July 1970.

—, 'The Vigilantes', *Builders' Labourer*, July 1970.

—, 'SPA "Analysis" of Builders Laborers: Mind-bending Distortion', *Tribune*, 19 Aug 1975.

Palmada, Joe, 'Trade Unions & Revolutionary Strategy', *Australian Left Review*, 37, October 1972.

Pocock, Barbara, 'Gender and Industrial Relations Theory and Research Practice', *Labour & Industry*, 8, 1, August 1997.

Pringle, Bob, 'War on Pollution Not on People', *Builders' Labourer*, March 1970.

—, 'The Black Awakening', *Builders' Labourer*, 1972 (also in leaflet form).

—,' Consumerism; It's No Way to a New Society', *National Times*, 18–23/10/76.

Robertson, Alec, 'Guilty Companies Ruining Historic Land', *Tribune*, 12/8/70.

Rushton, PJ, 'The Revolutionary Ideology of the Industrial Workers of the World in Australia', *Historical Studies*, 15, 59, October 1972.

Sandercock, Leonie, 'The BLF, Urban Politics and Inequality', in Mayer, Henry & Nelson, Helen (eds), *Australian Politics: A Fourth Reader*, Longman Cheshire, Sydney, 1976.

—, 'Citizen participation: the new conservatism', in Troy, PN (ed), *Federal Power in Australia's Cities*, Hales & Iremonger, Sydney, 1978.

Saw, Ron, 'A "complex" must never replace Jim Buckley's', *DM*, 17/10/72.

Shaw, David, 'Crisis in the Concrete Jungle', *International Socialist*, 8, Autumn 1979.

Souter, Gavin, 'The Glut in Skyscrapers', *SMH*, 7/9/71.

—, 'On the debit side of the green ban ...', *SMH*, 17/8/73.

—, 'Sacking the Boss', *SMH*, 28/7/73.

—, 'Steering Clear of Green Bans', *SMH*, 25/1/74.

Swancott, Neal, 'Builders will not knock history', *Australian*, 20/11/71.

Taft, Bernie, 'Communists and Workers' Control', *Australian Left Review*, 6, December 1969.

Tarbuck, Ken, 'Students and Trade Unions', in Coates, K, Topham, T & Barratt Brown, Michael (eds), *Trade Union Register 1969*, 1969.

Tennant, Kylie, 'Foreword for Battlers for Kelly's Bush Brochure', in Kalajzich, Pip (ed), *The Battlers for Kelly's Bush*, Cercus, Sydney, 1996.

Thomas, Pete, 'Brothers, Sisters and the Kids When the BLF Meets', *Tribune*, 17/6/70.

—, 'Why They're Attacking the Builders Laborers' Union', *Tribune*, 26/5/71.

—, 'Those Green Bans', *Shelter*, 1, 3, October 1973.

Whitton, Evan, 'Battle for Kelly's Bush', DT, 10/1/73.

—, 'The Greenies' Hero is Fighting for Survival – and so, some say, is Sydney', *National Times*, 29/10/73.

Wickham, Gary, 'The NSWBLF 1967–1975', *Local Consumption, Occasional Paper* 2, Sydney, n.d. [c. 1975].

Williams, Pamela, 'Gallagher's war with Mundey', *Business Daily*, 14/7/87.

—, 'Politics a pivotal force in building unionism', *Business Daily*, 15/7/87.

Yencken, David & Leader, Lyn, 'The physical setting', in Troy, PN (ed), *Federal Power in Australia's Cities*, Hales & Iremonger, Sydney, 1978.

Yeomans, John, 'A grand plan founders on the Rocks', *Melbourne Herald*, 26/3/74.

Young, PJ, 'The Last of the Tall Buildings?', *Australian*, 13/5/80.

BOOKS, BOOKLETS AND PAMPHLETS

Aarons, Eric, *Philosophy for an Exploding World: Today's Values Revolution*, Sydney, 1972.

—, *Oitr Party, Its Prospects and the Way Forward: Report to the National Committee Communist Party of Australia*, Sydney, 1977.

Aarons, Laurie, *Labour Movement at the Cross Roads*, Sydney, 1964.

ABCE & BLF, *Builders'Laborers Defend the People's Heritage*, Melbourne, 1975.

—, *Builders' Labourers' Song Book*, Melbourne, 1975.

ABCE. & BLF (NSW Branch), *Know Your Rights: Union Handbook*, 1980.

Allaby, Michael (ed), *Macmillan Dictionary of the Environment*, 2nd ed, Macmillan, London, 1983.

Altman, Dennis, *Rehearsals for Change: Politics and Culture in Australia*, Fontana/Collins, Melbourn, 1980.

Bellear, Robert W, *Black Housing Book*, Sydney, 1976.

Bonyhady, Tim, *Places Worth Keeping. Conservationists, politics and law*, Allen & Unwin, Sydney, 1993.

Boyd, Brian, *Inside the BLF*, Ocean Press, Melbourne, 1991.

Braverman, Harry, *Labor and Monopoly Capital: The Degradation of Work in the Twentieth Century*, Monthly Review Press, New York, 1974.

Brown, WJ, *What Happened to the Communist Party of Australia?*, Sydney, 1971.

Burgmann, Verity, *Power and Protest, Movements for Change in Australian Society*, Allan & Unwin, Sydney, 1993.

—, *Revolutionary Industrial Unionism: the Industrial Workers of the World in Australia*, Cambridge University Press, Melbourne, 1995.

Burton, Clare, *The Promise and the Price*, Allen & Unwin, Sydney, 1991 BWIU, *Some Notes on the Building Industry and the Need for Stronger Unions Through Amalgamation*, March 1970.

Caldwell, Lloyd & Tubbs, Mick, *The Harco Work-In: An Experience of Workers' Control*, Sydney Centre for Workers' Control, Sydney, 1973.

Calhoun, Craig (ed), *Habermas and the Public Sphere*, MIT Press, Cambridge, Mass. and London, 1992.

Castells, Manuel, *The Urban Question*, Edward Arnold, London, 1977.

—, *The City and the Grass Roots*, Edward Arnold, London, 1983.

Clarke, Tom, and Clements, Laurie (eds), *Trade Unions Under Capitalism*, Fontana, London, 1977.

Clegg, Hugh, *Trade Unionism under Collective Bargaining*, B. Blackwell, Oxford, 1976.

Coates, Ken, *Can the Workers Rim Industry?*, Sphere, London, 1968.

Coates, Ken & Topham, Anthony, *The New Unionism: The Case for Workers Control*, Penguin, Melbourne, 1974.

—, *Shop Stewards & Workers Control*, Nottingham, 1975.

Concerned Residents of the Inner City of Sydney, *The Rapier*, n.d. [late 1973).

Connell, RW, *Ruling Class, Ruling Culture: Studies of Conflict, Power and Hegemony in Australian Life*, Cambridge University Press, Cambridge, 1977.

—, *Masculinities*, Allan & Unwin, Sydney, 1995.

Connell, RW & Irving, TH, *Class Structure in Australian History*, Longman Cheshire, Melbourne, 1980.

Coombs, Anne, *Sex and Anarchy. The life and death of the Sydney Push*, Viking, Melbourne, 1996.

CPA, *Australia's Path to Socialism*, Sydney, 1958.

—, *Resolution, 20th Congress*, Sydney, 1964.

—, *Australia and the Way Forward*, Sydney, 1967.

—, *Modern Unionism and the Workers Movement*, Sydney, 1970.

—, *The Left Challenge for the '70s: Statement of Aims, Methods and Organisation*, Sydney, 1972.

—, *The Socialist Alternative*, Sydney, 1974.

—, *A New Course for Australia*, Sydney, 1977.

Curthoys, Ann, Spearritt, Peter, Eade, Susan (eds), *Women and Work*, ASSLH, Canberra, 1975.

Dahrendorf, Ralf, *Class and Class Conflict in Industrial Society*, Routledge, London, 1976.

Daly, MT, *Sydney Boom, Sydney Bust*, Allen & Unwin, Sydney, 1982.

Dubofsky, Melvyn, *We Shall Be All: A History of the Industrial Workers of the World*, Quadrangle Books, Chicago, 1969.

Dunne, John Gregory, Delano, Ferrar, Straus & Giroux, 1967.

Ellem, Bradon, *In Women's Hands? A History of Clothing Trade Unionism in Australia*, UNSW Press, Sydney, 1989.

Etzioni, Amitai (ed), *A Sociological Reader on Complex Organizations*, Holt, Rinehart & Winston, New York, 1969.

Faunce, WA (ed), *Readings in Industrial Sociology*, Appleton-Century-Crofts, New York, 1967.

Fletcher, Richard, *Problems of Trade Union Democracy*, Institute for Workers' Control: Pamphlet Series No. 21, Nottingham, n.d.

Foster, John, *Class Struggle and the Industrial Revolution*, Weidenfeld & Nicoloson, London, 1974.

Frances, Raelene & Scates, Bruce (eds), *Women, Work and the Labour Movement in Australia and Aotearoa/New Zealand*, ASSLH, Sydney, 1991.

Game, Ann & Pringle, Rosemary, *Gender at Work*, Allen & Unwin, Sydney, 1983.

Garden, Don, *Builders to the Nation. The AV Jennings Story*, MUP, Melbourne, 1992.

Gilpin, Alan, *The Australian Environment: 12 Controversial Issues*, Sun Books, Melbourne, 1980.

Gindin, Sam, *The Canadian Auto Workers: The Birth and Transformation of a Union*, J. Lorimer, Toronto, 1995.

Goodin, RE, *Green Political Theory*, Polity Press, Cambridge, 1992.

Goodrich, CL, *The Frontier of Control*, (foreword by RH Tawney), Pluto, London 1975.

Gordon, Richard (ed), *The Australian New Left: Critical Essays and Strategy*, Heinemann, Melbourne, 1970.

Gramsci, Antonio, *Selections from the Prison Notebooks of Antonio Gramsci*, Laurence and Wishart, London, 1971.

Habermas, Jurgen, *The Structural Transformation of the Public Sphere. An Inquiry into a Category of Bourgeois Society*, Polity Press, Cambridge, 1992.

Hancock, WK, *The Battle of Black Mountain. An Episode of Canberra's Environmental History*, RSSS, ANU, Canberra, 1974.

Hardman, Marion & Manning, Peter, *Green Bans: The Story of an Australian Phenomenon*, Australian Conservation Foundation, Melbourne, n.d. [1974–75].

Hickie, David, *The Prince and the Premier*, Angus & Robertson, Sydney, 1985.

Hinton, James, *The First Shop Stewards Movement*, Allen & Unwin, London, 1973.

Hinton, James & Hyman, Richard, *Trade Unions and Revolution: The Industrial Politics of the Early British Communist Party*, Pluto Press, London, 1975.

Holton, Bob, *British Syndicalism 1900–1914: Myths & Realities*, Pluto Press, London, 1976.

Horne, Donald, *Time of Hope: Australia 1966–72*, Angus & Robertson, Sydney, 1980.

Hutton, John, *Building and Construction in Australia*, Cheshire, Melbourne, 1970.

Hyman, Richard, *Marxism and the Sociology of Trade Unionism*, Pluto Press, London, 1973.

—, *Industrial Relations: A Marxist Introduction*, Macmillan, London, 1975.

—, *Strikes*, Fontana, London, 1975.

lnglehart, Ronald, *The Silent Revolution: Changing Values and Political Styles among Western Publics*, Princeton University Press, Princeton, 1977.

—, *Culture Shift in Advanced Industrial Society*, Princeton Unversity Press, Princeton, 1990.

Inner Core of Sydney Resident Action Groups, *Low Cost Housing*, Sydney, 1973.

Isaac, JE & Ford GW (eds), *Australian Labour Relations Readings*, Sun Books, Melbourne, 1968.

Johnston, Ruth, *Partners at Work: Building Workers, their Union and their Employers*, University of Western Australia, Perth, 1977.

Joll, James, *The Anarchists*, Methuen, London, 1964.

Kalajzich, Pip (ed), *The Battlers for Kelly's Bush*, Cercus, Sydney, 1996.

Karskens, Grace, *The Rocks. Life in Early Sydney*, MUP, Melbourne, 1997.

Kelly, Max, *Anchored in a Small Cove, A History and Archeology of The Rocks, Sydney*, Sydney Cove Authority, Sydney, 1996.

Kingston, Bev, *My Wife, My Daughter and Poor Mary Ann: Women and Work in Australia*, Nelson, West Melbourne, 1975.

Laclau, Ernesto & Mouffe, Chantal, *Hegemony and Socialist Strategy*, Verso, London, 1985.

Lenin, VI, *What is to be Done?*, Progress Publishers, Moscow, 1973.

Lester, Richard, *As Unions Mature*, Princeton University Press, Princeton, New Jersey, 1966.

Lipset, SM, Trow, MA & Coleman, JS (eds), *Union Democracy: The Internal Politics of the International Typographical Union*, Free Press, Glencoe, Ill., 1956.

Mandel, Ernest, & Novack, George, *The Marxist Theory of Alienation*, Pathfinder Press, New York, 1974.

—, *The Revolutionary Potential of the Working Class*, Pathfinder Press, New York, 1974.

Martin, Ross, *Trade Unions in Australia*, Penguin, Melbourne, 1975.

Marx, Karl & Engels, Frederick, Manifesto of the Communist Party, Progress Publishers, Moscow, 1965.

McCarthy, WEJ, (ed), *Trade Unions: Selected Readings*, Penguin, London, 1974.

McQueen, Humphrey, *Australia's Media Monopolies*, Widescope, Camberwell, 1977.

Mehnert, Klaus, *Twilight of the Young: The Radical Movements of the 1960's and their Legacy*, Hold, Rinehart & Winston, London, 1976.

Melucci, Alberto, *Nomads of the Present, Social Movements and Individual Needs in Contemporary Society*, Hutchinson Radius, London, 1989.

Michels, Robert, *Political Parties: A Sociological Study of the Oligarchical Tendencies of Modern Democracy*, Collier Books, New York, 1962 (1915).

Miliband, Ralph, *Divided Societies, Class Struggle in Contemporary Capitalism*, Clarendon Press, Oxford, 1989.

Moody, Kim, *Workers in a Lean World: Unions in the International Economy*, Verso, London, 1997.

Moorhouse, Frank, *Days of Wine and Rage*, Penguin, Melbourne, 1980.

Mundy, Jack, *Green Bans and Beyond*, Angus & Robertson, Sydney, 1981.

Neutze, Max, *Urban Development in Australia*, Allen & Unwin, Sydney, 1977.

Niland, John, *Collective Bargaining and Compulsory Arbitration in Australia*, UNSW Press, Sydney, 1978.

O'Donnell, Carol, *The Basis of the Bargain*, Allen & Unwin, Sydney, 1984.

Parkin, Frank, *Marxism and Class Theory, A Bourgeois Critique*, Tavistock, London, 1981.

Parkin, Sara, *Green Parties: An International Guide*, Heretic Books, London, 1989.

Probert, Belinda, *Working Life*, McPhee Gribble, Melbourne, 1989.

Ramson, WS (ed), *The Australian National Dictionary*, Oxford Unversiry Press, Melbourne, 1988.

Rawson, DW, *A Handbook of Australian Trade Unions and Employees' Associations*, (3rd ed), RSSS, ANU, Canberra, 1977.

—, *Unions and Unionists in Australia*, Allen & Unwin, Sydney, 1978.

Riach, Pam & Howard, WA, *Productivity Agreements and Australian Wage Determination*, John Wiley & Sons, Sydney, 1973.

Roddewig, Richard, *Green Bans: The Birth of Australian Environmental Politics*, Hale & Iremonger, Sydney, 1978.

Ryan, Edna, *Two-thirds of a Man*, Hale & Iremonger, Sydney, 1984.

Ryan, Edna & Conlon A, *Gentle Invaders: Australian Women at Work 1788–1974*, Thomas Nelson, West Melbourne, 1975.

Sandercock, Leonie, *Cities for Sale*, MUP, Melbourne, 1975.

Save the Public Transport Committee, *The Commuter*, n.d. [c. 1973].

Seidman, Gary, *Manufacturing Militance: Workers' Movements in Brazil and South Africa*, University of California Press, Berkeley, 1994. South Africa, Berkeley, 1994. (Publisher will be on hard copy list).

Sennett, Richard & Cobb, Jonathan, *The Hidden Injuries of Class*, Knopf, New York, 1973.

Sharkey, LL, *The Trade Unions*, CPA, Sydney, 1961.

Sheridan, Tom, *Mindful Militants: The Amalgamated Engineering Union in Australia 1920–1972*, Cambridge Universiry Press, Cambridge, 1975.

SPA, *The Socialist Program and the Constitution*, adopted at the Inaugural Congress of the SPA, 29–30 September and 1–2 October 1972.

SPA, Building Industry Branch, *Six Turbulent Years (Lessons from the rise and fall of the NSW Builders Labourers' leadership and building industry struggles 1969–75)*, Sydney, n.d. [mid-1975].

Stretton, Hugh, *Ideas for Australian Cities*, Georgian House, Melbourne, 1975.

—, *Capitalism, Socialism and the Environment*, Cambridge Universiry Press, Cambridge, 1976.

Summers, Ann, Bacon, Wendy, Morrisey, Dave, Gregory, Ruth & Shelton, Syd, *The Little Green Book: The Facts on Green Bans*, n.d. [c. November 1973].

Thomas, Pete, *Taming the Concrete Jungle: The Builders Laborers' Story*, NSW branch, ABCE & BLF, Sydney, 1973.

—, *The Nymboida Story*, Australian Coal and Shale Employees' Federation, Sydney, 1975.

—, *The Mine the Workers Ran: The 1975–79 Success Story at Nymboida*, Miners Federation, Sydney, 1979.

Thompson, Denise, *Flaws in the Social Fabric. Homosexuals and Society in Sydney*, Allen & Unwin, Sydney, 1985.

Tolson, Andrew, *The Limits of Masculinity*, Tavistock, London, 1977.

Touraine, Alain, *The Post-Industrial Society: Tomorrow's Social History: Classes, Conflicts and Culture in the Programmed Society*, Wildwood House, London, 1974.

—, *The Voice and the Eye: An Analysis of Social Movements*, Cambridge University Press, Cambridge, 1981.

Trotsky, Leon, *Leon Trotsky on the Trade Unions*, Merit Publishers, New York, 1969.

Troy, PN, *A Fair Price. The Land Commission Program 1972–1977*, Hale & Iremonger, Sydney, 1978.

True, Paul, *Tales of the BLF … Rolling the Right!*, Militant International Publications, Parramatta, 1995.

Turner, Ann (ed), *Union Power: Jack Mundey v. George Polites*, Heinemann Educational, Melbourne, 1975.

Turner, Ian, *In Union is Strength*, 2nd ed, Nelson, Melbourne, 1978.

Wallace, John & Owens, Joe, *Workers Call the Tune at Opera House*, National Workers Control Conference, Newcastle, 1973.

INDEX

Lightning Source UK Ltd.
Milton Keynes UK
UKHW010110130421
381871UK00006B/1571